SAVING JESUS

FORBIDDEN TRUTH SERIES

SAVING JESUS

By Míċeál Ledwith

Love is not a virtue to be practised, but an energy field in which to live

Edessa Code, LLC

SAVING JESUS

FORBIDDEN TRUTH SERIES

by Míċeál Ledwith

Published by Edessa Code, LLC

ISBN # 978-0-692-97305-9

Printed in the United States of America

Book Cover Design
by Paulina Amador of Holo-Graphics.net
Editorial Book Design
by Jaime Leal-Anaya of Hun Nal Ye Publishing

Edessa Code, LLC
P.O. Box 1100
Tenino, WA 98589
USA
micealledwith.com

This book is dedicated to

Ramtha

The Enlightened One

First and Greatest of the Master Teachers

And to His Daughter

JZ Knight

Who for more than Forty Years

Have Shone a Brilliant Beacon of Hope

Into a Dark and Troubled World.

CONTENTS

SCROLL THREE
THE CHEQUERED PAST OF THE HUMAN RACE

SCROLL FOUR
THE EVIDENCE FOR JESUS AND HISTORY'S IMPACT ON IT

THANK YOU!

An undertaking as significant as the production of this book could never have been accomplished without the support and encouragement of a very large number of people. I am deeply grateful to all those who made very significant contributions in so many ways to bring this book to its final form.

In the first place I want to thank Ramtha and JZ Knight. It was Ramtha who advised me to take the unusual step of speaking this book to a live audience, instead of writing it in the conventional way, and that formed the core of this volume. His wise guidance in so many forms about this book over the past few years has helped this work enormously.

This text is based on seventeen hours of talks which I delivered to a live audience over a period of four days. The conversational style has been deliberately retained. Max Laing and Janet Ballweber generously volunteered their skills, time and equipment, to record the four days of sessions professionally. They were ably assisted by Annegret Bürger and Frank Dabellein.

These seventeen hours came from a sampling of some of my talks in the "Conversations." My deepest appreciation goes to those who served as "Hosts" to those talks over the past six years, mainly in their own homes: Jenny Gifford, who founded the "Conversations" series, Linda Barnes, Michael Burke, Liza Bennett, Margaret Currie, Heidi Gould, Jayne of the Triad Theater, Dr. Conrad LeProwse, Jenise Mugler, Butterfly McCauley, Lucy Ryan, Terry Ryan, Elsie Sanchez, Jann Shia, Debra Sandusky Johnson, Jalene Smith, Sophie Sykes, Luke Sutton and Destiny Taylor.

Also of enormous support during the "Conversations" were Georgie Camacho, Bonnie Carey, Charles Folkerth, Helene Goslin, Susan Holler, Marie Krahn, David Ouellette, Diana Rae, and Lois Willman.

Lucy and Terry Ryan accomplished the marathon task of transcribing the recordings to serve as the outline for the text of the book. The proofs were read by them, Jenise Mugler, Elaine Oneil, Reza Leal-Smartt, and Nadja Galadram. Elaine Oneil provided many invaluable insights and much wise technical advice during the production of the book, as well as demonstrating enormous patience, which helped greatly to journey through the turbulence that inevitably accompanies the production of a volume of this scope! Paulina Amador designed the compelling cover graphics and re-designed the website. A great deal of artistic advice and insight was given by Melissa Peizer.

I am most grateful to my very good friends Dana Dabiri and YuChi Chu, Danesh and Andishe, Laura Eisen, Linda Evans, Dr. Terry and Carol Franks, Elizabeth and Eve Grigware, Robert Hillard, Steve and Yael Klein, Jaime Leal-Anaya, Reza Leal-Smartt, Menira Leal-Smartt, Tharetz Leal-Smartt, Linda McCallum, Dr. Ronald Overlie and Beverley Hallett, Diana Rae, Jean Sagan, Debbie Smartt and Jaymes Brandon, Colette Smartt and Robert Hawkins, Chalese Smartt and Peter Maus, Cherrie Spring, Dr. Rodrigo Vildosola Ulloa, Angela Izrailova and Alexandra, for their deeply valued friendship, counsel and support over the years.

Above all I want to acknowledge with deepest appreciation the substantial support for myself and this project in so many forms, which was given outstandingly by Chris Coleman, Dr. Conrad LeProwse, Jenise Mugler, Rebecca Oppenheimer, Pamela Roberts Aue, Sophie Sykes, Susan Janus, Nancy Driscoll, and Tony and Sheryl Clevenger. Without these people's support it simply would not have been possible at all to bring this work to completion. I appreciate your help and support deeply.

Finally, I am most grateful to Jaime Leal-Anaya who brought his wisdom and experience to bear with extraordinary skill and craft in designing every facet of this book, and in formatting the text and its layout in preparation for publication.

INTRODUCTION BY THE AUTHOR

a) Setting the Stage

Since the dawn of recorded history all the great sages and the spiritual movements they inspired have believed that everything subsists in God, the source of all that exists, and that it is possible and desirable for every human being to forge a more intimate and close union with that source from whence we all came.

Some traditions have believed we can best do this by shunning the world through acts of self-denial and mortification of the mind and body, and by focusing the spiritual energy within us on to a God "up there." This approach is usually known as "the ascetic path" and it does work, but it is not the only path, and despite all impressions to the contrary, it is certainly not the path that Jesus taught.

For centuries we have been brainwashed into praying to be healed, to be wealthy or happy. The programs related to these matters that run in our sub-conscious makes it enormously difficult to remember and to realize the implications of that crucial statement of Jesus in Mark 11:24.[1] That statement was based on the fact that we all have the power within us to do the remarkable and we now understand in terms of physics the mechanics of how that is possible. This is what we refer to as the quantum field responding to our observation, not our prayers.

Every person who has ever lived on this Earth has spent a lifetime manifesting reality out of what today we call "the quantum field." Even though the great sages of our history were always aware of that phenomenon, the terms used to describe it have varied down through the ages as humanity's knowledge and understanding of reality deepened. Whatever terminology we use, the bottom line is that whatever we believe and profoundly accept, will cause a similar reality to be magnetized to us out of the quantum field. If my attitude is "Woe is me" I will magnetize to me a reality to match that conviction. Fortunately, the opposite

[1] Mark 11:24 "Whatever you ask for in prayer, believe it is already yours, and it shall be so."

is equally true. Given how human history has unfolded with so much suffering, inequality, dis-empowerment, injustice, and broken dreams, it is no wonder that the propensity of the average individual is towards the negative, with its accompanying feelings of guilt, lack, fear, unworthiness, sinfulness and powerlessness.

To rescue the human race from this all-pervading negative mindset and its consequences, is what the mission of Jesus was really all about. He had a public ministry of less than three years, but it was the final three days of that short ministry that has always caught the public imagination. It was the lead-in to the major Jewish Festival of Passover. That Festival centered on the sacrifice of the Passover Lamb on the Altar of the Temple, and in the Jewish religious tradition, the blood of the sacrificed Lamb flowing down the altar was understood to wash away the consequences of our sin in the sight of God.

Sometimes we can forget that all of the Twelve Apostles were Jewish, that Jesus himself was a Jew, and that the first generation of Christians in Jerusalem who followed his message, were also Jewish. It was unfortunate, but very understandable, that due to the final few days of his public life in Jerusalem occurring on the eve of Passover, Jesus became seen predominantly by the Jewish early Christians in Jerusalem as the new and permanent Passover Lamb whose shedding of blood on the Cross would wash away our sins in the sight of God. Thus, it was that Jesus became our sacrificial lamb and "Suffering Savior."

Following on this tradition the Church's traditional recipe of sin, shame, guilt and repentance, ensures the persistence of victimization all life long. This engenders a massive dis-empowerment and is directly opposite to the intent of the teachings of Jesus, of which the Churches claim to be the guardian.

Down the centuries we have been persuaded that to make up to Jesus for all he suffered for us, it is imperative we should now be prepared to suffer and do penance in a mindset of sinfulness, worthlessness, and lack in the sight of God. We are told that if we do not do that we run the risk of losing our eternal destiny. So, it came about, tragically and ironically, that possessing those very states of negativity from which Jesus came to deliver us, became regarded as almost the very touchstone of our loyalty to him and his message.

Other less dramatic attempts to sum up Jesus are equally misleading, though not as obviously dis-empowering, such as the "Gentle Jesus, Meek and Mild" notion. A prominent Southern Baptist theologian once quipped that his whole Sunday School training could be summed up in one sentence: "Jesus is nice and he wants us to be nice as well."

All of these misleading attempts to sum up the mission and message of Jesus neatly have left an unfortunate legacy. In recent times, we have learned a lot about how sub-conscious programs control our lives. Apparently, such traits can even be passed on from generation to generation through our DNA.

If the vast majority of our normal everyday mental processing is under the control of the sub-conscious mind, we more than ever need to be aware that the sub-conscious mind is reckoned to be about a million times more powerful than the conscious in its impact on our everyday affairs. Only about 0.01% of all the brain's activity is experienced consciously, according to recent neuroscientific research.

Our life reflects the character of this sub-conscious programming. The sub-conscious mind is designed to create reality out of its programs and it will create a reality to match those programs. So, if we have negative programming in our sub-conscious mind, we will end up re-creating those negative experiences in our lives. If we are honest, we will realize that most of the programs in our sub-conscious are based on negativity: fear of what other people are thinking about us, fear of the unknown, fear of not being able to cope, fear of not being loved and respected for who we are, and so on. It is obvious that these are precisely the types of fears that the image of Jesus as a Suffering Savior continually engender.

However much we come to recognize that negative sub-conscious programs do enormous damage to any efforts we may make to live in power as Jesus taught us we should live, it's not simply a matter of recognizing that they are there and deciding to get rid of them. The primary duty of any sub-conscious program is to ensure its own existence, so any overt effort to dislodge them will only make things worse. While we continue to have those programs, even our most sincere and determined efforts to live as Jesus taught are rendered futile. It's like trying to fill the kitchen sink with water while leaving the stopper out. The sub-conscious programs drain away anything positive we may learn or understand if it is in opposition to those programs.

The only way we know in which sub-conscious programs can be removed is by going back as realistically as we can to where those programs first originated historically; getting to know every detail of those circumstances as perfectly as we can, and then assessing for ourselves whether the bases of such programs were really justified by how circumstances actually were, as opposed to how we were told they were. Simply being told that these sub-conscious programs are not based on fact will do very little. We have to make that assessment of the programs personally by reviewing the historical evidence ourselves.

Jesus came to deliver us from the pernicious effects of those sub-conscious programs, promising us that we could do all the wonders he did and more. Unfortunately, the circumstances of religious history turned him into someone who came to appease a God angered by our sins. So, it was that an agenda of empowerment and liberation was not so gradually turned into a mindset that exalts powerlessness, and praises wallowing in the consciousness of our faults and failings. All of this is supposed to be pleasing to Jesus, and by implication also to God. Obviously in such a modus operandi there is no way in which we can ever attain what Jesus so memorably promised us would be ours in John 14.[2]

Many Christian commentators have consistently pointed to these texts as some of the most difficult to understand in the whole of the New Testament. They know that doing some of the wonders Jesus did has been an extraordinarily rare thing in Christian history, and some of the things he did have never been repeated at all. When someone does any of these things, the tendency is to put them on a pedestal for veneration, instead of focusing on imitating them ourselves.

[2] The same teaching is found in John 15 and 17, 1 John 5:14-15, Matthew 21:22, Mark 11:24, and Luke 16:6.

The commentators who point to the difficulties they find with these statements of Jesus, never seem to realize that the very conditions of profound personal change which Jesus taught were a basic condition of accomplishing these wonders. Instead, being conscious of our sinfulness and unworthiness, is exalted as an ideal. How can we ever do the wonders if the conditions for accomplishing them are universally neglected? Jesus taught a way of being that involved profound personal change which centered on what we have to render in English by the poverty-stricken word "love." All of his mandates as to how we should live and behave were signposts to keep us in that state, or were realities that we would notice in a person who was living in that state. They were never intended as imperatives to be obeyed, for which we would get a 'reward,' and for which, if we did not obey, we would be punished later. As stated on the title page of this book, in the teaching of Jesus "'Love' is not a virtue to be practiced, but an energy field in which to live." Jesus was a Master whose message was based on acquiring a state of non-dual consciousness. When we begin to do that, and realize more accurately what Jesus was about, then John 14 will no longer pose such a problem as it apparently does now to so many commentators.

At the very beginnings of Christianity, just as now, the message of Jesus was often too much for those who heard it, so there was and is an instinctive urge to convert it into something similar, but more manageable. A great example is the statement of Jesus found in Matthew 16:25, Luke 9:24 and Mark 8:35: "For whoever would save his life will lose it; and whoever loses his life *for my sake and the gospel's* will save it." Most authorities agree that the words in italics were a later addition to this text. But these italicized words introduce a major change in context: in the original setting this statement was mandating a radical transformation of consciousness, but the italicized additions have turned the statement into what Cynthia Bourgeault once termed "a martyrdom, a set of sacrificial actions you can perform with your egoic operating system still intact."[3] In short, the italicized words change the meaning to the opposite of what Jesus intended.

---

[3] Cynthia Bourgeault, *The Wisdom Jesus* (Shambhala Publications, 2008), p. 75.

As mentioned earlier, the dominant model for personal spiritual transformation at the time Jesus was preaching was "ascetic mysticism," based on renunciation of the world. Through prayer, mortification and discipline the spiritual energy within the human person is sufficiently focused to fuse with and unify with the higher divine energies of existence.

The way to God is always 'up' with this school of 'Spiritual Ascent' and it does work, but it is not the only path, and as already stated certainly was not the path of Jesus.

He taught that the path to re-unification between the spirit within us and the spirit of the Creator or Source, was accomplished not by focusing upwards, but by focusing on the divine within. This approach is more familiar to us from the Eastern religious traditions, and it has sometimes been rather inaccurately labeled "the path of kenosis" or "self-emptying," rather than the path of asceticism. As explained in this book, "Agape" (poorly translated into English as "Love") is a state into which we are challenged to draw everything that exists. This is the focus that was really revolutionary in what Jesus infused into human consciousness two thousand years ago.

Jesus was preaching and teaching the purification and unification of consciousness. He was not preaching the path of asceticism, even though that is the form in which his message has been traditionally cast by conventional Christianity. By this process of the purification and unification of consciousness we become aware of what we deeply accept and believe, and thus eliminate any fractured and misguided attempts to create in the quantum field. Usually when we proclaim what it is we wish to create, it is a superficial proclamation, and consequently is undermined, because deep down, sub-consciously, it is the opposite state of affairs that we really accept.

The number of people in the world today who claim, in some form or other, to follow the message of Jesus, is now about 2.2 billion, or 31.5% of the world's population. For that number of people alive today, almost one third of the world's population, the way to God for them (another phrase to describe what human purpose on Earth is) is dictated by how they understand Jesus to have been, and what they were told he taught.

A very large percentage of these individuals who bear the name of 'Christian' today are sensing serious concerns with what they have been taught about Jesus' message. Most people do not have the knowledge to realize that possibly what they have been taught may not necessarily be the real thing, and that if they saw things from a better and more informed perspective, many of the difficulties they rightly sense would actually dissipate.

But even if someone has a better knowledge base, and recognizes the validity of the new case being presented, it is still not easy to step outside the box of one's own cultural conditioning and recognize that the problems do not come from the message of Jesus itself, but from the distortions to which it has been subjected almost right from the very beginning. The Christian Churches themselves, if they do not wish to fade into a shadow of their former selves, will soon have to come to the same realization.

In addressing the negative programs about Jesus that afflict us all, we have to make ourselves aware personally, as far as is possible, of what exactly happened during the life of Jesus, and in particular what his message actually was. Then we can start to look at what forces there were that continued to cripple his message right down the intervening centuries, but especially in the middle of the first millennium.

When we discover by patient and thorough investigation how the facts of the life and mission of Jesus actually were, then the foundations of the old dis-empowering programs will start to crumble of their own accord, and new, more accurate, and factually-based programs will be formed automatically to take their place. The stopper has been put back in the sink.

When those old and crippling programs are gone we have thoroughly cleaned house and then with a clear and unified consciousness we can really begin to change the character of what it is that we have always been creating in the quantum field.

This is why our process here involves going back to examine with a fresh mind what sources we have for the life of Jesus. We have four Gospels, which in the written form in which we have them, are in Greek, which was not the language Jesus normally used. Were there also possibly earlier written sources, or Aramaic or Hebrew memorized oral traditions, that might have been handed down, and that preceded all the written versions we have?

Some of the significant early Christian documents that we know existed, did not make it into the New Testament, but still exist, while others have been lost totally.

We also need to look at the circumstances that influenced the form of the Church's message down the centuries and how Jesus was eventually proclaimed to be an ethereal figure, Son of God and second Person of the Blessed Trinity, which made it completely impossible for us ever to imitate him as he desired.

So it is, surprising though it undoubtedly will be to most, that the magnificent message of Jesus does indeed need to be saved. Jesus did come here to be a Savior, but he certainly did not come here to save us from Hell fire as the consequence of our sins. He came to save us from the effects of what our own crippling attitudes are manifesting in the quantum field, how to profoundly alter those attitudes, and how thereby to accomplish monumental personal change.

This journey of empowerment is a difficult and detailed process, which is why it is necessary to traverse all of the areas detailed in this book, and is why a short snappy version is simply not possible. In addition to the written sources we need to ponder the influence of the family of Jesus, the attitude of his six siblings, who are mentioned in the New Testament,[4] the myriad of religious and political forces that influenced and warped the message down the centuries, the crippling religious controversies and divisions, the ultimate mistake of the Church beginning to function as an armed doctrine, and finding itself eventually in the curious position of preaching and practicing hatred in the name of the God of Love.

The tedious process of removing sub-conscious programs can also be greatly upsetting to many people who revere the name of Jesus, for they suspect some kind of wicked plot is afoot to undermine him. As a result, they can never summon up enough courage to look at the facts dispassionately, but instead try to kill

[4] The Gospel of Mark 6:3, and the Gospel of Matthew 13:55-56, names four brothers of Jesus, and also "sisters" whose names are not given.

the messenger, and so the game goes on.

The teaching of Jesus on how to create our own reality obviously has enormous implications for every aspect of human existence, and for the resolution of so many of the inheritances of a regrettable kind that we have acquired from history. It is not hard to see it is also the ultimate solution for all of the most intractable problems that we face in the world today, from hunger, injustice, want, disease, and discrimination, right down to personal unhappiness and lack.

In this coming decade, we will commemorate the 2,000th Anniversary of the beginning of Jesus' ministry. What an appropriate time to re-introduce what the real message of Jesus was, and sow the seeds of a profound world transformation that recognizes no lack or divisions of class, race or creed.

b) The God of the Home and the God of the World

I first went to school when I was five years old. We had a tiny one-room schoolhouse, with one teacher for all seven classes. The number of pupils during my six years there ranged from nineteen to a maximum of twenty-seven.

The school had been established by my great-great granduncle when that became possible in the years following the granting of Catholic Emancipation in Ireland in 1829, and my maternal grandmother had been a teacher there over fifty years before I enrolled.

With only three to five students in each class our school day was informal and enjoyable, in many ways an extension of our own homes, but we still managed to always maintain an excellent academic standard, as verified by the Government Schools Inspector on his annual visit.

Religious Instruction, or as we called it then, "Catechism Class," was one of my favorite subjects. My fellow students and I came from a religious background that never had any trace of the "Hell Fire and Brimstone" mentality that was such a prominent feature of religious belief in many other parts of the world, but nevertheless, on a couple of occasions in the year, both in religion class and in the sermons in our local Church, the awful subject of eternal punishment by God for sin came up. Even in those tender years it seemed to me that that posed enormous difficulties in how we thought about God. In recent times Paul Copan summed up this quandary well in the title of his 2011 book: "Is God a Moral Monster?"[5]

At home, it had always been conveyed that God was infinitely loving, and cared for us all individually with a love beyond all understanding. Now in School and at Church I am occasionally beginning to hear something that seemed radically at variance with that, even though it was put across in a very gentle manner. Even though God loves us, he can apparently also sentence us to a punishment in fire after death, not for a century or for a thousand years, but for all eternity! I could not get my mind around that; just could not see how both of those beliefs could be true: that God could love us and yet consign us to an eternity of torment? It seemed that if doing that God had to be sadistic. Nevertheless, just like everyone else who had no more information to go on beyond what we had been taught, I accepted that major contradiction at the heart of the Western religious belief systems.

Worse still, again according to what we were taught, God apparently became so infuriated with the sins of the human race, that about two thousand years ago he drew a line in the sand, and decreed that someone would have to make up to him for all of those offenses committed since creation began. The person chosen to make up to God by suffering, we were taught, was his only begotten and innocent Son, known to us as Jesus Christ, who on God the Father's diktat had come down here and incarnated on Earth to suffer the most cruel death imaginable because of how we had offended God. Now, not alone have we the burden of having mortally offended God, but, apparently, what happened to Jesus is also our responsibility.

If God is all powerful and all-knowing why did he choose the suffering and death of Jesus as the means of 'saving' us? Why is it that 'saving' requires suffering anyway? Surely an all-knowing and powerful-God could have chosen an entirely different plan,

---

[5] Paul Copan, *Is God a Moral Monster* (Baker Books, Grand Rapids, 2011).

and if not, why not? If the death of Jesus is so powerful that it can wipe all sins past, present and future, how come that a death has such power?

We have at least two monstrous issues here:

Firstly, what kind of being would be pleased by suffering, especially by the suffering of his own innocent son?

Secondly, how could the suffering of one individual make up for something done by another?

And, most important of all, surely a being who subscribed to such issues as these could never be God?

It is also blatantly obvious that there are serious deficiencies in a creation system where most creatures can live only by killing other creatures.

And what programs of guilt, fear, and powerlessness, the acceptance of issues such as these, would spawn among the human race?

In those far-off school days of childhood, of course, we accepted everything we were taught in School or Church about God, or about human purpose and destiny, as the truth, and accordingly revised downwards everything that we had been taught more sanely at home about Jesus and God.

I gained a Degree in Philosophy, and later a Degree in Arts, in our University courses. Well over fifty years ago I followed up by enlisting for a full University course in Theology, graduating after many years with Master's and Doctorate Degrees in the subject. I was appointed a Lecturer in Theology in 1971, and Professor of Systematic Theology in 1975. My appointment as President of the College in 1985 for the normal 10-year term, brought my academic research to a screeching halt for that decade! I mention all of this not with the aim of blowing my own trumpet, but to show I took no short cuts in all these years of research, and also to suggest I might possibly even know what I am talking about in this book.

In 1980, I was appointed to the International Theological Commission, which has been described as 'a group of theologians of international standing, charged with advising the Holy See on theological matters.' I remained a Member of the International Commission for seventeen years. Once at a public lecture I had given in France, a member of the audience approached me afterwards and said, "I hear you were an adviser to the Pope; you don't seem to have done a very good job?" I mention this range of involvements simply to illustrate that I took no short cuts in getting acquainted with the complex and multitudinous historical and contemporary sources underlying the issues discussed in this volume.

Over those fifty years or more I had an excellent opportunity to study in depth all the foundational documents testifying to the teaching and message of Jesus, the foundational sources of the surrounding religious cultures of the time, the puzzle of why there is so much convergence between the teachings of Jesus and the Eastern religions, as propounded by individuals such as the Buddha Gautama, Lao Tsu and Confucius, along with the way that message has been commented on by innumerable theologians and twenty Church Councils over the centuries. Then came the major revival in Biblical studies in the 19th and 20th Centuries, aided and inspired by the discoveries of collections of ancient documents of the ancient Near East, particularly in Egypt, Israel and Iraq. In particular a great deal of light was shed on the date of composition and authorship of the four Gospels of the New Testament.

When you have the opportunity to study these multitudes of sources and many other similar sources over a long period of years, you begin to see things very differently from those far-off days in childhood. More and more you begin to feel that all is not well, firstly, with the way in which the message of Jesus was originally understood, and, secondly with how he has been presented down the centuries as our Suffering Savior who saved us from the vengeance of a wrathful God. You know something is seriously wrong, but you can't quite put your finger on what the heart of the matter is.

Let me give an illustration that might help to clarify that feeling. Perhaps one day on-line, or in some book, I may come across an optical illusion. The caption says there is an image, a number, or a shape concealed there, but I can't see it at first. Then the brain somehow re-arranges the data coming from the eyes, and suddenly I "see" the 'hidden' image or pattern. The really interesting thing is, that while originally, I could not discern the image at all, having once seen it I can never "un-see" it again.

Over all the years of study of the vast body of knowledge surrounding Jesus and his message, at long last, just like with the optical illusion suddenly becoming visible, the penny drops and the inspiration strikes.

There are over 20,000 different Churches, Congregations and Communities in the world today that claim to follow the teachings of Jesus. Many of them hold views that are widely disparate from others, and some even claim to have the only true interpretation of what he taught. If one is in any way a thoughtful person, the existence of more than 20,000 different interpretations of the message of Jesus gives one serious pause.

Perhaps the real reason why we are faced with so many difficulties, misinterpretations, inconsistencies and disagreements about Jesus is because the mission of Jesus had nothing to do at all with being a Suffering Savior who came to die for our sins, but had everything to do with teaching human empowerment?

It has long been cliché to point out the injustices and atrocities carried out by the western religions at times like the Crusades and the Spanish Inquisition, but it has also to be recognized that these same religions have accomplished enormous humanitarian achievements down the centuries. All that being said, the unfortunate situation seems to be that the core of the traditional religious endeavor has come worryingly close to institutionalizing those very same things from which Jesus' message sought to free us.

It used to be said that shortly before the days of Nicholas Copernicus,[6] there were well over a thousand insoluble problems related to Ptolemy's[7] view that the Earth was at the center of the universe. When Copernicus introduced his new model of the solar system, with the sun at the center, almost all those ancient astronomical problems with Ptolemy were instantly resolved.

What made the difference – better knowledge, more information? Partly, but the main reason was that the viewpoint had changed; the paradigm was altered. No amount of improvement of the views of Ptolemy would have ever brought us to the system of Copernicus; the paradigm first had to change totally. For major

[6] 1473-1543, AD.

[7] 100-168, AD.

progress in human knowledge to take place it is apparently not just sufficient to continuously pile up evidence, as we have always tended to assume uncritically. The very pattern or paradigm within which we interpret the evidence must be altered before we make a major breakthrough. In short, real genius belongs to those who detect a new pattern or dimension of meaning in the facts before us, and realize the old program of interpretation no longer works. It's a good lesson to contemplate that at a certain stage of investigation a paradigm shift has to take place in order for us to progress in knowledge. Have we yet arrived at that point with the message of Jesus? It looks like the time is nigh.

In this regard, most important of all are those few but mysteriously tantalizing statements of Jesus, which are almost never commented on in preaching of catechesis nowadays, and never have been. If these statements of Jesus are referring to something very real in our situation, then they should be at the very heart of any presentation of his message, instead of being evidence to which reference is seldom if ever made. I don't ever recall Jesus saying in the four Gospels of the New Testament that he was going to be our Savior by suffering and dying for our sins, but I certainly can point out where he said clearly that we are all gods, and that we would do all the great things that he did, and that we would do greater things than he did. We would do that not by begging God or Jesus to fulfill our requests but by believing that these things were already ours: an essential condition for manifestation in the quantum field.

It is equally clear that none of those 20,000 Churches and Congregations that claim to be the heirs of Jesus' message today have yet done all of the things he did and more. Surely this is a clear indication that something has gone radically wrong? If the very attitudes from which Jesus sought to deliver us are now being put forward as at the very core of true belief, we are in serious trouble.

We have got used to hearing that we should do penance and make reparation to God for our sins, and to Jesus for what we are told our sins did to him. It is a system guaranteed to inculcate the maximum of guilt, fear, lack and unworthiness, but we are persuaded that we should endure all this if we want to faithfully follow Jesus.

The family of beliefs that descend from the conviction that Jesus is our Suffering Savior, contribute enormously to human dis-empowerment. Unfortunately, most of the damage is done in the form of sub-conscious programs that are created from holding such beliefs. The experts in neuroscience tell us that these sub-conscious programs will eventually take on a physical form and are transmitted from generation to generation in our DNA. One of the most important pieces of information that we have been given tells us that it is the first duty of every sub-conscious program to ensure its own survival. That means that any conscious assault on those sub-conscious programs to try and demolish them will only end up making matters worse. The supreme irony is that we are normally totally unaware of all this consciously.

The journey of eliminating dis-empowering sub-conscious programs is a much more subtle and skillful process than making a full-frontal assault. The neuroscientists tell us that the only successful way to remove a negative sub-conscious program is to go back and try to re-live the circumstances and belief systems that formed the sub-conscious programs in the first place. When we re-assess the realities of the situation and see from where the false impressions came from that created the negative programs, then a new and positive program will start to form. As it does, the old negative program will start to dissolve of its own accord. Obviously, this is not a quick fix, but it is a fix.

Paradoxically, if the majority of dis-empowering sub-conscious programs arise from the warped versions of the teachings of Jesus that have been handed down for centuries, then we have, in a sense, to go back to where the origin of our problem lies. In the case of understanding Jesus and his mission properly, that means going back to discover how Jesus really was, what his real teachings were and what his whole purpose was in launching his mission nearly 2,000 years ago. It will also involve probing to discover why his message was subjected to the distortions it suffered during the handing down of it to us through the ages.

That agenda has dictated the shape of this book. Reconstructing programs is not a linear and direct process. The old programs will do everything to ensure their survival if they sense they are under assault, so we need to be sensitive to how we can process matters without generating a total rejection of our efforts. We need to know when to back off and where and when to resume and go over matters once again so it has a chance to sink in. I liken the technique to the action of stretching an elastic band where we imagine the elastic band as our mind-set. We stretch the elastic band of our mind as far as it will go and then we relax it before it snaps. We take a different direction and repeat the exercise. As time goes on, the elastic band will stretch further and further as we gradually extend the scope of the investigation. We want to stretch the elastic band far enough to reform our fundamental beliefs. It is a slow and repetitive process. But it is necessary as I have discovered over the past 6 years during long 'Conversations' with people who are dedicated to uncovering their programs. This is the reason some of the material of this book may seem somewhat repetitive – it is by deliberate design. It is also the reason why a short and snappy presentation of this complex matter is impossible if we truly want to effect major change. Regular attendees to these 'Conversations' were invited to four days of recordings that provide the framework of this book. Most of the tone and conversational style of those recordings was maintained, with additional details pertinent to the major topics added where relevant.

This book sets out all the aspects of Jesus' ministry and the ways in which it has become warped down the ages. It is a complex matter bound up with all the most intriguing, puzzling and fascinating aspects of the human mind and consciousness, but every effort has been made to present this extremely complex field of the interaction between God and the mind, in as simple and direct a manner as possible.

c) The Enemy Within: Our Crippling Sub-conscious Programs

How often have we driven ten or twenty miles on a quiet, straight country road, doing all the right things so as to drive safely, but with no conscious recollection afterwards of having done so? All of a sudden, we arrive at our destination. Who was doing most, if not all, of the driving?!

Our conscious and sub-conscious minds are obviously capable of focusing separately on different things at the same time, and the conscious mind may have little or no awareness at all of what the sub-conscious mind is doing. G. W. Williams coined the term 'Highway Hypnosis' to describe this 'automatic' driving phenomenon in 1963.[8]

Take another example of this phenomenon. If we have been taught to type with all ten fingers on the normal keyboard of a desktop computer or laptop we can easily type 20-50 words per minute. But it's a different story if we are presented with a blank sketch of a computer keyboard and asked to write in the twenty-six letters of our alphabet on their proper keys – as represented by 26 blank circles. I tried this myself once and found that it took me nearly four minutes of typing imaginary words on a blank sheet of paper before I could fill in the correct position of the keyboard letters on the 26 blank circles on that piece of paper.

When learning to type we had to learn where each letter was on the keyboard and laboriously practice so as to memorize the position of each key on the keyboard until it all became automatic – that of course was long before the days of thumb typing! The day I tried to fill in the 26 blanks on the sketch of the keyboard, I realized that while I immediately knew where a few keys were on the keyboard, I did not consciously remember the positions of most of the keys any more. It was only by pretending to type words that I consciously discovered where most of the keys were. And it took me three or four minutes of very focused thought to figure it all out!

Yet, when we are typing, we are figuring it all out sub-consciously, with no effort at all – a few hundred times per minute if we are typing approximately 25 words per minute. As an aid to practice, people who are learning to type are often given specifically designed short paragraphs of text that contain all 26 letters of the alphabet. At 25 words per minute it would take us an average of five to six seconds to accurately locate all 26 letters on the keyboard.

---

[8] Williams, G. W: "Highway Hypnosis". *International Journal of Clinical and Experimental Hypnosis,* (103): 143–151. 1963.

Compare this to the three or four minutes (180-240 seconds) it took me to consciously figure out where the 26 letters were to fill in their positions on a blank diagram of a computer keyboard.

Obviously, this means that we know a lot of stuff sub-consciously of which we are not normally aware. The problem really begins however when that unconscious stuff starts to impact our everyday life in ways that are not benign and helpful, especially in regard to 'spiritual' convictions and practices. Usually we will be totally unaware, consciously, that these programs are having this influence, and probably we are going to resent it being pointed out.

Until well into the Middle Ages it was customary to write sentences with no spaces between the words. The Irish monks, during the 7th or 8th Centuries, invented the practice of dividing words by spaces to facilitate reading. They then exported the practice into Europe. Going back to the computer keyboard again...suppose I want to type a paragraph of text that I know by heart but decide, for old times' sake, to omit the spaces between the words as I type? How will I do? Not very well, because I have developed a sub-conscious program in me when learning to type, that insists on putting spaces between the words. Deciding to not put in the spaces between the letters now requires a major effort and will slow down my typing significantly.

Let's look at another example from a slightly different field. Destin Sandlin of Alabama is an engineer by profession and a YouTube educator.[9] One of his friends designed a bicycle with an interesting gear installed on the handlebars. When the handlebars are turned to the right, the front wheel of the bicycle turns to the left, and vice versa.

It took Destin Sandlin eight months of daily practice to learn to ride that 'backwards bicycle'. Nobody else who tried could ride it either, even though they were grimly determined to do so and understood perfectly well what was causing their problems. Destin explains that the skill of learning to ride a bicycle is an extremely complex affair. It involves the coordination of downward force on the pedals, leaning your whole body, "pulling and pushing

[9] He is the producer of the educational video series, "Smarter Every Day."

the handlebars, gyroscopic procession in the wheels; every single force is part of this algorithm."

Be as convinced as you wish that you can ride the 'backwards bicycle' and be as determined as you can that you will do it...the fact is that nobody can do so without a major amount of dedicated practice over a considerable period of time. If you do put in the effort and time then, quite suddenly, one day you can ride the 'backwards bicycle'. However, the really interesting thing is that you immediately discover, once you've learned that new skill, that you can no longer ride an ordinary bicycle. The inescapable conclusion is that once a program becomes embedded in our minds it takes a considerable amount of time and commitment to undo its influence. Once the time and commitment has been committed, however, the old program can disappear quite suddenly...but that happens only when it has been replaced completely by the new one.[10]

These are superb examples of how sub-conscious programs of all kinds rule the major part of our everyday affairs. It may have appeared in the previous few pages that I was laboring the point excessively by giving so many examples of this phenomenon. But if we should at some point decide that we wanted to get rid of a dis-empowering program, the essential first step is to profoundly accept that we have that program operating in our lives. It makes all the difference to know it in that way as opposed to being aware of it merely as some abstract piece of information that we have been told about by someone else. That will do nothing to help us move out of the effects of that crippling program. There is an oft-quoted saying from Horace[11] who was the major Latin poet at the time of Augustus: "Dulce et Decorum est pro Patria Mori." "It is a sweet and decorous thing to die for the Fatherland." It's written over the rear entrance to the Memorial Amphitheater at Arlington National Cemetery, and it was a favorite theme presented to High School children in Victorian days.

But that sentiment obviously meant very different things to a young man still in high school, than it did to a teenage soldier

---

[10] Go to Destin's website https://www.youtube.com/user/destinws2, where you can even purchase your own backwards bicycle.

[11] Died at Rome, 8 BC.

struggling to stay alive in the mud of Flanders on an horrific battlefield of the First World War. He was not seeing his case as possibly "dying for his country" but as dying for his fellow soldiers in the trenches with him. The high school student had what John Henry Newman used to call "a notional apprehension," whereas the young soldier had a "real apprehension" of what that line from Horace really implied. When setting out to remove religious or any other type of sub-conscious programs, a real apprehension of what they do and how they operate is required as a first step.

Some significant work done in this field over the last twenty-five years or so has demonstrated that only about 5% of what we do every day is under the control of the conscious mind. The remaining 95% is taken care of sub-consciously and automatically. The average person finds this a rather alarming piece of news and tends to reject the very suggestion that sub-conscious programs control vast areas of their everyday lives.

This is not to deny that sub-conscious programs are an extremely important part of our make-up and they make life considerably easier than if we had to take care of everything consciously and deliberately all the time. In fact, most of our day to day lives would bog down completely if we had to do this.

However, there is another side to these sub-conscious programs that can be far from benign. We are told by the experts in this field that most of our basic programs are embedded into our sub-conscious mind by the time we are five or six years old. These programs include the vast range of skills required for everyday living.

Of most importance to our discussion here, however, is that these fundamental programs also embody what we have been taught about God. This includes: why we are here in this world, what we should do while here and what we may expect from the whole enterprise of living in this world? In short, it encompasses the whole purpose and meaning of human existence. In the West all of these fundamental questions about meaning and life and death are intertwined with and formed by what we have been taught about Jesus. And these teachings were exported across the world as the Empires of the West spread their tentacles of influence across the globe down through the ages. Let's call these 'religious programs,' that deal with the meaning and purpose of life and what our destiny may be.

Jesus' message centered on all of these fundamental questions. Unfortunately, what he really taught and said and did has been considerably warped and distorted down through the many centuries since he was here, and right from the very beginning unfortunately. This was often done in by interested parties who subordinated his message to the purposes they wanted to accomplish at some particular point in history, but it got great assistance from some of the less worthy propensities we humans exhibit in some of our weaker moments: self-pity, fear, victimization, guilt and the sense of worthlessness.

To greatly simplify matters, we can say that the message of Jesus, as we know it today, has been turned on its head. Unfortunately, this is not just a matter of historical or antiquarian interest. Jesus taught us that many things, almost too wonderful and magical to believe, would be ours if we followed what he taught. How can this ever happen if we are getting only a garbled and warped version of his teachings?

If sub-conscious programs rule most of our daily activities, the same holds true concerning matters of fundamental belief. If the vast majority of our basic sub-conscious religious programs are based on what we have been taught about Jesus then we should be aware that some of these extremely misleading concepts about Jesus, and the programs they generate, are extraordinarily damaging to us. The prime example must be the model of Jesus as 'the Suffering Savior, who came here to die for our sins'; a model that has no basis in what the life and mission of Jesus was really all about.

The vast majority of our models about the purpose and meaning of human existence, and what we are supposed to accomplish here on Earth, are based on the warped and distorted versions of Jesus and his message that we humans have been fed for centuries...and from our earliest years. This creates an extraordinary collection of powerful and damaging negative programs in our sub-conscious mind — of which we are normally not even remotely aware. When we are trying to understand human meaning and purpose, the influence of these programs is as powerful as the influence we experience when trying to ride the 'backwards bicycle,' or when trying to type without leaving any spaces between the words.

The range of knowledge embraced by the study of theology as an academic subject is vast, ranging over a few thousands of years of history and its many related disciplines. I was a Professor of Systematic Theology during the 1970s and early 80s. At that time, we knew of the recent discoveries of many ancient texts in the Middle East, but did not yet realize how they might profoundly impact theological understanding. Up to that point in time, and despite the enormous corpus of knowledge in varying forms that already existed, there was almost no attention given beyond a very narrow focus, to an objective analysis of accepted theological positions and what valid foundations they may or may not have had.

In the past few decades we have learned an enormous amount about the circumstances surrounding the emergence of the foundational Western religious sources, such as the Old and New Testaments and contemporary documents, their dependence on secular sources, and how faithfully this collection of documents may have accurately represented the life of Jesus, even though written forty to seventy years or more after the end of his ministry. This awareness has created a renaissance, indeed a revolution, in all of the theological disciplines, but of course only for those who wished to recognize that the evidence to make that happen had emerged!

In a similar vein, it was only in the last few decades that an understanding of how the human brain works began to emerge as a related factor of great importance in the historical and contemporary religious field. This present work, which builds on these several disparate fields of inquiry, would simply not have been possible until the recent past. Using my expertise in theology, coupled with an exhaustive inquiry into how the human brain/mind works, I have been able to draw very significant conclusions in this book about an awareness of the workings of the 'human religious brain,' an artifact of 2,000 years of largely negative programming on human consciousness, and its profound effect on our religious disempowerment. In this book I look at those negative consequences, and investigate how we can begin to emerge from the miserable state generated by profoundly negative states of consciousness, relating to the mission of Jesus in particular, how to reverse their effects, and begin to emerge into the power to create our reality that Jesus promised us would be ours.

The name of Jesus figures in the title of this book. Jesus and his real message do indeed need to be saved, especially from those who most loudly proclaim their allegiance to him. That's why, mischievously, I had thought of a subtitle or amendment: 'Saving Jesus – from his Friends'.

There is another aspect to the 'Saving' in the title of this book. I'm sure you've been accosted by well-meaning and intense people on a street corner who earnestly ask you if you are 'saved'. I usually ask, in response to that question: "Saved from what?" I am still waiting for a reply. I suspect any hypothetical answer I might receive would include some threatening references to risking going to bottomless perdition at the end of my life. But most assuredly Jesus did not come here to 'save' us from that. There are a whole host of other things from which he might, with great benefit, have saved us. And at the top of that list I'm sure he would have to place saving us from belief in 'bottomless perdition' after death.

Even though the name of Jesus takes up 50% of the title, this book is not directly about Jesus at all. Rather it is about the dis-empowering programs that we have been burdened with as a result of the corruptions of his original and intended message.

Even more important is the question of how we effectively remove these programs from our sub-conscious mind. When we do accomplish that, they can no longer undermine every effort we make to accomplish what Jesus actually taught. Are we bold enough to accept that we even have these negative and dis-empowering programs? If we are not even aware that there are such programs, or if we are unwilling to concede that they exist and exert a major controlling influence over our lives, then our ability to move beyond these programs will be very limited or non-existent.

And we also need to know that trying to remove them by kicking and screaming will only make them more embedded and powerful. The 'backwards bicycle' and the other examples I gave at the beginning of this Introduction are superb illustrations of how religious programs also work. And they also illustrate how difficult it is for us to escape their influence...an influence that results in ever-increasing dis-empowerment.

This book is the first in a series called 'Forbidden Truth'. And there is an excellent reason for starting this series with a book that centers on matters related to Jesus. We have just briefly reviewed the power of sub-conscious programs, especially with respect to our fundamental beliefs. We will look at Jesus' real message and the many ways that his message has been distorted down through the course of Christian history. We will also explore how these distortions are now embedded in our sub-conscious minds as dis-empowering programs...programs that really do not have anything substantial to do with Jesus at all. Furthermore, we will see how these programs control our lives and prevent us from accomplishing what Jesus taught. The good news, however, is that there is a technique to disable those crippling programs skillfully and effectively. So, most importantly of all, doing just that is what this book is about.

Chapter 1
The Human Saga: How to Mess Up God

What Happens When God Hates All the Same People I do?

Anne Lamot said once: "I thought such awful thoughts that I cannot even say them out loud because they would make Jesus want to drink gin straight out of the cat dish."[12]

What does God love, or what acts or thoughts does God dislike? Divorce, gay marriage, fags, figs, workers of iniquity, homophobes, Democrats, Lady Gaga, remarriage, Ireland, techno, furries, war, cowards, Republicans, shrimp, lying lips, abortion, your outfit, bad manners, amputees, begging, Haiti, religion, complaining, Canada, haughty eyes, murmuring, mobile homes, haters... The internet is full of articles about things and people that God hates, and this is just a list of things I picked at random off the internet that some people affirm that God does not like. Some of them are with tongue in cheek, but the tragedy is that a remarkable number of them are not.

Where does this leave us: are we in a bottomless pit? Is it a fact that we're buried so deeply in these programs that a lot of individuals may very possibly never be able to muster the resources of mind to escape their clutches? Unfortunately, that is very likely.

When the weather starts to get better, people often ponder about invoking God before a football game. In a certain College, for which I have a great regard, there is a custom that when their football team goes out to play, they publicly invoke God's help in defeating their opposition, and make the sign of the Cross to seal it.

I don't know much about the other teams they have met, who may very well be far more nihilistic, atheistic, agnostic, and

---

[12] Anne Lamot, *Bird by Bird: Some Instructions on Writing and Life* (Pantheon Books, 1994).

irrelevant – or pious. But perhaps the other team is doing the same thing? This is obviously a problem for God. Which team is he going to support? But the real problem is for us: because if God makes a decision to favor one team, on what factors did he base his decision? And why?

Remember we are removing sub-conscious programs by pondering all of these apparently disjointed matters.

Let's also look at Grace before Meals, especially at times like Thanksgiving or Christmas. Who balks at grace before meals? Apparently only atheists, agnostics, nihilists and the damned. But yet, if we really believe that God loves all of his creatures equally, there should be consequences of that conviction. Take two children. One of them grows up in this country, surrounded by plenty. Maybe he had goldfish crackers with juice, cheese sticks, and peaches for lunch, and then an after-school snack. In another part of the world we have a child who has only had a thin helping of gruel for food since the day before yesterday.

Maybe if we were less self-centered, complacent and self-satisfied, then perhaps God would not be thanked in such a blasé manner for directing food to our dinner tables. Because it leaves us with the very awkward question as to why God didn't do the same for that starving child out in the middle of some desert in the Third World?

In a lot of things we do, like Grace before Meals, we give thanks for what God has done for us, and its assumed, unthinkingly, that God is doing the same for everyone else. But, obviously, "He" is not. This is not an *optical* illusion, but it operates in the mind in a similar fashion. It is a powerful illusion of the mind, and the consequences of that illusion are not flattering for God.

Courtesy of our sub-conscious programs God apparently has favorites. What do we do with that? There is a wonderful little piece of anonymous writing, publicized by Reata Strickland, called "Interview with God."[13] It's a profound meditation on

[13] Published, February 5, 2002. Full text also widely available on the internet, e.g., at http://rdoc.org.uk/eve/forums/a/tpc/f/109102483/m/106108316

someone who is pondering very deep and fundamental questions. Suddenly God manifests and asks: "Do you have some questions to ask me?" And God solves all of the problems that exist in the world of the person who has been doing that contemplating. Of course, that's all right in a suburban middle class, very happy home. But what about Darfur, Ethiopia, Syria, or the disastrous drought in the Horn of Africa in the Spring of 2017 that left close to 20 million people facing malnutrition and famine – including at least 6 million children.

We assume that God shares our views on everything else. This is an example of how the human mind operates in this sphere.

The image below is a famous optical illusion called the *Kanizsa Triangle.*[14]

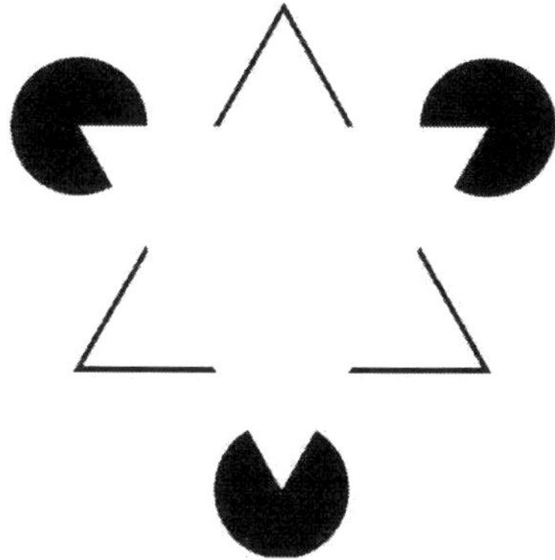

In the Kanizsa Triangle Illusion we readily perceive three black circles and two triangles, even though there are technically no circles or triangles in the image at all. We clearly see a white equilateral triangle in the center of this image, even though there are no lines or enclosed spaces to form such a triangle: in short, there is no white triangle in this image. Nevertheless, we see it, and furthermore, once we have seen it we can never "un-see" it again. The white triangle even appears brighter than the surrounding

[14] Devised by the Italian psychologist, Gaetano Kanizsa, in 1955.

white background, even though both the white areas are exactly the same shade.

No matter what efforts we make we still cannot help seeing that white triangle, which nevertheless we know does not exist. We are believing in things that never existed or perhaps cannot exist. In an odd way this illustrates how the mind behaves when it tries to grapple with issues such as the puzzle of God. We believe that God takes care of our needs, but we also believe he takes care of everyone else, when we know, if we would only look around us, that that is false. Can we ever begin to suspect that illusory convictions such as this have much more to do with assuring our own complacency, than they have anything real to convey about how God is?

How can we ever begin to properly understand our relationship to God, on which depends our realizing the Mandate of Jesus for us: "All the things I did, you will do, and greater than these will you do." Can I ever do anything meaningful to help starving people far away? More to the point, can I ever really manage to take control of my own destiny, as Jesus wished, if I persist in cherishing sloppy and sentimental versions of reality and of God's relationship to all who live in this world? Are we not embracing a make-believe world and a make-believe God? Maybe we need to face up to the fact that God is not taking care of the starving children far away. If he were, surely they would not be starving? But perhaps we may at last be on the verge of realizing that our cozy vision of God taking care of all his creatures is really far more about preserving our comfort zone than it is about understanding God's relationship to the people of the third world. Feuerbach put it so well when he said we have created God in our own image. We obviously do not like to be told that. But the reason why we did so create God is even less palatable: because it served the comfort and convenience of those who formulated and popularized such belief systems, instead of sticking to the message that Jesus uttered. While cherishing such illusions we have in essence crippled any hope of being able to manifest as Jesus did.

The Puzzle of Why Most Creatures Can Live Only by Killing?

Have you ever noticed that the vast majority of creatures who exist on this Earth can only continue to live by killing something else? Does this even remotely look like a situation that was exquisitely planned and supervised by an omnipotent, good, all-wise, and superintending deity? Is it not just one more inconsistency in our panoply of illusions? Again, the primary purpose of those illusions is to preserve us in our comfort zone, much more than it is to tell us something valuable about God.

The truth is that it is our responsibility, not God's, to evolve to such a state that we can rectify the all-too-obvious and pervading major problems that festoon this Earth and its inhabitants. Why are we looking "up" for help, metaphorically speaking, when the Creator apparently designed the solution to be in our own hands? Will we ever attain to such an ability if we continue to subsist on illusions and fairy tales about the most fundamental matters of our world, that in any case are designed primarily to create the mindset of a fool's Paradise? If you and I want to be masters of the quantum field; do we want to be able to extend our hand, or not extend our hand, and produce reality out of an invisible field as Jesus told us we could and should do? Is it possible? Yes. Are we going to do it with all of this mass of illusion and inconsistency ruling our brains and minds? The answer is emphatically in the negative.

How do humans treat fish? Are they less in the sight of God than creatures who have legs and walk on dry land, or who fly on wings? God doesn't seem to care. Jesus magically multiplied fish catches so they could be hoisted up in nets and subject to slow suffocation. How could God have such different views on how he regards his creation?

Fish brains are very unlike ours. And the more unlike our brains the brain of some species is, the less easily we can empathize with it. It's been pointed out that this might be why we concern ourselves less with the treatment of an octopus than with the treatment of chimpanzees, even though scientists tell us the octopus is one of the most intelligent creatures on the planet. What is at the core of this discrepancy? Chimpanzees in external appearances are more like you and me.

Unless we can somehow resonate with a creature's experience, meaning to feel it, at least at a tentative hypothetical level, then it falls outside our moral sphere — and outside God's priorities also, apparently. Isn't it curiously interesting how God's priorities seem suspiciously like something we would have dreamt up? Is this one of the programs in our sub-conscious mind? It most assuredly is. Can it stay there? Well of course it can stay there. But what do we want to do with our lives? If we want to do something wonderful, it cannot stay there.

There is something unique about human killing. It's not instinctual like it is with animals. The old Master Teacher asked me once: How do you feel about this world you are all in? I said I was depressed by one thing. It seems to me that, apart from the bees and few other species, nothing can live in this creation except by killing something else. I said there must have been some serious shortcuts taken when this setup was being processed.

Killing is part of survival here. We can choose why, and when and where we'll kill. And that gives rise to enormous complications in ethics. A person might become a vegetarian to avoid killing animals. Yet to eat and live we have to hack off plants from their roots and roast their bodies in ovens. Should the vegetarian eat eggs, the potentially unborn children of beautiful birds? Or drink milk, which may have been taken from cows whose calves have been slaughtered for veal? Why are those who campaign against abortion so often the same people who campaign for the restoration of the death penalty?

There is something radically illogical and incongruous in all of this set up, and the fundamental reason why that is so is that the illusions at the heart of most of the collections of religious beliefs have so radically dis-empowered us that we no longer even seem to be capable of envisaging what our true destiny here might be.

I am pointing out the very obvious fact that our ethical systems of belief, which are built into our programs, are normally illogical and a mass of inconsistencies. Are we ever going to heal the sick, walk on water and raise the dead while that's the case? Absolutely not! So, we have work to do. What ethical sense does it make to kill a murderer as an example to convince others that murder is wrong? We are in a rut of illogicality – to call it by a very mild term.

We find it so difficult to see beyond ourselves, or beyond what is similar to ourselves. We are far more likely to kill what's different from us than what is like us. The vegetarian feels guilty about killing animals but not about killing plants. Why? Plants are less like us. Some people will eat fish but they won't eat meat, and not for reasons of avoiding heart disease, but because of an unthoughtful assumption that fish have no feelings. There are fishermen who abhor the idea of hunting animals. And there are hunters who would shoot birds, but they would balk at killing a deer with its all too human eyes.

And the same is true when humans kill other humans. If you're a white European or American, it used to appear in times past that it was easier to kill a Black person or an Oriental than it was to kill another person who has a white skin and Caucasian features: that mindset fortunately has radically altered with the passage of time and hopefully soon will be no more.

The reverse is equally true. It used to be easier for an Oriental or a Black person to kill a White person of Caucasian decent. It's even easier when we throw highly offensive terms at them, and call them 'niggers', and 'wogs', 'rednecks' or 'kinks'. That vocabulary is aimed at dehumanizing.

It's easier for an Oriental to kill a European or an American than to kill another Oriental. But you know it's time to draw a line in the sand here if we are serious about really making a good use of this incarnation. And, especially since the message of Jesus was designed precisely to help us to do just that. That message has been turned inside out and on its head. Have we allowed ourselves to become so blind and illogical that the most basic of our convictions are actually mental illusions, and that the programs of our mind keep us pursuing that same goal? I'm afraid we have. What does that all say about the potentials of our evolution into Mastery?

A century ago it took a week to get a message from the United States to Europe and months to get in touch with China or Japan. The system of nation states was sensible in those days. Now, much of the system of nation states is outmoded and obsolete, but for reasons of comfort, for reasons of narcissism, we cling to them. It's only in such a climate that war can flourish. It's only in such a climate of alienation that we find it easier to kill those who are superficially different from ourselves. Hopefully, the increasing interaction between all races on this pitifully small planet will iron themselves out before we destroy ourselves completely.

It's usual these days for both sides in a war to proclaim themselves as victims. In former times people were less squeamish. You went to war to take what the other guy had. But nowadays we always seem to have to have at least a pretense of higher motives. Even Adolph Hitler, and several other well-known tyrants of the 20th Century, concocted reasons for their invasions. In the face of all of this it's all too easy to throw up our hands in despair, and say nobody is to blame for war. Nobody made the wrong choice. It all just happened — like spontaneous combustion.

And the same arrogance and the same blindness is in each of us that was in all of the great warring powers of history. Someone said to me one time, the Irish are a great people; they never made war on anyone outside their country. And that's true. But I replied, "Yes that's correct, but the only reason for it was that the canvas was too small." If we don't have the ability to do something, there is not much virtue or credit in refraining from it.

The same narcissism and the same inability to tolerate anything different is at the heart of our dis-empowerment. It's at the heart of our inability to create. We're just like chickens. Chickens will pick to death a chicken that has some disfigurement or some injury. We are exactly the same. We can't tolerate anyone who is different. And so many people who campaign for peace unfortunately are still carrying hatred in their hearts and either cannot see that, or see no contradiction in it.

Moral blindness, savagery, moral ambivalence, illogicality and narcissism. What has been the greatest force encouraging all this? The picture of our God that's been retailed into the three major religions of the West – Judaism, Christianity and Islam – in chronological order. Moral blindness, savagery, moral ambivalence, illogicality and narcissism, this is exactly what God is on the record for, even still today. Our religious and moral sense is totally dominated by a mass of illusions and inconsistencies, and our brains process those matters in fundamentally the same ways in which those optical illusions function, that we looked at a short while earlier in this book.

So why do I try to manifest and nothing happens? Why do I try to heal someone, but people don't get better? The reason is that I am conflicted within myself without really realizing it. And all of my knowledge and information about how the universe that I live in, functions; how I work towards my destiny; how I understand God; how I understand the message of Jesus Christ after 2,000 years: all of that belongs to a level of knowledge and awareness that was more appropriate in the Dark Ages than it is in the 21st century.

If we react in this way to entities that don't look like us what are we going to do if we have visitations of beings from other places? Given even the level of our present knowledge of the vastness of the universes, and even of how life on this planet came to be, is it not inconceivable to refuse to realize that there must be a multitude of other places besides this Earth where conscious beings have developed? The likelihood of them physically resembling our illusions of what makes an entity worthy of respect or love is very remote. Will we accept them only if they are blond haired, blue eyed beauties, from the Pleiades or Orion? Or is it the octopus and the chimpanzee all over again? Will we abhor other entities from Draco, or from Arcturus, who may be infinitely more loving, simply because they do not conform to our illusions of beauty? What are we going to do with all that? On even a cursory and honest examination we have to admit that we are really not fit to be let loose and that any sane race would probably figure the wisest course is for them to leave us strictly alone until we have managed to get at least some of our affairs on this Earth into a semblance of order.

A Muslim mystic, Imam Muhammed Baquir, had a little fable, which I found very appropriate: One day he found he could communicate with the ants. So, he approached one of the ants and said "What is God like? Does he resemble the ant? The ant said, "God? No, no indeed – we have only a single sting but God has two!" This is exactly what most people in the world believe: God is a human being enlarged.

Does someone think I am crabby or insecure or jealous? Does someone believe I am contented and I'm happy and I'm easily pleased? One way, surprisingly, would be to ask them. But an even more true insight would be gotten from watching how they interact with me.

Christians, I've often heard it said, spend a lot of time interacting with God, or at least attempting to. We may not be able to find out what's happening on God's side. But we know a good deal about the human half. How humans attempt to approach, influence or simply relate to God tells us a lot about how they actually perceive God. And the writers of the Bible, of course, have endless words on this. So, we know well how the authors of the Biblical books perceived God.

According to cognitive scientist, Pascal Boyer, most supernatural beings, regardless of their physical form, have human psyches, including emotions. And the God of the Bible is no exception to that. This is one of our biggest programs related to our dis-empowerment.

Biblical ideas about the anger of God might have come from how you and I would expect powerful people to behave towards people who were on a lower rung of the ladder. Sermons and texts that wax eloquent about God's anger are just one of the many clues about how the Old Testament writers related to God as a human being of higher status. That's all the Old Testament God is. And, of course, that assumption is fundamentally flawed. Most Christians since then have adhered to the human-being-enlarged version of God.

What gives God pleasure in the Bible? The counterpoint to the threat of God's anger is that certain ways of relating to God will please God, and so court favor with God. Making burnt offerings is a winner, apparently. I'm just going on the records we have today. Leviticus 1:9 gives us an example with regard to what is about to be burned in sacrifice to Jehovah: "He is to wash the inner parts and the legs with water, and the priest is then to burn all of it on the altar. It is a burnt offering, an offering made by fire, an aroma pleasing to the Lord." All of these matters are still on the books, and all over the place, not just in the Book of Leviticus, the Third Book of the Torah, Chapter 1, verse 9.

Besides burnt offerings, gifts or otherwise, what other kinds of attitudes please high-status people? I'm told that in the past in the Middle School world some pretentious students, affectionately called "Queen Bees," wanted always to be the center of attention. They liked being admired and imitated, which is of course the highest form of flattery. They like being exclusive and they reject students who spend time with outsiders to their clique. They like calling the shots. They like bequeathing special favors, and getting pathetic gratitude from the lowly in return.

If we think about this list it's remarkably, even painfully, similar to what the God of the Christians is supposed to desire from his followers. So, what does the God of the Christians want? This is a short list which it does not take much effort to draw up. The following are quotations from the Torah or Pentateuch (to use the Latin and Greek terms), for the first five books of what Christians call the Old Testament.

- Attention: "On thee I will meditate night and day" – in other words, I want praise and admiration – "For the Lord God is great and greatly to be praised."
- Subservience: "I will bow before the Lord my maker."
- Dependency: "Ask and it will be given." Given, not created.
- Uncritical compliance: "…receive the kingdom of God like a little child."
- Exclusivity: "Thou shall have no other Gods before me … For I am a jealous God."
- Gratitude: "…for this unspeakable gift … I give much thanks."

I recently came across this prayer by Mary Fairchild:[15]

Lord, in the morning I start each day,
By taking a moment to bow and pray.
I start with thanks, and then give praise
For all your kind and loving ways.
Today if sunshine turns to rain,
If a dark cloud brings some pain,
I won't doubt or hide in fear
For you, my God, are always near.
I will travel where you lead;
I will help my friends in need.
Where you send me I will go;
With your help I'll learn and grow.
Hold my family in your hands,
As we follow your commands
And I will keep you close in sight
Until I crawl in bed tonight.

I have underlined some particularly revealing words in her prayer. It's beautiful, poetic, comforting, and appealing — but like so much other pious material in this genre, unfortunately it's a recipe for spiritual disaster.

Submission Displays and the Downside of Person-Gods

Submissive displays are common in the animal kingdom. It helps to keep order. Submission displays are valued by powerful humans also. It is not confined to animals, because our species developed under conditions of insufficiency — never enough to go around, inadequate food supplies, not enough high-quality mates to get for every man as much as he wants, limited fertile lands and so on, so on, so on. Scarcity. Scarcity. Submission displays have

[15] June 21, 1855 — December 20, 1921.

always been very valued by those in authority and they still are, except of course the Lingua Franca has changed. Now their chief playgrounds are in the fields of business, high finance and politics.

These dominant hierarchies appear in all social animals if they need to compete for resources. Submissive displays from underlings will allow this hierarchy to be established and to be maintained without physical violence. For example, weaker chickens move away from food or off the more comfortable perch if their superiors in the pecking order arrive on the scene. With chimpanzees, a subordinate may crouch or hold out a hand, or squeak to acknowledge dominance.

Humans show submission through both words and behavior. And signals are so pervasive that actors are trained to incorporate hierarchy signals into every conversation. That's because acting and improvisation tend to fall flat unless the social hierarchy is established among the characters.

So as experts or specialists, or if we want to use that phrase, social information specialists, we depend on each other, and we also compete with each other. To minimize how much energy we spend on competition, we establish hierarchies. Hierarchies save energy, they get to the point. Our desire is to get as good a position as we can in the hierarchy but that leaves us emotionally insecure. We are not sure where we stand. If I am insecure, then unconscious signals that other people will submit to me, are reassuring and pleasing.

Little as we like to admit it, one of our great programs blocking the real message of Jesus taking effect in us is that dominance and submission are an integral part of human relations, and that is what we appear to have applied to our relationship with Jesus. The ultimate human illusions are to have turned Jesus into a Suffering Savior, and the Father into a Person-God.

Humans can be very creative, but some of our behavior may have very specific roots in biology. Do we realize when we bow our heads in prayer that it's a submission ritual? It's probably traceable to some posture that in olden times commoners had to exhibit when they approached royalty. The word 'grovel' in our language today means to show some kind of exaggerated deference or contrition to appease somebody or to gain their forgiveness or favor. It's believed to have roots in the ancient Norse phrase *á grúfu,* meaning 'face downward,' but its medieval roots also seem to be related to the word 'prone,' and may have to do with the physical posture required to approach a king.

A more obvious example in our terms today is the Chinese word 'kowtow.' It means to grovel before, to be obsequious, servile, and sycophantic; to cringe or bow and scrape; to ingratiate oneself, to suck up to, to curry favor. It derives from the traditional Chinese practice of bowing down so low that your forehead touches the ground. Essentially it means behaving with extreme submission to please an authority figure. In other primates, a bow communicates submission to an animal of higher status. It can be a means of avoiding a fight, when tensions are high.

If we understand our place, if we engage in submissive behaviors, then higher status people will let us hang around. And we ourselves gain status through proximity and osmosis. And Christians gain status, at least in each other's eyes, and in their own minds, because of how close they are perceived to be to God. I am not saying Christians are specifically arrogant, because I don't think that's factually accurate. But all of us are wired by nature to orient ourselves according to hierarchy and to seek advantage within the hierarchy. This is very unpleasant stuff to hear and it's even more difficult to put words on. Why? Because it is so close to the root of our problems.

These hierarchy relationships were mediated by emotions. So we instinctively expect them in any being with a humanoid psyche, such as the Old Testament and Christian God is. Since the Christian Bible describes a person-god who relates to humans, it's inevitable that people who believe in that kind of God are going to respond in this kind of way.

If the world were different, and if we had properly understood what the message of Jesus Christ was all about, then Christianity might instead center on release from desire, or ethical studies, or acts of compassion, such as you have in some forms of Buddhism.

You might even focus on ahimsa, or nonviolence towards all living things, as in the philosophy of Jainism and the main branches of Buddhism. Ahimsa, ironically has suffered somewhat the same fate as the teachings of Jesus. It is generally understood as avoiding violence towards others and perhaps even having compassion for them. But the much deeper meaning of Ahimsa is to avoid violence towards oneself. This gives us a clue that the deeper meaning of ahimsa has more to do with thoughts rather than with anything we do. In short, it means the absence of violence in any of the three main realms of our being, the body, the mind, and the spirit. It is relatively easy to abstain from violent actions, especially if we are comfortable and well off, but much more difficult to abstain from violent thoughts, especially when we are confronted with situations of extreme injustice, of which there is no shortage in our world. In fact, there is an insidious movement of thought that teaches it is desirable to get intensely worked up about injustices on a global scale. However, when we realize that our thoughts and experiences profoundly change the brain, in a very literal sense, at the neurological level, then we should have second thoughts about that, for the effect on the brain is dis-empowering. The first focus in the practice of non-violence ought to be towards ourselves, for if we do not accomplish that, our ability to manifest out of the quantum field is stillborn.

This is similar to the ways in which the teachings of Jesus became transformed into a purified and exalted system of ethics – which they certainly are. But those ethical mandates and ideals were taught by him as the signs that manifest when we are on the right track towards personal empowerment. But none of those ideals were meant to be ends in themselves, which is how they have been presented to us, but only ways by which our power to interact with the quantum field would be freed up.

Like the God of Islam, the God of the Bible is interested mainly in worship. That's what the texts tells us, and that's how believers respond. As a consequence, intellectual assent and submissive behaviors and displays of devotion are at the heart of both religions. The way that believers interact with God, tells us who those people are talking to. And unfortunately, our ideas about God fall victim to what we accept about big-cheese humans. That means that we see a God who not only has emotions, but many emotions that are far indeed from noble.

We often find ourselves arguing with people and voices inside our heads; made-up people who live only there, cartoonish and two dimensional. Real world people might grow and change, but my internal version of them usually will not. In fact, psychologists tell us that our perception of other people all too often is manufactured from issues up to which we ourselves have not faced, and those failures to own our challenges have now become physical in the neuronets of the brain, many of them unfortunately in that critical rear section of the brain.

Getting people out of our heads is not easy. Why? Because they got in there so early on. I am referring to the sub-conscious programs, the illusions that roam the mind. While most animals have their behavior largely programmed by instinct, humans rely on information handed down from one generation to the next. So it is not surprising that one of the chief characteristics of human childhood has to be credulity. If trusted authorities say it, like our parents, like our teachers, like someone we revere, then children believe it.

"Sinners in the Hands of an Angry God" was a famous sermon preached by Jonathan Edwards,[16] over two and a half centuries ago. He said:

> "[Wicked men] are now the objects of that very same anger and wrath of God that is expressed in the torments of Hell. And the reason why they do not go down to Hell each moment is not because God, in whose power they are, is not then very angry with them; as He is with many miserable creatures now tormented in Hell, who there feel and bear the fierceness of His wrath. Yea, God is a great deal more angry with great numbers that are now on Earth; yea, doubtless, with many that are now in this congregation, who it may be are at ease, than he is with many of those who are now in the flames of Hell."

[16] Preached to his own congregation in Northampton, Massachusetts, on an unknown date, and again on July 8, 1741 in Enfield, Connecticut.

It's a fine example of this type of preaching, which was very popular in colonial times in this country, and which indeed probably inspired much of that tradition. It was found that that to which individuals responded best, in terms of a sermon's effectiveness, was the fear of everlasting damnation in Hell fire.

Anger is an activating emotion. It is a response to pain or from being thwarted. When we are in danger, or our goal-oriented activities are blocked in some way, and anger can make us more focused, more persistent and more determined. So socially it serves us to get our bodies ready for defensive action by making us stronger, more alert, more aggressive and more intimidating. It can be almost like the function of the amygdalae, a programmed instant response to threats that happens faster than the conscious mind can assess the situation. That means that there is both a positive side and a downside to anger.

If someone is powerful enough then he or she really has no need to ever be angry. If that's the case with some humans, then surely the force that created the universe will have no need for it? Why would God need it? He is already as powerful as can be. What would God gain from being angry? To be better able to focus? To break through inhibitions? Surely neither of these apply to God? And yet we still find no problem whatever with expressing a belief, that either implies or directly affirms, that God could be angry. On the face of the matter it's one thing that God should find impossible to be. In fact, one distressing thing that eventually confronts us is that the list of atrocities attributed to God in our Sacred Writings actually makes it impossible for that entity ever to be God.

Can the True God Be a God of Power?

Where then did all this stuff come from that is applied to God, but that seems symptomatic of the worst sides of human nature? Why is all this so much at the heart of religion? Take the Bible writers. Their image of God as the most powerful person imaginable was based on Iron Age Chieftains or Kings who wielded absolute power over their subjects and were beyond accountability.

Look at the example of Job, who was a pawn between God – Jehovah or Yahweh – and Satan. As a test of the loyalty of Job, his children are taken from him in death, and everything else that he had – friendship, wealth and health, are taken from him also. When Job complains that he hadn't done anything to merit this treatment, God says, "Will the faultfinder contend with the Almighty? Let him who reproves God answer it." (Job 40:2).

Absolute power allows caprice and cruelty. It is always maintained, partially at least, by fear, a level of fear that is virtually impossible to perpetuate without anger's unpredictability.

We often think of anger being the domain of powerless, frustrated people. But the opposite may be true. Anger often functions as a bargaining tactic. It increases formidability and, consequentially, when someone gets angry, people pay more attention to the one who is angry, and pay less attention to their own concerns. But that only works if you stick around. Most people don't like being around angry people and most people don't like the sensation of 'walking on eggshells'. So, we generally try to avoid others who are chronically irritable, in particular if their anger is unpredictable or dangerous.

But the equation changes if the angry person is powerful. Powerful people are ones who can inflict penalties if we don't pay attention to their wishes. Or who, on the other side, can confer benefits if we do. They can reject us, they can injure us, they can even kill us, or they may be able to give us special favors. With powerful people we want to avoid their anger by staying connected. So when we figure out what makes them angry we tend to be more compliant by learning to avoid those delicate areas.

This is a sublime analogy of the illusion in the way we relate to God. Maybe it's that we are biologically predisposed to be anxious about God's wrath. But the fact that I am disposed to expect something doesn't necessarily make it real. Nonetheless, our minds are designed to help us anticipate and adapt to the feelings, emotions and behaviors of other humans, especially powerful ones who can make our lives wretched or easy.

It is all too easy to acquire this template, and then project it onto the universe and to the whole of the supernatural. It appears then that the Biblical writer's belief in an angry God reduces down to an artifact of human information processing. So, with due respect to Jonathan Edwards, are we sinners in the hands of an angry God, or rather sinners in the hands of angry humans?

A lot of scholars have decided long ago that the earliest Biblical texts give an indication that the ways in which God/Yahweh or Jehovah was pictured was almost identical to how an ancient Near Eastern tribal deity would have been treated.

The Song of Moses in Deuteronomy 32 indicates that Yahweh was believed to have been one of the children of the Canaanite deity, El Elyon (God Most High). The song describes how the nations were formed and it says the peoples of the Earth were divided up according to the number of El Elyon's children. Yahweh was Israel's patron.

In other words, the best evidence suggests that Yahweh or Jehovah did not begin as the "only true God". He did not begin by being regarded as the Creator of the world. Yahweh began as a young and up and coming tribal deity whose prowess among other gods mirrored the aspirations of Israel *vis-a-vis* surrounding tribes and nations.

But over time Yahweh and El Elyon are conflated, merging into one. Jehovah starts by being seen as a Creator-god. But during that period, the people of Israel still believed in other gods. They are forbidden to worship other gods, because they owe their allegiance to Jehovah, their patron deity. He was supposed to have a wife Asherah. It is clear that she was worshipped by the people of Israel as his consort. That seems to have been acceptable till about the 7th century BC, when the people of Israel were in captivity in Babylon.

Unfortunately, human sacrifice was a rare but nevertheless widespread practice in the Near Eastern religions. It continued in Israel up to about the seventh and sixth centuries BC as an acceptable part of placating God, for example, so that he would give them victory in their battles. The Israelite warrior Jephthah sacrificed his virgin daughter to God in fulfillment of a promise to secure Jehovah's help in battle. Some of the earlier accounts in the conquest of Canaan showed the same pattern. Jehovah gave the Israelites victory against the enemy armies and they in turn slaughtered all of the women and children that they captured in payment for his aid.

There is also evidence that Jehovah commanded human sacrifice in the Law of Moses. And when the practice of human sacrifice began to fall into disrepute, the prophet Ezekiel[17] complained about the people of Judah burning their children to death. He tells us that from the time when the people of Israel were in the wilderness, to his day, they sacrificed their sons by fire.

He confirms that Jehovah did command human sacrifice, but he claimed that Jehovah ordered them to kill their first-born sons only as a way of getting back at them for their lack of faith. All this was to horrify them and show them he is the Lord. Ezechiel tells us, beginning in Chapter 16: "And, you took your sons and your daughters, whom you had borne to me, and these you sacrificed to them to be devoured. Were your harlotries so small a matter that you slaughtered my children and delivered them up as an offering by fire to them?"

> Ezechiel, Chapter 20:
>
> [25]Moreover I gave them statutes that were not good and ordinances by which they could not have life; [26]and I defiled them through their very gifts in making them offer by fire all their first-born, that I might horrify them; I did it that they might know that I am the LORD.[18]
>
> [30]Wherefore say to the house of Israel, Thus, says the Lord GOD: Will you defile yourselves after the manner of your fathers and go astray after their detestable things?
>
> [31]When you offer your gifts and sacrifice your sons by fire, you defile yourselves with all your idols to this day. And shall I be inquired of by you, O house of Israel? As I live, says the Lord GOD, I will not be inquired of by you.

---

[17] Born 622 BC. He was among those deported in 597 BC to Babylon.

[18] Ezek. 20:25-26.

No illusions here.

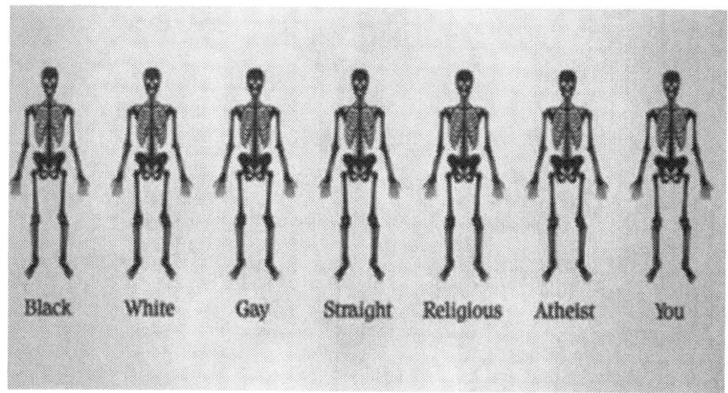

Courtesy of Blaze Press

Emotional Reaction versus Rational Processing

The reason that an emotional reaction can happen faster than rational processing is that it literally bypasses the cerebral cortex, the part of the brain that handles conscious thought. That's why we use all those phrases such as, "trusting your gut", "gut instinct", etc. So as the human brain took on its present form there was no point at which the whole thing got designed from the ground up. Rather, new layers were added on, old parts got repurposed, upgrades followed upon upgrades. Imagine a house that has had the back porch enclosed, another porch added, a family room tacked onto the side of the building, cables poked through the framing around the basement door, dormers popped up to convert an attic into a bedroom. That is the brain of the human being.

That said, it does assume that if we have sufficient natural explanations for natural events, then we don't assert supernatural causes as well. So if schizophrenia can be explained and controlled by the presence or absence of certain neurotransmitters in my brain, then we don't bother talking about demons possessing schizophrenics. This assumption is basic to the study of psychology, but not uniquely so. In fact, except where it threatens religious dogmas, it is considered true. If I think my car runs on gasoline, I don't need to draw magical signs or pray over it after filling the tank. Gallons of hydrocarbons will suffice nicely, thank you very much.

If I think that locking my door will keep out thieves I don't bother with sprinkling protective herbs around the door. If I think bullets will kill enemy soldiers I don't need to employ a voodoo specialist before going into battle. When we find natural cause and effect relationships that are sufficient to explain, control and predict phenomena, then we should let it be. And that's the bottom line.

So, what does all this set of feelings do, what does it mean for a God who is supposed to be all knowing, all powerful, all benevolent, but apparently still has these all-to-human emotions?

Bishop John Shelby Spong once said "Christians don't need to be born again. They need to grow up". He was reacting to the fact that many believers never outgrow their childhood concept of God as a kind of mean daddy in the sky; one who needs our admiration, can be cajoled for favors, and covers or beats our backs when we get ourselves into trouble.

Unfortunately, we often acquire all these religious beliefs when we are too young to process abstractions. When children are taught that Jesus loves them, they have no way of understanding love except as they experience it from other humans, especially their parents. As we get older most people don't stop to re-evaluate our childhood ideas. Believers rarely ask themselves, "What does the statement 'Jesus loves me' actually mean?"

If you look at God's alleged emotions through the lens of affective science, we get that into our adult minds. It puts us in a state from which our adult selves can get a glimpse of a deeply layered set of concepts about God that are embedded in us, whether we believe it or not. Fundamentally they have no bases in reality, but does that make the situation acceptable? Far from it, but it's hard to remove these programs. Some of these concepts come of course not from our own childhood, but from the childhood of our species.

While it's very necessary, it's also very disheartening to have to talk about this kind of material. And it's also very often the stage at which people give up, largely from having some type of deep, atavistic, and emotional reaction, to contemplating these kinds of thoughts.

Or they lapse into the old pitfall of blaming the messenger. That's fine. Perhaps that's as long or as far as they can go in this incarnation. But they will come again, and maybe the next time they will have more capacity to challenge what's unpleasant in the interests of their spiritual evolution and empowerment.

Chapter 2
The Hijack of the Message of Jesus

It is certainly not very original to point out that Jesus of Nazareth is the most influential person who has ever lived in the course of recorded human history. More blood has been shed in his name and more good done, than in connection with any other person; more movements have claimed him as patron, and more books have been written about him, than about any other person who has ever lived.

Tragically, however glorious his message undoubtedly was, it suffered the fate of many another glorious message in the ways in which it was warped and damaged almost beyond recognition down the centuries. But in the case of Jesus this seems to have happened almost from the very beginning.

Given that the arrest and torture of Jesus took place a day and a night before Passover, and that his early followers were Jewish, it was almost inevitable that his message would have become interpreted through the major themes of Passover, and later of Yom Kippur, the pre-eminent Jewish Day of Atonement to God for our sins. Thus, even very early on, the main elements of his teachings were already side-tracked.

Before the destruction of the Jerusalem Temple in 70 AD, the ceremonies of Passover culminated with the sacrifice of a spotless lamb on the altar of the Temple. The flowing of the lamb's blood down the stone of the altar was seen as a symbol of our sins being washed away in the sight of God. In the traditional accounts of the Passion of Jesus there was no shortage of the flowing of blood. After the crown of thorns was pressed into the head, Pilate ordered a scourging way beyond the legal limit, in the hope the Priests and mob before him would be appeased by the sight of so much blood and suffering. The first Epistle of Peter testifies that that scourging was particularly savage. Against this powerful and dramatic background, the role and message of Jesus almost immediately came to be understood as intimately related to blood sacrifice for the atonement for sin, about which he had not said a word during his public ministry, even though blood sacrifice was prominent in Jewish tradition. The authenticity of the so-called ransom statement of Mark 10:45[19] is much disputed, and it is apparent that, in the context of the narration of the Last Supper in Matthew, Mark and Luke, the only blood Jesus has in mind is the red wine of the Eucharistic meal.

As will be explained in more detail later, in the ancient mystical traditions the symbolic meal of a great spiritual Master with his disciples, was designed to celebrate their incarnation and evolution through life's journey. This mystical meal was focused on bread, wine and water, symbolizing the three elements that constitute the human being: the spirit, symbolized by the wine, the physical body, symbolized by the bread, and the water, symbolizing the soul that keeps the memory of the spirit's journey. It was believed that in such a ritual meal the Master could transmit his DNA into the bread and wine the disciples consumed. Any suggestion of even implying a literal blood sacrifice is light years away from any of these historic sacred enactments, and most especially from the one that was enacted with Jesus and his disciples.

In effect, right at the very start, the message of Jesus was already hijacked.

After the Passion, the followers of Jesus largely remained in Jerusalem, under the leadership of the brother of Jesus, James the Just, even though the message began to spread quickly much further afield, even as far as Rome. It seems most of those early followers

[19] "For even the Son of Man did not come to be served, but to serve, and to give his life as a ransom for many."

of Jesus around Jerusalem did not see any conflict between being followers of Jesus while remaining orthodox Jews. Consequently, they continued to attend the Temple and Synagogues, while celebrating the Eucharistic Meal among themselves as the central ceremony establishing their link with Jesus.

However, with time, the early Christians' were formulating more and more explicit statements of a unique way in which Jesus related to God. This was largely due to the influence of Paul, whom, we can't forget, had never met Jesus during his ministry. This expression of a unique relationship of Jesus to God, does not seem to have been nearly as prominent at the core of the faith early on in the Christian movement, compared to the form it took twenty or thirty years later.

Mainstream Judaism became convinced that the inclusion of Jesus in the Godhead, as expressed by Paul, was threatening the Jewish belief in monotheism. As the Christian movement spread more and more to the Gentile world, the Jewish dietary laws and the practice of circumcision were also being progressively abandoned by the early Christians. Eventually, the day of reckoning came, and sometime in the period 85-90 AD, the alleged Jewish Synod of Jamnia expelled the "Nazarenes," as they were called, from mainstream Judaism, and it seems at around this time the Christians were banished from the Synagogues.

Obviously, this exaltation of Jesus to being a member of the Godhead was based on a misinterpretation of what he taught: that we "are all gods." The real reason for his mission was to blaze a trail so we could follow him and do everything that he did, including, as he stated explicitly, all the 'miracles.' He was most certainly not here to suffer and die for our sins so as to appease the vengeance of a savage God.

One does not have to search very far or wide in human history to find stories of angry gods who needed a human sacrifice to calm them down: the Incas, the Mayans, the ancient Hawaiians, the worshippers of Moloch in ancient times, even in Israel. The list is long. The Second Book of Kings, and the Book of Jeremiah the Prophet, tell us of a god to whom child sacrifice was made in the Valley of Hinnon, south west of Jerusalem. A large idol would be heated red hot, then new-born babies would be placed on the arms of the idol, and the participants would watch them burn to death. Such activities were explicitly prohibited by Jehovah.

While it is still very common in Christianity to believe that God demanded a blood sacrifice of Jesus in reparation for the sins of humanity, we should at the minimum at least be alert to the implications for God, if we are ever tempted to interpret the events on Calvary in this way.

Dr. Benjamin J. Corey expressed it well: "If God needed the blood sacrifice of an innocent human, then he is similar to primitive versions of god … we are simply describing another version of an angry god who needs a virgin thrown into the volcano."

Returning from this grisly topic, we note it is only one of the warped understandings of God that happens to instinctively repel most people today. Nevertheless, to see Jesus as a Suffering Savior steers very close indeed to some of these very unwelcome implications about God that still manage to seem relatively innocuous on the surface, until we probe a little deeper and see the atheism lurking not far beneath.

We would instead express the whole matter today using some of the insights quantum physics has given us into the nature of reality: that we live in a sea of energy that comes from the Creator, and depending on how we interact with that force determines the type of life we experience.

It was a message of power and freedom. It's ironic that the all-pervasive emphasis on Jesus as a Suffering Savior that gradually came to dominate early Christian belief, is calculated to create nothing but powerlessness, guilt, shame and lack: the very opposite of what he had intended. The basic message of power and freedom has become warped into something that largely serves only pious self-gratification, and our further spiritual enslavement.

We know that a great deal of our lives is ruled by sub-conscious programs. Many of these serve very useful and indispensable functions in our lives, as already noted, but because of our particular religious history the influence of our religious sub-conscious programs can be very pernicious. Unfortunately, most of the programs which the history of religion has given us about

Jesus are extraordinarily dis-empowering; again, the very opposite of what he intended.

As already emphasized, it would be a bad mistake to directly oppose, much less attack, those sub-conscious programs that we now realize we would be better off not having. It cannot be stressed sufficiently that the first priority of a sub-conscious program is to ensure its own survival. That means that direct confrontation of our programs obviously will only serve to empower them. There is a very effective technique to free ourselves from the negative influence of these damaging programs. It consists in getting to know, as profoundly as we can, the actual historical situations out of which those crippling programs first grew, as opposed to what we have been told the situations were like. In short, the techniques consist in examining who and what we came to believe Jesus was, and how we understood what was his agenda during his public ministry.

When we begin to strip away the accretions of history and see what the historical facts really were, we are in effect now creating a set of new and positive programs, and when we do, the old and damaging ones will fade away of their own accord.

This realization is what has dictated the shape of this book. It involves, however, not just recognizing the existence of these programs as some kind of abstract item of information, but coming to realize in a very personal way that they really do exist, and how they can do enormous damage to our spiritual journey. Attempting to gain for ourselves the spiritual power over reality of which Jesus spoke, while leaving those negative sub-conscious programs untouched, will have about the same success as trying to fill the kitchen sink with water while leaving the stopper out. The programs will drain away all the results of our endeavors, as they have been so well designed to do.

If we want to correct our negative sub-conscious programs about Jesus and his message, we need to look once again at all the facts, but this time with an open and fresh mind — which can be a very threatening thing for someone whose whole religious life has been dominated by such programs and the mindset they produce. We will be looking afresh at the life of Jesus and his real message, with the emphasis he came to give, and how the subsequent and often tumultuous history of the Church proposed for belief many elements that were seriously at variance with those fundamental realities.

They say the age of robots is about to dawn. A very large amount of our own activity has always been highly robotic, which has been largely to our great advantage, but when applied to the realm of fundamental religious belief it is a major obstacle to understanding the real message of Jesus.

Let us commence with the heart of Jesus' message to see more clearly how the hijack occurred.

Jesus put his finger on the central problem that has plagued humanity for a very long time, but perhaps never more urgently than today. He promised that those who put his teachings into practice *would do all of the wonders that he did and greater.*[20] This was not an inspiring aside, or some form of optional extra which Jesus might have said it would be wonderful to have. It was the very core of his message.

While this was a glorious promise of what our destiny was meant to be, it was, in equal measure, a very uncomfortable touchstone, yardstick, barometer and litmus test, all rolled into one. Jesus said that manifesting these abilities would be an indication of whether those who followed him had really understood what his message and ministry was all about. It was the very issue that had plagued him since those very first days around the Sea of Galilee in his less than three-year-long ministry.

In the closing days of the last millennium I was invited to speak at the Conference for a Parliament of World Religions, at Cape Town, South Africa.[21] Over seven thousand people attended. I am not easily surprised at matters in this field, but nevertheless I was somewhat shocked to hear at that Cape Town Conference that

---

[20] John 14:12.

[21] 1 to 8 December 1999. "At the 1999 Parliament over 7,000 people from around the world – teachers, scholars, leaders, believers and practitioners – came together to experience astonishing spiritual and cultural variety, to exchange insights, to share wisdom, to celebrate their unique religious identities; in short, to be amazed, delighted, and inspired." Statement from Parliament of the World's Religions.

there were then more than 20,000 Churches, Congregations and Denominations that claim to bear the name of Jesus and follow his teachings ... some of them even claiming to possess the only authentic interpretation of his message.

We can cut to the chase about the competing claims of various religious organizations as to which best represents his teachings and his legacy, and simply note that, as the two thousandth anniversary of Jesus' ministry now looms close, there is still no notable sign of what Jesus promised (John 14) happening in any of those 20,000 present-day churches, congregations and communities that bear his name.

As noted earlier, it is obvious that something has gone seriously wrong.

The quotation from the Gospel of John — *"All the wonders I did, you will do and greater"* — summed up Jesus' whole ministry and message. Jesus was speaking about our ability to manifest reality as the ultimate test of whether we really got what he came here to do or not, for to teach us how to manifest reality is why he came. But that message has been lost almost totally. Instead, his mission has been mostly construed as Jesus being a Savior who came here to suffer and die for our sins so as to appease the vengeance of a Savage God — or, what's worse, to be a 'Gentle Jesus, Meek and Mild.' Throughout the centuries, those who had a different view of him were relentlessly pursued — and very often burned alive at the stake — all in the name of loyalty to the status quo, but little else.

But if we could only realize and embrace Jesus' true message — that we have the ability to manifest reality — it would take us out of the apparently endless cycle of guilt, fear, unworthiness and lack that characterize the lives of the vast majority of people across the entire world today. And not just the lives of the two billion people in the Christian world, this includes the lives of most of the people on Earth. For no matter what religion one espouses, including atheism, the power of those distorted versions of Jesus' message is in our sub-conscious minds.

What follows as a consequence is one of the greatest problems we have: manifesting what we desire — whether it be health, wealth, happiness, or something as simple and solid as a fulfilling personal relationship. There are a whole series of unconscious blocks in our way. And we don't even realize that they are there.

To make matters worse, the central message that most of the Jesus-orientated organizations preach today is that we should constantly recognize our sinfulness, acknowledge our guilt and beg God's mercy and pardon for our sins. All of these messages serve to strengthen those unconscious blocks that limit our ability to manifest reality. As already stated, it really does not matter greatly what we attempt to do; if we do not first address and get rid of those blocks it's like trying to fill the kitchen sink with water when we have neglected to put the stopper in the drain. Our efforts are futile because no matter what we try to do, the effects are drained away before they can ever accomplish anything.

Recognizing that these blocks exist, and how potent they are, is the first step in the process of removing them. But the blocks won't go away by cursing and swearing at them, or by trying to expel them by force. The good news is that there is an approach and technique that will do it. And it is that process that will be addressed in this book.

In the first place, we need to address the ways in which we have pictured Jesus; how we have understood who Jesus was, what he taught, what he said and what he wanted to accomplish. Those preconceived images of Jesus act as molds or filters which shape or interpret every other piece of information that we try to process. The ways in which Jesus is understood in the Western world, and the Christian world in general, are highly inaccurate in many important respects. And there are a multitude of reasons historically why all this happened. We will explore some of these in subsequent chapters.

These images of Jesus are misleading, dis-empowering, filled with guilt, apprehension and unworthiness. The images themselves present us with major blocks to being able to manifest reality to our liking.

We have major work to do. The technique that I will be using involves looking at the various ways in which those distorted images have come about. As I mentioned already, it is impossible to get rid of these programs by simply wishing to get rid of them or by attacking them. Why? Because they are in what we call "the sub-conscious" ... and one thing we find really hard to get into our heads is that the sub-conscious mind and the conscious mind work in an almost entirely separate mode from each other.

The process we will use here may appear to be tedious and it is slow, but it is very effective. Basically, it is an uncovering of 'myths' and 'misunderstandings' that we have believed to be true. We will be addressing the customary ways in which Jesus has been understood by those who claim to follow him. And we will be addressing the precise forms in which most of the damage has been done to the spiritual empowerment of those who follow him.

If we cast an objective eye over the early sources of Christianity it appears that the message of Jesus seems never to have been properly understood ... and as the centuries went on things only got worse. There is no doubt that Jesus' message was extraordinary and powerful and many-faceted. Precisely because of that, it was possible for different people to understand aspects of it in highly divergent ways. Many individuals and the movements that followed them pulled out his secondary messages and made them primary. When we encounter something extraordinary, it is all too easy to become dazzled and lose sight of the fact that the extraordinary thing we have understood may not have been the core of the matter. It's highly likely that the reason the extraordinary makes such an impact on a particular individual is because of hidden issues, needs and longing, that may have never been addressed by that individual. What strikes that individual as extraordinary may have only been a stage that was meant to lead on to something even more wonderful, powerful and fundamental. Instead we focus on the extraordinary as an end in itself and never are led on to the really extraordinary that lies beyond.

Whether people are followers of Jesus or not, it is clear that everybody reveres him. In any survey that tries to discover who is regarded as the most influential person in all of human history Jesus is always at the top. The second spot is usually held by Mohamed. However, even though the influence of Jesus has been enormous, we are still crippled by the ways in which we understand him. It's hard for us to realize that what he was teaching was a very different matter from what he is remembered as having taught. This discrepancy in our understanding of Jesus and his actual teachings will dictate the pattern of what we are doing here in this book.

The design for this book's cover was inspired by a quotation from Dorothy Sayers, the renowned British writer who died in 1957. She put her finger very precisely on the problems we have with Jesus.

> "To do them justice, the people who crucified Jesus did not do so because he was a bore. Quite the contrary; he was too dynamic to be safe. It has been left for later generations to muffle up that shattering personality and surround him with an atmosphere of tedium. We have declawed the Lion of Judah and made him a house cat for pale priests and pious old ladies"
>
> — Dorothy Sayers

As each century goes by tastes differ and situations alter. After a huge catastrophe like the Holocaust, or a war that makes life unlivable for an entire people, or a devastating famine, people gravitate to a different facet of Jesus than they do in peacetime. During a long period of peace and contentment people prefer a different kind of Jesus that harmonizes with that peace and contentment. So, Jesus becomes a type of buffet or smorgasbord: the aspects of him that appeal largely depends on the circumstances of the age.

Dorothy Sayers' statement is poignant because the real person behind all those swings of taste has been very badly obscured. Jesus was called the 'Lion of the Tribe of Judah'. There were lions in ancient Israel and, in fact, the lion was one of the really great images applied to prophetic figures in ancient Judea. But our tastes have turned Jesus into a lamb, which in itself says a lot about our proclivities.

When we set out to remove crippling programs it is essential to be very aware of what we have done; basically we have turned Jesus from a lion into a 'house cat'.

SCROLL ONE
THE MIND AND MANIFESTATION

Chapter 3
The Labyrinth of the Mind

The Rise of the Inaccessible One

Almost a century ago Dr. James Allan Francis[22] made the following well-known statement about Jesus in one of his sermons:

> "All the armies that have ever marched,
> All the navies that have ever sailed,
> All the parliaments that have ever sat,
> All the kings that ever reigned, put together,
> Have not affected the life of mankind on Earth
> As powerfully as that one Solitary Life."

If that is so, it's all the more important to ensure that Jesus' influence was what HE would have wished his influence to be. I think we can say without apology, it has not turned out that way ... because his less than three-year public ministry, to all intents and purposes, failed, in the sense that he didn't get through to those closest to him, who were the ones who in the end handed on their understanding of his message.

Jesus is generally regarded as the person who has done the most to alter human history for the better. We date our calendars from the year we believe he was born. All of history goes back and forward around the date of his birth. And yet, even if Jesus is the most significant individual in the whole of human history – what do we really know about him? And is what we think we know

[22] James Allan Francis, D.D. (1864–1928).

even true? Or is it the situation that we have been fed censored versions of his life and teachings, for God knows whatever number of reasons?

Christians believe that Jesus has a 'unique significance' in the world. But some of the things that have been believed about Jesus down through the centuries, and are still believed today, would surprise him more than any of us. One of these beliefs is that he was conceived by the Holy Spirit; and that he was born of a virgin who, by the way, was not a virgin just in his conception, but remained a virgin during his birth as well. Quite an interesting conception, at least from the physiological point of view.

Christian doctrines also include the beliefs that Jesus performed miracles, that he founded a Church and that he died by crucifixion as a sacrifice to achieve atonement with God. As if that weren't enough, he rose from the dead just to show them he could, and then ascended to heaven in a blaze of clouds and light. Furthermore, he's coming back a second time to teach everyone a lesson because of what they did to him. But where Jesus himself would probably be taken by surprise most of all is that the majority of Christians worship Jesus as the Incarnation of God the Son. He began to be spoken of as the second of three Persons of the Blessed Trinity, who are distinct from each other, but not separate — not a plural but a singular three. A baffling puzzle, to say the least.

Without too much exaggeration we can begin to suspect that the views of what Jesus was and is underwent an enormous amount of change as time went by. Jesus got a lot of really major promotions, during the first 350 years after his Passion.

He started off as an itinerant preacher in Galilee and Judea and then he became regarded as the expected Messiah; although I don't ever remember Jesus saying he was the Messiah.

Then he was graduated to being the Son of God, although, again, I don't ever remember Jesus saying that he was the Son of God without accompanying it by the statement, "You are all Gods."[23] He certainly didn't go around campaigning to have people accept either of those former two fundamental statements

---

[23] John 10.

from St. John's Gospel. He was on to more.

Then he was promoted to divine status in his own right due to his Resurrection.

Not only that, he then became regarded as someone who had pre-existed his life as Jesus. He actually did pre-exist his life as Jesus, but not in the sense that is believed by Christianity today.

This 'pre-existing Being' came down to Earth and incarnated as a human. Eventually he became regarded as the Incarnation of the Word of God, a Divine Being who existed with God the Father before all things came into existence, and it was through Him that God created the entire physical universe ... not just this Earth.

These are a lot of promotions to get, even spaced out over 350 years. Jesus himself was probably the most surprised of all to hear about this collection.

The problem is that these beliefs, that on the face of it seem to superficially exalt Jesus, are in fact the most powerful and effective barriers to our own empowerment that could ever be imagined. This is why I have deliberately given you this rather tedious list of "promotions" that Jesus received, as they emerged over the first 350 years of Christianity, and in the chronological order in which they were first applied to Jesus.

It is not hard to see that as each of these stages was reached, Jesus became more remote, more difficult to imitate, more inaccessible and more utterly removed from anything that we are. As he rose up, we sank down into more unworthiness, more guilt and more fear. In short, if we contemplate this list, the more Jesus was exalted the farther away and more unattainable his purposes for us became. It constituted the '*Rise of the Inaccessible One*'.

So it was that the person who came here to make a huge break with what had happened in human history up to that time, especially in Judaism, had his message, and everything that he stood for, turned on their heads. No doubt the intentions of those who re-framed Jesus' message were good, but unfortunately the belief system they created has served as an absolutely perfect set of blocks to our spiritual empowerment, and to our own evolution as masters of the quantum field. Ironically, the picture of Jesus evolved by the Church in the first four centuries very effectively blocked us from imitating him, which, unfortunately, was what the heart of his message was about.

In those first four centuries after Jesus had finished his mission, the early Fathers of the Church endlessly debated conundrums about how Jesus related to God the Father and how he related to the Holy Spirit. They also debated how all three (the Father, the Son and the Holy Spirit) are equal and yet distinct from each other … but were still not separate. They basically took on the rather doomed task of trying to prove that three equals one.

How can you have something that is distinct from another without being separate from it? It makes no sense. Not even when you allege that the difficulties we have in understanding how these realities can exist is because they belong in a realm beyond our capacity to understand.

It was also alleged that there can't be any superiority or inferiority in these three categories of being — the Father, the Son and the Holy Spirit. On good days, we know that two and two make four, but we certainly know that three is not equal to one no matter in what transcendent language the statement is cloaked. We are in trouble when we do that. But that's essentially what the views of the early Fathers of the Church amounted to.

When they did resolve the matter finally, it was a compromise that was to the satisfaction of nobody, for they still couldn't agree. It was only because of their apprehension about the power of the Emperor Constantine that they produced some semblance of unanimity at the Council of Nicaea in 325 AD. At that point, the centuries-old process of redefining Jesus ground to some sort of a merciful pause. But by that stage any hope of ever truly imitating Jesus, as he wished, was doomed. And the path of following Jesus was dominated by the urge to see how much we could repent and suffer to expiate our sins.

If we make mistakes, the message of Jesus had been that we should learn from the experiences, change, and then move on wiser and empowered. There was no room in his system for wallowing in guilt, shame and repentance. It was designed to be all about learning. When we focus on guilt and fear we re-create the monsters of our past who will return and devour us all over again. When we learn and move on wiser we have removed the magnetism that draws our monsters back to us again. Unfortunately, the Church's system of sin, guilt, fear and repentance, while no doubt well-intended, was a serious misunderstanding of Jesus' message that has caused catastrophic consequences down through Christian history so that the heart of his message was lost. Eventually, to even ponder becoming what Jesus was, began to smack of irreverence or even blasphemy.

The Conscious Mind Is a Minority Partner in Our Daily Thinking

Over the last forty years or so a range of studies by leading molecular biologists has shown that our conscious mind contributes only about 5% or less to our daily cognitive activity. And that's for individuals who are more aware and active in mind. The majority of people they say operate at only about 1% of the consciousness potential. Dr. Daniel J. Siegel[24] and Dr. Bruce Lipton[25] have done excellent work in this field.

It used to be believed that it was our genes that controlled who we are, but Dr. Lipton says that the new science of epigenetics shows that how our minds see and interpret our environment controls and manipulates our genes. According to these new discoveries, how we interpret situations that happen to us can change many things about how we are.

Our everyday thoughts usually revolve around where we have suffered some mental injury in the past, so our thoughts normally

[24] Dr. Daniel J. Siegel, Professor of Clinical Psychiatry at the UCLA School of Medicine and Executive Director of the Mindsight Institute. *The Developing Mind: How Relationships and the Brain Interact to Shape Who We Are* (Guilford, New York, 1999).

[25] Dr. Bruce Lipton, *The Biology of Belief* (Hay House, Santa Rosa, California, 2005), pp. 166-170; *The Wisdom of Your Cells – How Your Beliefs Control Your Biology,* (Sounds True, 2006); *Spontaneous Evolution: Our Positive Future and a Way to Get There from Here,* co-author Steve Bhaerman (Hay House, 2009).

gravitate to our weaknesses, and those thoughts, unless corrected, unfailingly create more of the same. The Church's traditional recipe of sin, shame, guilt and repentance, is tailor-made to ensure the persistence of victimization all life long, and is the direct opposite intent to the teachings of Jesus, of which it claims to be the guardian.

Dr. Lipton's research claims that our DNA is controlled by signals from *outside* the cell, including the energetic messages emanating from our positive and negative thoughts. This implies that our genes are controlled and manipulated by how our minds perceive and interpret our environment. Not surprisingly, Dr. Lipton's views have yet to attain acceptance in mainstream medical circles.

According to Dr. Lipton, the sub-conscious mind processes about 20-40 million bytes of information per second. In contrast the conscious mind, which we regard as being in charge of everything, operates only at about 40 bytes per second.[26] That means the vast majority of our normal everyday mental processing is under the control of the sub-conscious mind, and we need to remember that the sub-conscious mind is about a million times more powerful than the conscious in its impact on our everyday affairs, for only about 0.01% of all the brain's activity is experienced consciously.

Dr. Lipton explains that it's helpful to visualize everyone having two separate minds that control the body. The conscious mind can think freely and create new ideas. The sub-conscious mind however, is more akin to a super-computer loaded with a database of programs that control our behavior. Most of that database was acquired in our early years – before we reached the age of about six. Fundamentally the sub-conscious mind is the sum of our genetically programmed instincts and our beliefs.

It appears then, that most of what we believe or feel depends on that significant major part of our brain activity that is beyond our conscious awareness. In terms of our interest in this book, that means the root of our empowerment is outside the conscious sphere, and our effective ways of increasing our empowerment must also lie in that field.

---

[26] *The Biology of Belief.*

The sub-conscious mind reacts to situations automatically with its previously stored behavioral responses. It cannot move outside its fixed programs. All of this occurs without the knowledge or control of the conscious mind.

Our life reflects the character of this sub-conscious programming. The sub-conscious mind is designed to create reality out of its programs; in short, its job is to prove that its programs are true. So, if we have negative programming in our sub-conscious mind, Dr. Lipton says we will end up re-creating those negative experiences in our lives. He also points out that, if we are honest, we will realize that most of the programs in our sub-conscious are based on negativity: fear of what other people are thinking about us, fear of the unknown, fear of not being able to cope, fear of not being loved and respected for who we are, and so on. It is obvious that these are precisely the types of fears that the image of Jesus as a Suffering Savior continually engender.

In essence, this means that the biggest blocks to manifesting our dreams are the limitations programmed into the sub-conscious mind. One of the most powerful sources of this type of program has come from the ways in which Jesus and his message have been corrupted. In fact, one might legitimately say that perhaps in a sense the world would have been better off if Jesus had never come, or, more accurately, if the distortions introduced by religious authorities into his message, could have been prevented. These distortions have very negatively affected the course of Christian history.

So, the alarming fact is now emerging that those beliefs and convictions we accepted at a deep level continue to function at an sub-conscious level. This is especially true of the ones that come in when we are very open and receptive — as in our early years. Apparently most of the programs that direct our fundamental behavior patterns were downloaded unquestioningly by observing others when we were young children. These programs then began to control the way we reacted to new situations in our lives. In this way the programs themselves are reinforced.

If new information or insights come into our awareness, and it is at variance with one of these sub-conscious programs, that new information is going to have an extremely difficult time getting through to where it can do some good … if it manages to get through at all. That information will not be allowed to make any impact where it matters because the programs will sense the danger the information poses to their continued existence. Based on this we can see that the bastion of our sub-conscious programs is almost impregnable.

This fact holds true in all areas of life but nowhere more than in the area of our fundamental religious belief systems. Take a simple and obvious example: let's say in childhood I have been told that Jesus came here to suffer and die because of my sins against God. The whole orientation of that program in the sub-conscious mind will be to direct me to constantly attempt to make amends to Jesus because of all he suffered for me personally and for the totality of human kind. As a result of this belief, I have to be constantly on the alert to not recreate the state of affairs that brought about this tragedy in the first place. I must not offend God … indeed, a savage God who did not hesitate to exact such a terrible vengeance on his only begotten and totally innocent Son. I need to feel guilty because of what Jesus had to suffer for me, I need to fear the vengeance of God and be careful to keep God placated. I believe that the best way to do this is to constantly proclaim, in a thousand ways, that I am basically a worthless sinner, whose best hope is to cast myself on the mercy of God: in short, guilt, fear, powerlessness and worthlessness, and the hope that God will overlook my worthlessness. Unfortunately, that precisely constitutes the very heart of a great deal of traditional moralistic preaching.

What chance do I have?

Obviously, when we gain new information, we will morph it to fit in those molds dictated by the programs in control. All our knowledge and understanding of Jesus has to do with suffering, reparation, guilt, and above all fear of a vengeful God. That's how our reality is created out of our basic programs. It's like the ancient Greek Myth of Sisyphus.[27] Those programs are in control, and if they are deficient, and mostly they are extremely deficient, then we are back with the myth of Sisyphus. We may think we are making

[27] See Homer, *The Iliad,* Book VI, and the *Odyssey*, Book XI.

progress but, like Sisyphus, for every one step forward, we slide back two. So, we are doomed. Incarnation after incarnation, after incarnation, we make no significant progress. Unless we address these programs, we just chalk up mileage lifetime after lifetime, a mileage that takes us nowhere.

All We Need Is Power

As mentioned earlier, in the Western world almost all of the religious programs that we have about fundamental reality and our destiny and purpose, have come in some warped form or another from Jesus, or to put it more accurately, they have come from the way Jesus has been misunderstood and misrepresented. Where do we come from? What should I do while I'm here? What's expected of me? And what may I expect after the death of the physical body?

The Beatles once famously sang "All You Need Is Love" But what the world needs far more than love is power, not power over other people, but the particular brand of power that is able to create the kind of reality and experience we desire out of the quantum field. Without that kind of power behind it love can degenerate into a mawkish and sentimental reality which has little in common with what Jesus actually spoke about. One of the major difficulties facing us as a species is that we have so little, if any at all, of this kind of personal power, and the philosophical and religious belief systems that might be expected to generate it, with the best of good intentions, end up doing precisely the opposite.

As a result, we normally find ourselves victims of chance circumstances, of influences from outside, of all sorts of programs and coercions that affect us for the worse. We are our own jailers. We have got to come to grips with this situation and change it.

There is good news, however. In some branches of modern physics, we have been provided with the tools to at least begin to understand how reality works, and to apply that understanding in our creation of reality. Imagine the potentials of an alliance between Quantum Mechanics and the Gospel?

We can all recall hearing of the chaos there was in scientific circles when quantum theory first reared its head. It seemed too ghostly, too ephemeral and subjective for traditional hard-core scientists to accept. According to quantum theory, the physical reality which we perceive as solid and objective is not actually so. It is all a reality that emerges out of, and is held in existence by, the quantum field.

The particles of matter play out all possible realities simultaneously. Each particle is represented by a "probability wave." It is only when the wave is observed or focused on, that the particle takes on a particular solid form. In short, in quantum mechanics it's our focused thought that dictates which form reality takes. But if we recall what was mentioned a page or so ago, the sub-conscious mind has an enormous influence on the quality of our conscious focused thought, but it is also operating all of the time, even when having a focused thought to create reality is not even in our awareness at all. In short, the sub-conscious programs are continually broadcasting to the quantum field and that field will reflect back precise the kind of reality that we have projected onto it. It would be harder to find a more succinct expression of what Jesus tried to alert us to, and what he intended to teach us. If our basic condition of thought is guilt, worthlessness and fear, it hardly needs pointing out what the consequences inevitably will be – irrespective of what words we utter.

However, the upheaval that quantum mechanics began to cause in the scientific world about a century ago has yet to significantly affect the realms of theological and religious thought and practice. But at least we are beginning to realize at long, long last, that the heart of Jesus' teaching was in reality all about teaching us how to control and interact with the quantum field, however blasphemous or irreverent that statement will undoubtedly be judged in certain predictable quarters.

Most of the varied audiences that Jesus addressed in his short public mission of less than three years, were unsophisticated. "Literate" is of course far from an univocal term since degrees of literacy vary so much. People who can read might not necessarily be able to write. The literacy rate in Israel at the time of Jesus is estimated to have been about 3%, so most of his audiences would have been illiterate,[28] as were most, if not all, of his Apostles. People who had heard Jesus' teachings would have passed on what they had heard by word of mouth. A multitude of theories abound as to whether any now unknown written source came before the earliest Gospel (of Mark) appeared, about the year 70 AD, a generation after the time of Jesus. That Gospel is anonymous and its attribution to John Mark, a disciple of Peter the Apostle, is now regarded as dubious.

Later we will address whether the poetic forms of the statements of Jesus imply that his teachings were memorized by eyewitnesses, and these memorizations would obviously then ante-date any of the written texts we possess today.

The teaching of Jesus was couched in basic and homely terms for the benefit of the type of audience to which he spoke. Discourses on profound matters at the very heart of human life and purpose were powerfully woven from everyday realities like casting nets for fish, sowing the seed for crops by hand, and harvesting grapes from vines. It was the only way a first century illiterate peasant could begin to understand how reality functions, in what we now recognize under the much more dignified and impressive range of titles collected under the umbrella of quantum physics.

Jesus' message was all about how the mind interacts with reality so as to create and shape it, a message whose importance to the human race is impossible to exaggerate. That was why he came. His mission had nothing to do with suffering and dying for our sins so as to appease the anger vented on us by a vengeful God. That type of belief, unfortunately so rampant throughout most of the history of Christianity, is an insidious intrusion, and far indeed from an innocent and pious position; in fact, it takes little scrutiny to recognize it for what it really is: a thoroughly atheistic stance.

One is shocked to find it figuring so much at the very heart and core of those who claim to follow Jesus and love his message. It is why the crucifix has become such a prevalent and misleading symbol of what he stood for.

---

[28] As estimated for example in W.H Kelber, *The Oral and Written Gospel* (1997); *Jesus and Tradition: Words in Time, Words in Space* (1995).

If we want to diminish the influence of unconscious programs on us, a good place to start would be to ask what kind of Supreme Being could make any such demand of a human person as God the Father is supposed to have asked of Jesus? "I have been greatly offended over a vast period of time. I need someone to make up to me for all these offenses. No mere creature could ever make up to me for the enormity of these offenses by the human race over thousands of years. I will have to find someone who is capable of doing it. The obvious candidate for this role is my only innocent Divine Son, incarnate in Jesus, who is acknowledged by all to be without blame?"

What kind of mental depravity could it take to be pleased by the prospect of one's own innocent son suffering unimaginable torments to make up for offenses that others have committed? How could the sufferings of any innocent person ever make up for the offenses of the unjust? How could a being with such a mindset ever be imagined as the Supreme Being, the God of Love, who is the Creator of the Universe? Instead this is the mindset of a psychopath, badly in need of urgent and major psychiatric help.

That's where it all went wrong, right at the very beginning.

So we now can see that most of our lives are ruled by sub-conscious programs. If we want to benefit from learning any new information we have to get that information we have learned into the sub-conscious mind – much like Destin Sandlin famously did with successfully riding the 'backwards bicycle'. Once he practiced enough and mastered the new skill, he effectively turned the lights off on the old program. He could ride the 'backwards bicycle' – but then could no longer ride a 'normal' one.

Praying: The Best Way to Ensure We Do NOT Get What We Want

As we saw earlier we can't kick out those old sub-conscious programs. Ranting and raving against them accomplishes no improvement either. Above all we shouldn't say: "Oh, I wish

I were well again". Because once I say "I wish...," my efforts to change things are doomed.

Begging, asking, beseeching, hoping, imploring, and above all praying, are the most effective ways to make sure we do not get what we want. The quantum field reacts only to what my mind holds as present. If I fervently ask, beg or pray to God for, say, a new car, I am obviously seeing that new car as hopefully being part of my reality in the future, but not part of it now. In brief, my requests to God will manifest the hoping and wishing for the car that dominated my mind when I was praying for it, but that mindset will not ever generate the circumstances that will manifest the car itself.

What will be the result of my prayer if done in this fashion? The manifestation of the absence of what I really desired. Why? Because, in effect, what I presented to the quantum field for manifestation, what I was really present with, was the absence of the reality that was the subject of my prayer. I don't have the car now and I am praying to get it in the future. The quantum field reacts always only to what is present, and we are rarely present with that for which we pray.

In fact, praying, wishing, hoping or desiring, have become defined as asking God for what we do not yet have: in this case it is focused on the absence of a new car and hoping we will get one. If we have placed the states of wishing, desiring, hoping or praying before the quantum field, then those states are what will manifest. But wishes, desires, hopes or prayers will not manifest that new car. We have forgotten the central message of Jesus on this point.

Jesus did not recommend that we 'Ask to be healed'. His fundamental teaching on this point was very extraordinary, and like several other lessons he taught it was too much at variance with the current mindset to have been transmitted in its integrity to the grassroots belief systems of those people down the ages who cherished his name. He said that when you want something you should "Believe it is already yours, and it will be so."[29] Believing something is so now, is a process that is the direct opposite of asking, hoping or praying.

[29] Mark 11:24.

Jesus did not teach us to pray to be well if we were sick. He taught us how to create our wellness. Instead we have descended into a mind state that sees all such states, such as delivery from catastrophic illness, as a gift bestowed by God in response to our humble petitions. Unfortunately, we have been misled into thinking that the more we demean ourselves and proclaim our guilt and worthlessness, the more God will be pleased, and the more likely God will be to grant our request. Unfortunately, this mindset is the highway to disaster.

In fact, if a person is seriously ill, it can do a lot of damage to pray to be healed if we are doing it in this fashion. We first must become what it is we wish to manifest. Unfortunately, in the way we have been taught to seek relief from catastrophic illness, we make it progressively less and less likely that we will be healed. This is because the traditional way of doing it makes the fatal mistake of conveying that we are less worthy and deserving, and therefore less able to heal ourselves. We believe we are at the mercy of a God, out there, instead of claiming our own personal power to be well, which is the only way that works. Responses to such God-oriented requests are not made by some being "up there" who will do an auto-correct on our heartfelt utterances. The response is made by the quantum field, and made precisely in the mindset we are holding at that moment.

This fundamental shift is diametrically opposed to what has become deeply ingrained in us for centuries, so it bears a little repetition for the sake of emphasis. When I am praying, beseeching, hoping or wishing for something I am presenting to the quantum field the absence of what it is I wish to attain. What will the quantum field give me in response? Exactly what I asked for – the absence or lack of what I say I want. So, if I'm short of cash, or if I am in a tough situation in my family, or I'm dying of incurable cancer, begging God to change that situation not alone will not work, but it may actually make the situation worse. And yet it is what most people normally and instinctively tend to do. Not alone have we all been brainwashed into believing that proclaiming that we are worthless and powerless is the way to get God to answer our prayers, and to add insult to injury, we have been indoctrinated by the monstrous lie that it is pleasing to God and Jesus for us to be that way.

Take cancer, one of the worst of all illnesses. If I'm begging to be healed from cancer, or I'm saying: "Oh my beloved God, please heal me from cancer ... I'll be very good, and I'll walk around the block five times a day pronouncing your praises". What have I manifested by praying to be cured of cancer? I have very likely created an intensification of the disease – because that disease was what was in my 'Present' when I addressed the quantum field in an attitude of wishing, hoping and desiring.

It can't be emphasized sufficiently how difficult it is to say and profoundly accept that we are already healthy, if we are laboring under a serious illness. It seems like hypocrisy, or living in cloud cuckoo land. If I'm wracked with severe pain and nausea from a major illness it seems like the ultimate in self-deception to say that "I am radiantly healthy" and to profoundly accept it with every fiber of my being. Saying, "I am radiantly healthy" is not as assertion to be assessed for its truth or falsity, which is how we instinctively judge matters. Instead it is a technique for manifesting in the quantum field. Furthermore, it is the only method that works in the quantum field.

If I hear this insight and am enthralled by it, I may cease to be a sceptic for a while, and say "I'll give it a try." Don't waste your time. All you will manifest is trying.

I know this personally because I've been in situations of severe sickness such as this. In those circumstances, it was very hard to convince myself that I was already well. But until we can manage to get ourselves into this mindset, we are going to accomplish nothing significant in terms of self-healing. Is it difficult for us to rise to this state when ill? Enormously so, and we have the programs in our sub-conscious to thank for most of the difficulty we experience ... and for our inability to properly grasp what Jesus taught.

Once we start to 'pray' in the traditional sense, not alone is that power gone, but what is even more serious is that, without realizing it, we are also highly likely to exacerbate the disease or the situation we are attempting to change.

A Case History

Serious consequences can come from not realizing that in the realm of manifestation in the quantum field, the law of cause and effect works in reverse: in short, the effect has to come before the cause.[30] It had never been expressed more powerfully than by Jesus himself in his memorable teaching on manifestation in Mark 11.34. A lot of disappointed hopes, shattered dreams and human tragedy, hover around the failure to realize this basic fact. It is even more tragic if it dawns on us that it could all have been avoided and that each of us could much more powerfully manifest into our lives the things and situations we would like to see there, if one only made the basic shift involved in this realization.

It's a very salutary reminder that the quantum field does not respond to our prayers, but to what we "observe" at the deepest level within us.

Many years ago in Ireland I knew a beautiful woman, happily married with a wonderful husband and young family. At the age of thirty-three she developed breast cancer which tragically soon brought her life to an end and left behind a desolate husband and two children of tender years.

In any scheme of assessment this lady would certainly have qualified as a "spiritual" person of a very high order. She was absolutely conscientious in everything she did and took the greatest care to pass on to her children the highest ideals and ways of behavior that she knew. One would expect in such a person that because of what's often called their "closeness to God" that their prayers would be answered in a speedy and direct fashion.

The real key to understanding this tragedy came to me in a quiet few moments some weeks after her case had been pronounced hopeless. She said to me: "I can't believe how I ever got cancer, because my mother died of cancer when I was

30 See Míċeál Ledwith, "Poisoned Prayer: Reversing the Law of Cause and Effect."

eight, and every morning and night since then I have asked God fervently to protect me from ever getting that horrible disease. Now here I am not alone having it, but my case is beyond all medical help? What did I do wrong, or what was it that I did that was not pleasing to God?"

It was extraordinarily painful to try to sort out all the tangled web of emotions, regrets, fears and disappointment that lurked behind those grief-filled, agonized sentences. Faced with the agony of soon having to leave behind her two beautiful children and husband, she was not interested in the least in the tongue-tied standard platitudes of comfort we all tend to utter at times like this, when the shallowness of our own spiritual understanding has left us with nothing helpful to say. Her grief at the awful separation that death brings was overshadowed by something even more tragic: the fear that she had lived her entire life in a way that was displeasing to God, since apparently an entire lifetime of prayer and sterling moral character, was still not sufficient to secure an answer to her request from God in prayer. What she wanted to know, in order to set her soul at peace for her transition, was in what way she had lived a life displeasing to God, for it was only in those terms that she was able to grapple with it in some fashion.

To brutally summarize a very long exchange between us, I said to her that I knew that she wanted to understand, not to be comforted by platitudes, or, to put it more accurately, that she knew the only satisfactory comfort comes when we understand. Over a period of several hours that evening, and as gently as I could, I managed to convey that, unfortunately, by following the practice she had all her life, there really was no way she could have avoided getting cancer. She had had the thought of cancer before her, in fear of what happened to her mother, every morning and night, in her prayer for every day, for well over a quarter of a century. The quantum field makes no distinction between what we present to it in love, or in fear.

All great spiritual masters that ever walked this Earth always insisted that the first priority when anyone decides to make a stand and own the stuff that is keeping them held back, is to get rid of fears, for fear is a far more powerful magnet in the quantum field than love is. It terrifies us and chills us to the core of our being. We find it enormously more easy to become analogical with fear than with most other emotions. Whatever we are focused on manifests. Whether it is feared or loved is irrelevant.

The tragically early death of this beautiful wife and mother is a classic case of what can happen when we have never been really informed about the true nature of God, the form of true prayer and how what we profoundly accept manifests infallibly to us out of the quantum field. She saw her prayer to God over all those days and nights as not having been answered. The reason is she saw God as a being modeled on the sultans and potentates of the Ancient Near East, as so many of us did and still do. "He" could be cajoled into dispensing us from a fate that might otherwise endanger us, or "he" might not. There was no coming forth of the true teaching of Jesus on this matter. She did the best she could, as far as we can humbly judge, and what she focused on manifested perfectly. So, there is a tragic sense in which her prayer was perfectly answered, but it was because she did not realize the true form of prayer that she was expressing.

If we understand the nature of cause and effect are related in reverse in the quantum field, then we have to watch every thought like a hawk intent on its prey, until we have made the change habitual. I have to absolutely become what it is I want to manifest. If I am intent on manifesting something wonderful and beautiful, then I must absolutely become that completely and thoroughly, in a way that has nothing at all in common with the superficiality of "positive thinking."

If I am terrified at the prospect of contracting a terrible disease from which I saw my own mother die, then assuredly that thing that I fear has taken possession of me to such a degree that I am in acute danger of manifesting it into my own life. The effect is already in place and has preceded the cause.

Moving away from the personal level, this is equally true when we campaign against something — whether I am against war or for civil rights, or the dignity of women or whatever. When we fight against something there is always a grave danger that we have already become analogical with that against which we protest, and when we fight in this way we almost always end up only further empowering what it is we oppose. Traditional understandings of what we are doing when we pray had none of this awareness unfortunately. I quote a classic source in the pages that immediately follow here: the famous survey of Sir Francis Galton.

"Does Prayer Work?" — Sir Francis Galton

A prominent element in the Pauline strain of Christianity admonishes us to pray for forgiveness of our sins and for everything else we may desire to have in our lives. In that respect, I once came across an interesting study by Sir Francis Galton,[31] who was a Fellow of the Royal Society in England. Galton excelled in a bewildering array of specializations. He was an explorer, polymath, anthropologist, inventor, eugenicist, and psychologist. His reflections are just as relevant today as they were in the mid 19th Century.

Growing up he was a very unusual child. He could read at the age of two and a half. He wrote his first letter at the age of four, and learned to do multiplication at the same age. The average mortal learns to do that around the age of six or seven.

Galton was inspired to do a study into whether prayer worked or not.[32]

> "Despite constant prayer vigils for the sick and dying, the devout — including the devout Christians — have a similar life expectancy to everyone else."

> "In aggregate, research on prayer shows no overall effect or one so weak that the most that can be said for God is that he — maybe — operates at the margins of statistical

---

[31] February 16, 1822 - January 17, 1911.

[32] "Statistical Inquiries into the Efficacy of Prayer," Fortnightly Review, Vol. 12, pp. 125-35, 1872.

significance: not a very impressive claim for an omnipotent, interventionist deity."

In the chart that follows Galton records the mean age attained by males of various classes who had survived their 30th year, from 1758 to 1843. Deaths by accident are excluded, apparently because Galton's God was not in charge of accidents? Strange, because he was supposed to be all-powerful and all-present?

The first column in the chart gives the number of individuals surveyed. The next column gives the average age at which they died. The third column gives the average age at death of "eminent men." Note that for Galton 'men' obviously did not include "women!" It was, after all, only 1872!

MEAN AGE ATTAINED BY MALES OF VARIOUS CLASSES WHO HAD SURVIVED THEIR 30TH YEAR, from 1758 to 1843.
Deaths by accident or violence are excluded

	Number	Average	Eminent Men*
Members of Royal Houses	97	64.04	--
Clergy	945	69.49	66.42
Lawyers	294	68.14	66.51
Medical profession	244	67.31	67.07
English aristocracy	1,179	67.31	--
Gentry	1,632	70.22	--
Trade and commerce	513	68.74	--
Officers in the Royal Navy	366	68.40	--
English literature and science	395	67.55	65.22
Officers of the Army	569	67.07	--
Fine Arts	239	65.96	64.74

* The eminent men are those whose lives are recorded in *Chalmer's Biography,* with some additions from the *Annual Register.*

These are people who survived their 30th year. People in Literature and Science lived an average of 67 years; Officers of the Army — 67 also. Those in Fine Arts lived an average of 65.96 years. So basically, it doesn't matter whether you are an atheist, an agnostic, clergyman or bishop, everyone dies at roughly the same age, give or take a few years.

He says "The sovereigns are literally the shortest lived of all who have the advantage of affluence." Are they neutralized by the effects of public prayers? Every session of Parliament is preceded by a prayer for the sovereign in Britain, for example. He also collates the longevity of clergy, lawyers and medical men. The clergy are a "...more prayerful class than either of the other two. It's their profession to pray." They've gotten into a habit "...of offering morning and evening prayers. A reference to any of the numerous published collections of family prayers will show that they are full of petitions for temporal benefits."

"But we don't find that any of the clergy lived longer despite all of this prayer.[33] Now they have a life value of 69.49 years as against 68.11 years for the lawyers and 67.31 for the medics. (Refers to 'Eminent Men' column).

"But the easy country life, and family repose of so many of the clergy, are obvious and sanitary conditions in their favor."

"But now when you compare members of the three classes, persons of sufficient note who have their lives recorded, the value of life among the clergy, lawyers and medics is 66.4, 66.5, and 67.0 respectively, the clergy being the shortest lived of all three despite their numerous prayers." Galton's bottom line is that the numerous prayers of the clergy for protection against the perils and dangers of the night, for protection during the day, and for recovery from sickness, appear to be futile.

A question I would pose is this, when someone stands up and faces an audience on national television to say: 'Praise God! He made me late for the plane that crashed'. We have seen some of that sort of thing over the last few years. What is that person saying about the people who arrived on time for the flight?

---

33 Page 129.

Coming back to football again, when a sports team gives thanks to God for their win, what are they saying about the other team? And when we sit around a dining table and thank God that he has blessed us with pork roast and potatoes, what are we implying about the approximately 20,000[34] kids who will die that very night of hunger? Is not God in charge of both groups? What are we thinking and, more importantly, why?

For those of us who were raised in religious families, there's another set of authority figures: Gods and their messengers, I mean pastors, priests, Sunday school teachers, Bible study teachers, youth ministers and Christian College Professors. I also mean the writers of the sacred texts, whose words we have heard with reverence repeated over and over. One of the most effective tools for creating belief in something especially when there is no evidence, is to keep on repeating it. I suppose those who practice these techniques believe that eventually we'll scream "Uncle" and submit. Just like the Fathers of the Council of Nicaea: "For God's sake let us go home: we'll sign anything."

May we now use the word 'gods' in the plural? Even people who are raised believing in one God have multiple conflicting God ideas that can be switched on to suit different circumstances. The judgmental God can be switched on. So, can the abstract God, or the Jesus-buddy God.

I thought there was too, too much to miss, to not quote what follows. The most powerful sermon ever preached on American soil was given by Jonathan Edwards to whom I referred earlier. "Sinners in the Hands of an Angry God," was preached on 8th of July 1741, a classic of the Hell, fire and brimstone religious genre. It's a rant, among many other things, against the "Negro" rebels who were then being hanged and burned at the stake for a suspected plot to destroy the city of New York by arson. From May to August in 1741, at a market place described as lying in a grassy valley, thirteen slaves were burned at the stake and seventeen were hanged. The executed were interred within a six-acre burial ground, a stone's throw southwest from a marshy

[34] Hunger and World Poverty Sources: United Nations World Food Program (WFP), Oxfam, UNICEF.

ravine. Hundreds were jailed, seventy-two transported to certain death in the West Indies. Contemporaries compared these events to the 1692 Salem witch hysteria.

The printed version of his sermon runs to 28 pages. It requires no commentary for it speaks for itself.

If you search the internet of course you are going to find all sorts of Christians arguing that God is really not angry or fierce or wrathful. He's just bound by the obligations of justice and aggrieved. God is saying, "This hurts me more than it hurts you." Now Edwards's vision was closer to many of the Bible writers than Oral Roberts, or contemporary celebrity preachers like Rick Warren or Joel Olsteen. Here are some examples that Edwards quotes:

> "I will tread them in my anger, I will trample them in my fury, and their blood shall be sprinkled upon my garments and I will stain all my raiment." (Isaiah 63:3). These are some of their favorite texts. Jesus wasn't even heard of at that time.
>
> "Therefore, will I also deal in fury, mine eyes shall not spare, neither will I have pity; and though they cry in mine ears with a loud voice, yet I will not hear them." (Ezekiel 8:18). Again, these are the words of Jehovah himself.
>
> "What if God, willing to show his wrath, and make his power known, endured with much long-suffering, the vessels of wrath fitted to destruction?" This is Saint Paul, (Romans 9:22).

Coming out of his mouth is a sharp sword with which to strike down the nations:

> "He will rule them with an iron scepter. He treads the winepress of the fury of the wrath of God Almighty." (Revelations 19:15).
>
> "Therefore, will I also deal in fury; mine eyes shall not spare, neither will I have pity: and though they cry in mine ears with a loud voice, yet I will not hear them." (Ezekiel 8:18).

Towards the end of his marathon Sermon Jonathan Edwards says:

> "But alas! how many (of this congregation) is it likely will remember this Discourse in Hell? And it would be a Wonder if some that are now present here, should not be in Hell in a very short Time, before this Year is out. And it would be no Wonder if some Person that now sits here in some Seat at this Meeting-House in Health, and quiet and secure, should be there before tomorrow Morning. Those of you that finally continue in a natural Condition, that shall keep out of Hell longest, will be there in a little Time! Your Damnation don't slumber; it will come swiftly, and in all probability very suddenly upon many of you...."[35]

That Sermon of Jonathan Edwards has been highly praised, in predictable quarters, all through the best part of the almost three centuries it's been in circulation.

I refer elsewhere in this book to the "Amygdala Hijack." It's been shown that the amygdala can act in response to a threat before any possible instructions can be received from the conscious brain (the neocortex). The reason an emotional reaction can happen faster than a conscious reaction is because the danger signal bypasses the cerebral cortex, the part of the brain that manages conscious thought and goes straight to the amygdalae. That's why we use phrases like 'gut instinct'. Throughout the entire history of the human brain taking on its present form, there was no point at which the whole thing got designed afresh. It was built up in layers. The old parts sometimes got repurposed, but it is basically an ancient system that was constantly being added to, rather than being totally updated and re-designed. Hence the old programs have a very safe retreat in which to dwell!

The reason for the success of the Edwards type harangue is because the threat of everlasting damnation, that could befall us at any moment, probably ranks close to the top of all vestigial human

---

35 Edwards, Jonathan and Smolinski, Reiner, Editor, "Sinners in the Hands of an Angry God, A Sermon Preached at Enfield, July 8th,1741." (1741). Electronic Texts in American Studies. Paper 54. http://digitalcommons.unl.edu/etas/54

fears, particularly in the case of sensitive individuals. There is a perverse form of thrill, in any case, in closely avoiding disaster, as is apparent in so many forms of adventures favored by our culture.

Chapter 4
The Ability to Manifest Is Confronted by Thousands of Years of Negative Indoctrination

We are told that programs in our sub-conscious mind control about 95% of our daily thinking, and we know that many of those programs are negative and dis-empowering because they have their roots in fear, guilt and unworthiness. The process of using new and more enlightened information from our conscious awareness to rebuild and replace those crippling programs in our sub-conscious mind, is a crucially important skill. It is vital to learn this if we are ever going to stand up and take control of our destiny in this world.

To do so, we cannot afford the luxury of accepting that the physical is the only form of reality that exists. Rather, we need to realize that the physical shape of reality is something that descends from an anterior state of higher frequency in the quantum field. That state always interacts with my fundamental belief system to create reality in accordance with the basic insights of quantum mechanics and quantum physics. Realizing this is a hard task that goes against every fiber of our being, mainly because it goes against thousands upon thousands of years of indoctrination, both secular and religious. For most of the last 2,000 years, in particular, with so much misplaced emphasis on Jesus as a suffering savior, these attitudes have in effect become fossilized within us. To change these programs is a subtle and major task — but it can be done.

The Program of Jesus As a Suffering Savior: Awkward Questions for Genesis

In no place is all of this more painful than in the areas of fundamental belief systems. If it has been ingrained into us from childhood that Jesus came here to suffer and die for our sins against God, then the whole orientation of that program will be to tell me that I have to make up to Jesus for all of the suffering that my sins brought to him which needless to say only deepens immeasurably my dis-empowering sense of guilt and unworthiness.

Of course, we never ask ourselves if Jesus was actually sent down here for that purpose. He would be the first to be surprised at this invention. But if Jesus were sent down here approximately 2,000 years ago with the sole purpose of suffering the most cruel death imaginable – crucifixion – what would be the purpose of it? We should ask that question frequently – until our programs are gone. Normally we won't go there, because once we do, immediately the alarm bells start to go off, and above all the hellfire and brimstone trumpet starts to sound forth. Because if we do go there, maybe we are offending God in an even more major way, and may end up going to Hell to burn for all eternity?

This brings us back to examining the programs that make us so afraid to go there and question those long unquestioned forms of belief. Where does the power of these programs come from? The people who propose that Jesus came here to appease the vengeance of a savage God by his suffering have also quite an interesting collection of other beliefs that fall into the same category.

One of them is the conviction (according to the Irish Anglican Archbishop, James Ussher writing in 1650 AD),[36] that on a particularly busy week in the year 4004 BC, beginning on the 23rd

---

[36] *Annales Veteris Testamenti, a prima mundi origine dedvcti: una cum rerum Asiaticarum et Aegyptiacarum chronico, a temporis historici principio usque ad Maccabaicorum initia producto.* London, 1650. Modern English translation; "Annals of the World."

of September,[37] at 9.00 a.m., to be exact, God created the world and everything in it. And He finished it all in one week; quite an achievement, you'll admit, even for God.

According to Archbishop Ussher, human history is only about 6,000 years old. However, for the first 4,000 years of human history, according to Archbishop Ussher, things didn't go so well. In fact, things went to pot almost right from the very start. God placed the first man and woman in a garden and told them they could eat from any fruit tree there, but they were not to eat the fruit of one particular tree. At that early stage of human history, God apparently did not yet know much about human psychology.

God had hardly left the company of the original human couple, before that awful serpent arrived. The serpent tempted the woman to eat exactly the fruit that God had forbidden. She gave the forbidden fruit to Adam ... and there you have it. According to Genesis, the first woman was the origin of all the world's woes and difficulties, and women have been punished and diminished for it ever since, because of what that famous 'rib-woman' did.

The day of reckoning always dawns. God came back and asked the first man – "Why did you eat that fruit that I forbade you to eat?" (It's a 'fruit' in Genesis, not an 'apple'). Adam said: "She gave it to me." And when God said to the woman "Why did you eat the fruit? She said: "The serpent gave it to me." In other words, the serpent is ultimately to blame for it all. The serpent, of course, in ancient Mesopotamia, was the symbol of immortality – since serpents shed their skins,[38] which in early times was understood as the serpent taking on a new body. In other civilizations, the serpent had a very different symbology, being the symbol of the kundalini energy[39] – meaning 'the coiled one', representing the primal force lying at the base of the spine.

[37] Ussher calculated October 23, apparently believing the Autumn Equinox occurred in Biblical times on that date.

[38] Nowadays we know that even all mammals, including humans, shed their skins.

[39] The term "kundalini" is found as far back as the Upanishads, 9th - 3rd century BC.

It is patently obvious that the negative view of what Jesus came to do was formed by the very early Christians against this background in the early part of Genesis. As we will see later, Jesus had to become a Suffering Savior, just as the sin and imperfection of the creation had to be made the responsibility of the first humans. The reason is the same in both cases. However, no matter how we regard Jesus or what he was, there are some significant questions that still have to be asked of the authors of Genesis.

Traditional Christianity maintains that God offers us eternal life instead of the everlasting punishment we deserve, only because God's only Son died in our place to make amends for our sins. St. Paul expressed it classically: [21] God made him who had no sin to be a sin offering for us, so that in him we might become the righteousness of God."[40] In this perspective God seems to have always been intent on a sentence of death for the sinful members of the human race. But can the death of a single individual, even one who was a Divine Being as well as a human, really make up for over 4,000 years of sinning by ordinary mortals? I think this is a reasonably fair statement of the problem.

Even accepting Archbishop Ussher's charming chronology, many questions arise: by the time of Jesus, hadn't 4,000 years of sinners already died? Did they escape punishment by God at the time they died because God was not quite as upset earlier on as he became later – particularly around the time of Jesus – when matters apparently came to a head? Or were the benefits of the suffering and death of Jesus retroactively applied to them? If so where were those individuals housed until those benefits could be applied to them? They could not be said to be in Hell, from which there is apparently no escape ever. To make this scenario work they needed to have been kept in some sort of holding situation till Jesus was ready to die.

In an attempt to get some perspective on all this, may we ask what kind of sense would it make to have Jesus come 'down' here to make appeasement to God for the disobedience of the first human couple and for all the other offenses the human race is supposed to have committed during that alleged first 4,000 years of its history?

---

[40] 2 Corinthians 5:21.

What about sins committed after Jesus is supposed to have gone through his Passion to appease the vengeance of God? We are now 2,000 years into that situation with a world population rapidly approaching 7.5 billion. Obviously, there is no demographic data available on what the Earth's population was for 99% of its history, but it's estimated the population of the world at the time of Jesus may have been about 300 million. It's similarly estimated that the total human population that has ever lived may be about 108 billion, with between six to seven percent of all the people who have ever lived alive today. Whatever the true statistics may be, the fact seems to be undeniable that only a tiny fraction of all the human beings that have ever lived had sinned and lived and died before the time when Jesus is supposed to have gone through his passion to "save" them.

So, on this understanding will Jesus have to die again, since apparently he is the only one capable of making reparation on such a massive scale? Or does the suffering of Jesus anticipate those sins of the future and pay for them all in advance? If that is so, does this belief then steer dangerously close to appearing to be a license to sin?

What kind of Supreme Being, much less one whose very essence is love, would find any meaning or satisfaction in the death of others, especially of the innocent? Further, what kind of Being would decree that he whom Christianity has for so long called "God's Only Son,"[41] and who is acknowledged to have been totally innocent and without sin, should come 'down' here to undergo the most cruel form of death imaginable? There are enormous difficulties in understanding how a Being who might deserve to bear the tile 'God' could ever wish to instigate such a process, and even if we do concede that this was done, even greater difficulties remain.

For what purpose would all this be done? Apparently to appease God's vengeance. Let's take an analogy. Assume some

---

[41] 1 John 4: 9. Written at Ephesus between the years 95–110 AD. Also see, John 3: 16: "God so loved the world that he gave his only begotten Son..." The Greek word that is normally translated as 'only begotten' is "monogenes," which could also be translated as "one and only" or simply 'only.'

human father was gravely offended by somebody. Would the death of that father's only child, who was completely innocent and unconnected with the offense, appease that father's anger against the offender? How would we assess such a father? Obviously at a minimum it would be someone whose moral values were in absolute chaos or who was suffering from some extreme form of mental illness. Are these the terms in which we would like God to be envisaged, or could we even envisage accepting such a being as 'God'?

This paradigm of the redemptive death of Jesus, to appease the vengeance of a God against the masses of humanity, does not present a picture of the kind of God Jesus spoke so much about. He spoke of a loving God, who was not just a loving being, but whose very essence was love.

Instead it's a picture of a savage, cruel, neurotic and vindictive and psychotic being. The last description we would ever dream of giving such an entity would be the title: 'Creator God'. There is something seriously wrong with this picture of a savage God who didn't hesitate to exact vengeance on his only begotten and innocent Son. Note carefully that I am not saying there is something seriously wrong with the Creator. What I am saying is that there is something very seriously wrong with our acceptance of such pictures and models of the Creator...models which are the origin of so many crippling programs in our sub-conscious minds. The whole notion of the redemptive death of Jesus for our sins has been a treasured part of the belief systems of most Christians for a very long time, but it takes only a little awareness to see how in reality it might actually be a poisoned chalice.

Obviously, Genesis did not say that Jesus had to come down here and stand in for us by living and suffering as a human being in order to appease the vengeance of a vindictive God against us. But most, if not all, of those 20,000 Christian Churches, Congregations and Communities, to whose delegates I spoke at Cape Town in 1999, and who understand the message of Jesus against the background of Genesis, unfortunately do say that nowadays, and have been saying it for a very long time.

Where does all of this leave the human race? It leaves us with a colossal burden of guilt, unworthiness and fear. Once we take that on and accept it we can say goodbye to hopes of spiritual empowerment or to becoming a master of the quantum field. If as a test of our loyalty to Him, God desires us to be immersed in guilt and dis-empowerment, fear and unworthiness, then how can we be loyal to that God and at the same time achieve the empowerment that Jesus taught? We cannot.

Should belief in the redemptive suffering and death of Jesus for us all, instead be recognized for what it really is — a thinly disguised form of atheism, since a being behind such a bizarre system of beliefs could never qualify to be the Creator?

How Did Jesus Redeem Both Those Who Lived before and after Him? The Problem of After-Life Storage: Limbo, Purgatory

Perhaps this puzzle, about how to retroactively apply the saving benefits of the suffering of Jesus to individuals already long dead, eventually gave rise to belief in the two renowned "in-between" states, Limbo and Purgatory. Limbo, in effect, was abolished by the Pope in April 2007 on the advice of a 41-page Report from the International Theological Commission,[42] but the decision was hedged about with so many qualifications that it is difficult to ascertain what exactly the status of Limbo now actually is. On the other hand, Purgatory is still clearly in a state of Limbo.

I think it can be fairly said that the document of the International Theological Commission seemed somewhat less concerned with the fate of unbaptized infants than it was with not implying that the Church had changed its teaching.

In the Pope's decision about Limbo there was no mention of the state of agony endured by the countless mothers of newborn babies who died at birth without being baptized. According to

[42] Originally commissioned by Pope John Paul II. *The Hope of Salvation for Infants Who Die without Being Baptised,* International Theological Commission, April 22, 2007.

the Church's teaching, such children could never see the face of God for all eternity. This belief held sway in the Catholic Church for about eight hundred years. It is just one particularly poignant example of the extent of human suffering that can be caused by a misunderstanding and distortion of the reality and teaching of Jesus. It especially highlights the absurdity of theologians long ago generating ill-founded theological postulates. Those theologians didn't really know their business, and could not see that those postulates create far more difficulties than they could ever hope to resolve. If they had recognized the need for a paradigm shift things would have been very different, and much suffering of grieving mothers spared down the centuries.

The factor that most likely dictated the particular shape the New Testament writers put on things was this line of reasoning about the need for reparation to God for our sins by Jesus and by Jesus alone, and where to "store" those who had died without sin in other faiths before the time of Jesus, or those who died without baptism after the time of Jesus. Once again, it is a powerful example of many such postulates that generate many more enormous problems, that far outnumber any difficulties they might have hoped to resolve.

The document of the International Theological Commission on Limbo came to this tentative conclusion: "Our conclusion is that the many factors that we have considered above give serious theological and liturgical grounds for hope that unbaptized infants who die will be saved and enjoy the beatific vision. We emphasize that these are reasons for prayerful hope, rather than grounds for sure knowledge. There is much that simply has not been revealed to us."

Ironic, given that nobody has ever claimed that belief in Limbo was something revealed by God.

However, I am sure the members of the august body that produced that document in 2007 would be the first to express relief that the fate of infants who die without baptism, before or after Jesus, will not be decided by a paper from the International Theological Commission, even when issued with, admittedly, a very tentative Papal approval.

Chapter 5
The Ultimate Embarrassment: Realizing "I" Am Not in Control

Are We Really All Gods?

Where does all of this confusion leave us? And where does it leave us especially with respect to the fundamental statements of Jesus such as: "*You are all Gods,*"[43] and "*All these things which I do, you will do, and greater than these will you do.*"[44] This is not a peripheral issue. In fact, Jesus insisted that it was only when we did even greater works than he did that we would be sure we were understanding what his message really was about.

If we really are all Gods we've never shown much evidence of it. Throughout the history of the world we have been consistently victims of circumstances and of the manipulations of powerful forces and other human beings. Furthermore, we are constantly assured by all forms of religious authority that to say we are God or divine or to say that we are acting as Gods would be construed as the ultimate form of blasphemy.

Are we all Gods? Yes. Why? Because we have all come down from Point Zero — the source of all that exists. This is certainly a much more civilized picture of the Creator God than the savage God of the Old Testament. But we're making a really bad job of matters and it's urgent that we change that.

The real message of the real Jesus was that as Gods we have the power to create our own realities. That was the heart of the message he came to teach. Where did Jesus ever say in the New Testament that he was coming here to suffer and die for our sins?

The real message of Jesus addressed the crippling programs that are still alive and well in the sub-conscious mind of the

[43] John 10:34.

[44] John 14:12.

majority of the people in the world today. Those programs are related to matters of fundamental concern, such as we have been discussing in these pages. Those negative programs have been indoctrinated into us almost since the time of Jesus, and they will not allow us to go where he directed or accomplish what it is he wished. Above all they will not allow us to make sense of and apply those two central statements of his quoted above, which were the bedrock of his message.

He wanted us to become masters of the quantum field and do the things he did. Unfortunately, the old sub-conscious programs prohibit us from accomplishing that, and lead to the classical dis-empowerment and unworthiness that is all too evident in even the most wonderful and enlightened branches of Christianity today.

I am not in any way, shape or form denying that there are wonderful and profound things in Christianity. Some of the most enlightened and uplifting insights that ever appeared in human history are penned in the pages of the New Testament. Some of the most uplifting humanitarian work on a grand scale down through human history has been performed by Christians in the spirit of applying the mandate of Jesus '*to love your neighbor as yourself*'. No-one is denying these wonderful things. What we are talking about is the unfortunate context in which it was all put across, and especially the failure to realize that all these wonderful things were signs that we were on the right track towards the state he taught about. These will be signs that we are on the right path towards attaining the state, but they are not the state itself, which is where most of the confusion lies.

Returning to the issue of the sub-conscious mind and the ultimate embarrassment of not being in control — even after I make the difficult discovery that these programs are alive and well in me, they still will not release their hold on me just because I may decide I no longer want them. It's not that easy. A different method is required. That realization is what dictates the basic structure of this book. We are looking at the central issues that relate to our knowledge and understanding of the teachings of Jesus, which were all about teaching a new and empowering way of living.

They were absolutely not about repentance from sin, conversion and making up to God for our offenses.

Tragically, most of our religious programming not alone does not support that shift into being powerful divine beings. It actually works powerfully against that ever occurring.

The Clash of Two Minds: I say, "I want to heal myself" but yet nothing happens

You may well ask: "What has all this about Jesus and his times got to do with us, now that we are well into the 21st century?" You may be thinking that all these things happened so long ago. Its fine for historians or students of the Bible, but we are busy and practical people. Why is this important?

And I will respond to that by saying — Is it really important for you and me today to delve into all these matters and try to find out what really happened when our fundamental belief systems were originally generated? It matters enormously because the only way to remove a dis-empowering program is to re-visit where those programs originated and assess whether the right empowering message ever got into our sub-conscious programs.

Why is it so difficult to say with great conviction that I want to heal myself — but yet nothing happens? The reason is because 'I' am not in control. The conscious mind is not in control of these matters. It is the sub-conscious mind and its programs that are. As discussed earlier in these pages, 95% or more of my mind has not been affected at all by my conscious decision to heal myself.

There is an old adage in psychology that there are always at least two people who come for a therapy session, both living in the same body ... the person who wants to change and the person who does not. These are really just two labels for the conscious and the sub-conscious mind. But it is the sub-conscious mind that is in control of almost all of what goes on.

Let's contemplate this for a moment. Imagine that you are doing some repetitive and routine stuff like mowing the grass or driving a car alone for miles on a road you know like the back of your hand, which I mentioned earlier. For how much of that long drive were you fully aware and conscious of what you were doing? Or was it the sub-conscious that was doing most of the driving? Was the rest of you preoccupied with something else?

Even if the psychologists say there are always two people who come for a therapy session, the situation is actually much worse than that, because most of us walk around not just with two people, but with a whole committee in our heads. And usually the opinions of the committee are like the opinions of any group — widely divergent. And a divergent mind is relatively powerless to create anything positive ... although it is excellent at creating more divergence.

As stated earlier, most of our basic beliefs we took in verbally or by observation, before the age of about six years. Children learn from what they see and from what they experience much more than from what they hear. We take in these basic messages and then everything else that comes into our minds for the rest of our lives is molded, assessed, sorted and filed, in accordance with those original beliefs.

Whether we are really aware of it or not, there is a subtle filtering system — a subtle censorship system that's always switched on. If new information comes to us, for instance in High School, or College, or I have an experience in the daily work place or anywhere else in life, it will be filtered out if it is not in accordance with our already deeply-entrenched programs. What is really crucial to realize is that we won't even be aware of this happening. The primary business of the sub-conscious mind is to ensure its own existence and to prevent any change to its programs. We can spend an entire lifetime reinforcing these early beliefs without ever realizing it.

Take an example. A little boy or girl is told that he or she is stupid and useless. "You're exactly like your good-for-nothing Uncle Jeff ... just like him. Everyone knows he's a bum and you are just like him". At that tender age, that message instantly becomes a powerful lifelong program of worthlessness in that little person's mind.

In the later years growing up, that program of worthlessness in the young person's mind is reinforced by any criticism or mockery. In fact, he or she will distort messages to conform to the belief that "I am worthless" even if that was not the intent of the person speaking to him or her. The message becomes a program for failure. Even if the little child did manage to accomplish something worthwhile, more than likely there will always be the nagging insecurity – "Maybe I'm deceiving myself" or "Maybe when people tell me how wonderful I'm doing, they are just being hypocritical; they just want to get on my good side, or they may want something from me". We can't accept there is something valuable in us when our program is that we are worthless and a failure. And it can all come from what seemed to be such a small matter at the time.

Maybe the child's parent made that statement – "You're good for nothing" – when exhaustion or frustration was the main reason it was ever expressed. It was not at all based on any worthlessness of the child. But the effect of these offhand remarks can last for a lifetime. Unfortunately, at those tender stages of our lives, these remarks quickly form themselves into life-long programs. This little boy or girl may be prone to experience failure most if not all of his or her life, because the child's basic belief system in the sub-conscious mind has now been programmed to failure.

Take another example. A little child is given something sweet to eat every time he or she falls and cuts himself or herself, or goes through some bad experience at school. Every time there is some discomfort, every time there is a failure, every time there is a catastrophe, or a threat, or a major disappointment, the parent gives the child something sweet to eat. If this is so, it's almost inevitable that the child begins to turn to sugar and sweetness to bolster self-esteem and to avoid all these feelings of sadness, failure or depression.

All these beliefs – the ways of acting and believing that we picked up from our parents and those close to us during childhood – become like computer programs in our sub-conscious mind. They remain there and they are going to call the shots for the rest of our lives. There is nothing that the conscious mind can do in any direct way to combat these feelings.

That's why it's so hard to stay on a diet, for example, if you have been programmed to equate food with self-worth, comfort and esteem. When one has this type of program and is trying to diet or follow some disciplined regimen, it is very difficult because there is a feeling that I am fighting myself. Actually, I am.

If we leave aside the homely little examples I've just given and go on to greater things, such as when we try to empower ourselves in relation to the quantum field, it is even worse. Then it is no longer me fighting myself on the very humble level of candies and cookies and schoolyard bullies or exhausted parents. Now I'm fighting myself and much more profound issues are at stake: such as colossal lack of self-worth, dis-empowerment and the inability to create. And the more we scream and protest against those programs the worse the situation becomes.

We are only effective if we are wise enough to know that when we want to address the removal of a program the only effective method is to first create a replacement for it, built from the ground up. And this needs to be done from the same source of information from which the foundations of these crippling programs first arose – with no assumptions. Until that task is addressed every opposition to the program makes the program stronger, because, as already noted, one of the primary tasks of every sub-conscious program is to ensure its own survival and empowerment.

This is why, if we want to get past the crippling programs into which most of the misunderstanding of the message of Jesus has been crushed, then we need to know personally all of the facts we can about how Jesus really was and what he really taught. It is no longer about facts and statistics from a long gone by era. We will build up a new program based on the truth of the situation, and when we can do that, with absolute openness and integrity, the old crippling program will start to fade away of its own accord, and with it will go our dis-empowerment in the area that was bedeviled by that program.

The lower down on the scale of life a species is, the less complex its nervous system, and the more that creature depends on sub-conscious programs. For instance, hummingbirds migrate enormous distances, as do geese. Turtles come back from thousands of miles to their birthplace to lay their eggs. Salmon return to where they were born to do the same. None of them have any understanding, at least in our sense of understanding, of why they do these things — but they do them perfectly.

We are supposed to be higher up on the scale of life. We have bigger nervous systems and bigger brains which enable us to learn from experience. But actually, in this respect, we are worse off than the creatures who have all those sub-conscious programs that enable them to do all those useful things. Our programs don't do anything useful for us on that scale. They don't even tell us where to go to lay our eggs! But they do take care of a lot of day to day "automatic" behavior for us, such as driving my car while I'm abstracted. Very often because so much of our life's experiences and fundamental programs are grounded in worthlessness, negativity and lack, especially in the religious realm, they tell us we have offended God or betrayed Jesus, and if we don't do something about it we are going to Hell to burn for all eternity.

What should we do? The religious authorities tell us in effect to make ourselves even more worthless. Why is this? Because, unlike the swallows or the geese, we humans have a level of intelligence that can empower us to alter the sub-conscious programs that dictate the course of our lives. And maybe, if we do that, we will no longer have a need for the form of negative guidance often offered by religions.

Unfortunately, most of the sources of our sub-conscious programming arise from dis-empowerment, lack and worthlessness. So if we are looking for guidance in times of depression and despair, the standard religious form of guidance will tell us to make up to God for our doubt and other sins. Thus, the last state shall be worse than the first.

Unfortunately, our main source of religious beliefs and customs come from how we imagine Jesus to have been. I am repeating this fact many times, and I am doing that deliberately, because it is essential to the creation of a new program. His message has been turned on its head, from being a primordial message of empowerment to being a colossal mindset of worthlessness, guilt, powerlessness and fear. Worse still, in our most susceptible years, we have been emphatically told that these crippling states are pleasing to God and that we should cultivate them.

If we believe that the whole of the mission of Jesus was designed to culminate in his gory suffering and death to appease the anger of a vengeful God, can we at least dare to realize at last that loyalty to this caricature of things is, in fact, a not so obvious form of atheism? Further, can we realize it is impossible to create meaningfully in the quantum field while we remain in such a condition? Atheism is unfortunate, not because God might perhaps find it offensive, but because it dis-empowers humanity.

So, to review again, the difference between all the species on the scale of life is actually not very great. The only difference is that the creatures lower down on the scale of life have unconscious motivations that work for them. Our unconscious motivations usually work against us. We, in our early years, take in all of the attitudes, convictions, beliefs and ways of judging and acting that we observe in our parents and others around us. These are now the 'tenants' which control our biology for the rest of our lives unless we learn a way to replace the crippling programs that are normally alive and well in our sub-conscious. All the instincts that come from our genes, and the behavior we have observed in our early years, have now formed this sub-conscious mind.

It's all about a set of programs. And it's all about stimulus-response ... when the stimulus is applied the reaction or response results. There's no judgment in the sub-conscious mind. No questions are asked. At the same time, the conscious and the sub-conscious minds do cooperate. The sub-conscious takes over when the conscious mind is not paying attention. We saw a sublime example of it with the 'backwards bicycle'.

How will our sub-conscious mind take care of things? Exactly in the way it was programmed to do. No amount of temper tantrums or persuasion can change the 'tenants'. Dr. Bruce Lipton tells an amusing story in one of his books.[45] During his college days one of his fellow students, who was seriously inebriated, was trying to get the jukebox in their recreation area to play a certain

---

45 *Biology of Belief*, p.170.

song. Lipton tells this story to illustrate that the jukebox in many ways operates in a similar fashion to our brains. There are certain programs installed in the juke box and if you press the right button you get the desired result in the form of playing the song you wish to hear. If you press a different button you will get a different result. But the student was too drunk to operate the machine properly, so in exasperation he finally started kicking and abusing the juke box, but of course got no results apart from the damage sustained by the machine. It's a good illustration of the futility of ranting and raving against a program in the sub-conscious that we want to get rid of. It accomplishes nothing. Yet ranting and raving against such unwanted programs is exactly what we usually do because we have never been accurately informed about how these processes work.

All of the homely analogies and comparisons in the teachings of Jesus were designed to inspire, awaken and enlighten us at a deeper level than the superficially obvious. But instead of probing to understand what the images and stories convey, we normally just note the superficial details and circumstances of the narratives. Good examples include the story of the miraculous draft of fishes,[46] the house built on sand[47] and the parable of the sower.[48] All these anecdotes, of which Jesus was so fond, were not about improved methods of husbandry or house construction, but about the deeper truths those situations conveyed.

For example, the account of the miraculous draft of fishes in John 21 was about letting down the net on the right-hand side of the boat into the deep, which in the terms of those days was a metaphor for accessing the sub-conscious mind. The yield from metaphorically delving into the sub-conscious was a draft of 153 fish. Jerome[49] claimed he was quoting the Roman writer Oppian[50]

---

[46] Luke 5:1-11, John 21:1-14.

[47] Matthew 7:24-27, Luke 6:46-49.

[48] Matthew 13:1-23, Mark 4:1-20, Luke 8:1-15.

[49] 347-420 AD.

[50] Oppian of Anazarbus, in modern Turkey, a Greco-Roman poet during the reign of the Emperors Marcus Aurelius and Commodus. Born 183 AD.

while commenting on Ezekiel 47,[51] and he said that the Greeks had identified exactly 153 species of fish in the sea, hence John 21 was using a metaphor for a catch that could not be surpassed. Unfortunately, no such reference can be found in the works of Oppian. The previous attempts of the Apostles had caught nothing all night. The metaphor in the Gospel perhaps conveys that those who do not access the sub-conscious mind gain no insights at all.

In areas that are devoutly religious, people are often wonderfully kind and supportive of each other, but they do not take that all important further step. Jesus taught that this wonderful way of acting was a sign of something much deeper that was occurring within us if we had the wit to see it. Most of us do not; we pause at the good works, and do not explore any deeper.

The conflict between our conscious mind and the programs in the sub-conscious mind is manifested in another familiar phenomenon: muscle testing. When there is conflict between the two minds it manifests itself in a weakening of the muscles. All of us on the path to evolving have run into at least minor versions of this. We find jobs that we fail at but we remain in them. We stay in circumstances that we really don't like. We think we deserve better, but somehow are not able to create an improvement. Or worst of all, in terms of deception, we stay with something that is killing us because we think it is more 'spiritual'. After all, Jesus put up with a lot during his three-year mission in Israel we are told. Therefore, we also apparently, should follow his example and put up with a lot as well.

Thus money, wealth, having a positive influence over people or thinking deep questions about God and the brain, is regarded as 'ungodly' and unspiritual, and therefore regarded as forbidden or somehow disloyal: most definitely inappropriate ponderings for a true and faithful believer. So, no matter what we do, we remain poor, because somehow we have persuaded ourselves it is more godlike than wealth. We don't make any changes because we live in fear of the unknown. No matter what we do we don't make a 'mark' on anything. No matter what we do we will certainly not

[51] Commentary, Ezekiel, PL 25:474C.

get within light years of making manifest what Jesus referred to in those two famous quotations from St. John's Gospel..."*You are all gods*" and "*All these miracles I do you will do, and greater than these will you do*". We certainly will never evolve or gain the power Jesus told us was our birthright. We'll never do that as long as our sub-conscious mind is in conflict with our conscious mind. In some cases that conflict can have catastrophic consequences. And we never suspected why!

DNA and the Emotional Children of Fear

In the study of the human genome a sensation was created in 2012, when a group of scientists working with the ENCODE[52] project, announced that 80% of human DNA was active and performing some function. However, two years later a group of scientists at Oxford[53] also analyzed the human genome and claimed that less than 10% of our DNA is functional. Of course, the precise definition of 'functional' remains unclear, and much of the gushing coverage over the redefinition of 'junk' DNA that followed the 2012 announcement, did not help to clarify matters.

DNA is the physical mechanism behind the attitudes and beliefs in both our conscious and sub-conscious minds.

It has been well established that emotions have a vibration or frequency attached to them. Our thoughts and emotions send out signals — just like a radio signal. Several pioneering scientists in this field, such as Dr. Rudolph Tanzi,[54] the late Dr. Mitchell

---

[52] The Encyclopedia of DNA Elements (ENCODE) is a public research project launched by the US National Human Genome Research Institute (NHGRI) in September 2003. It was intended to be a continuation of the work of the Human Genome Project, and it has the aim of identifying all the functional elements in the human genome.

[53] Chris M. Rands, Stephen Meader, Chris P. Ponting , Gerton Lunter. PLOS Genetics, July 24, 2014, http://dx.doi.org/10.1371/journal.pgen.1004525

[54] Professor of Neurology at Harvard University Medical School.

Gaynor,[55] and Dr. Randy Jirtle,[56] now say that this signal directly affects the structure of our DNA.

It is hardly necessary to note that allowing emotions to get out of control and play total havoc with our lives is reckless and unwise. It's a luxury we can't afford if we are serious about taking charge of our existence. While we await more clarification from the field of divided experts may we ask if distortions in Jesus' message alter our emotions and thus impact our physical bodies through our DNA?

The Human-Machine Interaction Network on Emotion (HUMAINE) classifies a bewildering array of 48 emotions.[57] But there are apparently only two basic ones: Fear and Love. All the other 'emotions' originate directly or indirectly from these two. We often say to people, "Don't be so emotional". What are these emotions, and why should we be concerned about them? Because they broadcast a vibration that can either turn on or turn off important receptors in our DNA.

Let's ponder for a moment these two basic emotions: Fear and Love. Both are often misunderstood. Let's first look at Fear. 'Real' or acute fear is the result of a real danger or threat; such as when there is a saber-toothed tiger on your heels, or you have narrowly

---

[55] President of Gaynor Integrative Oncology and Gaynor Wellness in New York City. Died in suspicious circumstances, 16 September 2015. The Gene Therapy Plan: Taking Control of Your Genetic Destiny with Diet and Lifestyle, Nurture Nature, Nurture Health.

[56] Professor of Epigenetics at the Department of Biological Sciences, North Carolina State University, Raleigh. Environmental Epigenomics in Health and Disease—Epigenetics and Disease Susceptibility and Epigenetics and Complex Diseases.

[57] "HUMAINE: Emotion, Annotation, and Representation Language, 2006. Shaver, P., Schwartz, J., Kirson, D., & O'Connor, C. (1987). Emotion Knowledge: Further Exploration of a Prototype Approach. Journal of Personality and Social Psychology, 52(6), 1061. Parrott, W. (2001), "Emotions in Social Psychology", Psychology Press, Philadelphia. Plutchik, R. "The Nature of Emotions." American Scientist, 2011.Robinson, D. L. (2009)."Brain function, mental experiencer and personality," The Netherlands Journal of Psychology. pp. 152—167.

avoided a serious car crash. We don't have saber-toothed tigers anymore, but we still have the genetic response to that ancient history within us. Recall the physical sensations we experienced when in similar situations – racing heart, rapid breathing, enhanced strength and heightened awareness to name a few. This is a healthy reaction – it saves our lives.

But the fear we are referring to here now is different, it is a long, slow emotion: a symptom that we are feeling unworthy and powerless. These 'Children of Fear' run the gamut of unpleasant emotions including insecurity, guilt, unworthiness, depression, and apprehension of punishment ... and of course nothing makes us more apprehensive than the thought of eternal punishment. And lastly but by no means least, the belief that there isn't enough to go round.

While 'real' fear is fleeting, and actually helpful, the fear we refer to here is chronic and lingering. It results in low self-esteem and harmful alterations in our DNA.

The other basic emotion is usually called 'love'. The term has not had a good history, and has become so abused and disempowered that it's probably no longer a good word to describe this second basic emotion at all. When we use it nowadays we nearly always feel the need to add some other term to it to give it some impact – such as 'altruistic' or "unconditional" love. 'Love' was at the heart of what Jesus was talking about. But nowadays it has degenerated into either a mawkish, sentimentalist kind of attitude that weak and spineless people often exhibit, or it may express something crude or of a sexual nature. So it appears we really don't have a clear picture in our minds of what either fear or love really mean anymore – if we ever did.

I have been at the bedside of quite a few individuals when they were dying. Some of these were absolutely blameless individuals, outstanding on every level – humanly and spiritually. But to my great surprise some of them died in terror. Terror of what, you might ask? Terror of the judgment of God. They had become brainwashed by the notion of the savage God as depicted in so many places in the Old Testament, and by the implications of the Passion which it is alleged Jesus had to endure as something exacted by God for our sins. It seemed to them that there really wasn't any way, no matter how heroically they had lived, that they could escape Divine Judgment and Punishment in the hereafter. They believed that no matter what good work they did, it was never enough, because this unfortunate version of God makes demands that can't ever be satisfied.

We may think that we have gotten rid of all that and that we are now beyond those crippling mindsets. But, if we were ever a part of that kind of belief system, and most people in the West have been, it is not that easy to shake off its effects, no matter how much we may wish to. Unfortunately, the very great likelihood is that when we get to our weakest state, as with the people I mentioned above on their deathbeds, those programs are very likely to re-emerge with full force. When the conscious mind's defenses are at their weakest, the sub-conscious programs all come rushing back. Then we are in dire trouble.

It is crucial to be aware that living under the influence of programs based on grief, insecurity, unworthiness and lack prevents the receptors on our DNA from opening up to a higher level. And that higher level is the physical mechanism that we are aiming to accomplish. Whatever focusing we are doing, and whatever program we are trying to replace, the physical correspondence of that is what happens with our DNA.

If we are living in a state of unworthiness or guilt or fear, these attitudes are not going to stay in our mind at that level. Mental attitudes very quickly become physical in the synapses of our brains, and drain into programs of the sub-conscious. But what is even more troubling is that they will filter down into the neuronets of the brain and into our DNA.

This of course opens up a huge can of worms, because if we realize, even with the very limited amount of knowledge that we have, how our DNA works and how it is transmitted from one generation to the next, we are faced with a colossally depressing realization. To our horror we now know that we have inherited crippling attitudes from our physical ancestors right back to the very beginning. And we also now know that the alleged origin of the human race took place considerably farther back than

Archbishop Ussher's 6,020 years ago, so we have a much more massive inheritance of insecurity with which to cope.

How long has it been since our race was first formed? Let's say a quarter million years. That's quite a lot to inherit by way of a legacy. When we make an effort to address what's keeping us from living in a state of joy, which is much closer to what Jesus was speaking about than what the word 'love' conveys today, then we have to realize we are carrying with us those attitudes that have been ingrained in our race for perhaps a quarter million years or more. That's going to make our task much harder.

The Cosmic Christ: An Alien Scenario

Our problem is not just about informing ourselves, or getting correct or better information about the facts of our existence. What do I mean by better information? Well, realizing that the Earth was not created just 6,020 years ago on the 23rd of September, 4004 BC, would be a good start. We realize now that that is not what happened at the beginning of things. But it is even more catastrophic for us to realize that this Earth is not the be-all and the end-all of everything as we have normally assumed. In terms of the length of recorded human history it is really not all that long ago that this Earth was regarded by most people who lived on the planet, as the center of the entire Universe. It is quite a come down from that mindset to begin to suspect today that we probably are living on the fringes of a modest sized rural galaxy, in the very boondocks of the Universe.

Remember that Jesus was first thought of as being the Savior of this World (when this was thought to be the only world) in order to free us from these crippling emotions we call the 'Children of Fear'. In the light of our new knowledge does he now need to be a Cosmic Christ as well?

What if, after all, there is some truth behind that mass of UFO related material we have heard so much about? And what if we should painfully discover someday that instead of being the master race, such as we have for so long uncritically assumed, that we are actually one of the more backward races in the entire universe? And how would Jesus fit into that scenario if he died to rescue the whole of creation (which I assume would include aliens) from God's vengeance? Did Jesus suffer to appease God's vengeance against the first humans and all their descendants? That was the traditional teaching of the Church and it was a comfortable scenario when the Earth was considered to be the center of the universe and the people of Earth the only human beings that existed. It was still even reasonably comfortable when we tentatively moved with Copernicus in 1543 to seeing our Sun as the center of the universe.

We now have a more expansive view of things and know that our Sun is just one of approximately 100 billion stars just in our own Milky Way Galaxy. It's estimated there are about 10 trillion Galaxies in the observable universe. That would give an estimate of 100 octillion (1 followed by 29 zeros!!) stars in the universe.[58] As yet, we have no way of knowing how many planets of a habitable kind may orbit those stars. But according to traditional belief Jesus is supposed to be the Cosmic Christ rather than just the Christ of this human race. Does he then have to do something for all of those hypothetical inhabitants of numberless planets, leaving aside all questions of multiverses that were not known to exist when that belief or its equivalents were formulated? If so, then the work of Jesus as Redeemer has not even begun, and questions about the real meaning of Limbo and Purgatory will occupy the International Theological Commission for many centuries to come.

Or maybe, instead, it's time for a Copernican revolution in matters of belief. Maybe the first humans did not sin in the way it's been traditionally understood. Maybe the scenario of the fall of the first human couple was the best the authors of Genesis could do to square their beliefs in an all-powerful Creator God, who was said to be good, but who made such an imperfect creation. The only way out was to blame the kind of creation we have on the first humans so that God could be acquitted. To be fair the world we live in bears

---

[58] David Kornreich, Ithaca College, New York State. Founder of the "Ask An Astronomer" service at Cornell University.

all the signs of something that was intended to be much better, but in which something serious has gone wrong. Obviously, all this leaves even more unanswered questions – about the Creation itself in the first place, but much more ominously about God.

Maybe the role of Jesus here on Earth was of a dramatically different and more wonderful kind than we have been traditionally told? Maybe the intelligent races elsewhere originated entirely separately from us? Maybe they had a different vision of how to make sense of the apparent clash between a good and all-powerful God and a radically imperfect creation. Maybe they didn't need to blame their own first humans for everything that had gone wrong. Maybe they started from an entirely different set of presuppositions than did our first people who tried to make sense of existence here on Earth long ago. Maybe we need an entirely new paradigm and maybe that is exactly what Jesus came to bring us almost 2,000 years ago. Unfortunately, that never started to dawn on us until recently.

But when the first indications began to appear that there might be intelligent beings living on other planets in our solar system or galaxy, or even beyond that, this posed enormous problems for the Church's tradition that viewed Jesus as the Universal Savior.

It is said that President Dwight D. Eisenhower had a council with aliens at Muroc Field (now Edwards Air Force Base) in California on 20 February 1954. He invited James Francis Cardinal McIntyre, then Archbishop of Los Angeles, to come along with him as a spiritual advisor. The Cardinal a few days later, and against President Eisenhower's wishes, reportedly went to the Pope and briefed him on the President's meeting with the aliens. It is also reported that subsequent meetings with those same aliens, took place with Pope Pius XII in the Casa Pio IV in the Vatican on three separate occasions. That, of course, is an enormous topic in itself, and outside the scope of this present volume.

For now, we will focus on the implications that the discovery of alien life would have on certain aspects of the Church's teachings, particularly on its view that Jesus was the Universal Savior of all intelligent life in the Universe. As I mentioned earlier, that view sat well with a culture that believed the Sun was the center of the universe and the Earth was the only home of intelligent life anywhere. However, these new findings have presented a dilemma for theologians who have almost turned themselves inside out in their attempts to square their beliefs about Jesus with these new facts.

Many questions arise. If intelligent beings live elsewhere, how does Jesus relate to those beings if indeed he is the Universal Savior as the Church teaches? Would Jesus, as Universal Savior, have to incarnate in all of those civilizations and suffer and die for them there as the Church insists he did for us here? And can there then be the equivalents of the Garden of Eden and First Couples on every other habitable planet as well as on Earth? Would Jesus have to go to all those places where intelligent life exists in the universe and do something for them as he is supposed to have done here for us?

Adopting a more realistic stance than that scenario, some have suggested that what Jesus did for us 2,000 years ago during his Passion was more than sufficient to take care of all intelligent beings on any planet, anywhere, at any time. The former Vatican Astronomer, Monsignor Jose Gabriel Funes,[59] apparently thinks so, for when asked a few years ago what the Church would do if intelligent life were discovered outside this Earth, he responded that the Church's first duty would be to baptize those aliens![60] Obviously this is the familiar old view of Jesus as some sort of funnel for a commodity called 'salvation' that can only come through him ... presumably because he, as a divine being, is the only one who could make reparation for our sins.

Of course, that makes a huge assumption that everything is about that original sin in the Garden of Eden for which we are all trying to make amends. It is clear that the authors of Genesis were trying to square their beliefs in a good and all powerful God, who created the world, with the factual observation that the world was

[59] Vatican Astronomer from 2006. On September 18, 2015 Pope Francis replaced him, to the surprise of nobody in particular, with fellow Jesuit, Brother Guy Consolmagno, from Detroit. Funes was the first Argentinian born Jesuit Director of the Vatican Observatory, at the time when the first Jesuit, Jorge Maria Bergoglio, also from Argentina, ascended the throne of Peter.

[60] Article in *Osservatore Romano.*

a mess of imperfections and injustices. But there are other ways to resolve such an impasse, which is not an impasse generated from God, but by erroneous conceptions imposed on God from human starting points.

There is a wonderful legend about God sending an angel down to this Earth. The angel is coming from the vast gloriousness of the universe, light years upon light years away from here. Glorious planets and all sorts of wonderful things appear as they glide through the cosmos, and then suddenly as they travel along, God takes the angel by the arm and they see this dull, murky, tiny little orb in the distance, where no-one would ever want to go. To the angel's great surprise God said: "I want you to go there." "What!?" says the Angel. "No way am I ever going to that dull insignificant spot."

Anyway, the point of the legend was that this is where we are; and it's by no means the jewel of the entire universe. It took us an awfully long time to figure that out. And when we did it was the ultimate and humiliating brush with sanity. We didn't figure out even much lesser things for a long time. But when we did, it was as always due to a few very gifted individuals.

Maybe there really wasn't anything to take care of, and maybe the work of Jesus was about something entirely different? Sometimes new information gives us a much more informed insight into the background and validity of ancient beliefs.

Does Belief in Jesus As a Savior from Sin Need a Copernican Revolution?

The first of the gifted individuals who upturned our view of reality was Aristarchus of Samos[61] who lived in Greece more than two hundred years before the time of Jesus. When Aristarchus was sitting out on his deck one night having a glass of wine, he realized that the heavens were not rotating around us, as it seemed, but that it was we who were rotating beneath the heavens. In the traces of our relatively recent history, he was the first to place the Sun at the

[61] c. 310 – c. 230 BC.

center of the known universe — with the Earth revolving around it. It wasn't until seventeen hundred years later that Copernicus figured it out all over again for the Western world.

Let's put Aristarchus' history into a little broader context. He was born on Samos, a Greek island one mile off the western coast of Turkey. He lived most of his life in Alexandria in northern Greece: a town often confused with Alexandria in Egypt. Aristarchus was a contemporary of the noted philosopher Epicurus,[62] also a native of Samos. Pythagoras (c. 570 — c. 495 BC), the noted philosopher and mathematician, was also from Samos, although more than two hundred years earlier. It might interest you to know that wine from the island of Samos was well known in antiquity, as it remains today. It was often credited with being the inspiration for the ground-breaking ideas of its three renowned native sons — the founding fathers of Western thought: Pythagoras, Epicurus and Aristarchus. Perhaps we could use some more of that wine in current times!

Claudius Ptolemy,[63] was a Greco-Egyptian astronomer, mathematician and geographer who lived in Alexandria in Northern Egypt. He was born 350 years after the death of Aristarchus, but does not seem to have either heard or heeded Aristarchus's revolutionary ideas. Ptolemy lived and died where he was born, in Alexandria, and throughout his life reposed in the belief that the Earth was the center of the universe.

The shift from the views of Ptolemy to that of Aristarchus/Copernicus (1473—1543 AD) seventeen hundred years later was enormous in the field of astronomy. At that point the old paradigm of the Earth being the center of the universe radically shifted and a sun-centered universe emerged.

Unfortunately, we never achieved a similar paradigm shift in the ways we understand other dimensions of reality. The move from Ptolemy — who believed that the Earth was the center of everything — to Copernicus was a complete shift. No amount of improving Ptolemy's view could ever produce the ground-breaking paradigm of Aristarchus or Copernicus. All the

[62] 341 — 270 BC.

[63] 90 — 168 AD.

assumptions of the Ptolemaic view had to be jettisoned before making a new beginning with an entirely new paradigm.

Have we learned anything from this experience? It seems to provide us with the ultimate paradigm of how real advances are made in knowledge, in whatever field we are exploring. Do we really understand yet that knowledge painfully advances by constructing paradigms, frames of reference, manufactured out of the best fragments of knowledge we may happen to have at the time? As more knowledge is gained we may come to realize that the paradigm we constructed was defective and may not be repairable. Copernicus realized that the Ptolemaic view of reality was not repairable as its fundamental presuppositions were wrong, so he had to jettison everything and start from scratch.

It is blatantly obvious that if we begin with the wrong presuppositions about reality we can never get the right answers, but yet we do it over and over? The presuppositions we start with seem to have assumed some form of sacred quality and often seem to be regarded as above question.

We now badly need another Copernican shift; but this time in the field of fundamental religious beliefs. That kind of shift has in fact already been done for us by the teachings of Jesus. But his message was warped by the old molds of thought, the old paradigms concerning God and mankind. This was done especially against the background as portrayed in the Book of Genesis and by the doctrinal chaos of the Christian world in the centuries following the Ecumenical Councils of Nicaea[64] and Chalcedon.[65] We must now re-visit these issues with fresh minds if we want to escape the dis-empowerment of those crippling programs.

In spite of the Western world's widespread adoption of the Copernican view of things, in many other ways we have stayed stuck in the old-world view. In 'religious' terms we still appear to think we are the center of everything. We could say that we still have a 'Ptolemaic' Religion. Are we wondering why the Aliens

[64] Acknowledged as the first Ecumenical Council of the Church, held at Nicaea, now Iznik, Bursa province, Turkey, from 20 May to 19 June, AD 325.

[65] Fourth Ecumenical Council of the Church, held at Chalcedon, (modern Kadıköy, now a district in Istanbul), from October 8 to November 1, 451 AD.

don't turn up more promptly? Perhaps we haven't done anything to our belief systems about fundamental reality that would accelerate such a meeting!

Let's consider some of our fundamental beliefs including our convictions about: why we are here; what we should be doing while we are here; and where we may anticipate we are going after death? I wish we were as comparably advanced in those beliefs as Ptolemy was in his astronomy, however limited and mistaken he was. But, unfortunately, despite the message of Jesus, in the sphere of fundamental beliefs it seems we have not yet even arrived at the equivalent of a Ptolemaic system.

As said above, if we start with the wrong presuppositions we can never get the right answer. For millennia we have been fed a web of fables, instead of the truth, about fundamental reality. The only way out of the mental prison we find ourselves in is to basically re-program our DNA at a fundamental level and replace the crippling programs in our sub-conscious mind with new and improved ones based on the mindset Jesus told us we should acquire.

As I stated above, the conscious mind cannot do anything directly to alter the programs of the sub-conscious. We need a more clinical approach. That approach involves rebuilding these crippling programs from the ground up. This process will not work unless we become profoundly aware of the limiting programs that we already have in our sub-conscious mind and understand as fully as we can how they got there. We can then consciously work to replace them with new programs constructed with more accurate information about how reality actually is.

In that re-building of programs nothing can be assumed and nothing can be taken for granted. Furthermore, there can be no break in the chain of logic in the step-by-step reasoning of what's presented. Once we make an assumption that is not justified by the evidence, then the sub-conscious mind will reject that assumption and scatter everything. The sub-conscious program has discovered a chink in the armor of what is trying to destroy it. After all, the sub-conscious program is fighting for its life. It has been programmed to protect itself. If, indeed it controls up to 95% or more of what our mind processes, then we begin to see what strategy will be needed to break free of this prison of limitation and dis-empowerment.

In essence, the very faculties of mind needed to enable us to break free are the same ones that control our imprisonment. And that is one of the main reasons why it is so hard to make meaningful and fundamental change. The sub-conscious mind will dismiss our entire enterprise given the slightest chance. If there is any doubt, the sub-conscious is always going to rule in favor of the status quo and against any change. These distortions have framed most of our fundamental religious conceptions, so to alter them effectively is a task that requires great skill, wisdom, patience and accurate knowledge. And that has been a rare combination in human history to date.

If we need a Copernican revolution in terms of what we believe, and we have grasped the fundamental process by which revolutions in fundamental patterns of thought occur, it is obvious there is no point in re-hashing the tired old platitudes that so often constitute what we believe about Jesus. Above all there is no point in rigidly and blindly adhering to them as some form of warped proclamation of loyalty to Jesus.

SCROLL TWO
A FRESH LOOK AT JESUS AND HIS FAMILY

Chapter 6
The Jesus We Lost: Did the Gospels Ever Really Get the Heart of the Matter?

Russell Moore, the well-known author and speaker once said: "If we've ever had a really nasty stomach virus, wracked with fever and chills and vomiting and diarrhea, we get upset because we have no control over the most disgusting of our bodily functions when they go wrong in illness."[66] In that context, we have to admire – and that's a very, very, mild word – the efforts of people who look after the old, the sick and the infirm when the most disgusting and degrading aspects of human nature predominate.

Having a bad stomach virus or some similar complaint that makes us feel really awful, is not just awful it's undignified, which is probably the biggest difficulty in this sad scenario.

If we were to think of Jesus in relation to all of these embarrassing and humiliating aspects of bodily existence, it seems to us to border on the ultimate in disrespect if not blasphemy. Somehow or another, individuals whom we have on a pedestal, people we look up to and revere, we feel they are exempt from all of this. Does the Pope or the Dalai Lama have a bathroom? If you find yourself wondering about such irrelevant things in some odd moment, does that mean you disrespect the Dalai Lama or the Pope? Or that you are cultivating a prurient and disgusting mindset? No. I raise this only to highlight that there is an unconscious element in our minds which wants to assert that great beings are fundamentally not human in the normal way.

[66] Delivered the 29th Erasmus Lecture in 2016

A central tenet of Christianity has been that Jesus is truly human as well as divine. In fact, several people went to the stake for denying that he was human. This could be a serious matter in the wrong circumstances. But while the official line is that Jesus was both truly human and truly divine, in practice Christianity has spent most of its history in denying his real humanity

The Councils of Nicaea and Constantinople effectively put Jesus totally, completely and utterly out of our reach to imitate. This is a great catastrophe, because the guiding principle of the Mission of Jesus was to ask us to imitate what he did so that we could become as he was.

We can never recall too often his immortal words: "You are all Gods…all these wonders, these miracles that I do, you can do and greater than these can you do". But of course, after Nicaea and Constantinople there wasn't, no pun intended, a chance in hell of that happening.

When we feel it's not kosher to ask embarrassing and inappropriate questions about great beings, not least Jesus, it shows us that we are not comfortable about accepting that they are truly and fully human. The reason why Christianity has in effect spent most of its history denying the real humanity of Jesus was because it was feared it might diminish him. But if he really wasn't human, but just looked like he was, what hope have we of imitating what he asked us to do?

The early Fathers of the Church[67] struggled to reconcile the fact that Jesus was divine with his equally real humanity. In the terms in which they discussed it, being human and being divine were cast as almost inevitable competitors. If you were really human, that seemed to make it impossible to be truly divine, and vice versa. The Fathers of the Church got into difficulties because their presuppositions about divinity and humanity were defective. The molds, the paradigms, in which they were trying to frame the question were erroneous. Jesus was divine in the same sense that he taught you and I are also. The difference between him and us

[67] A term used to describe the outstanding theologians and teachers who analyzed and expounded the message of Jesus in the early centuries. It is usually applied to such people who lived up to about the year 700 AD.

was that he had removed the garbage that was blocking the effects of his divinity emerging into material reality. In short, he had emerged into existing permanently in the state of agape.

If we really accepted that Jesus was truly human we wouldn't think such disrespectful questions as Russell Moore asked were either inappropriate or blasphemous. But it appears that right from the start, we've lost Jesus: even in our own day to day affairs, leaving the Councils of Nicaea and Constantinople aside for a moment.

We're more at ease apparently when we see Jesus in terms of godliness and almighty power. We're more comfortable when we see Jesus as utterly remote and inapproachable, and vastly different from us — some kind of strange, ghostly, ethereal figure from a supernatural realm. This is a catastrophe, because if we don't feel it's right to think of him as having flesh and blood, and growing in wisdom and age and grace, as the infancy narratives of Luke's Gospel tells us he did, then where does that leave us?

The Childhood of Jesus: Most of the Early Christians Knew Nothing about It

The earliest Christian believers in Jesus knew nothing about his childhood. In the sources we have, Saint Paul was the first person to write a word about him. That was in the First Letter to the Thessalonians. The Roman Province of Macedonia included northern Greece, and parts of present-day Albania, Bulgaria and Macedonia. Its capital was Thessalonica, and it was to the Christians in that city that Paul's Letters to the Thessalonians were addressed. The first Letter was occasioned by the fact that Paul's disciple, Timothy, had returned from visiting the early Christians in Macedonia, and had reported to Paul that some serious matters needed to be addressed there. The Letter was probably written by Paul from either Corinth or Athens in the year 51 or 52 AD, which makes it the oldest book of the New Testament, dating from about two decades after the Passion of Jesus.

It was another twenty years or so after 1 Thessalonians that the first Gospel appeared. In fact, all the letters of Paul were written before anyone had ever seen or heard of a Gospel, so we begin to realize there was nothing known about the early years of Jesus from the earliest layer of preaching from the Apostles themselves. The focus was on what followed his baptism at the age of about thirty years.

It is also very easy to forget how differently a message was conveyed in Ancient Near Eastern times from what are the customary forms of such narrative today.

When the Gospels did appear, two of them did contain narratives about the early years of Jesus, Luke 2:1-39, and Matthew 1:18-2:23, which are usually referred to as "The Infancy Narratives." I want to look at those infancy narratives briefly. They do contain some historical data, but their motive was not to tell us what happened in Jesus' childhood, and the sooner we disabuse ourselves of that notion the better off we will be. The concerns that Matthew and Luke had, dominate everything. They had different ways of approaching the matter dictated by what they wanted to emphasize in Jesus. It is a relatively easy thing for us today to see that Matthew and Luke's Infancy Narratives contradict each other on several points. But daring to point out such matters is usually dismissed as an attempt to undermine the message of Jesus itself.

Unfortunately, it's even harder nowadays for us to work out what happened in the childhood years of Jesus because in our religious culture in the West the two accounts of the childhood of Jesus in the Gospels of Matthew and Luke have in effect been put into the blender and combined.

There is no childhood material at all in either Mark or John.

What we have is a combined story in which, to take one example, the Magi who appear only in the Gospel of Matthew, are combined with the account of Jesus in the manger in the stable at Bethlehem, which appears only in Luke's account.

Is there any place where its stated in the New Testament that the Magi came to visit Jesus lying in a manger? No. It's a combining of elements from the two different traditions. For purpose of clarification in the next section let's look at the differences in the two Infancy Narrative accounts.

Comparing the Two Accounts of the Infancy of Jesus

Note that the consensus among New Testament scholars is that Matthew was written somewhere between the years 75-90 AD. Luke was written between 80-95 AD.

1. Where did Mary and Joseph live?

On this matter the two Infancy Narratives contradict each other:

According to Matthew they lived in Bethlehem.

According to Luke they lived in Nazareth. They go down to Bethlehem for a census, because it was their family ancestral place.

Remember the Gospels were written between forty to seventy years after the event. How would we fare if we were only now writing about things that happened at the end of World War II, approximately seventy years ago, (or even at the end of the Vietnam War, well over forty years ago), at this distance in time, which is the exact same time difference that separates the writing of the accounts of the Infancy Narratives from the actual events?

2. Where did the birth take place?

According to Matthew, it took place in a house. Matthew 2:11.

According to Luke, Jesus was born in a stable. Luke 2: 7.

3. Who came to adore him?

The Magi, according to Matthew. They were Gentile Philosophers. How many? The text doesn't say.

According to Luke, who came to visit? Shepherds: in other words, the lowest of all classes in society. How many Shepherds? No numbers are given.

4. The Star of Bethlehem

In the account of the Gospel of Matthew it is stated that an unusual star appeared in the heavens at the time of the birth of Jesus. Viewed from the Earth there actually was a coming together of heavenly bodies at that time that could have given the appearance of an unusually bright star.

However, while Matthew says there was a star, Luke does not mention any star.

5. Angels

Matthew mentions no angels but Luke does.

In summary:

Matthew (75-90 AD)	**Luke (80-95 AD)**
Birthplace: Bethlehem They go to Bethlehem only for the Census	Birthplace: Nazareth
Place of birth: a house (2:11)	Place of birth: a Stable (2:7)
Adoration: By Magi. Gentile Philosophers. (Text does not say how many.)	Adoration: By Shepherds. (Low place in society). Text does not say how many.
Star	No Star
Angels	No Angels
Massacre of the Innocents	No Massacre of the Innocents
Journey into Egypt	No Journey into Egypt

Let's look at Matthew's account of the infancy of Jesus.

Herod the Great had died when Jesus was very young, and Herod's son, Herod Antipas, became ruler of Galilee and Perea. That's the person Jesus called a fox, as we will consider later. According to the story in Matthew's Gospel, Herod Antipas had heard from the Magi that the heir to the throne of Judea had been born. Herod was paranoid about any threat to his rule, and consequently, as the story goes in Matthew, he killed every infant under the age of two years in the vicinity of Bethlehem.[68] In Luke's Infancy Narrative it is puzzling that there is no mention at all of what must have been an horrendous massacre.

In Matthew, before the massacre of the innocents, Mary and Joseph were told to flee into Egypt with Jesus for their own safety, and then the infants were massacred. But in the version of Saint Luke there was no massacre, or at least it wasn't mentioned. And there was no trip to Egypt. They simply went back peacefully to Nazareth.

What do we make of this? According to Matthew's account they went back to Nazareth instead of back to Bethlehem where they had lived, for fear of Herod Archelaus.[69] He was the new ruler of Judea after the death of his father, Herod the Great[70]. (Matthew 2:19-23). In Luke, they returned to Nazareth where they already lived, which was the obvious place where they would go. No trip to Egypt (Luke 2:39-40).

There is a large number of traditions about the journeys of the Holy Family through Egypt and through the Temples there, which is interesting in the light of what Jesus did later when he came back from Tibet and Nepal about the age of twenty-seven.[71] He went back to Egypt where he had been previously in his infancy and early years.

In the Gospel of Luke, Mary and Joseph are from Galilee. They traveled to Bethlehem because of the census of Tiberias. The newborn Jesus is placed in a manger. They go back to Nazareth. They stop at the Temple in Jerusalem on the way.

But in Matthew, by contrast, Joseph and Mary are introduced as natives of Bethlehem. In other words, Jesus is born at home. After fleeing to Egypt to escape the murderous designs of Herod the Great, they relocate to Galilee. In short, they simply moved house.

---

[68] Matthew 2: 16.

[69] Ethnarch of Judea, Samaria and Iudemia from 4 BC to 6 AD. Died c. 18 AD.

[70] Matthew 2:19-23.

[71] For an account of the travels of Jesus in Egypt, India and Tibet, see my DVD set, *How Jesus Became a Christ*, published by Edessa Code, LLC, 2006.

Luke repeatedly compares Jesus with John the Baptist. But John the Baptist is not mentioned at all in the infancy narrative of Matthew.

In Matthew's narrative Jesus' birth is detected by foreign astrologers, the Magi. In Luke, it is lowly shepherds who first hear the news.

In Matthew's narrative King Herod in Jerusalem hunts throughout the region to find Jesus and when he couldn't find him he decided to be on the safe side and kill every infant of tender years. In Luke's narrative, by contrast, the child is publicly proclaimed without incident in the very heart of Jerusalem by Simeon and Anna.

Luke says that Jesus' family went into Jerusalem and went to the Temple, but in Matthew they avoid the city entirely.

In Matthews's narrative, the spotlight shines on Joseph. It is he who receives the divine guidance in a series of dreams. In Luke's account, it is Mary who predominates. She is the one who hears and keeps God's word.

Matthew starts his account of the infancy of Jesus with a genealogy of Jesus from Abraham down to Joseph and Mary. Luke's genealogy is presented at the beginning of Jesus' public ministry but it runs backwards from Joseph to Adam, which is a heck of a lot farther back than Abraham.

Luke's Gospel was probably composed somewhere around the Aegean Sea, the sea between Greece and the Balkans. As has been noted, the Gospel is reckoned to be the first of a two-part work, the second volume being the Acts of the Apostles.

It seems that Matthew, or whoever Matthew was that wrote the Gospel, and Luke, whoever Luke was who wrote the Gospel, were not aware of each other's work, which is very understandable for the time.

The Gospels of the New Testament we are told are "the inspired, written word of God" but it is disconcerting to find after even such a brief investigation as this, that there is so much difference in the two versions of the infancy of Jesus.

Luke: Jesus, Healer, Reconciler, and the Ultimate Prophet

Luke has a wider perspective than Matthew.

Luke had two items on his agenda. To the non-Christian, non-followers of Jesus in the Roman Empire, he wanted to convey the Christian movement as a philosophically enlightened, politically harmless, socially benevolent and philanthropic organization. In other words, it's a religion for Jew and Gentiles which the Roman Empire would be well served by recognizing. That state of affairs of course did not manifest until a long time afterwards, with the Edict of Milan in 313, issued by the co-Emperors Licinius and Constantine.

One embarrassing fact that Luke had to deal with in implementing his agenda was that the founder of the Church, if you want to call him that — to wit, Jesus — had been executed for sedition by a Roman Prefect and had been very barbarously treated in advance of that, by being mocked, insulted, scourged and crowned with thorns, and then sent back and forth during the night between the Courts of Pilate and Antipas.

Luke offsets this by saying that Pilate declared Jesus innocent three times — you remember the old story of how he washed his hands, etc.[72] In Luke's Gospel the Roman Centurion at the foot of the cross, says, "Surely, this man was innocent" (23:47), unlike the account in Matthew and Mark.

It is also surely not an accident that every Roman character in Luke-Acts is portrayed favorably.

But for those who were not already "members of the church," Luke has a second agenda item. In his time and place the church's proclamation to the Jews was running into difficult circumstances, but by contrast it was succeeding remarkably with the Gentiles. Some were apparently wondering if God had remained faithful to his promises to the Jews, so that they would remain blessed, or was God about to abandon them? If the blessing through Jesus was

[72] Luke 23:4, 14, 22.

shifting to the Gentiles, then what about the promises to the Jews made by Jehovah? Or was the Church an heretical deviation from Judaism, as some were now charging?

Luke responded that the Church began among pious, law-abiding Jews – including Jesus! – and the Jewish-Christians formed the heart of an increasingly Gentile Church. As it says in Chapter 2:32; through them comes "a light for the revelation to the Gentiles and the glory of the people of Israel".

The way Luke portrays Jesus relates to these purposes. For Luke, Jesus is the bringer of authentic peace, of spiritual and physical wholeness, and of healing and reconciliation. When Jesus was born, angelic messengers proclaim, "Good news of great joy for all the people: today is born to you a Savior! Peace on Earth among those whom God favors!" (2:10-11, 14).

As I pointed out earlier these words echo actual inscriptions from that period that still survive today. They praise Caesar Augustus, the Emperor, as "God" and "Savior" in exactly the same terms: the bringer of the Roman Peace, whose birth "marks the beginning of the good news, through him, for all the world." Luke seems to be claiming that Jesus completes the work of the Emperor.[73]

Similarly, in Luke's Gospel, John the Baptist is said to be the one who will "guide our feet in the way of peace" (2:14).

In summary, in Luke's Gospel, Jesus is surrounded by an aura of healing and reconciliation that affects everybody who comes into contact with him. You can see that clearly in several passages in Luke dealing with the Passion. It's only in Luke, for example, that we have the incident in the Garden of Olives, where Jesus went after the Last Supper, and where he was arrested. Peter, impetuous as ever, took out his sword and cut off the ear of the High Priest's servant Malchus. Jesus restored the ear and told Peter to put away his sword.

Herod Antipas and the Roman Governor Pontius Pilate were bitter enemies prior to their encounter with Jesus, but after being

[73] Augustus died on 19 August 14 AD.

in his presence they became fast friends.[74] This is told only in the Gospel of Luke. And it's only in Luke's Gospel that Jesus asks for forgiveness for his crucifiers (23:34). It's only in Luke's Gospel that one of the two thieves crucified with him expressed faith in Jesus (23:39-43) and was promised he would be with Jesus in Paradise that same day.

There is also a theme in Luke that portrays Jesus as the Ultimate Prophet. If he is the Ultimate Prophet, he, of course, has to die in Jerusalem, as all the prophets before him did. Connected with this is the concern that Saint Luke has for the marginalized people of the first century: the poor, the oppressed, the diseased, and women, especially, all receive special attention in Luke. Christians are expected to address the needs of the sick, the lonely, the poor and the depressed, particularly the disadvantaged. They are expected to see to it that nobody goes hungry.

The rich are portrayed in Saint Luke's Gospel as finding it really hard to detach themselves from their possessions, even though the few who do are praised (e.g., Acts 4:32-37).

The main perspective on Jesus with Saint Luke is that Jesus brings peace, *shalom*, healing, reconciliation, forgiveness and wholeness. He brings God's promises of blessings. And if you want to really follow this message than you promote the well-being of all the marginalized by fostering peace and unity.

Why am I going through all this? To undermine a program. Despite all these wonderful ideas with Luke, how far are we already from Mastery of the quantum field? Is there a word about it? No, it's all about being nice. Is there any word about being teachers of the mechanics of creation? Most people, as I go through this list for the last few pages, start to get bored. I'm stretching the elastic band. "We've heard all this before and it's wonderful, but it's boring." You are right. It doesn't cut it.

So, what are we undermining here in terms of a program? The program that these Gospels managed to get the nitty-gritty, the heart of the matter about Jesus. I'm afraid it's apparent that they did not get it.

---

[74] Luke 23:12.

Matthew: Jesus the Fulfillment of All Previous Jewish History

This Gospel was apparently written somewhere in the period 70-90 AD, very likely in the middle 80's. A lot of scholars believe it was written in Antioch, located in south central Turkey, close to Lebanon and Syria. Others consider it to have been written in Damascus, or even in Galilee. It was obviously written by a Jewish scribe who was very familiar with the scriptures of the Hebrew people. He says he is a "scribe trained for the kingdom of Heaven who brings out of his treasure what is new and what is old." (13:52).

He's writing in a very Jewish community or Jewish church. There are Gentile members, but they are expected to toe the line of Judaism (22:11-14), including being circumcised. Needless to say, the prospect of circumcision was always a deterrent to adult conversions, as Paul himself eventually recognized.

Matthew is writing for a predominately Jewish audience who believe in Jesus as Lord. He's competing with other Jewish leaders for influence in the chaos that ensued after Titus had destroyed the Temple and the city of Jerusalem. The Jewish people were scattered to the four winds and the seven seas.

So Matthew's church constitutes one strand of first century Judaism after that catastrophe. He considers himself Jewish, and more authentically Jewish than other Jewish groups, because he follows the Torah as taught by Jesus.

Other people, after the destruction of Jerusalem in the year 70, interpret the Torah in different ways. The Pharisees and their tradition gave birth to what's now known as Rabbinic Judaism. Matthew is thus in competition for the heart and soul of Judaism. With whom is he in competition? The local Pharisees. That's why they are so negatively portrayed in the Gospel of Matthew.

One notable thing that occurred after the Jews were scattered, is related to a nation called the Khazars, who ruled a vast territory stretching from the southern end of the Black Sea and Caspian Sea, far north into modern Russia. The Khazar Empire was at its height from about 650-850 AD. It is reported that at a certain time the whole nation, as was common enough in those days, converted to Judaism. The matter, needless to say, is contested by Jewish scholars. However, according to DNA results recently obtained, the descendants of the Khazars constitute the majority of the population of Israel today.

In other words, most of the population of Israel today are not descendants of the Hebrews in Palestine prior to the destruction of the Temple. Because even though the Khazars are Jewish in terms of faith and in terms of ancestry, they are not children of Abraham.

Matthew says Jesus "comes not to abolish the Law, but to fulfill it," to bring it to perfection (5:17). Those who advocate the negation of the least of the commandants in the Torah are the least in the Kingdom (5:19). Mark's gentile context led him also to show Jesus as not having great respect for crippling laws of a boringly detailed nature.

The Gospel of Matthew is geared for instructional purposes. There are five sermons of Jesus (5:1-7:29; 10:1-42; 13:1-52; 18:1-35: and 23:1-25:46) that are apparently designed to imitate or mirror the five books of the Torah – Genesis, Exodus, Leviticus, Deuteronomy and Numbers.

Jesus is seen by Matthew as somebody who sums up the whole of previous Jewish history in himself. For example, the infancy narratives hold this genealogy (1:1-17) who have four notable women (1:3, 5:6); and a number of "fulfillment" passages that connect Jesus with prophecies (1:22-23; 2:5-6, 14-15, 17-18, 23); and allusions to famous Hebrews of the past (e.g., Joseph) who like this Biblical forebear receives dream messages (1:20; 2:13, 1, 22); and Moses who, like Jesus, was rescued as an infant from a murderous king (2:16-18). Remember that Moses's natural mother had to leave him in a basket in the weeds and he was found by Pharaoh's daughter.

Jesus begins his ministry with three temptations that correspond to the three major temptations of Israel in the desert when they were fleeing from Egypt. But where Israel, the son of

God failed, Jesus, the Son of God succeeds. You may recollect that famous incident when Mary, when she was pregnant with Jesus, goes to visit her cousin Elizabeth. The account is rich in Old Testament echoes. Elizabeth, in the words of Saint Luke, says the infant in her womb leaped for joy when she heard Mary's greeting: "...when the sound of your greeting came to my ears, the baby in my womb leaped for joy.[75]

ἐσκίρτησεν τὸ βρέφος ἐν τῇ κοιλίᾳ αὐτῆς, as it says in the Greek original.

To 'Dance for joy' (ἐσκίρτησεν), is a very rare verb in Greek, but it corresponds to an even more rare word in Hebrew.[76]

That word is used in the account of the birth of Samuel where the infant danced for joy.[77]

The word is also used in the account of King David dancing before the Ark of the Covenant to acknowledge the divinity present in it.[78]

"[14] And David danced before the Lord with all his might."

All of these are looking backwards. Jesus is looked upon as a re-embodiment of the whole first five books of the Old Testament. That's what Luke intends to convey. Therefore the teachings of Jesus must be observed and if you don't observe them you will not enter the kingdom. The only ones who will enter are those who obey the Fathers will.

Jesus is presented as the Torah in practice, with an emphasis on reconciliation and forgiveness (5:23-24; 18:23ff), and there is only hellfire and brimstone if everything else fails (18:15-17). Jesus is the Torah. His instructions are love and forgiveness. We've got to put those into practice, so if I want to be a real follower of Jesus I have to do what Jesus commands

To recap, the infancy narratives, in the only two Gospels that have them, contain certain historical data to tell us what happened, even though they contradict each other in parts. They

---

[75] Luke 1:44.

[76] ריקוד משמחה

[77] 1 Samuel.

[78] 2 Sam 6:14-16.

are driven by theological interests, and the writer's concerns and issues predominate in those infancy narratives. But both of them, are poles apart, light years away from anything to do with what Jesus really was about which is "imitate me, and then you will do all the wonders that I do and greater". In other words, these were not commandments. And the lack of observing them, therefore, was not sinful. They were things that you've got to put away if you are ever going to embrace Agape, and if you're ever going to create reality in the fashion in which Jesus himself did.

What did Jesus do, for example, when on several occasions he healed the withered hands of paralyzed people? He observed the hand from a state of unconditional love that was completely in the flow from Point Zero. What did he do? He interacted with – as the Old Master Teacher called it – the six levels of frequency above this one, and particularly the sixth plane of reality.[79] He put a new idea of the reality into that frequency and accelerated its decent down through the intervening levels of frequency between the physical body, and where the origin of all physicality begins. That's how he did the miracles. Are they miracles? They are rare and wonderful and highly unusual obviously, but they are not miracles. They are accessing the physics of creation at a very deep level, but they're not exceptions to the higher laws of physics, but rather their most sublime exemplification. They are what we should all be doing, as he himself said. But if we persist in viewing them as 'miracles' then we will never come to imitate him as Jesus asked.

His Mother, Mary

So far we have said very little about an extraordinary person, Mary the Mother of Jesus. Mary was a very popular name in first century Judaism, calculated to have been borne by about 20% of all Jewish women at the time of Jesus, but Mary the Mother of Jesus

---

[79] Ramtha, *A Beginner's Guide to Creating Reality,* Third ed. (JZK Publishing, 2004).

was a very uncommon person. She is mentioned nineteen times in the New Testament, mostly during the Christmas story in the Infancy Narratives.

The first reference to Mary is in Luke: "Jesus increased in wisdom and age and grace before God and men". And he says about Mary his mother, that she "...continued to keep all these things in her heart". There is definitely a hint of an inter-personal growth between Jesus and Mary.

There are not many hints of it, but there is a tantalizing suggestion that they didn't always get on well together. There are only two recorded conversations between Jesus and his Mother in the New Testament. The first took place in the Temple when Jesus was there at the age of twelve, presumably for his Bar Mitzvah. Jesus was lost for three days and then was found.[80] In those circumstances it could easily happen. Usually people took care of each other, especially the children, when they were at the Temple for big ceremonies such as this one. It was only after they were part of the way home that Mary and Joseph realized Jesus wasn't with the big crowd of people that was moving back home. They had to scramble to get back to the city and try and find their twelve-year old precocious child. They found him talking to all these learned men attached to the Temple. They were amazed at his answers. That's what he had been doing for the three days. When Mary asked him, "Where the heck were you? We were worried out of our skins." He said very curtly, "I have to be about my father's business." In other words, "Don't bother me."

The second conversation is narrated in John 2:1-11. It took place at the wedding feast of Cana. These are the only two conversations between Jesus and his mother that we know about. Paul, who wrote more than half of the New Testament as we have it, never mentions Mary at all. Intriguing?

In the second conversation Mary approaches her Son with a request, probably on behalf of embarrassed newlyweds. She alerts Jesus to the fact that the hosts have run out of wine. Probably they didn't have a lot of money. No one knows who the hosts were, so

[80] Luke 2:41-52.

obviously no one is quite sure who was being married. Some even say it was Jesus himself, and that it may have been Jesus' marriage to Mary Magdalen which was being celebrated, which is what a lot of people in the New Age tradition suggest.

Some say it might have been Mary herself, or some say it might have been one of the brothers. Nobody knows for sure.

In any event Mary would be most unlikely to have taken the initiative if she hadn't been connected in some way to the people who were celebrating the marriage. She says diplomatically to Jesus that "They've run out of wine." Jesus preferences his response with "Woman," in Greek "Gune," (γυνή) which is not as disrespectful as 'Woman' sounds to us in an English translation today.

"Woman, why are you involving me?" His question is not answered: Mary says nothing. She was a very wise woman. Instead she turns to the servants and says to them, "Do whatever he tells you."

Jesus tells them to bring some large stone containers of water and then he turns it into fine wine. Those serving the meal were astonished, because the wine was superb, far superior in quality to what they had had up to that moment. How did he do it? By agape and the focus of energy into the realms of frequency and accelerating its arrival into the Hertzian plane. Is that easy to do? No. Is it impossible? By no means.

By the time that Mary intervenes it's quite likely that Jesus was surrounded by people who were drunk or heading that way. The master of the banquet says to the bridegroom in verse 10, "Everyone brings out the choice wine first and then the cheaper wine when people are too drunk to notice the decline in quality."

The problem in John Chapter 2, however, is that both the good wine and the cheap wine have apparently run out, it's all gone. And it's in that context that Jesus said, "Okay, you've run out of booze. Why do you want to involve me? We don't know why Mary thought her son should intervene. The only reasonable conclusion is that it was to save the hosts embarrassment.

John says that this was the first spectacular deed that Jesus did to show what he could do, or rather what the following of his teaching and the imitation of him could bring about in every man and woman on this planet. Basically, John is telling us that the glory of God was first and foremost revealed by Jesus in what the Puritans would regard as a very inappropriate manner. The Puritans would have taken Jesus aside into a corner quietly, and said, "Do you really think it's appropriate that you should encourage even deeper levels of drunkenness in those who are already so drunk?" Do you really think this is the best time to make your move? Couldn't you start out your mission at a more opportune and appropriate time than this? Jesus ignored such prim advice, and always would.

Controversial, extraordinary, extravagant, yes, it was all of those. What was the purpose of this first "miracle?" Not to put Israel on the map, or to tighten up the moral fiber of the entire country. Rather it was something designed to keep the party going. In other words, it was about giving people something they really enjoy. More wine and more of the best, more goodness, more fun, more life, more reasons to celebrate. He gives them more, when the sober minded probably judged they had already had more than enough, seeing all the wine had run out. What was this? Was it mindless excess, or did it show Jesus operated in an over-abundance of life? We're going with the latter.

In both accounts in the New Testament of conversations between Jesus and his mother, Jesus asks his mother a question. In the Temple, at the age of twelve, he asked, "Why did you seek me? Did you not know I should be about my father's business?" And at the wedding, "Why are you involving me?"

Both of these two replies are not really questions. They are "conversation stoppers." In Ireland, we have several useful phrases you can use when a conversation has irretrievably broken down: "The peacock is a wonderful bird." Basically, Jesus in both cases is saying to his mother, "The peacock is a wonderful bird."

In neither case does Mary answer her son. But what she does is very different in both cases. It's really hard to put a label on this definitively, but both stories I think portray Jesus and his mother as fundamentally not in agreement.

For now we can note that there's possibly a foothold of friction between mother and son, and it helps to move the narrative forward in Luke's Gospel.

Can we also contemplate for a moment, that Jesus left home with his twin brother at the age of twelve? What does this tell you? How would you or I react if our twelve-year old left home to go to somewhere at the ends of the Earth? Jesus and his brother were obviously difficult children.

In the Temple Jesus had the last word presumably. Mary and Joseph were left speechless. But in Cana at the wedding the response was different. Mary takes charge of the situation and says to the stewards, "Do whatever he tells you." This was the beginning of the signs he did, and it shows the growth that had taken place between them over the intervening eighteen years between his Bar Mitzvah and his arrival at the Jordan to be Baptized by his cousin John at the age of twenty-nine.

Can we contemplate something beautiful about the problems between mothers and precocious incarnations! Because it's only if we understand this that we'll really be able to get rid of programs that limit its manifestations in ourselves.

Jesus remains the most influential person who ever lived in the whole of recorded human history.

Because of that it's not surprising that a whole plethora of documents arose about Jesus in the first couple of centuries, working backwards from the first miracle at Cana, to a past of copious miracles in his childhood that probably never occurred. This trend in early Christianity distracts our attention from the fact that Jesus was growing in spiritual power throughout his life, and that was how he was able to operate these phenomena.

If you regard Jesus as God's only Son, let down fully formed from Heaven, then of course you would tend to attribute all sorts of miraculous phenomena to him from the earliest years of his life.

The Quran[81] states that Jesus as a child did all sorts of miraculous deeds, including healing lepers, raising the dead to life, restoring the sight of those blind from birth, and creating living birds from mud. The list of miracles the Quran gives is suspiciously close to a similar list given in a document called "The Infancy Gospel of Thomas," which is dated to about 150-190 AD, but it also adds

[81] Surah 005.110.

in some mischievous and even mean-spirited acts. The Infancy Gospel of Thomas circulated widely in the Coptic communities all across North Africa from the second century onwards, so there is little doubt the author of Surah 005 would have known that text.

However, the Infancy Gospel was written well after the four Gospels of the New Testament, and does not seem familiar with Jewish practices and customs. The information quoted by the Quran seems to come from that single source. The early Church Fathers were convinced of its falsity, and Iraeneus, writing about 180 AD, lists it among the historically unreliable documents he is discussing.

These fictional accounts of the early years of Jesus tell us of all sorts of wonders he is supposed to have accomplished. One report is that when Jesus was in the manger of the stable at Bethlehem, one of the oxen had a bad cold, but when he nuzzled the infant Jesus he suddenly got better. With reference to the making of clay birds in the Quran, Joseph his father – or foster-father or step-father or step foster-father, or however far your theology requires you to distance Joseph from Jesus' reality – came out and admired them. Jesus then blew on them and the clay birds became alive and flew away, etc.

What is most significant is that accounts of Jesus working miracles as a child go against the testimony we have in the canonical Gospels. Luke tell us in Chapter 4 of his Gospel that the people of Nazareth were greatly surprised by what Jesus said and did when he began his mission as an adult, and asked in puzzlement if this was not the craftsman's son that they had known in his earliest years?

In John's Gospel we are explicitly told that the miracle of the wine at Cana was the first miracle of Jesus.

Some people interpret all this as Jesus waiting until he was an adult to reveal his power. Waiting until he was an adult to do the miraculous was not a strategy of Jesus: he had not developed his abilities until then. When he began his public ministry, his intent was to teach us how to imitate what he had done. He came to show the way, and the method was self-empowerment. He did not come to 'save' helpless sinners.

Jesus was able to accomplish the miracles he did because of the work he did to remove the mental garbage, the crippling programs, that were blocking his power. The same crippling programs he confronted are the same that are blocking us. The accounts of the alleged wonders he accomplished in his very early years, such as contained in the Infancy Gospel, are based on the old deception that Jesus was a divine being from day one, who was lowered down into this world from Heaven, and could perform countless wonders precisely because he was a supernatural entity. This is an insidious belief system, however initially attractive, because it takes the focus off where our real power can come from, which is what Jesus came to teach us. It's insidious because it takes the focus off imitating Jesus and replaces it with worshipping him. Fundamentally it ignores the fact that Jesus had to process an incredible amount of personal growth to do what he did in terms of the 'miraculous.' To fantasize about him doing wonders as a child fundamentally fails to understand what Jesus was here to do, and it is all based on the false supposition that he was a divine being who descended fully formed onto this Earth.

He did not do any of these things. You might say, maybe he came into that incarnation with the ability already earned to do these miracles. I assure you that the previous incarnations of Jesus were not of the kind that would have allowed him to do those miracles. In other words, whatever he did, he earned his ability to do, in that extraordinary life two thousand years ago.

What does that mean? It means there's hope for you and me. The previous incarnations of Jesus were not always a past of which to be proud. But whatever he did do, he accomplished greatly in that life. If he did it, you and I can do it too.

His "Father," Joseph

The family of Jesus bore Joseph's name. Surnames only came into use in the Western world at the end of the 11th, or early 12th century in Europe, mainly with the spread of Norman influence.

Before that there were no family names. There were certainly no surnames, in our sense, in use in the Holy Land at the time of Jesus.

The family of Jesus, as was the custom, bore their father Joseph's name for ease of identification. Jesus was known as "Yeshua Ben Joseph," which means in Aramaic, "Yeshua, son of Joseph".

Matthew and Luke both say that Joseph was not the biological father of Jesus, which is true. But who the biological father of Jesus was is another day's work.

He was understood to be Joseph's son. In the Synagogue at Nazareth, when he first started attracting unwelcome attention — and according to some, breaking his mother's heart — they said, "Isn't this Joseph's son?"

Matthew 13:55 adds an interesting detail. We speak of Joseph being a carpenter, but in Matthew 13 they do not say, "Is not this the carpenter's son?" Instead they say, "Is this not the craftsman's son?" The word in koine Greek is "tekton." It means a craftsman, a builder or some class of skilled worker, maybe even a blacksmith. It means somebody who made stuff with his own hands, maybe even a contractor who builds a house. Jesus was a "tekton". So was his twin brother Jude Thomas. In the latter's mission in India he left behind several structures that he had built with his own hands.

Mark surely recognized the irony of calling Jesus a "tekton" in the context of his miracles (Mark 6:2-3), which Jesus always described as his "works."[82] This is super tekton-ity. Mark states: "What wisdom is this which is given to him, that such mighty works are performed by his hands. Is this not the tekton?"[83]

As stated earlier, in two of the four Gospels, Luke 2:1-39 and Matthew 1:18-2:23, we have an account of the very early years of Jesus, but nothing in the other two. Then we have a gap until he is twelve years old. He appears for his Bar Mitzvah, and we hear something about him for approximately three days. When the three days are over we hear nothing about him for the next eighteen years. When he does emerge after the eighteen years he is able to change water into wine; he's able to heal withered hands,

[82] See John 14:12.

[83] Mark 6:2.

heal sicknesses of all kinds, walk on water, produce food out of thin air and raise the dead.

Are you and I on the wrong track? Perhaps we should all be taking up carpentry or whatever role "tekton" describes. Why, because, according to the traditional account of things, supposedly after eighteen years of apprenticeship in the carpenter's shop in Nazareth, he was able to do all these wonders. But was he actually in the carpenter's shop in Nazareth for eighteen years? To swallow that fish you really would need to be gullible in the extreme.

Joseph, the father whom we are looking at here, had a difficult task. Was he the father of Jesus? No. Could he then be excused for feeling very anxious or insecure? However, in what we do know of him from the Gospels, Joseph is not insecure, worked up, anxious, or about to have a nervous breakdown. He appears in five scenes in the Gospel of Matthew, and every single time he is sound asleep. (Matthew 1:20-24, 2:12, 13, 19, 22). So, whatever we can say about the problems Joseph had in dealing with a precocious stepson, it did not include insomnia. Praise God for small mercies!

Jesus' Message Warped into a System of Exalted Ethics: Does God Really Need 'Submission Displays' from Us?

The historical order of the Books of the entire New Testament is reversed in the forms of the New Testament we have today. Paul's fourteen letters were written, or attributed to him, from approximately the year 51 or 52 up to 63 AD, when he came to a sudden and unprovided end as a result of losing his head in Rome. In all of that time no single Gospel existed, but Paul had created the early New Testament.

The Gospels were the late books. The earliest Gospel wasn't composed until well after Paul had been murdered, and after the great fire at Rome in 64 AD. That means that, as mentioned earlier, the material that we now read in the Gospels was probably unknown to most of the early Christians.

There were obviously traditions and reminiscences and probably small documents like the famous 'Q' document[84] that is alleged to have been used by the Evangelists as one of the sources to form their own Gospel. So, between the time of the Passion of Jesus, say about the period 29-32 AD, until at least 65 or 70 AD, very few who followed Jesus' message knew anything about what he did during his early years or during his public ministry. Unfortunately, in that period the message he taught had been morphed into a very, very sophisticated and exalted system of ethics, which is how we know it today, but it was not what he had delivered. An enlightened teaching was converted into the avoidance of sin and the doing of good.

What is the message of Jesus? Basically, as was given in the Sermon on the Mount, "Love one another as I have loved you". Did he say all these things? Absolutely he did, but they were only clues to people who had no understanding of the quantum field and its operation in creating reality.

This was Jesus' way of teaching in homely terms. Do you want to be free? Do you want to accomplish that for which you came into this incarnation? Well look, here is how you do it. If you want to do that, which involves living in the state of agape, then you do not do this and you don't do that, and don't do the other thing. Does that mean if you do do them that you'll go to Hell and burn? No.

This is the problem that arises with person-gods, and when we model God on ourselves. If God is modeled on ourselves God gets angry if we ignore him, don't like him or don't practice true worship to appease him. Animals often practice 'submission rituals' after dominance displays. It's uncannily similar to what is often proposed by traditionalist groups as pleasing behavior on our part towards God. Apparently, we need to exhibit submission displays to God in order to be accepted by God. If this proposal were true, what would that say of God?

---

[84] 'Q' stands for the German word "Quelle" meaning 'source.' Matthew and Luke were written separately, both of them using Mark and a second hypothetical source document now known as "Q." "Q" describes the material found in Matthew and Luke but not in Mark.

God is infinite — the Zero Point. There is nothing that can add to or subtract from God. No amount of sinning, even by Adolf Hitler, Ivan the Terrible or Attila the Hun, or any other monster that you can think of in human history, can do one whit to offend Point Zero. On Point Zero's radar it is so insignificant that it wouldn't even emerge as a blip. Does that mean we should do all these awful things? Absolutely not, but Hell is not the motivation for avoiding them. God's anger is not the motivation for avoiding these courses of action, and if you and I get into this bottomless pit of thinking that God is watching us, we are fully into the situation which I pictured on the cover of my first DVD, "The Hamburger Universe." In this image God is watching every move we make and noting it on his laptop, because he has moved with the times, and is no longer using the Book of Life in which to register our faults and failings, and anything positive we do. With all our performance data on his laptop all he has to do when we die is press 'Enter,' and the resultant score apparently decides whether we go down or up. If we get into that bottomless pit of the Hamburger Universe mindset, we might as well have not come into this lifetime. We've wasted our incarnation so far, and we're still wasting it.

How hard is it for us to get from regarding the message of Jesus as not just a system of ethics of the most sublime and exalted kind, and to realize that this is not what Jesus was here to teach. The goal was not the system of ethics but what those exalted maxims were pointing towards. Unfortunately, almost nobody got it. As a result, now you and I are crippled by all these programs.

It may seem impossible that in one short life we can deal with all this stuff in the time at our disposal. The problem seems insurmountable. It's not. All it needs is one vast, catastrophic, act of decision: "I am going to let this go." I'm not going to fight it, because I know I cannot remove crippling sub-conscious programs by opposing them or fighting them. I'm not going to oppose them. I'm simply going to embark on a focused life that is aimed at causing me to live in the state of agape.

When I have done that, and I have eschewed all this urge and imperative of taking vengeance and settling old scores — "by God I will teach them a lesson they will never forget!" If I can give up all that, that's the real asceticism. The real asceticism is not about fasting or wearing, like the Opus Dei members in Dan Brown's novels are reputed to do, a torture chain around your legs. Nor is it about wearing a hair shirt. All that stuff is just a convenient distraction from what's really going on. It's about something entirely different.

So, are we going to hold onto our thirst for vengeance? Or nurse our dented egos? Or all of the other little things that preoccupy us? Are we going to cherish those at the expense of attaining the state of agape? We would be fools if we were to do that. But, of course, we already know we're fools. And we already know the teachings of Jesus have been warped into a complicated system of do's and don'ts that have no result except radical dis-empowerment, while the positive paths which the teachings laid out, are never heard of.

Is it our fault? Not entirely, because the whole tradition that turned the message of Jesus upon its head for the last 2,000 years is what's created it. The whole tradition of Paul, long before any Gospel had ever appeared, saw Jesus as a replacement of the sacrificial lamb of Passover or Yom Kippur in the days of the Temple Sacrifices. From there came the whole tradition of suffering and atonement to make up for the offenses we have offered to vengeful and insecure models of God. Add that to the baffling array of stuff that we've got from the Church – largely dominated by Paul – that succeeded the Church of James, the brother of Jesus, after the destruction of Jerusalem, and which had those three elements that I mentioned earlier. That was what was presented at the time of the Council of Nicaea almost 300 years later. That is what became enshrined as quintessential Christian belief.

Jesus got a series of rapid promotions from being an extraordinary itinerant preacher in the first century, to being something entirely more than the Messiah, to being something more than just the Son of God, who was promoted again at Nicaea. He wasn't just the Son of God, he was a member of the blessed Trinity, which is a pagan idea. And he is then promoted not alone to being the second person of the Godhead, but he was also stated to be equal to the Father. The Son and Father being declared equal left another question: The Blessed Trinity.

There is a story told from some early missionary in Japan a couple of centuries ago, that a Christian priest was trying to explain some Christian teachings to a very revered figure in the Japanese religion. He was explaining who the Father was, who the Son was, and how the Holy Spirit related to the two. He was trying to explain who the Spirit was. The Spirit he said was like a dove with beautiful wings outstretched above us, and then he went on to explain who Jesus was and how he fitted into this whole system. He explained that even though there were three beings in God, they were actually one. Having gone through this bizarre complexity at length the missionary asked the Japanese official, "Do you understand?" And he said, "I think I do, I think I understand the Father. I think I understand the Son, but I don't understand the Honorable Bird."

Neither do we. We don't understand the distinguished bird, but we don't understand the Son either. And we don't understand the Father. I assure you the reality of the life of God and our connection with it is not captured in any of those three terms that were defined at Nicaea and elaborated on at Constantinople.

The net effect of all of those was that we were left with the Jesus who had always been difficult to reach, because of all of the programming of the Pauline view of who he was. Paul had never even spent five minutes with Jesus. He had never met him, save that incident on the road to Damascus. But difficult as it was to access and imitate the Jesus of Paul, after the definitions of Nicaea and Constantinople three hundred years later, it became totally impossible. Yet that is the version of Jesus and his mission that was normally marketed, and is still being marketed to all of us today.

> "We believe in one Lord Jesus Christ, the only begotten Son of God, begotten not made, of one being with the Father through whom all things were made. Who for us men and for our salvation came down from heaven, was incarnated from the Virgin Mary (despite those seven children) and was made man, Who for us suffered and died under Pontius Pilate, was crucified, rose again from the dead,

from whence he will come to judge the living and the dead, and his kingdom will have no end."[85]

With what are we left? Can we insert ourselves into this program? No. We're outclassed. We're out of our league. Fortunately, this is not what Jesus was. But how do we get back to what he really was?

Chapter 7
The Family of Jesus and the Infant Church

"Born of a Virgin"

Seventy years after Constantine's Council at Nicaea another Council was called, that met close to where Nicaea had been held. The Council assembled in Constantinople itself in the year 381. In the period immediately after this Council there was what I can only describe as a rush to prove that Jesus was celibate.

Most of us from Christian backgrounds will know the Creed of Constantinople well. Speaking of Jesus, it said, "...who for us men, and for our salvation, came down from heaven, and was incarnate *by the Holy Spirit of the Virgin Mary*, and was made man".

As part of the realms of belief associated with the message of Jesus, by the time of the Council of Constantinople, the Virgin Mary syndrome had become a major issue, and obviously for us it is still a major program. As has been stated many times in this book, we need to know where programs come from, and how they developed, in order for them to begin to fade away. Directly assaulting programs is counter-productive, as we well know.

The belief in the perpetual virginity of Mary has three central elements:

1. First of all, "the Virginal Conception." It's often thought to refer to the conception of Mary herself, but in

[85] Nicaea-Constantinople Creed.

fact it refers to the circumstances of the conception of Jesus in the womb of Mary.

2. Number two, the Virgin Birth.

3. Number three, the Perpetual Virginity of Mary

People have died for these beliefs.

What does belief in the Virginal Conception assert? It means that Jesus was not conceived in the normal way. His mother was still a virgin after his conception. Is that impossible? No, it's not. Did it occur? Shall we say for now, that we will not go beyond the evidence we have at hand at this stage of this work.

Secondly, what exactly does "the Virgin Birth" mean? It means that Mary gave birth to Jesus while remaining a virgin. In other words, after you have given birth to your baby you still have a hymen. You may say that's impossible, but I am simply clarifying what those three words mean.

Thirdly, the Perpetual Virginity of Mary. That means that Mary remained a virgin for the rest of her days, and that she had no other children.

Catholics, Assyrian Christians, the Eastern Orthodox Churches and the Oriental Orthodox, as well as sections of Anglicanism and Lutheranism, believe in the perpetual virginity of Mary. Even the main Protestant Reformers from the time of the Reformation onwards, for example Martin Luther,[86] Huldrych Zwingli,[87] John Huss,[88] and John Wesley[89] also believed in it. Unfortunately, there are some skeletons in the closet: nine skeletons to be precise. I'll refer now to these texts in the New Testament.

---

[86] A German priest and Professor of Theology. A major figure in the Protestant Reformation in Germany. November 10, 1483 – February 18, 1546.

[87] Leader of the Reformation in Switzerland. January 1, 1484 – October 11, 1531.

[88] Born in Czech Republic 1369, died in Germany, 6 July 1415.

[89] Anglican minister and theologian. Founder of Methodism. June 17, 1703 to March 2, 1791.

1. Mark 6:3

"Isn't this the carpenter? Isn't this Mary's son and the brother of James, Joseph, Judas and Simon? Aren't his sisters here with us?" And they took offense at him."

2. Matthew 12:46

"While he was still speaking to the people, behold, his mother and his brothers stood outside, asking to speak to him."

3. Luke 8:19

"Now Jesus' mother and brothers came to see him, but they were not able to get near him because of the crowd."

4. Mark 3:31-32

"Then Jesus' mother and brothers arrived. Standing outside, they sent someone in to call him. A crowd was sitting around him, and they told him, "Your mother and brothers are outside looking for you."

5. Matthew 13:54-56

The brothers of Jesus are named again. All this was meant to bring Jesus down to the ordinary level – who the heck is this guy who is preaching all this esoteric stuff? Don't we know him, he's just one of us; he's the carpenter's son? And we know his four brothers.

They are named again in Matthew 13: James, Joseph, Simon and Jude Thomas and "all" his sisters. What does all mean? How many would there have to be for them to say all? At least three, maybe more.

6. John 7:1-10

"After this, Jesus went around in Galilee, purposely staying away from Judea because the Jews there were waiting to take his life. But when the Jewish Feast of Tabernacles was near, Jesus' brothers said to him, 'You ought to leave here and go to Judea, so that your disciples may see the miracles you do. No one who wants to become a public figure acts in secret. Since you are doing these things, show yourself to the world.' For even his own brothers did not believe in him."

7. Acts 1:14

"They all joined together constantly in prayer, along with the women and Mary the mother of Jesus, and with his brothers."

8. Galatians 1:19

"But I saw none of the other apostles except James the Lord's brother."

9. 1 Corinthians 9:5

"The brothers of the Lord" are referred to again by Paul in 1 Corinthians 9:4-6. And what's worse — oh God forbid — Paul said the brothers had wives![90]

Were the Mother of Jesus and His Siblings against His Mission?

Almost all scholars today agree that the Gospel of Mark was written about the year 70 AD, thus making it the first Gospel. It is similarly agreed that Mark's Gospel was relied on heavily by Matthew and Luke in composing their own Gospels.

There is some sort of half-accepted rumor in Christianity that the family of Jesus was largely against his mission. That view is, in the main, based on a well-known passage in the third Chapter of Mark's Gospel.[91]

> "[20]Then Jesus entered a house, and again a crowd gathered, so that he and his disciples were not even able to

[90] 1 Corinthians 9:4-6: Don't we have the right to food and drink? Don't we have the right to take a believing wife along with us, as do the other apostles and the Lord's brothers and Cephas? Or is it only I and Barnabas who lack the right to not work for a living?

[91] Mark 3:20-21.

eat. [21] When his family heard about this, they went to take charge of him, for they said, 'He is out of his mind.'"

Because of statements such as this in the New Testament it is understood that the family of Jesus disapproved of his mission, and it has been taken as an historical fact that he was rejected by his family. If so, how did it happen that members of Jesus' family assumed leading roles in the early Christian movement soon after the Passion of Jesus. That would be very difficult to explain if they had been hostile to his movement all during his ministry.

The easiest and most obvious answer seems to be that they were not opposed to his mission, but in fact were deeply involved with him all along.

If this seems an apparent contradiction perhaps the resolution will come from taking a closer look at the text quoted above from Mark 3:20-21: "When his family heard about this, they went to take charge of him, for they said, 'He is out of his mind.'"

The original Greek in which Mark wrote these sentences, holds a number of surprises for us. This is the full sentence in the original language in which Mark wrote, with the English translation beneath:

Mark 3:21

καὶ ἀκούσαντες οἱ παρ' αὐτοῦ ἐξῆλθον κρατῆσαι αὐτόν ἔλεγον γὰρ ὅτι ἐξέστη.

"When his family heard about this, they went to take charge of him, for they said, 'He is out of his mind.'"

We can break down the translation as follows:

καὶ ἀκούσαντες	and hearing (this)
οἱ παρ' αὐτοῦ	those with him
ἐξῆλθον	set out
κρατῆσαι αὐτόν	to seize him

ἔλεγον γὰρ	for they said,
ὅτι ἐξέστη.	he is out of his mind.

Notice that there is no word for "family" in this sentence. "Those with him" could apply to anyone who happened to be in his company at the time. Ten verses later his mother and his brothers do show up, and then they are named. It would be strange if the writer meant to refer to the family of Jesus ten verses earlier, but did not name them, when he did name them ten verses later.

There really is no justification from this text for concluding that the family of Jesus were of the view that he was out of his mind. If, as is generally accepted, the writers of the Gospels of Matthew and Luke depended on Mark as a source, it is interesting to compare their version of this same incident as told in Mark, with Matthew and Luke's version in their Gospels, Luke 8:19-21, and Matthew 12:46-59. Any possible negative interpretation towards the family in Mark's phrase "those with him" is removed by Luke and Matthew, especially any mention of questioning Jesus' sanity. Both Luke and Matthew have excised that ambiguous phrase of Mark from their own account of the same incident.

Indeed, it has been suggested that Mark may have intentionally tried to cast the family of Jesus in an unflattering light, and that that might reflect on the central role and powerful influence which the Apostles and the Jesus family exercised in the early Christian community, in Jerusalem up to the cataclysm of 70 AD. Early Christianity in Jerusalem was by no means a unified movement, with various groups holding different understandings of Jesus; some of whom wished to continue to be practicing Jews, while other groups strongly disapproved of Paul extending the message to the Gentiles.

All this came to an end when Trajan ordered the total destruction of the city of Jerusalem, and the construction of a new city on the ruins, to be named "Aelia Capitolina". That remained the official name by which Jerusalem was known up until the time of the Arab conquest nearly six hundred years later.[92]

[92] 638 AD.

By the Emperor's orders everyone but Jews were allowed access to the new city. This would have marked the end of whatever authority the relatives of Jesus might have had in the Jerusalem early Christian community. By the third century the blood relatives of the family of Jesus had come to be known as the *Desposyni*.[93]

What is to be made of those nine references to the brothers and sisters of Jesus?

Tertullian, (c. 160 - c. 225) maintained that these children mentioned in the Gospels were the children of both Mary and Joseph.

A third century group called the Antidicomarianites (They were known as the "Anti-Mary" Group) maintained that, when Joseph became Mary's husband, he had six children already from a previous marriage, and that subsequently he had normal marital relations with Mary. That did not come from any mystical insight but presumably is a calculation from the references in Mark 6 etc., where four brothers and all of the sisters are mentioned, so a minimal estimate would be six children.

Later the Antidicomarianites changed their minds and held that Jesus was not conceived and born in the usual way.

I mentioned already that after the Council of Constantinople in 481 there was a rush to prove Jesus was celibate. Later there was a further rush to go beyond that and prove that the way he came into existence had nothing at all do with sexuality, because, as you know, sexuality is suspect. We are asked to accept that the method by which every human being in recorded history came into existence is from the Devil! If so, God has been off duty for considerable blocks of time.

Epiphanius, bishop of Salamis in Cyprus, who died in the year 403, said that the four brothers and the sisters of Jesus were children of Joseph by a previous marriage.

Bonosus, bishop of Sardica, modern Sofia, capital of Bulgaria, said at the end of the fourth century that Mary had other children after Jesus. The other bishops of his province condemned him for this. He was slapped with a writ and threatened.

[93] From the Greek δεσπόσυνοι, (Desposunoi) plural of δεσπόσυνος, meaning "of or belonging to the Master or Lord."

Helvidius, writing about 383, asserted that Mary and Joseph had other children. The writings of Helvidius are lost and he is known only though the criticisms levelled against him by St. Jerome.

In the late 4th century Jerome stated the general view at the time that Mary remained always a virgin; he held that those who were called the brothers and sisters of Jesus were actually children of her sister, another Mary, whom he considered the wife of Clopas, or children of Joseph's brothers and sisters.

There is a perfectly good word for 'cousin' in koine Greek: "anepsios," ανεψιός. In the original Greek text of the Gospels do we see that word used to describe those who are alleged to be the 'cousins' of Jesus? Is "anepsios" there? No. The words used are 'adelphoi' and "adelphes" ("αδελφοί" 'αδελφές') — "brothers, sisters."

It's obvious the authors of these nine texts in the New Testament, cited above, were quite happy to say that Jesus had brothers and sisters, and didn't see any need to feel concerned about it. If they had wanted to say they were "cousins" of Jesus, not brothers and sisters, there was a perfectly good word with which to express it. It is obvious these New Testament texts are asserting that Jesus had brothers and sisters. If we imagine that position conflicts with other beliefs we have, then it is those other beliefs that we should first examine. It's amazing how often individuals trumpet abroad that the New Testament is "the inspired, written Word of God" — until it says something that they don't like.

What is coming to the fore here? All of these problems that have been foisted upon you and me to try to wrestle with, are false programs that increase our already significant burdens. Early on it was felt that it would demean Mary or contaminate her, to have conceived Jesus in the normal way. So, it had to be miraculous. If you are determined to teach that Mary was a perpetual virgin, obviously, you have to block any evidence that Jesus had siblings. We just can't take it. A virgin having seven children is hard enough to swallow, but please remember that figure is a minimalist assessment. It might have been eight. But, needless to say, all of this controversy began to pale in comparison when individuals began to dig up the association that Jesus had with Mary of the Magdalene's.

Of the four brothers of Jesus that we have listed in these Gospels, only two of them joined Jesus, Jude Thomas Didymus, and James, and became members of the Twelve. The first brother was named "Jude," "Judas" in Aramaic. 'Thoma' in Aramaic means "Twin." 'Didymus' in Greek and Latin means 'the twin,' so the full name of the first brother has now become: "Jude, the twin, the twin" — in case you missed it the first time. "Didymus" was added for the benefit of those whom he met later in parts of the world where neither Aramaic or Hebrew were known.

When Jesus ran foul of the authorities on that famous week, we are told in the New Testament that he was arrested, scourged, crowned with thorns, and then crucified. The fifth Chapter of the Quran, *Al-Ma'ida,* the table, refers to a meal Jesus had with his disciples, (Sura 5:114), but the Quran makes no connection between that meal and a crucifixion. In fact, the Quran insists that Jesus was never crucified.

Some say that he was substituted for by someone who physically resembled him closely. Whatever happened during that fatal Passover week, Jesus disappeared from the scene. James took on the oversight of the group who claimed to follow his brother. James is highly likely to have been one of the two Apostles named James in the traditional lists. He remained in charge of the nascent Jesus community until his murder by the Pharisees and Sanhedrin. Eusebius of Caesaria says James was murdered by being thrown from one of the towers of the Temple, and then beaten to death with a club, somewhere in the period 62-69 AD.

It appears then that it was James the brother of Jesus who took over the Jesus movement originally, not Peter, as is often assumed. It is credible that much of the shape of the early Christian community, with its strong mixture of Jewish elements, was formed in Jerusalem under James in this early period.

But it wasn't too long until the former persecutor of the Christians, the newly converted Paul, joined efforts with Peter. It's they who preach the Gospel to the entire world. Not James, who was in charge. What happened? Basically, the message of Jesus has already been hijacked.

This was done in the first place, by a person who, on his own admission, as we will see here shortly, could never reach or even understand the question "Are you able to reach the state of Agape?" On the other hand, we have a second person also coming to the fore, who had been persecuting Christians all his life. As a result of a confrontation with an apparition of Jesus on the road to Damascus, he became a zealot.

The shape of the message of Jesus, whatever chance it had of maturing, even under the administration of his brother, had no chance at all once Peter and Paul took over.

The original form of Christianity, which is what James his brother was presiding over, was very, very different indeed from the new form of Christianity developed by Paul and Peter. The Jesus movement at Jerusalem, headed by James, continued to live as Jews. They followed the Torah. They went to the Temple. They went to the synagogues as long as they were permitted to do so. They honored Jesus who had been martyred for what he preached.

In particular, note that they didn't 'divinize' Jesus, in other words they didn't turn him into "God," the being at the top of the pyramid or Triad. Secondly, they did not see him as a Savior who died and rose for our sins.

What were they focused on? The "Kingdom of God" which they believed had now arrived. And what was the heart of the state of the "Kingdom of God"? The habitual state of Agape, which is fundamentally a matter of physics. How do I create reality? By getting into this state.

This version of early Christianity was never very well known and most of its adherents were Jewish. It vanished altogether with the destruction of Jerusalem by Titus, and that siege down on the shores of the Dead Sea at Masada, which wiped out the remaining traces of the Jewish people in Israel in the year 70 AD. If you go there today you can still see this rock fortress which had been a palace of Herod. The Roman soldiers spent two years building an earthen ramp so they could surmount the walls of that rock fortress. That in itself shows you the hatred of the Jews that the Romans had. The night before the Roman besiegers were about to come over the top of the rampart, almost all the Jewish defenders committed suicide, except a couple of people who survived and told the tale.

The razing of Jerusalem to the ground, the fall of Masada, the banishment of the Jews from Israel, and the building of a new city on the ruins, Aelia Capitolina,[94] were just stages in a single campaign to remove all traces of the Jewish people from their homeland.

This series of calamities in the first century was the end of the influence of the family of Jesus on the Jesus movement. Josephus tells us that "Jerusalem ... was so thoroughly razed to the ground by those that demolished it to its foundations, that nothing was left that could ever persuade visitors that it had once been a place of habitation."[95]

After the Jews migrated northwards a significant number of them congregated around the city of Jamnia (Yavne in Hebrew). In 1871 Heinrich Graetz proposed that a Council or Synod had been held at Jamnia in the decades after the destruction of Jerusalem, probably about the year 90. His contention that the Council of Jamnia had established the canon of the Hebrew Bible is no longer sustained by scholars in the field[96] but it is agreed that several other significant matters of importance in Jewish history and identity were decided there.

As the Jewish people were being widely dispersed, it is obvious they wanted to have their religious affairs in order before they were about to spread across the world. They established the order of the Old Testament books with which we are familiar today. That ordering would have made no sense even 100 years before because all the documents then were scrolls. Whichever book was first was the one you first took out of the scroll storage

[94] 'Aelia' derived from Hadrian's 'family' name (Aelius, from the gens Aelia), while Capitolina refers to the cult of the Capitoline Triad, Jupiter, Juno and Minerva. A Temple to Jupiter was erected on the site of the Jerusalem Temple which had been levelled in 70 AD.

[95] Jewish War, 7:1:1.

[96] McDonald & Sanders, editors, The Canon Debate, 2002, Chapter 9: Jamnia Revisited by Jack P. Lewis.

box. But by this date Codices were coming into being, books, like ours, that were tied or bound on the left-hand side, like the codices discovered at Nag Hammadi in Egypt in 1947. About the year 90 AD, the Jews at Jamnia established a sequence of the Old Testament documents, and they worked the sequence out logically, starting from the beginning with the accounts of creation in Genesis, and then working forward through the history of the Jewish people in their relationship with Jehovah. The journey out of Egypt was recounted in Exodus, the system of laws governing God's people was in Leviticus, the giving of the Covenant, the law, the prophets and the histories. It's interesting for us to note that in terms of date of composition Genesis is two thirds of the way down the list of Old Testament Books, so while it is known as the first book of the Bible nowadays, it is by no means the first book of the Old Testament in terms of date of composition.

Even if the canon of the Old Testament was not decided at Jamnia, nevertheless many other significant things were enacted there. It was certainly the occasion when the Jewish authorities decided to ban the followers of Jesus from the Synagogues.[97]

Assimilation of the Message of Jesus into Passover and Yom Kippur

During all of these decades after the destruction of Jerusalem, instead of the early understanding of the message of Jesus which flourished under the leadership of James his brother, the new focus was on the teaching journeys of Peter and Paul. This new brand of Christianity was based on the mystical and ecstatic experiences of Paul, who was prone to these experiences. The elements as they evolved are familiar, we know them very well from our own experience.

Jesus became our sacrifice of Passover and Yom Kippur. Yom Kippur is the Jewish Day of Atonement. Before the destruction

---

[97] Expulsion of the early Christians from the Synagogues is attested by John 9:22.

of the Temple in the year 70, the early Jerusalem Christians blended Jesus into the Jewish observances of these two major Jewish Festivals. Central to the observances in those times was the sacrifice of a lamb on the altar to Jehovah. The blood of the sacrificed lamb in the sight of Jehovah symbolized the washing away of our sins. The goat of Yom Kippur was traditionally laden with symbolic baggage, representing the burdens of our sins, and was driven out to meet its fate in the desert of Judea. These two elements of Yom Kippur were grafted on to Jesus by the early Jerusalem Christians. It was almost inevitable given how close to Passover the Passion of Jesus had occurred. Given the central meaning of Yom Kippur in the religious awareness of the early followers of Jesus, the prominent emphasis was always on our sins and appeasement of God, and the role of Jesus became seen through those lenses. Jesus became our Sacrificial Lamb, making up to Jehovah for all our sins and offenses. He also became our Goat of Yom Kippur, taking on our burdens, and carrying them away into the forgetfulness of the wilderness.

John's Gospel makes that explicit. The other Gospels say that Jesus sat down for a Last Supper with his disciples and that it was the Passover meal.[98] It could not have been the Passover Meal because the next day they would have been absolutely forbidden to do work of any kind, and yet the day following the Last Supper

---

[98] Matthew 26:17: "On the first day of Unleavened Bread the disciples came to Jesus, saying, 'Where do you want us to make the preparations for you to eat the Passover?' ... The Teacher says, 'My time is near; I will keep the Passover at your house with my disciples' … So the disciples did as Jesus had directed them, and they prepared the Passover meal."
Mark 14:1-2: "It was two days before the Passover and the festival of Unleavened Bread. The chief priests and the scribes were looking for a way to arrest Jesus by stealth and kill him; for they said, 'Not during the festival, or there may be a riot among the people.'"
Luke 22:7-15: "Then came the day of Unleavened Bread, on which the Passover lamb had to be sacrificed. So Jesus sent Peter and John, saying, 'Go and prepare the Passover meal for us that we may eat it.' When the hour came, he took his place at the table, and the apostles with him. He said to them, 'I have eagerly desired to eat this Passover with you before I suffer.'"

the leaders of the Jews were heavily involved in parading Jesus back and forth between Pilate, themselves and Herod Antipas. John's Gospel is more insightful. It says the meal of Jesus with his close disciples took place the day before the day of the Passover Meal (namely our Thursday).

- Fundamentally Jesus has become our Paschal Lamb and Goat and everything is about sacrifice for sins and reparation to God for them.
- The second element is: He will send us the Holy Spirit and the gift of eternal life if we believe that he rose from the dead.
- And the third: We will reign with him forever.

The last two elements are not Jewish, but were added from the preaching of Paul. These were not the teaching of James or of the primitive Christian community in Jerusalem, nor were they the teaching of Jesus.

There were two Rites that go along with that new set of beliefs.

The first was the ceremony of Baptism. Baptism is an extremely ancient ceremony. It is rooted in the ancient Hebrew belief that all creation emerged from water. We will see later the two contradictory accounts of the emergence of the world in the first two chapters of Genesis. One account says everything emerged from water, the primeval substance. The other account says everything came from a dry place.

The idea that everything came from water came to predominate over time. Thus, in the Jewish tradition, if I want to reform myself and have a profound change of heart, it is like being born again. I do that symbolically in a ceremony where I descend and dissolve into the original substance, water, and I emerge a new creation. That was the original form: descent into water and emerging in a new state of being. Nowadays of course, the ceremony of baptism normally consists of pouring or sprinkling – and other ways of saving water, I presume. But originally baptism goes back to those roots, and while Jesus used the ceremony he didn't invent it.

At the River Jordan he himself was baptized by John the Baptist at the start of his public ministry.

Secondly, "The Lord's Supper" was not a Passover meal. If it were a Passover meal it would reinforce the conviction that Jesus had died for our sins.

John again clarified matters. In the Passover ceremony, the lamb was sacrificed in the middle of the afternoon. In the Jewish calendar the day began at sunset, not at midnight, as it does with us. If the lamb was sacrificed at, say, 3 o'clock in the afternoon, then the next day began at dusk which in those latitudes would have been about 6.00 or so in the evening at that time of year. You then brought home the remains of the lamb that was sacrificed that afternoon for your Passover Meal, and you ate that along with bitter herbs and unleavened bread. The Last Supper of Jesus with his disciples was not a Passover Meal, because if it had been, then none of the frenzied things that happened to him the next day would have been permitted under Jewish law.

However, it suited the Yom Kippur mindset about Jesus that the early Jerusalem Christians had, to conflate the death of Jesus with the death, as an atonement for sin, of the sacrificial lamb at Passover and Yom Kippur. Therefore, the Last Supper should be located a day after it had actually occurred, so that it would be a Passover Meal, which in fact the three Synoptic Gospels state it to have been.

The two rites, Baptism and the Eucharistic meal that commemorate these three elements have dominated Christianity for the last 2,000 years. Was this what Jesus taught should happen?

The Acts of the Apostles is the only early history of Christianity that we have. It was probably written by the same person who wrote the Gospel of Luke as we noted earlier. It exalts Peter and Paul and their version of the message. It marginalizes James the brother of Jesus, or hides him entirely, in spite the fact that he was the one, de facto, who succeeded Jesus as head of the movement.

Let's look again at the list of the brothers and sisters of Jesus in Mark 6:3: "Is not this the carpenter, the son of Mary, the brother of James and Joseph, and Simon and Jude, and are not his sisters here with us?"

Now look at what the author of Luke's Gospel and of the Acts of the Apostles has to say. As pointed out earlier in this book the author of the Gospel of Saint Luke uses the Gospel of Mark as a source. But in narrating this exact same incident the author cuts out the name of the brothers of Jesus.

> Mark 6:3:
> "Is not this the carpenter, the son of Mary, the brother of James and Joseph, and Simon and Jude, and are not his sisters here with us?"

> What does Luke's Gospel say, narrating the same incident?
> "Is not this the son of Joseph?" (Luke 4:22).

No mention of the brothers and sisters. Joseph was safely dead so I suppose you could mention him as he can't do much damage.

At the Crucifixion Scene, in Mark, it says: "The mother of James and Joseph was present." And "Mary Magdalene and Mary the Mother of Joseph" were present at the burial as well as the crucifixion.

What does Luke say recounting exactly the same two incidents? He simply states: "the women," were present, with no mention of who they are, and no mention of their son or sons.

The agenda seems all to obvious: diminish the role of the family of Jesus and exalt the role of Paul and the brand-new slant which he gives to the message.

That was the brand of message that went to the Councils of Nicaea and Constantinople. But that was 300 years later. However, in those intervening three centuries this was the brand of the message of Jesus that was approved for circulation: sacrifice, sin, making up for it, and being rewarded if we were good. That trend formed the programs from which you and I are now trying to escape.

You would not have warmed to the Emperor Constantine, but he didn't assassinate any bishops at Nicaea to get a vote to pass a particular formula, as is often alleged. Constantine didn't give a hoot what the Bishops voted to accept as long as they agreed on something. He had put a lot of money, time and effort, into holding this gathering and his principal motive was not to benefit the Church but to remove dissensions about religious matters which were such a disruptive feature of his unsteady realm. But he didn't physically force anyone during the debates, didn't assassinate anyone and he certainly didn't decide the Canon of the New Testament by throwing the books on the table and seeing which ones would fall off, as a lot of New Age writers have contended.

When they had come up with a formula about the reality of Jesus and his relationship to God the Father — which most of the bishops there did not want and did not feel comfortable with — he told the bishops they would have to sign that they agreed with this formulation. The price of not signing would be banishment into exile. Two bishops did not sign and were banished. It wasn't exactly a free vote, but the main impetus in hurrying some decision was not just that Constantine was running out of patience with discussing trivia as he saw it, but that the bishops wanted to go home.

Given the kind of unsatisfactory agreement that was clobbered together at Nicaea it is no surprise the issue boiled up soon again, and to quell that controversy another Council was called in 381 AD, this time twenty miles up the road at Constantinople itself. We are told in the words of the Creed that came from the Council at Constantinople that Jesus was "the first born of all creation. God from God, light from light, true God from true God, begotten not made, one being with the Father from whom all things are made... who for us men and our salvation came down from heaven, was born of the Virgin Mary, and was made man, suffered under Pontius Pilate ... etc., etc."

People from Christian backgrounds were taught all these elements as little children, and these elements became deeply ingrained and established programs. It is easier to pull back teeth than to get rid of those programs. Consequently, if an opinion contrary to those of the Council of Constantinople is expressed about Jesus, no matter how well based, it almost inevitably arouses deep feelings of unease in those who have grown up in those beliefs.

I've just noted that when Luke[99] lists the twelve Apostles, he distances the Apostles from the Jesus family. In the very beginning of the Book of Acts (1:13-14), Luke is describing what happened after Jesus' crucifixion: "All devoted themselves to prayer, together with certain women and his brothers (unnamed of course). And the pillars of the Christian movement are James, Peter and John." James was the head of the community! But in Luke Chapter 6:14, when he is mentioning this list, the author of the Gospel of Saint Luke places Peter first and John after him. Where is James? Conspicuous by his absence. It is unlikely the Gospel was written after the death of James, so we are left wondering.

It's extremely likely that the author of the Epistle of James was James the brother of Jesus himself. The Epistle is not focused on Jesus himself, but on what he taught. That's an interesting deviation from the norm, because it recognizes that Jesus' mission was to teach us something that would empower us to do the same things that he did.

But the Pauline approach was completely different. It exalted Jesus to an unattainable level of being, to where we could only worship and venerate him from afar, instead of doing what he came to teach us to do. Which was certainly not to put himself on a pedestal.

The Epistle or Letter of James has no teaching on those three main points of Paul that are outlined above. Neither has it anything from the traditions of the author of the Gospel of Mark or the Gospel of John. Instead it's a reflection on the traditional Kingdom teaching of Jesus, which is based on agape, the fundamental mindset, or state of frequency, into which we must move for the creation of reality to become something feasible for us.

This is extremely interesting seeing that the document is almost certainly from James himself, and thus it shows that this was the original form of the beliefs of the Christian community.

Unfortunately, it is not the mindset displayed by the writings

---

[99] Or the author of Acts, who was probably the same person.

of Paul. Paul is credited with being the author of most of the books of the New Testament as we have it, and the influence of those writings down through Christian history has been enormous. Thirteen of those twenty-seven books bear his name, even though most scholars believe he only wrote eight of them, Romans, 1 Corinthians, 2 Corinthians, Galatians, Colossians, Philippians, Philemon, and 1 Thessalonians. I assume his name was attached to the others to ensure acceptance by the early Christian communities, or as we might put it today, to increase sales. All thirteen books, however, were written along the pattern of those three major themes of Paul that are noted above.

What might have happened if, instead of the influence of Passover, Yom Kippur and the similar tenets of Paul – with all the emphasis on sacrifice, sin, reparation, unworthiness and guilt – the Christian community had instead been focused on achieving a state in which the ability to create reality would be taken for granted?

When Are We Going to Have That Copernican Revolution in Christian Belief?

Looking at the histories of cosmologies can teach us a lot, especially if they reflect the world view of the Medieval Europeans.

In depictions of the schema of Ptolemy we see depicted the outer firmament where all the stars are stuck onto the surface of a big sphere in which we are all contained. The Earth is at the center of everything. Above us is the air, and above that is fire. Next, we have the moon, and the planets, and then the sun. It's worthwhile to look at a diagram like this because it's a sublime example of how knowledge grows. Surprisingly, it does not grow by the mere accumulation of fuller and more accurate knowledge of facts, for the real insights only come when we can jettison the old paradigms entirely, and replace them with the new. In short, the most productive way in which human knowledge grows is by revolution not evolution.

By the late Middle Ages experts had become aware of a huge number of problems with the Ptolemaic understanding of the world – huge and unsolvable problems. What created the problems? The paradigm that was being used: that the Earth is at the center of everything.

It was observed that the planets weren't arriving where they should be according to Ptolemy's charts, and over time a host of major problems had accumulated, well over 1300 of them, and all to do with this view of things. When Nicolas Copernicus decided to change the paradigm, in one fell swoop almost all of those problems disappeared. I think there were only two left unresolved out of the 1389.

Fundamentally, a similar Copernican Revolution in terms of our belief systems is what is now badly needed. But we are so immersed in sub-conscious programs about Jesus, thanks to the Pauline version of the message of Jesus – as I noted above, he never met Jesus – that it's not quite as easy as moving from Ptolemy to Copernicus, because Ptolemy to Copernicus was just about the physical universe.

The Copernican theories weren't about matters of ultimate concern: Who am I? Where did I come from? What should I do while I'm here? Where do I go when the physical body dies? What if anything takes place after death? This collection of belief systems is a different kettle of fish entirely from whether the sun goes around the Earth or vice versa.

But actually despite the differences, there is still much in common. We can struggle with problems seemingly endlessly, but at some point it may eventually dawn on us that the problem is not with me. Neither are my beliefs the main problem. The real problem is I am starting with the wrong set of presuppositions.

The main group of erroneous presuppositions is grouped around what we believe we are here to do. Do I believe that I am here in some form of a not so neutral testing ground, and that in the end I will be judged on the basis of my performance throughout life? Do I believe that if I do "good' things" they will cancel out my record of 'bad' things? Do I believe that I will get a 'reward' if I do virtuous things in my life? Do I believe that if I do bad things I will have to pay for it after death? Do I believe that a superintending God may send me unfortunate circumstances to punish me for things I shouldn't have done? Of all the sub-conscious programs, this one is the closest to being in tune with reality, for there is a god manifesting into my life's path, but it is I myself who am the god in charge of my life, and my proclivities and deep convictions magnetize to me out of the quantum field the type of situations that match my basic intent.

Do I picture God as some sort of human being enlarged, and that Jesus was sent down here by God to try appease God's anger against us? What are the foundational beliefs behind such a scenario? An insecure and moronic God, and the conviction that you and I will be fortunate to escape the potential of an eternity of punishment?

That's the Ptolemaic version of religious belief.

If we change it back to the message that Jesus actually spoke about, which was all about living in a frequency of agape, then we can begin to change those self-destructive viewpoints.

Is that the end of the story? No, because there was little or no baggage, little or no programs, attaching to the transition from the views of Ptolemy to Copernicus.

While the switch from the views of Ptolemy to Copernicus didn't carry a lot of emotional baggage, our required shift in relation to our beliefs about matters of ultimate concern, carry an enormous amount of orbiting programs. How do we deal with them? This is what we are doing in this book, and that's what dictates its method of unveiling something as far as we can tolerate, then relaxing that trajectory, and then taking another tack, and then another, and another. In this way, the makings of a new program are gradually instilled into the sub-conscious mind and the old sub-conscious programs will start to dissolve of their own accord, like frost in sunshine.

One helpful strand for consideration in achieving this is to take a look at the development of our main cosmologies. Why? Because it tells us what the world view of those Medieval Europeans was like, and by osmosis we tune in to their mindsets behind the world views. Of most interest is how their beliefs about the nature of the universe were influenced by earlier Greek philosophies, and how that got mixed up with Christian beliefs and theologies about God, Jesus and human destiny — all through a labyrinth of historical circumstances. Eventually this process, so immersed in the perceived emergencies of each passing age, made it almost impossible to separate the beliefs themselves from the passing thought patterns in which they were being expressed.

The physical universe, in the days of Ptolemy and company, were thought to be centered around the Earth, even though Aristarchus, a long time before, had already said what it took Copernicus another 1,700 years to say. The psychological universe of Medieval Europe revolved around humans. Having an understanding of the psychology and the behavior of individuals requires a consideration of the desire for eternal salvation.

For Medieval Europe time had two divisions: The brief insignificant one in which the people of those times lived out their sinful lives, and the cosmic one in which the suffering or joy of their souls would occur. You had to make sure which one you were going for. In Medieval Europe, there was no room for any abnormality or non-conformity, because EVERY deviation was in general regarded as the work of the devil.

Hierarchy was set up everywhere, in all things, and people accepted their place in the social order, no matter how low a place it might have been. And everything in the world could symbolize something supernatural. People saw messages from God in a way that you and I would regard today as extremely superstitious. Constantine, Emperor of Rome, was an <u>extremely</u> superstitious man. It is hard for us to credit the interest he had in placating the most powerful God around, and make no mistake, he regarded the Jewish Christian God as just the most powerful of the Gods that were then doing business on this planet. They were only part of a multinational that did business on other planets as well.

People in those times tended to perceive God in virtually <u>every</u> natural and human event. I think if you ever are sufficiently deluded and free of worldly concerns, you could do no better than read the history of The Venerable Bede,[100] an English monk

---

100 673-735 AD.

of prodigious learning, whose classic work "Ecclesiastical History of the English People" is regarded as one of the great historical works of all time. Most of the English people wouldn't like Bede today, any more than they did while he was alive. That book spells out how the world view that was in power at the time affected the lives and people of the time, and we can infer how its influence can still be felt by those of us who are living in the 21st century.

We've basically taken over, unexamined, the belief systems that grew up in an entirely different worldview from the one in which you and I are living now. In that vast collection, if we were to isolate one particular instance that needs reworking, it is that whatever else God may be, God is definitely not some form of human being enlarged, sitting on the upper floor of the Hamburger Universe, scrutinizing and evaluating everything that goes on "down" here.

I referred to the well-known anecdote of the Creator taking a Senior Angel on a tour of the galaxies. They went through all beautiful realms of magnificent glory, thousands of light years from here. Suddenly as they were going far away from the center of things, right into the boondocks, away in the murky darkness they saw this badly illuminated murky planet, and to the great distress of the Angel, the Creator said to the Angel, "This is where I want you to go." And the Angel said, "Oh please!" Anyway, that's another perspective on the way our universe and our planet is regarded from the outside. The illustrations are mythical but the message is true. We really are in the boondocks of creation. Is it a beautiful planet? Absolutely. But, are we the center of everything?

But if we were to realize that we're not at the center of everything, but are in fact living in what is most likely a rural galaxy situated way out in the boondocks of the universe, is the only reaction to collapse in grief, disappointment and despair? By no means, we are each as powerful as the other or anyone who exists anywhere. Why? Because our significance is not based on where we inhabit, geographically, in the universe. We have all come from Point Zero and are all incarnations of Point Zero into physical matter. In the much more simple phrase of Jesus, we are all Gods.

The problem is that we've crippled ourselves. And unfortunately, the method used to do that was to turn the message of Jesus inside out, and on its head, so that we mistakenly believed that that was what he taught and that we had no choice but accept it. In the light of all that, is Jesus coming back? Absolutely not; once was far more than enough.

But at least we can give him something that might bring him some consolation — if it's at all appropriate to speak of an ascended master deriving hope or joy or gratitude from the input of others? We should at least give Jesus something, and it would be most appropriate, even at this late stage, if we indicated at long last that we had finally got what he was saying. And also, that we are determined to set about removing the major obstacles in the many historical perversions of his teachings, with which we have been left to deal. When we have done that, then we will truly be, as he himself said, all Gods, because there will be no block to the effects that agape will create in the whole of the material creation. It's a wonderful destiny. Our grasp of it previously was often hideously distorted, but this time we see far more clearly, and what is more, this time we're going to accomplish it.

An Enlightened Teaching Converted into Avoiding Sins and Doing Good

In the Gospels we are told of the famous encounter after the Resurrection between Jesus and Peter on the lake shore early in the morning. What Jesus was asking Peter was, "Can you access the state of being where you love unconditionally?" If you can manage to love one person or one thing unconditionally, then you're on the way to loving all things unconditionally. Why is that so important as I've stressed so often in these pages already? Because this is the state which in the quantum field facilitates manifestation. It brings about creation because it is imitating and tapping into the energy that brought about the whole of creation in the first place. What Jesus was asking Peter did not arise out of some form of insecurity, in short it was not to find out if Peter really loved him or not, or was loyal to him or not. Rather the question was "Can you get yourself into the state where you can become a Master of the Quantum Field?" Because, if you can attain to that state habitually, then whatever you say is.

What's another way of expressing that state in terms of what we're discussing here? Another version of it is that if I can neutralize all my sub-conscious crippling programs, then I am in the agape state. If I'm still under the control of programs I am not in the agape state.

If I'm still thinking of Jesus as a Suffering Savior, and believe that my job here is, as Saint Paul put it, to imitate the sufferings of Jesus in order to gain a reward later, then I'm as far away as can be imagined from the agape state.

All the other things that Jesus spoke about, such as love your neighbor, do good to those who hate you, do this, do that and do the other thing, all of these have long, long ago morphed into being S-I-N-S in the Western tradition. In the teaching of Jesus these weren't commandments to be obeyed, which if you didn't obey, you had sinned against God. No, no, and no! We have turned God into an idol — a human being enlarged — and we have turned the empowering statements of Jesus relating to activating change in the quantum field into a set of do's and don'ts that are supposed to please or displease an all-too-human style Deity. This has been the great tragedy of the fate the teachings of Jesus suffered.

God is love. Agape is infinite. There is nothing that can add to the greatness of God. And the corollary of that is there is nothing that can subtract from it either. God doesn't give a hoot about our "sins." They don't impact him/her/it, whatever term you choose. God cannot be offended. Only a being or beings who are masquerading as the Creator can be offended, and this offense-taking is then used as a technique for control. These are all terms from the Hertzian plane, and grossly inapplicable to the Creator. The real problem with our "sins" is that they impede us from accessing the agape state of spiritual power.

This is not at all to say that if we do what are currently regarded as 'sins' that there are no consequences. There are very many consequences, for we are magnetizing back to us more of the same stuff that we have just meted out to others. The main point being stressed here is that 'sins' are not to be avoided because they displease God, but because such a way of life is a catastrophe in terms of the destiny we are creating for ourselves. Apart from the repercussions we are magnetising back to ourselves, the 'sinful' state totally blocks us from attaining this state of 'agape.'

Magnetising back to myself what I mete out to myself or to others, is a far more serious repercussion than going to Purgatory or Hell could ever be. Why do we persist in working with a world view of God and human destiny that was all the human race could manage to attain to, thousands of years ago? In what other area of life would we tolerate working with a view of things that not alone has been surpassed, but has been discredited for centuries? Why do we assume that it is perfectly all right to accept these misunderstandings of human purpose and destiny, when it is crippling the very process that we came here to activate?

It's crucial to understand that what Jesus came to teach was getting into this state where we become masters of what we say, when we say it in truth. Then there is no more division. So, are we to avoid this particular sin and that particular sin and the other particular sin? Yes, not because they are sins but because they prohibit the agape state. I lose if I go down this track. If I hold a grudge against somebody, I can't get into the agape state. If I cheat somebody, if I'm dishonest with somebody, it's not that it's a sin and I'm to go to Hell and burn for all eternity if things get really bad. No, there is no such place, unless I am convinced of it, and if I die in fear and apprehension of the judgment of God and Hell fire, then I may actually experience such a place for a while after I leave the physical body. But leaving all that afterlife expectation aside for now, what does happen is that if I hate or cheat or hold grudges I can't become a Master. And that is not because some exalted being somewhere will not allow me to become a Master as a punishment for what I've done. No, it is I who am short-changing myself. It is I myself who am doing myself in.

Do I prefer to hold a grudge rather than the ability to be able to stretch out my hand and produce food out of pure energy, which is the way all matter originally emerged? Without realizing it very clearly that's exactly what we're doing when we hold grudges, malign or hate. Do I prefer to hold on to my pettiness, my nasty, mean little miserable attitudes, instead of becoming a glorious and powerful being? I can't give up my desires to even up scores, I can't give up my petty resentments, nor can I forget my ego being snubbed, even though I know the price that I pay for those petty attitudes is enormous. Please keep this in mind as we continue on this topic. Jesus' teaching was all about empowerment. Almost every element of the many religious traditions has turned his teachings into something quite different, whose net effect unfortunately is dis-empowerment.

Our intent here in this book is to move on dissolving those subconscious, crippling programs. We pursue a line of investigation into how these programs originated, how deceived we have become about how they originated, and to realize that very often there is not a shred of credibility to them. Then we begin to see how catastrophic they are for our journey. We can only go so far with this process until it becomes counter-productive, because the ego will eventually begin to resent it if too much reality is forced upon it all at once. I often use the analogy of stretching an elastic band as far as it will comfortably go and then relaxing it, and having some repose before trying again. It is also almost universally true that once individuals begin to feel threatened in this sort of process, they withdraw, so we must relax our attendance.

We discuss a theme, we uncover the truth. It's a very uncomfortable process. We see where we went off the beaten track, we stretch the elastic band, and stretch it and stretch it, until just before we can't take any more. If we are saying these things to other people, the audience may be just about to walk out or kick over the TV screen, or do something equally dramatic. Just before that happens we need to relax the rubber band. But if we don't get close to that condition, we are not making any impact on the subconscious programs. I have often attended public lectures where an individual in the audience gets very upset or angry with the speaker, and very often speakers resent that. However, the truth of the matter is that the person is upset and angry because he or she has really got what the speaker was putting across, and has realized its implications for the belief system by which the angry person has lived most of their life. In short, very often it is the angry people in the audience who have got what the speaker was trying to get across, and very often those who remain silent and appropriately well behaved, have missed the point.

Using the analogy of stretching the elastic bands, what we are doing is approaching the same reality, the same process, from different standpoints. This is how negative sub-conscious programs are disabled. As I pointed out earlier, they cannot be directly attacked or dismissed, only built up from the ground with different, and more positive and true insights into reality. These complimentary different approaches can look like disorganization, but actually it's all a very sinister and deliberate process! It's called sneaking up on enlightenment. The old Master Teacher once used a famous analogy to describe people on the spiritual path. He said we are like bullfrogs in a wheel barrow. He is trying to wheel us towards enlightenment but we keep wanting to jump out. So it is with the undermining of sub-conscious programs. If we stretch the elastic band too far all at once, people will jump ship!

Why do we have this innate propensity to run away from enlightenment? Because it's too uncomfortable. All the hits and thrills of our emotional dramas have to be transcended as a prerequisite.

Chapter 8
The Lion of Judah Declawed?

"Gentle Jesus; Meek and Mild"?

On a Sabbath day Jesus went into a Synagogue and a man with a shriveled hand was brought before him. He was asked to heal the man's hand. For Jesus to perform this miracle would have been an infringement of the Sabbath and, according to the Law, breaking the Sabbath was a capital offense. As expressed in the Book of Exodus the Law stated: "Six days work shall be done, but on the seventh day you shall have a Sabbath of solemn rest, holy to the Lord. Whoever does any work on it shall be put to death."[101]

But apparently, to be about to witness an extraordinary physical healing that defied all the known laws of nature, was of less importance to the Pharisees than upholding an ancient moral prohibition whose meaning and purpose had long been lost. To try to entrap Jesus they asked him: "Is it lawful then to heal on the Sabbath?" Jesus said to them: "If any of you had a sheep and it falls into a hole on the Sabbath will you not take hold of it and lift it out? How much more valuable is a person than a sheep! Therefore, it is lawful to do good on the Sabbath." Then he said to the man with the crippled hand: "Stretch out your hand." The man stretched it out and as he did so it was completely restored. But without marveling at what had been miraculously accomplished in the twinkling of an eye, and trying to figure out what the implications of it might be for their own belief system, the Pharisees instead went out and started to plot how they might kill Jesus.

This is perhaps one of the very best texts in which to see the method Jesus used to deal with those whom he knew were planning his demise.

The "Gentle Jesus"

If we look back at the course of Christianity down through the ages it's not difficult to notice major differences in the way Jesus has been perceived and understood over the centuries. It's hard to resist saying that he has been used as if he were some kind of religious smorgasbord, and that those smorgasbord choices are a reliable barometer of the longings in people's hearts at a particular time in history.

It is obvious that certain aspects of Jesus proved more appealing to people depending on how the circumstances were in

[101] Exodus 35:2.

particular times and places in history. The reverse is true as well: certain aspects of Jesus were ignored, forgotten, or soft-pedaled, or enthusiastically accepted, depending on the tastes or the quality of experiences of the times.

When anyone opens up the four Gospels, what probably strikes one most about Jesus is his compassion, his gentleness and his authenticity. However, one of the main issues of concern with the Gospels of the New Testament is that the smorgasbord method was apparently already in action at the very beginning. As a result, what Jesus actually came to do and say and teach was morphed into something related but different. What was that 'something else' into which the real message was turned? An extremely exalted, purified and rarified system of ethics, that was probably best expressed in his Sermon on the Mount[102] – a magnificent and beautiful system of how belief should work out in practice; one which would transform the world radically if more people decided to live by what he taught there. But to convey such a marvelous system of ethics was not the primary purpose of the ministry of Jesus. Instead that system of ethics was presented as one of the consequences that would follow once you grasped and implemented what his message really was. In short, the system of ethics from the Sermon on the Mount was not a set of ideals to be aimed at directly: these qualities described in the Sermon come to us as a consequence of acquiring a state that is even deeper and more extraordinary than these qualities.

It's only when we realize this that we can begin to see the real basis of his message, and understand that it had a far more fundamental purpose than just to make us become extraordinarily nice people.

This is the reason why we need to look at the whole question as to whether the texts of the New Testament that we have today correspond to the original autograph texts of those works. Despite the massive number of variants in the surviving manuscripts, we will see clearly that most of those variants are trivial, and that we can remain confident that the New Testament text as we know

[102] Gospel of Matthew, Chapters 5, 6, and 7.

it, is substantially what the authors intended to convey in the autograph copies.

In short, our difficulties with the New Testament, if we can call them that, go far more deep than the issue of whether our modern translations convey what the authors intended at the time of composition.

That Jesus was gentle and compassionate is blatantly obvious all through the four Gospels. We can look at several examples. One text, which could serve as a sort of chapter heading for his gentle kindness, is found in Matthew 11:29: "Take my yoke upon you and learn from me, for I am gentle and humble in heart, and you will find rest for your souls."[103]

In another incident, narrated in Chapter 12 of the same Gospel, Jesus was walking through some fields of grain on the Sabbath day. His disciples were hungry. They began to pick some of the heads of wheat and eat the grain. The Pharisees criticized the disciples for "harvesting grain" — as they termed it — on the Sabbath. These individuals believed their unique role was to enforce the very strict Jewish law of not doing any work on the Sabbath, even though they had long before entirely lost the understanding of why that prohibition was put there in the first place. Their ultimate motive of the Pharisees at the point we are referring to here, was to use anything they could to undermine Jesus.

The Bible itself does not specifically list all forms of work that are prohibited on the Sabbath, although it does allude to field labor.[104] These details are spelled out in the Mishnah[105] where thirty-nine categories of labor are enumerated. So technically, in accordance with the declaration of the Book of Exodus,[106] Jesus'

---

[103] New International Version.

[104] Exod. 34:21; Num.15:32-36.

[105] The Mishnah is first major written account of Jewish oral tradition. After the destruction of Herod's Temple in 70 AD there was a fear that the Jewish traditions of the Pharisees would be lost. Rabbi Yehudah HaNasi made a collection that formed the basis of the Mishnah before his death around 217 AD.

[106] Exodus 20:8-11. "Observe the Sabbath day, to keep it holy. Work six days and do everything you need to do. But the seventh day is a Sabbath to GOD,

disciples were indeed breaking the Sabbath. In the eyes of the Pharisees that was not a small matter. Exodus 31:14-15 pronounces a number of times that death is the punishment for anyone who violates the law of Sabbath rest.

In response to the accusations of the Pharisees, Jesus taught that the prohibition of work on the Sabbath was not an unthinking, rigid and absolute rule independent of all other considerations. which is indeed what the message of Exodus seems to suggest. He pointed out that circumstances could dictate exceptions that were in accord with common sense. He cited examples: "Haven't you read what David did when he and his companions were hungry? He went into the house of God and ate the consecrated bread, which was not lawful for him to do, but only the priests. Or haven't you read in the law that the priests on Sabbath duty desecrate the Sabbath by working and yet are innocent? I tell you something greater than the Temple is here. If you had known what these words mean, 'I desire mercy and not sacrifice', you would not have condemned the innocent. For the Son of Man is Lord of the Sabbath."[107] What was the heart of this teaching? Rules have a purpose that help to organize matters, but they are not unthinking absolutes that must be adhered to, especially long after the purpose for which they were put into place has vanished.

A few pages back we recalled the account of how on a Sabbath Day Jesus went into a Synagogue and a man with a shriveled hand was brought before him. He was asked to heal the man's hand. For Jesus to perform this miracle would have been an infringement of the Sabbath and, according to the Law breaking the Sabbath was a capital offense.

I'm sure the man whose hand was healed by Jesus would have a different perspective. But as I pointed out a few pages back, without marveling for even a moment at what had been

---

your God. Don't do any work—not you, nor your son, nor your daughter, nor your servant, nor your maid, nor your animals, not even the foreign guest visiting in your town. For in six days GOD made Heaven, Earth, and sea, and everything in them; he rested on the seventh day. Therefore GOD blessed the Sabbath day; he set it apart as a holy day."

[107] Matthew 12:1-8, Mark 2:23-28 and Luke 6:1-5.

miraculously accomplished in the twinkling of an eye the Pharisees instead went out and started to plot how they might kill him.

In Matthew 10 Jesus sent out his twelve disciples and told them: "Don't go among the Gentiles or into the Samaritan territory. Go to the people of Israel and tell them the Kingdom of Heaven has come. Heal the sick, raise the dead, cleanse those who have leprosy and drive out demons. Freely you have received; freely give."

And in Matthew 9 we are told he went into a boat and came to his own town. The people brought him a paralyzed man lying on a mat. When Jesus saw their faith, he said to the man: "Take heart, son, your sins are forgiven." Then the Teachers of the Law said to themselves: "This fellow is blaspheming for he is putting himself in God's place. Only God can forgive sins." Jesus, knowing their thoughts said: "Why do you entertain evil thoughts in your hearts?" In effect he was saying, "If I can miraculously heal his hand surely I must be closer to God than the individuals making this shallow criticism? Which is easier to say, 'Your sins are forgiven' or to say 'Get up and walk'? But I want you to know that the Son of Man has authority on Earth to forgive sins." He said to the paralyzed man, "Get up, take your mat and go home." And the man got up and left.

This is the quintessentially well-known, meek and mild Jesus, the worker of extraordinary miracles, the loving, the compassionate one. The predominance of this aspect of Jesus became particularly noticeable in the English-speaking world of the 19th century and has thoroughly permeated the religious culture, of the West especially, in the interim. A remarkable change began to happen in the focus of religion on texts such as those I have just quoted. The focus was no longer on God, as it used to be, in most of the English-speaking world. The focus shifted from God to Jesus. But also to a very specific brand of Jesus — a Jesus who was strongly sentimental, gentle and emotional. He was always forgiving, tolerant, patient, compassionate and welcoming… all of which he undoubtedly was. But that was most certainly not the whole story of Jesus; unfortunately, it almost became the whole story.

The emphasis in the United States in the middle of the 19th century noticeably moved away from doctrines and abstract belief systems. God had to be near, almost tangible and relevant. God had to be loving. What we were all supposed to be aiming at here in this life was understood to be a life of spiritual intimacy with Jesus … a gentle, meek and mild Jesus chosen from the smorgasbord. It became the very heart of the Christian faith in the West. Christianity was no longer about aligning your mind and heart with the presence of God within. Instead it was all about having Jesus in your heart. That became the dominant theme in the prayer books and devotional manuals of that era.

Charles Wesley, brother of John Wesley who founded the Methodist Church, wrote more than six thousand hymns. One of his best known was written in 1763 and has had a profound effect on most popular forms of Christianity:

> Gentle Jesus, meek and mild,
> Look upon a little child;
> Pity my simplicity,
> Suffer me to come to Thee.
> Lamb of God, I look to Thee;
> Thou shalt my Example be;
> Thou art gentle, meek, and mild;
> Thou wast once a little child.
> Loving Jesus, gentle Lamb,
> In Thy gracious hands I am;
> Make me, Savior, what Thou art,
> Live Thyself within my heart.[108]

Or take another example from the hymn "Once in Royal David's City". I am sure we have all often sung this verse in our better years! It was written in 1848 by a renowned lady, Cecil Frances Alexander, and put to music by Henry Gauntlett.

> "And through all His wondrous childhood
> He would honor and obey,
> Love, and watch the lowly maiden,

[108] Charles Wesley, "A Child's Prayer," First published in *Hymns & Sacred Poems,* 1742.

In whose gentle arms He lay:
Christian children all must be
Mild, obedient, good as He."[109]

So we see that some of the most beloved American evangelical hymns see our ideal relationship to Jesus in completely individualist terms on the smorgasbord ... as a friendship almost, or sometimes even as a relationship between lovers. A lot of these sources speak of this relationship in terms of having a walk with him; having a chat with Jesus; embracing Jesus ... Jesus is my companion ... Jesus is always by my side.

The very popular hymn "What a Friend We Have in Jesus" is an excellent example of this. It was published in 1855 and remains one of the most popular hymns in the English-speaking world today.

Have we trials and temptations?
Is there trouble anywhere?
We should never be discouraged –
Take it to the Lord in prayer.
Can we find a friend so faithful,
Who will all our sorrows share?
Jesus knows our every weakness;
Take it to the Lord in prayer.[110]

Sentiment in religious belief and practice was really given a boost when Ira D. Sankey published his "Gospel Hymns" in 1875.[111] That volume is still a very popular book of hymns today. It's difficult to escape getting the impression that the Jesus of the English-speaking, nineteenth century world, was, over and above everything else, a meek, mild, weak, inoffensive, forgiving and harmless individual. Unfortunately those same qualities are then put forward as the marks of a true follower of Jesus.

---

[109] Cecil Frances Humphreys Alexander, (1818-1895), *Hymns for Little Children,* 1848. Put to music by Henry Gauntlett (1805-1876) in 1849.

[110] Joseph M. Scriven, *What a Friend We Have in Jesus* (1855).

[111] "Gospel Hymns," by Ira Sankey, Philip Paul Bliss, 1838-1876; James McGranahan, and George C. Stebbins (George Coles), 1846-1945.

Yet it's often been noted that of all the adjectives that could be applied to Jesus from the smorgasbord, these are probably the least appropriate. J.B. Phillips[112] noted that this version of Jesus, which was normally portrayed in that evangelical tradition from the 19th century onwards, gives the impression of someone who would let sleeping dogs lie; someone who would avoid trouble wherever possible; someone who is a bit of a nonentity, uninspired and uninspiring.

But there is another kind of Jesus which is not as well known, or as popularly attractive, as the familiar gentle Jesus.

Ponder this text from Matthew's Gospel (18:15-17): "If your brother sins against you, go and tell him his fault, between you and him alone. If he listens to you, and reforms, then you have gained your brother. But if he does not listen to you, take one or two others along with you, that every charge may be established by the evidence of two or three witnesses. If he refuses to listen to them, tell it to the assembly. And if he refuses to listen even to the assembly, let him be to you as a Gentile and a tax collector." In other words – "Kick him out".

This is one of the first hints we get of what may be strange news for people who believe that Christianity is all about non-confrontation. Or that Jesus himself was about non-confrontation and peace at any price. You may find it interesting that this kind of text has been used a lot in the context of excommunication. Indeed, it was one of the fundamental texts that used to justify the Inquisition when it was at its height.

So what was Jesus and his message really like – behind the smorgasbord? If we do not get ourselves straight on what he was really like, we will not hear the real content of his message. And if we do not hear that message we have little hope of removing those dis-empowering programs of guilt, fear, unworthiness and sin. Can we restore some balance to this picture?

---

[112] J.B. Phillips, Your God Is Too Small. A Guide for Believers and Skeptics Alike (Simon and Schuster, 1952).

Another Kind of Jesus

Let's explore the 'other' side of Jesus.

Some of the Pharisees approached Jesus and said: "Go away from here for Herod, (Herod Antipas, son of Herod the Great), wants to kill you."[113] Jesus said in reply: "Go and tell that Fox, behold I cast out demons and perform cures today and tomorrow, and the third day I will reach my goal."

Now the one thing above all that was not a career move in those far off days was to call Herod Antipas a fox. He was ruler of Galilee and Perea all during Jesus' ministry and had learned the ropes growing up in a very perilous household. Two of his brothers, and his mother, the Hasmonean Princess, Mariamne, had been killed by his father. He had learned early on how to keep a low profile, and to nip any possible threat to his power in the bud.

He was the person who had John the Baptist beheaded at a dinner party to fulfill a drunken promise to a teenage dancer.[114] We are told Antipas was greatly distressed when the dancing girl was prompted by her mother to ask for the head of John the Baptist because Antipas was fascinated by John and also had a superstitious fear of him. However, but he did not want to lose face in front of his guests. He had John beheaded and his head brought to the banquet table on a platter.

Now if Antipas was fascinated by John, he was fascinated much more by Jesus, whose mission was eminently more remarkable than John's had been. In fact, there was a rumor that John the Baptist had re-incarnated in Jesus, which made the superstitious Herod even more wary of him.

An ironic note here is that a lady named Johanna was the wife of Chuza, the Manager of the Household of Herod Antipas. Chuza presumably had a good income from his position as Manager of the King's household. His wife, Johanna, was one of the women who

---

[113] Luke 13:31-32; Mark 6:14—29.

[114] Salome, daughter of Herodias.

accompanied Jesus on his travels, and helped sustain his mission financially. It is scarcely credible that Antipas was not aware of the financial support that his Steward's wife was providing to the small group that followed Jesus everywhere.

Herod the Great, Antipas' father, was the only one of the Herods who ever held the title 'King'. A contemporary Jewish author describes him as "a mad man who murdered his own family and a great many rabbis."[115]

It's interesting to note that, like Abraham himself, King Herod the Great of Judea was not a Jew. His father was from Idumea, a region south-east of the Dead Sea, outside of Judea. To help legitimize his throne Herod the Great married Mariamne, who was of the Hasmonean Dynasty of Judea. This Dynasty was the second Royal House of that territory, and descended from Judas Maccabeus[116] who achieved independence for Judea from the Selucid Empire that had been part of the Empire of Alexander the Great. Mary Magdalene was of this same family. Herod's main reason for marrying Mariamne was to strengthen his grip on the throne of Judea. However, it appears, he was also madly in love with her, although she hated him.

There was much to hate in Herod the Great. The Jewish Encyclopedia states: "above all, he was prepared to commit any crime in order to gratify his unbounded ambition". Mariamne's particular grievance against him was the sinister murder of her brother Aristobulus.[117] Josephus tells us that Herod had conferred the High Priesthood on Aristobulus at the age of 17, but shortly afterwards, fearing his growing popularity as Heir of the Hasmonean Dynasty, had him drowned in a bath during a celebration in Herod's house at Jericho in 36 BC.

Later, in 29 BC, in a rage Herod ordered Mariamne's immediate execution. This ruthless and paranoid ruler also killed their two

---

[115] Rabbi Ken Spiro: A Crash Course in Jewish History: The Miracle and Meaning of Jewish History, from Abraham to Modern Israel. 2010.

[116] 191-160 BC. Killed in battle at age 29. The Jewish feast of Hanukkah marks the restoration of Jewish worship at the temple in Jerusalem in 164 BCE after Judas Maccabeus removed the Greek statutes.

[117] Hebrew name 'Jonathan.'

sons, Alexander and Aristobulus. The Emperor Augustus, said of Herod: "It's apparently safer to be Herod's pig than Herod's son." Even though Herod had executed two of his own sons, nevertheless as a Jewish King he didn't eat pork. It appears there is always some redeeming feature in even the worst tyrants!

Returning to the time of Herod Antipas ... the person most responsible for the beheading of John the Baptist was Herodias. She had been the wife of Herod Antipas's half-brother, Phillip. Under Jewish law at that time it was not permitted to marry your brother's wife, even if the brother had died. John the Baptist had criticized Antipas in public for marrying Herodias.

All this goes to show that Antipas was not the sort of person who would relish being called a 'fox' by Jesus, and he had the means to make his displeasure felt unimpeded by any awkward realities like Constitutions, Laws, Judges, Juries or Courts of Justice. His word was law. For Jesus to stand up in public and call Herod a fox in his own Kingdom took an uncommon level of courage, and was, by no stretch of the imagination, something a meek and mild individual would ever contemplate.

The Violent Jesus

Large numbers of Jewish people from all over were accustomed to come to Jerusalem every year for the major Festival of Passover, celebrated in the early Spring: from the 15th through the 22nd of the Hebrew month of Nisan. It commemorated the journey of the Hebrew people out of Egypt. At the stroke of midnight on 15 Nisan in the year 1313 BC, Jehovah visited the last of the ten plagues on the Egyptians, killing all their firstborn. He spared the Children of Israel, "passing over" their homes—hence the name of the Festival.

The Israelites departed in such haste that the bread they baked as provisions for the way did not have time to rise. It is said that six hundred thousand adult males, plus many more women and children, left Egypt on that day, and began the trek to Mount Sinai and their birth as the Chosen People of Jehovah.

In memory of the unleavened bread that the people of Israel took with them on their flight out of Egypt Jewish people don't eat or have in their possession any *chametz* from midday of the day before Passover until the conclusion of the holiday.

Chametz means any leavened grain, that is any food or drink that contains even a trace of wheat, barley, rye, oats, spelt or their derivatives, and which wasn't guarded from leavening or fermentation. Included in this list is bread, cereal, cake, cookies, cereal, pasta and most alcoholic beverages. Any processed food or drink is assumed to be *chametz*.

When it was assumed, incorrectly, by most of early Christianity that the Last Supper of Jesus with his disciples was a Passover meal, the Christian commemoration of that which we call the Eucharist, was celebrated also with unleavened bread. In ancient times when a great spiritual teacher broke bread and gave it to his disciples, he had the ability to transform the bread into his own DNA: hence the statement of Jesus at the Last Supper "This is my Body," which was of course literally true.

The early Christians used unleavened bread for the distribution of the Eucharistic hosts used in the celebration of Mass or the Eucharist. In fact, the title "Mass" itself is most likely to have come from a Latinization of the Hebrew term *matzâh* (מצה), meaning "unleavened bread," despite many other less likely explanations.

In the time of Jesus, the normal attendance at the Temple in Jerusalem has been estimated as being between 300,000 to 400,000 pilgrims. The Gentiles' Court of the Temple would have been where all transactions took place. It was crowded with livestock for sale to be used in the Temple Sacrifices. One can only imagine the noise, the stench and the filth. Those visitors who had come from abroad for the Festival would probably have their funds in Greek and Roman coinage, which could not be used for purchases in the Temple, so their funds would have to be changed into Jewish money to purchase animals for the Sacrifices. Great numbers of money changers, who operated at a handsome profit, had set up their tables in the outer Court of the Temple. It must have been a scene of unparalleled chaos and confusion. To describe it as unbefitting in the Temple itself would have been the understatement of all time.

Jesus made three visits to the Temple for Passover during his public ministry. On his first visit, he had not been to the Temple for about eighteen years, and he was appalled by what he saw in the Court of the Gentiles. He made a whip of ropes and drove the sheep and oxen out of the Temple, and then he turned on the money changers themselves. He threw their coins into the air and kicked over their tables. The account of this incident is in each of the three Synoptic Gospels.[118] Matthew 21:12-13 tells us: "Jesus entered the temple and drove out all those who were buying and selling in the temple, and overturned the tables of the money changers and the seats of those who were selling doves. And He said to them, 'It is written, My House shall be called a House of Prayer', but you are making it a Robbers' Den."

I presume the traders in the Temple to at least some degree must have already known that what they were doing was inappropriate or even sacrilegious. So, it was unlikely that they would have ceased their activities if someone had simply pointed out the error of their ways in a calm and measured fashion.

This was the first visit of Jesus with his disciples to the Temple for Passover. I would imagine that the following year business might have fallen off somewhat in the Court of the Gentiles, or at least a closer watch would have been kept on the arrival of unpredictable itinerant preachers into the city!

The rich were able to afford to offer a lamb or an ox at the Passover sacrifices. For the benefit of the poor, the Book of Leviticus, Chapter 5:7 says, "Anyone who cannot afford a lamb is to bring two doves or two young pigeons to the Lord as a penalty for their sin — one for a sin offering and the other for a burnt offering."[119]

It is interesting to note that while Jesus kicked over the tables of the money changers, scattered their coins everywhere, and used a whip on them, he didn't physically attack the people who were selling doves and pigeons. He simply asked them: "Why

---

[118] Mark 11:15-19, 11:27-33, Matthew 21:12-17, 21:23-27, Luke 19:45-48, 20:1-8.

[119] The burnt offering was meant to make up to Jehovah for intentional sins, the 'sin offering' for unintentional sins.

are you turning my father's house into a market place?" and told them to get out. He didn't accost them physically because doves and pigeons were the offerings of the poor, so they had some redeeming feature.

In light of these incidents, can we still say that Jesus was gentle, meek and mild? We are beginning to see that indeed there was much more on the smorgasbord than that.

Insulting Confrontations with the Pharisees

The Pharisees represented what might be called blue-collar Jews…in contrast to the more aristocratic Sadducees. The third major party in Judaism at the time of Jesus was the Essenes, a group that emerged from disgust with the other two.

To say Jesus did not have a good relationship with the Pharisees is an understatement. He referred to them in the most unflattering of terms: "You brood of vipers, how can you being evil speak what's good, for the mouth speaks out of that which fills the heart."[120] Since the Jews intensely hated and feared these venomous snakes, it was the worse insult that could be offered to them. This was especially so for people who felt they were the bee's knees and perceived themselves as forming the top stratum of Jewish religious society. Everyone knew the viper was the most dangerous and treacherous of snakes with double forked tongues and venomous fangs. Once they bit they did not let go. Obviously, these same traits Jesus saw metaphorically in the Pharisees. They taught a rigid and unthinking interpretation of the Law to others, but did not observe it themselves.

So Jesus didn't mince his words. If you were to ask the Pharisees of Jesus' day, or if you were to ask the money changers in the Temple: "Was Jesus gentle, meek and mild?" I doubt that you would have gotten an affirmative answer from them. Was Jesus against violence? You had only to consult those money changers to get an illuminating answer.

[120] Matthew 12:34.

We read in Luke Chapter 4:29-30 of the reaction when Jesus preached in the Synagogue at Nazareth. In his day, the Second Temple at Jerusalem, built by King Herod, was still standing and was the focus of Jewish religious life.[121] Beginning in 833 BC the First Temple had been built by King Solomon on Mount Moriah in Jerusalem, during the United Monarchy of Israel and Judah; the site made notable as the place where Abraham had declared his readiness to sacrifice his own son to Jehovah as a pledge of loyalty.

That Temple had been destroyed in 587 BC after the siege of Jerusalem by the Babylonian King Nebuchadnezzar II.[122]

However, during the previous two hundred years before the time of Jesus, and before Herod had built the Second Temple,

---

[121] The city has been claimed by Christians, Jews, and Muslims, and the oldest portions of the city have been long been divided for a very long time into the Armenian, Christian, Jewish, and Muslim Quarters. It should be noted that the Jerusalem of the time of Jesus is about 10-15 feet beneath the level of the present city. After World War I, the United Kingdom was given a mandate for Palestine, which it had conquered from the Ottomans during the first World War. In 1937 the Peel Commission suggested partitioning the territory of Palestine under Mandate into an Arab state and a Jewish state, though the proposal was rejected as unworkable by the government. The collapse of that proposal was a major factor in creating the 1936—39 Arab revolt. The State of Israel was established after the 1948 war. West Jerusalem was captured by Israel, while East Jerusalem was captured by Jordan. In the Six Day War, which was fought between June 5 and 10, 1967 by Israel and the neighboring states of the UAR, (or Egypt), Jordan, and Syria, Israel captured East Jerusalem and annexed it, but the international community still sees it as Palestinian land under military occupation, which is why, for example, the Embassy of the United States to Israel has been located in Tel Aviv not Jerusalem, a situation which Donald Trump seems determined to change. Israel captured the West Bank (including East Jerusalem) from Jordan in the 1967 War, and the Golan Heights from Syria. The building of settlements in those captured areas remains a major problem.

[122] Reigned c. 605 BC — c. 562 BC. Both the construction of the Hanging Gardens of Babylon and the destruction of Jerusalem's Temple are ascribed to him. He is mentioned in the Book of Daniel and in several other places in the Hebrew Bible.

synagogues had been established throughout the land where people could come on the Sabbath to hear the scriptures formally read aloud and to discuss the readings. It was customary to ask any distinguished scholar or teacher in attendance to read from one of the Prophets.

On this particular day Jesus was handed the scroll of the Prophet Isaiah. He searched for the place we now refer to as Chapter 61 and read: "The Spirit of the Lord is upon me. Because he has anointed me to preach good news to the poor. He has sent me to proclaim freedom for the prisoners and recovery of sight to the blind, to release the oppressed, to proclaim the year of the Lord's favor."[123] He then said to them: "This day this scripture is fulfilled in your hearing."[124] A little later he said: "I tell you the truth, no prophet is accepted in his home town. I assure you that there were many widows in Israel in Elijah's time, when the sky was shut for three and a half years and there was a severe famine throughout the land. Yet Elijah was not sent to any of them ... And there were many in Israel with leprosy in the time of Elisha the prophet, yet not one of them was cleansed—only Naaman the Syrian."[125] In reaction to these statements: "All the people in the synagogue were furious when they heard this. They got up, drove [Jesus] out of the town, and took him to the brow of the hill on which the town was built, in order to throw him over the cliff. But he walked right through the crowd and went on his way."[126]

With reference to the episode cited above, Luke states that it took place in the Synagogue at Nazareth. But, many questions have been raised as to whether a place called Nazareth existed at the time. If it did, it must have been a very small hamlet that could scarcely have afforded its own synagogue? Further, the nearest cliff to the traditional site of the Nazareth Synagogue is apparently two and a half miles away. It is unlikely that even the most murderous mob would have dragged Jesus that distance just to throw him over the edge, when more expeditious means of dispatching him

---

[123] Isaiah 61:1-2.

[124] Luke 4:21.

[125] Luke 4:24-27.

[126] Luke 4:28-30.

were available far closer to hand.

And if we look at the 'Nazareth' issue a little more closely we see that it is highly likely that the phrase '*Jesus of Nazareth*' is actually a bad translation of the original Greek '*Jesous o Nazoraios*'. A much better translation would be "Jesus the Nazarene", where the word "Nazarene" has no connection to a place. The 2nd century "Gospel of Philip"[127] helps to clarify this issue and offers this explanation:

> 'The apostles that came before us called him Jesus Nazarene the Christ ... "Nazara" is the "Truth". Therefore 'Nazarene' is "The One of the Truth."[128]

Polycarp of Smyrna,[129] had personally known several of Jesus' Apostles and had spoken with several other people who had known Jesus during his public mission. In fact, Polycarp had been a disciple of John the Apostle and is the author of some of our most renowned ancient Christian sources.

Apparently one of the abilities that Jesus taught his followers was how to affect material reality by focused thought. Polycarp had a great affinity with fire and he may indeed have been taught this skill by John. There was a major fire once in the city of Smyrna which had gotten completely out of control. We are told that Polycarp extinguished the fire by just focusing on it. That gets attention!

About the year 153 AD Polycarp was preaching to a large assembly, but his audience took great exception to what he was saying. As had happened with Jesus at Nazareth, Polycarp was seized and brought before the civil authorities. At length, it was decided that his punishment was to be burned alive at the stake, because he refused to curse Jesus or offer incense to the Emperor as a god. He was brought out, tied to the stake, and the wood kindling was lit around him. But though the flames grew higher and higher they never touched him inside the bonfire. "The fire made the shape of a vaulted chamber, like a ship's sail filled by the

---

[127] The only known copy was found at Nag Hammadi in Egypt in 1947.

[128] Gospel of Philip, 47.

[129] Smyrna was an ancient city situated about half way down the western coast of modern Turkey.

wind, and made a wall around the body of the martyr." (15:2).[130] Eventually, in exasperation, one of the executioners shoved a long spear through the flames and stabbed him to death.

Jesus had used his ability to repel danger on several other occasions besides the time he escaped from the murderous mob that had seized him at the synagogue. On some of these occasions the people who tried to attack him reported that they were repelled by some kind of invisible force.

After the Last Supper with his disciples Jesus had gone across the valley to the Garden of Gethsemane. The soldiers of Pilate came to arrest him. Judas had offered to identify Jesus to the Romans, for a complexity of reasons, including the hope of provoking Jesus into action against the Roman occupiers and re-establishing an independent Kingdom of Judah, in which Judas hoped to have a senior position. However, other plans were also afoot, and the Teachers of Jesus, while bound by the laws of non-interference, were still not disposed to allow him to be killed when he was so close to attaining his full mastery so they devised another plan.

Jesus was physically indistinguishable from his twin brother, Jude Thomas, so it was necessary for someone who knew him well to identify him — or deliberately mis-identify him — to the soldiers. When an individual had been pointed out to the soldiers by Judas they approached that person and he said to them: "Who is that you are looking for?" They answered: "Jesus the Nazarene." And he said to them "I am He". When he said, "I am He" they all fell to the ground.[131]

Once again, let me refer to Dorothy Sayers: she expressed the whole matter of the true reality of Jesus exceptionally well:

"I believe it to be a grave mistake to present Christianity as something charming and popular with no offense in it. Seeing that Christ went about the world giving the most violent offense to all kinds of people it would seem absurd to expect that the doctrine of His Person can be so presented as to offend nobody. We cannot blink [at] the fact that gentle Jesus meek and mild was so stiff in His opinions, and so inflammatory in His language, that He was

130 "Martyrdom of Polycarp," sections 12-16.

131 John 18:5-6.

thrown out of church, stoned, hunted from place to place, and finally gibbeted as a firebrand and a public danger. Whatever His peace was, it was not the peace of an amiable indifference; and He said in so many words that what He brought with Him was fire and the sword."[132]

We find in Luke a statement of Jesus that comes closest of all to best summing up how he was in reality: "I have come to cast fire on the Earth, and how I wish it were already ablaze!" (Luke 12:49).

Given all of this evidence, how did the image of "gentle Jesus, meek and mild" come to dominate everything else about him in the middle of the 19th century? And to this day that stamp has left its mark on us. Christianity, in claiming that the message of Jesus is actually something mild, inoffensive and loving, is missing the major part of his reality.

The real Jesus was far, far different indeed, and his intent was certainly not to come here to die for our sins, as if anyone could do that, much less without realizing the catastrophic implications for our image of God that such a notion entails. Do we realize the implications of maintaining that Jesus came here to die the most cruel and painful death imaginable in order to appease the vengeance of a savage God? To be appeased by the sacrifice of the life of an entirely innocent person would imply a God who was monstrous, warped, unjust and catastrophically insecure. As said already elsewhere, the notion of the sacrificial death of Jesus for our sins, far from being an exceedingly pious belief that is so central to much of Christianity today, is actually in essence an atheistic belief.

If we are going to remove these dis-empowering blocks in our sub-conscious this is something, above all else, that we must attend to: getting his message straight. If we get his message straight it is apparent that 'being nice' is not how we imitate what he was. Or how we aspire to accomplish the many so called 'wonders' that he did ... not wonders at all really, however extraordinary, but in reality what we might term nowadays, the exercise of a higher form of physics.

---

[132] Dorothy Leigh Sayers (1893-1957), Creed Or Chaos?: and Other Essays in Popular Theology (Methuen, 1957), p. 36.

Jesus "the Suffering Savior"

Let's look again to the notion of Jesus as a 'Suffering Savior' who is supposed to have come here to appease a God mortally offended because of our sins. As I've stated earlier, there is no way to avoid classifying this as an atheistic stance, though I'm sure most Christians would be shocked by that statement. The reason for the shock is that they have never teased out the implications of what they are affirming. From where did that program come from? What is that all about? The answer to these questions is the focus of this chapter, and the following chapters which deal with the Book of Genesis, which is from where the framework for understanding guilt and forgiveness first came.

Mel Gibson's movie "The Passion of the Christ" was a good example of what we are discussing. I went with a friend to see the movie on the night it was released. There were only about ten people in the theater, and we spent the entire night criticizing the movie. In short, we wasted our money totally ... apart from everything else. You probably remember that there wasn't a word of English spoken in the entire movie. It was in Aramaic with English language subtitles, or at least the closest we can come today to Aramaic. It was apparent from the movie that the more blood the better ... and it is equally understandable that Mel Gibson did this in order to bring home to people the enormous suffering that he believed Jesus had endured for them.

The lurid images in that movie only helped to reinforce an already major misinterpretation of Jesus' message and the enormous amount of damage it has already done in distorting human destiny and our ability to answer questions about why we are here on this Earth in the first place. This trend in spirituality is all rooted in gross misunderstandings of what Jesus was and did, and especially in the excessive emphasis placed on his suffering. Unfortunately, Mel Gibson interpreted that suffering as something voluntarily endured to make appeasement to a jealous God for our sins, whereas nothing could be further from the truth.

And as a result of this misunderstanding we've heard a lot about the redemptive value of suffering for centuries. That phrase, which comes right out of the devotional manuals, began to float around extensively in the middle of the 19th century. The message is that it is a wonderful thing to suffer in imitation of Jesus and that we should actually be looking for opportunities to suffer…so that we can make up to Jesus for all he suffered for us. In fact, there are some religious organizations in existence today that actually wear devices on their bodies to cause them physical pain. They believe that this practice is actually pleasing to both God and Jesus.

Apparently, the background to this belief is that there is some kind of personal hard drive running in God's heavenly kingdom, recording everything that each individual does. You are chalking up credits for yourself on that storage device by suffering. These credits can be harvested or cashed in when you die. So, while you are here, suffer as much as you can, because you are imitating what Jesus did. And he will be mightily impressed that you are willing to put up with so much pain for his sake. Is it any wonder that Jesus is not coming back? Once was much more than enough.

Jesus would, of course, be the most horrified of all to hear that this message was being put forward in his name. Guilt mechanisms, as you know, pursue us from the cradle to the grave. This is a huge factor in the way the message of Jesus has been distorted and it is a huge program for us to try to surmount. It is perhaps the greatest of all the distortions about Jesus with which we have been burdened by the major religions. We need to realize that accepting Jesus as our Suffering Savior is actually an atheistic belief.

Chapter 9
To What Kind of God Did Jesus Relate?

All of the twelve Apostles, the seventy-two disciples, Jesus himself, and almost all closely associated with him during his public ministry, were Jewish. Until the annihilation of Jerusalem in the year 70 under the Roman General Titus, the core of the early Christian movement was in Jerusalem, focused on James the brother of Jesus. It is not surprising, as a result, that the standard early Christian belief was that the Old Testament was a preparation for Jesus' mission and not a stand-alone collection of documents. Hence the early Christian division of sacred texts, into the "Old Testament," which became the new Christian name for the Hebrew Bible, and the "New Testament" which referred to the documents that witnessed, even at second or third hand, to Jesus' ministry, even though it took some considerable time to clarify what documents should be regarded as part of the New Testament Canon.

But is it possible to sustain a view that the Old Testament was a preparation for the ministry of Jesus? In what sense, and to what kind of God did Jesus relate? He never addressed "God" by that name throughout his teaching ministry, but always referred to him as "The Father." The modus operandi of Jesus is well summed up in this statement at the Last Supper which comes from John's Gospel.

"A new commandment I give you. Love one another. As I have loved you so you must love one another. All men will know that you are my disciples if you love one another."

This is generally taken to express the heart of the message of Jesus. But in fact it is not the core of his message, even though this 'brotherly love' as it is called, is the phenomenon by which his message is probably best known. In reality, it is a preparatory stage for what the heart of his message really was all about: "I said, 'You are "gods"; you are all sons of the Most High.' He also said: "Very truly I tell you, whoever believes in me will do the works I have been doing, and they will do even greater things than these."

In order to do those wonderful things, he taught that we would have to drop all the endless list of crippling attitudes we can have; judgment, resentment, hate, jealousy, vengeance, and spite; the list can appear to be almost endless and discouraging in its enormity. The Christian Church today condemns these attitudes and their related behavior, because they have been condemned by Jesus and others, and are now labeled "sins": for which it is assumed there will have to be a day of reckoning. But Jesus did not condemn these things because they were 'sins' that offended God, and for which we would have to pay the price eventually unless someone interceded for us. He told us to avoid these crippling attitudes for an entirely different reason that is light years away from the 'sin and forgiveness' paradigm. We need to avoid these states and attitudes because these attitudes block the fundamental flow of energy and power that permeates the whole of creation. What is that energy? He called it "Love." Not any mawkish sentimental form of love, but what was rendered in the original Greek text of the New Testament by the word "Agape."

We have no equivalent for that word in English, but it describes the energy that flows out from the Creator God and permeates the entire creation, creating a state of being. When we allow that energy to flow through us by "loving one another as I have loved you" that is what makes it possible for us to create the marvelous, which we can never do when immersed in crippling attitudes of limitation and deceiving ourselves that they are just "sins" for which we can easily get something glibly called "forgiveness," and then the problem is over. The task hasn't even begun at that stage of awareness.

What Jesus taught was much more than a way of behaving towards others, much more than being nice, or kind or compassionate, however wonderful those things undoubtedly are. It is actually a state of being. When you realize that, you begin to understand how great a gulf there is between what the Christian churches state Jesus' message to have been – sin, guilt, unworthiness, repentance, forgiveness – and what the message actually was about.

This state is engendered when you make sure you are in the flow of what God is. It allows us to accomplish the marvelous, or as we call it, the "miraculous," whereas in fact the state of "agape" is simply permitting us to access a deeper level of the physics of reality than is normally attainable. In short, it is not "miraculous" at all, but 'normal' in the context of the dimensions of a new world whose wonders we cannot even begin to imagine at first.

But a huge barrier immediately looms before us. When we look at many of the images of God which we have in the Old Testament we see sublimely portrayed in those images the very crippling attitudes which Jesus demands we give up in order to be powerful. Where does this leave us, and can the Old Testament in its entirety be really seen as a preparation for the mission of Jesus? We saw earlier a selection of texts that show the Old Testament God as behaving in ways we would regard as intrinsically immoral and which would debar such an entity from ever being regarded as the Creator. How are we supposed to wrestle with this? Did Jesus in any way, shape or form, ever relate to this kind of being?

Here is a short sample of what the Old Testament God is on record as having commanded, and which has been pointed out by many distinguished authors.

- Warfare
- Genocide
- Mutilating corpses
- Raping virgins
- Committing genocide
- Murdering innocent children
- Committing pederasty
- Selling into slavery
- Wife beating
- Thievery
- Human sacrifice

All of these can be found in the major texts of the Old Testament.

This God of the Old Testament…what kind of Being is he? Fortunately, we have a list of works that tell us how he was and is. I have already summarized the list. No one disputes this list. The Jews accept it as much as we do.

What kind of God is portrayed in these Old Testament Texts, and is this the God to whom Jesus related?

The Old Testament God

a) The Old Testament God Commands Genocide

Deuteronomy 2:32-35

"The Israelites utterly destroy the men, women, and children of Sihon."

Deuteronomy 3:6

"The Israelites utterly destroy the men, women, and children of Og."

Joshua 6:2 (Joshua 6 and Joshua 8:1 to 30)

"And the Lord said unto Joshua, See, I have given into thine hand Jericho, and the king thereof, (and) the mighty men of valor."

Joshua 6:21

"And they utterly destroyed all that was in the city, both man and woman, young and old, and ox, and sheep, and ass, with the edge of the sword."

b) The Old Testament God Does Not Believe in Showing Mercy

Deuteronomy 7:2

"And when the LORD thy God shall deliver them before thee; thou shalt smite them, and utterly destroy them; thou shalt make no covenant with them, nor shew mercy unto them."

Deuteronomy 20:13-14,16

"When the LORD your God delivers it into your hand, put to the sword all the men in it.

[14]As for the women, the children, the livestock and everything else in the city, you may take these as plunder for yourselves. And you may use the plunder the LORD your God gives you from your enemies. [16]However, in the cities of the nations the LORD your God is giving you as an inheritance, do not leave alive anything that breathes."

Judges 18:27

"Then they took what Micah had made, and his priest, and went on to Laish, against a peaceful and unsuspecting people. They attacked them with the sword and burned down their city."

c) The Old Testament God Does Not Believe in Morality

Numbers 31:17

"Now therefore kill every male among the little ones, and kill every woman that hath known man by lying with him.18. But all the women children, that have not known a man by lying with him, keep alive for yourselves."

This is exactly what it sounds like – kill everyone except the virgin girls....

d) The Old Testament God Demands Human Sacrifice

Numbers 31:31-40

Note that amongst the plunder are 32,000 virgins. Read verse 40 carefully to figure out that they seemed to have sacrificed 32 of these to the Lord.

Judges 21:11-12

"This is what you are to do," they said. "Kill every male and every woman who is not a virgin."

They found among the people living in Jabesh Gilead four hundred young women who had never slept with a man, and they took them to the camp at Shiloh in Canaan."

Judges 21:14-23

The 400 virgins captured above prove to be insufficient, so the Benjaminites hide in the vineyards and kidnap "the daughters of Shiloh" as they come out to dance and celebrate.

In the Book of Judges 19:22-29 we find more of this type of behavior. A group of sexually depraved men beat on the door of an old man's house demanding that he turn over to them a male house guest. Instead, the old man offered his virgin daughter (this was before woman's liberation) and his guest's concubine (or wife). *"Behold, he said, here are my virgin daughter and his concubine: let me bring them out now. Ravish them and do with them what seems good to you; but against this man* (the guest) *do not do so vile a thing"*. The man's concubine was ravished and dies. The man then cuts her body into twelve pieces and sends one piece to each of the twelve tribes of Israel.

e) The Old Testament God Apparently Believes in the Mutilation of Corpses

When David married the daughter of King Saul, the King asked for 100 foreskins of dead Philistines; David brought him 200 as a dowry (1Samuel 18:25-27).

Joshua 5:2-3

"At that time the Lord said to Joshua, "Make flint knives and circumcise the Israelites again. So Joshua made sharp knives, and circumcised the children of Israel at the hill of the foreskins."

f) The Old Testament God Believes in Slavery

Joel 3:8

"And I will sell your sons and your daughters into the hand of the children of Judah, and they shall sell them to the Sabeans, to a people far off: for the LORD hath spoken."

g) The Old Testament God Is Bloodthirsty

Deut. 32: 39-42

"I put to death ... I have wounded, I will render vengeance to mine adversaries and repay those who hate me. I will make my arrows drunk with blood, and my sword shall devour flesh."

h) The Old Testament God Is a Vengeful Child Murderer

Psalm 137: 9

"Happy is he who repays you for what you have done to us – he who seizes your infants and dashes them against the rocks."

i) The Old Testament God Threatens to Cause Cannibalism As a Punishment for Disobeying Him

Leviticus 26:27-29

"If in spite of all this you still do not listen to me I myself will punish you for your sins seven times over. You shall eat the flesh of your sons and the flesh of your daughters."

These descriptions of the immorality of a being passing himself off as the Creator God, are not taken from marginal, doubtful or suspect sources; they are taken from the very heart of the Old Testament narratives that are still as revered today as they ever were in history. Is it not inconceivable that this being was the God to whom Jesus related?

A Survival of Sexism into the New Testament?

If we take a look at the New Testament there are certain things in the writings of Paul that deserve a second look, just in case you think the entire New Testament is exempt from all of the matters listed in the previous section. We'll take a glance at what the writings of Paul have to say about Sexism.

1 Corinthians was written by Saint Paul. It was one of the books he did write as opposed to the six or seven books in the New Testament that were forged in his name.

1 Corinthians 11:7-9 7

> "A man ought not to cover his head, since he is the image and glory of God: but the woman is the glory of man." [8]"For man did not come from woman, but woman from man." [9]"neither was man created for woman, but woman for man."

And moving on to Chapter 14: 34

> "Woman should remain silent in the churches. They are not allowed to speak, but must be in submission, as the Law says. 35 "If they want to inquire about something, they should ask their own husbands at home; for it is disgraceful for a woman to speak in the church".

Can you imagine the situation that some enlightened beings would be contemplating when this state of affairs had been going on for hundreds of years? Would some move be made by them to try to bring it to an end...and to advance the human race into a more enlightened and empowering way of believing and living?

That was why the mission of Jesus occurred. As a result of his mission and message, we are rebuilding better programs here now, which was what he himself did during his public ministry of less than three years in ancient Israel. This is not pleasant material to be rehearsing. But if we are going to address those crippling programs we've got to start to re-build from the ground up. If we want to be successful in this endeavor we need to see how these ideas originated, what the background was, and to understand as a result at what the message of Jesus was really aimed.

Two Names for God in Genesis: What Does This Imply?

If we look at the Hebrew original text of the opening chapters of Genesis we will notice something of great significance.

Genesis 1:1 launches with the well-known phrases, "In the beginning God created the heavens and the Earth. Now the Earth was formless and void, and darkness was over the surface of the deep, and the Spirit of God was hovering over the waters." The account ends at Genesis 2:1. "Thus the heavens and the Earth were completed in all their vast array." All is completed, the process is at an end.

But in Genesis 2:4 apparently a second account of the creation begins all over again:

> "This is the account of the heavens and the Earth when they were created. When the Lord God made the Earth and the heavens, no shrub of the field had yet appeared on the Earth...."

The two accounts are very decidedly different. The Genesis 1 story is written in poetic meter, and was probably intended to be sung as a chant. The Genesis 2 version is a prose work.

The language of the Genesis 1 account is lofty and sublime and aimed at conveying the majesty and order of God and the creation. In Genesis 2:4 and following we leave behind the majesty of the heavens where a disembodied Spirit of God broods over the waters and creates effortlessly. By contrast in Genesis 2:4 ff. God is working with the soil of a garden and builds the first man from the mud.

In the Genesis 1 account God creates many men and women simply by uttering the word. In the Genesis 2 account God carves a single human being from the mud, and then takes a rib from the man and fashions a companion for the man from the rib. But God does not breathe his essence into the female companion; he did that only for the man.

The down to earth God of the Genesis 2 account is very different from the transcendent deity of the Genesis 1 account. In Genesis 2 God gets tired and needs rest. He needs help from Adam to tend the garden which he has created by planting, not by speaking a creative word. He waits till the sun goes down to walk in the evening, presumably so as to avoid the heat. He doesn't know where Adam and Eve are hiding, so he has to call out to find them.

In the Epic of Gilgamesh and also in some of the other ancient Mesopotamian creation stories, several of the foundational images used by the Genesis 1 account are found, more than a thousand years before Genesis was written. Both in ancient Egyptian and Mesopotamian sources the original state of the cosmos is pictured as a disordered, watery place; the same imagery as used in Genesis 1.

In fact, a very sound case has been made that the ancient background of the Genesis narratives is far more likely to be Egyptian rather than Babylonian, reflecting the influence of the ancient Egyptian creation accounts as contained in the Pyramid Texts, the Coffin Texts, The Book of the Dead, The Memphite Theology, the Wisdom texts and various hymns.

But despite this background the Genesis texts often take up a stance against the Egyptian sources from which they borrow. For example, God's creation of light on day one, before the creation of the sun and moon on day four, is often pointed out as an absurdity. However, this sequence takes on a different appearance if we see it instead as an incisive and profound argument against the position of Atum-Re, the sun god. This seems to be intended to show that the source of light does not originate with the sun or the moon (i.e. Re, the sun-god or Thoth, the moon-god), but with the Hebrew God, who exists separately from both the light and the creation.

What is even more interesting is the names of God used in these creation stories. Chapter 1 uses "Elohim" which despite all claims of the use of plurals of majesty, is a plural form on the word "El" or "Powerful One," certainly an odd choice for a people so insistent on the reality of only one God. The second name for God, used in Chapters 2 and 3, is: "Yahweh Elohim" (Never 'Elohim' on its own).

In the English language we have only one name for describing God in himself, so we will not notice this double name in an English translation.

Are the Hebrews talking of two Gods, who have very different perspectives on creation, as we can see in the two creation stories, (Genesis 1-2:4a and 2:4b-25)? Was one of these the God who committed all those atrocities we looked at a short time ago? Was the other God one more in keeping with how Jesus seemed to envisage a loving Deity? Or is there a more simple solution?

In 1878, the German Old Testament scholar Julius Wellhausen published his "Prolegomena to the History of Israel," which is reckoned to be the most significant book in Old Testament scholarship in the modern era. It became the starting point for most of the scholarly work that followed in that field. Wellhausen noticed sections in Genesis, and in the Pentateuch in general, that showed similar characteristics, and eventually he postulated that these groupings of text found in Genesis were originally independent documents that were combined together about the middle of the 5th Century BC, after the Jews were able to return home from their Exile in Babylon. The redactor who produced the Book of Genesis laid the two creation accounts side by side, in the first two chapters of Genesis, or alternatively he tried to weave the two accounts together, as he did with the Genesis Flood story (chapters 6-9).

This line of investigation began to shed light on some very interesting features in Genesis. Since it is the paradigm about how things became as woven by Genesis, that determines the way we understand what the mission of Jesus is all about, (Creation, Fall, Redemption) it is worthwhile taking a closer look at these narratives and from where they may have come.

All the significant accounts in the Old Testament, which were formerly considered to be original and unique to the Hebrew Bible, the creation of humanity, the creation of the Earth, the Great Flood, the destruction of humanity, and the Tower of Babel, are all found in these ancient collections that antedate Genesis by many centuries.

It is also worth remembering that the general belief in Christianity, up to the high Middle Ages, was that there was a single author for the Torah, or Pentateuch, the first five books of the Christian Old Testament, and further that that single author was Moses, even though the death of Moses is chronicled in Deuteronomy 34!

Several texts in the New Testament affirm that belief. See for instance, Mark 10:3, Luke 24:27, and John 1:17.

But the bigger question is not whether Moses wrote the Pentateuch, for it is obvious there was no single author at all.

A Further Look at the Dependence of Genesis on Earlier Sources

In more recent times the influence of the ancient Egyptian cosmologies has been emphasized more than the Mesopotamian cosmologies. The Egyptian cosmologies are found mainly in the Pyramid Texts from Heliopolis, the Shabaka Stone from Memphis, and the ethos of the cosmogony of the Ogdoad from Hermopolis.

The Egyptian sources describe the primordial state in the same way as the Genesis 1 account, and the means by which the Egyptian creator gods accomplished their goals is also the same as that narrated in Genesis. As with the two contradictory accounts of the creation in Genesis, the ancient Egyptians also seemed comfortable holding two contradictory views of the emergence of the creation.

The great works of literature of ancient Mesopotamia were completely unknown in the West until the middle of the 19th century of our era: The Epic of Ziusudra, the Epic of Gilgamesh, the Epic of Athrahasis, the Enuma Elish, the Descent of Innana and the Myth of Etana. They were written in cuneiform, which began to be deciphered in the first half of the 19th Century by brilliant scholars such as George Smith and Henry Rawlinson. The major find occurred in 1846 when the Library of Ashurbanipal was discovered at Nineveh. It was calculated recently that the total number of clay tablets from Sumer that have been recovered is now over one million.

There are six ancient near-Eastern Flood myths. To take just one prime example, the story of the Flood in Genesis, (a mere three chapters), and the Flood story from "The Epic of Gilgamesh," have twenty major points in common. The only realistic explanation has to be one of the following:

- Genesis was copied from Gilgamesh and the Egyptian texts.
- Gilgamesh and the Egyptian texts were copied from Genesis.
- They were all copied from an earlier source.

For obvious reasons, the first option is the most likely, but the possibility came as a great shock to religious authorities who had believed that the Biblical accounts had been dictated by God directly, and who in some cases believed that the entire Pentateuch had been written down by Moses personally. (Despite the fact that his death is described there).

Many of the 'gods' in these accounts are named, and the accounts tell how they helped the humans learn about agriculture, about the care of agricultural animals, about astronomy, the creation of calendars, and the science of irrigation. The Sumerian rulers never claimed to be discoverers of this knowledge themselves, instead attributing it to their Gods, the Anunnaki, meaning "Those who from Heaven to Earth Came."

Did the Hebrews Really Believe in One God?

While in general terms all throughout, the Hebrew Bible seems monotheistic, nevertheless there is evidence that the people of

Israel as a whole were not monotheists before they were taken into exile in Babylon in the 6th Century BC. The Bible itself tells us that many of the people chose to worship idols and foreign gods instead of the God of the Bible. In the 8th Century BC the monotheistic worship of the God of the Bible was in competition with several other cults that were not monotheistic. In fact, some have asserted that their religion at that early period consisted of the recognition of many gods, but with the regular worship of only one divinity. It's been pointed out that even the First Commandment may reflect such a belief system: "Thou shalt have no other gods before me." The oldest books of the Bible such as the Book of Hosea and the Book of Nahum, portray a similar situation, probably from the 7th Century BC, where the people of Israel are upbraided for their worship of many gods.

There are also instances in the Old Testament where "Élohim" the name used for God in the opening verse of Genesis, refers to deities that are not related to Israel.

It has also been suggested that angels are what became of the false gods once monotheism became established in Israel.

These are intriguing points for us to ponder on our journey to discover the real Jesus and his real message.

Intriguing Evidence Relating to the First Verse of Genesis

An "Acrostic" is defined by Merriam-Webster as "a composition usually in verse, in which sets of letters (as the initial or final letters of the lines) taken in order form a word or phrase or a regular sequence of letters of the alphabet." One of the best known acrostics in history was made in Greek for the proclamation), "JESUS CHRIST, SON OF GOD, SAVIOUR." The initials spell ἰχθύς (ICHTHYS), which means "fish" in Greek, and it inspired the familiar symbol of the fish, often used on business cards and bumper stickers today to proclaim allegiance to the message of Jesus. In early Christian times Christians are said to have used the symbol as a code to identify friends, or to mark meeting places in a confidential manner. A Christian meeting a stranger, who might be Christian, would draw one side of the fish symbol in the dust. If the stranger were a Christian then he or she would complete the symbol.

The sentence "Jesus Christ, Son of God, Savior," (in Greek: "Ιησοῦς Χριστός, Θεοῦ Υἱός, Σωτήρ") has the same number of letters as the first verse of Genesis in Hebrew.[133] Acrostics were beloved in ancient Hebrew writing, being used extensively in the Books of Psalms, Proverbs and Lamentations (Lamentations is a complete acrostic poem, the verses of which begin with successive letters of the Hebrew alphabet).

In an echo of acrostic there was a convention in the Hebrew tradition that in writing about fundamental matters, such as Genesis is doing preeminently, the first letter of a book dealing with origins ought to be the first letter of the alphabet. But Genesis does not begin with the first letter: it begins with the second letter of the Hebrew alphabet.

However, if we add in the first letter of the Hebrew alphabet, which I am suggesting ought to be there, (or, more suspiciously, may have been there originally), what happens then? Something remarkable. The entire meaning of the first verse is altered: "In the beginning God created the Heavens and the Earth," now changes to "The Father of the Beginnings created the Elohim, the Heavens and the Earth."

Efforts down through history are legion to explain why the Hebrews, almost fanatical believers in monotheism, used a plural word for "God." Maybe they didn't originally? Maybe the replacement of this acrostic beginning letter reveals the truth of what actually happened?

Recently Professor Ellen van Wolde, a respected Old Testament scholar and author at Radboud University in The Netherlands, claims that the traditional view of God as the Creator is untenable, and that the English translation of the first sentence of Genesis "in the beginning God created the Heaven and the Earth" is not a correct translation of the Hebrew.

---

133 בראשית ברא אלהים את השמים ואת הארץ

She maintains that the Hebrew verb "bara", which is used in the first sentence of the book of Genesis, does not mean "to create" but to "spatially separate".

She states that Genesis says that "God did create the humans and the animals, but not the Earth itself." In conclusion, she maintains that the text of Genesis does not say that God created, but that he "separated: the Earth from the Heaven, the land from the sea, the sea monsters from the birds and the swarming at the ground.

Most significantly of all, she states in her thesis that the new translation fits in with the approach of ancient Sumerian texts with regard to the creation.

The Name "Jehovah"

Who was the Creator God if he was not the God of the Hebrew Bible? We are up against a major problem. While there is nothing in the Torah to outlaw the speaking of the name of God, nevertheless modern Jews never pronounce it, but instead say "Adonai."

The term "Jehovah" for God's name only came into the English language with the translation of the Bible by William Tyndale in 1537.

The tetragrammaton[134] – YHWH – is how God's name appears in the Hebrew Bible. Written Hebrew originally possessed no written vowel signs, though obviously, the vowels would have been pronounced in reading. Long after the Jews returned from the Exile in Babylon, by about the 3rd Century BC, and with a dramatic rise in the superstitious fear of God in Jewish religion at the time, the Divine Name became forbidden to pronounce, not because it was forbidden in itself to pronounce it, but for fear of the punishment from God that would follow for mis-pronouncing it. What does even this small detail this tell us about this entity as God, and was this entity the God of Jesus?

---

[134] Literally meaning "having four letters."

The name of God that was permitted to be spoken in Jewish tradition was "Adonai," which means "Lord." Because the pronouncement of the name was forbidden, and only the consonants were written, after a time nobody knew how the name should be pronounced. When the Masoretic scribes produced their text of the Hebrew Bible in the 9th and 10th Centuries, they inserted vowels into the Biblical text for the first time. The vowels were written below the consonants. Of course, the Masoretics did not know the proper pronunciation of God's name either, nor did they believe it should be pronounced, but they inserted some vowels into the tetragrammaton. However, the vowels they inserted were the vowels of the word "Adonai." The purpose of these vowels was to prompt the reader to say "Adonai" when they came to God's name, instead of pronouncing God's real name.

In the time of the Renaissance the Ancient Languages became very popular, including the Hebrew text of the Old Testament. But when the Renaissance people came to the tetragrammaton in the Biblical text they pronounced it with the vowels the Masoretic scribes had inserted a few centuries before, not realizing that these vowels did not belong to the tetragrammaton itself but were just a prompt to say "Adonai." Consequently, in the Renaissance period they began to pronounce God's name as "Yehowah," but obviously there never was such a name.

When Tyndall produced his English language Bible in 1537 he transliterated the tetragrammaton into English using the Masoretic vowels. This was how the name "Yehovah" for God first appeared in the English language. The switch to an initial "J" did not emerge until the late 17th Century, and it is only since that date that the name for God in English tends to be pronounced "Jehovah."

Whatever way we pronounce his name, who was this being?

Chapter 10
The Book of Genesis Gave Us Our Traditional Paradigm of Reality

As pointed out earlier, we didn't get this Parable of the Serpent, the Tree and the Fruit, from those Hebrews in exile in Mesopotamia who put the Book of Genesis together as far back as the seventh and sixth centuries BC. That parable is far, far, more ancient than the times of Genesis, and very few are even aware of that.

However, where this famous parable about the origins of the creation came from is not our major issue here, but rather the way in which the text of Genesis is normally divided. In fact, it is clear to anyone who cares to investigate with an open mind that the traditional way in which this opening part of Genesis is divided into chapters and verses significantly distorts and obscures what the authors intended to say.

Since the meaning and significance of Jesus and his message are usually understood against the pattern of what the first few chapters of Genesis attempt to tell us, a misunderstanding of these chapters will inevitably compromise a correct understanding of Jesus and his mission as well. Since these misunderstandings of Jesus now constitute for us a set of crippling unconscious programs this investigation we are engaged in here is not an abstract academic issue relevant only to the remote past, but a crucial element in dealing with our present spiritually and physically dis-empowered state.

The Problems Caused by Early Writing Techniques

The earliest writing systems only used consonants. For example, the sentence "The Bible is a collection of books" would read "Thbblscllctnfbks." In those writing systems obviously some form of designation of where words began and ended was crucial in trying to deciper what was written Sometimes a vertical line was used to separate words, sometimes a single, double or triple dot, called "interpunkts" were used.

When the Greeks started using vowels it became easier to recognize where words began and ended, but at more or less the same time, the designation by some sign in the text of where words began and ended, fell into disuse. This was the practice in vogue when the New Testament was written in "koine" or street Greek.

Thus, the opening sentence of St. John's Gospel in its original form "In the beginning was the Word and the Word was with God." would have appeared like this in its original form, (if we use the Latin alphabet to illustrate it instead of the Greek alphabet):

"Inthebeginningwasthewordandthewordwaswithgod."

The Irish monks in the seventh century began to separate words by using blank spaces between them. They introduced this commonsense practice into Europe, and by the eighth or ninth centuries it had become the general usage everywhere across the continent.

We know from the earliest surviving manuscripts of the Hebrew Bible that those works did have some form of division in them originally, but they did not have any division into numbered sections or any alphabetical sequence. In short, the books of the Bible were not divided into chapters or verses when they were written. To facilitate ease of reference these chapter divisions were inserted for the first time only around 1227 AD by Cardinal Stephen Langton, Archbishop of Canterbury at the time of King John of Magna Carta fame. In short, the chapter divisions in the book of Genesis were inserted for the first time nearly two thousand years after the book was compiled. With regard to the first chapter of Genesis, in particular, we have to assert that the job was very badly done which is a very serious matter, because inserting chapter divisions, or even verse divisions, into the Biblical text, is of course a perilous process, because inserting a division in the wrong place can change the intended meaning.

The division of the chapters of the Bible into verses came later still with Robert Estienne (Robert Stephanus). His verse numbers entered printed editions of the Bible, in 1551 for the New Testament, and in 1571 for the Hebrew Bible.

A group of Jewish Scholars called the Masoretes produced a definitive text of the Hebrew Bible, called the Masoretic text, probably in the 10-11th Centuries AD, with the main purpose of removing inaccuracies that had crept into the texts, mainly during the Jewish Captivity in Babylon, a thousand to fifteen hundred years before. In the Masoretic text the Old Testament was divided into verses; however, the verses were not numbered. The verses were marked by the soph pasuq, which is a double point (:). In 1448 AD the Hebrew Old Testament was divided into verses by a Jewish Rabbi, Isaac Nathan ben Kalonymus, largely following the chapter divisions of Cardinal Langton.

Rabbi Nathan numbered the soph pasuq markings of the Masoretic text to give us the familiar Old Testament verse numberings we still use today. Over a century later, in 1528, a Dominican Scholar, Santes Pagnino, also inserted a somewhat different set of verse markers into the Old Testament.

The second phase took place in 1551 when the renowned French printer, Robert Stephens, (also known as Robert Estienne, or Stephanus), published his Greek edition of the New Testament, inserting verse numberings or markings into the New Testament for the first time.

It has been rather unkindly stated that Robert Stephens inserted the verse markings into the Biblical text while in his carriage, on the way to and from his printing works. (His work certainly bears all the signs of it!). However, the more likely story comes from his son Henri, who tells us that his father put in the verse numbers in 1551 during a journey "by horse" from Paris to Lyon – a distance of about 280 miles.

Scholars point out that the chapter and verse divisions are often incoherent, confusing and inappropriate, and that they can enable the quotation of passages out of context. They are therefore best understood as a system of technical references that enable us to quickly locate a precise section of the Scriptures. However, they do not assist in the correct interpretation of particular texts and sections of the Biblical books, and in fact often make that task difficult and confusing. This is particularly true of the early part of Genesis.

But it goes beyond that, for if in fact chapter and verse divisions are inserted into the wrong places in the Biblical text they can radically alter the meaning that the ancient authors intended to convey. There are many places in the traditional Biblical text where it is obvious that this has happened.

An often-quoted example is John 9:1-7.

> [1]"Now as he passed by, he saw a man who was blind
> from birth. [2]And his disciples asked him, saying, "Rabbi,
> who sinned, this man or his parents, that he was born
> blind?" [3]Jesus answered, "Neither this man nor his parents
> sinned, but that the works of God should be revealed in
> him. [4]"We must work the works of Him who sent me while
> it is day; the night is coming when no one can work."

This customary division of verse 3, that I've adhered to in the paragraph above, indicates the man was not blind because of any sin his parents committed, nor because of any sin he had committed himself before he was born (an interesting revelation that Jesus' disciples believed in reincarnation). But it seems to imply, aided by the efforts of innumerable preachers down the ages who have taken this interpretation, that God caused this person the suffering and misfortune of being born blind so that Jesus could work a miracle and heal him. It's obvious that this interpretation would raise very serious questions about the moral character of God.

So, let's take verse 3 and divide up the text differently. Put a full stop and end the sentence after "Neither this man or his parents sinned."

Then join the remainder of verse 3 to verse 4.

We now get:

> "But that the works of God should be revealed in him, we must work the works of Him who sent me while it is day."

Now with this simple change, only one of punctuation, there is no longer any implication that God sadistically caused the blind man this life-long suffering so that Jesus could create a stir by healing him. Rather the text asserts that marvelous accomplishments of healing can be enacted by those who follow Jesus' teachings. The disciples' question shows they were more interested in what sin was being punished by God than in the process, or the "how," of his healing by Jesus.

This shows that even dividing the text into wrong sentences can seriously alter meaning for the worst, as we see in that example.

However, that is nothing to the level of misunderstanding that can happen when whole chapter divisions are made in the wrong place. As already mentioned, the traditional way in which this opening part of Genesis is divided into chapters radically distorts and obscures what the ancient authors intended to say.

This is tragic because these texts of Genesis greatly illuminate what the mission of Jesus Christ really was.

As already stated, Cardinal Stephen Langton, Archbishop of Canterbury, is credited with devising the chapter divisions of the Bible that we accept today. The dispute between King John and the Pope over his election is what reputedly led to Magna Carta. If we adopt a different division of these early texts of Genesis than the one adopted by Cardinal Langton, it is not difficult to see what the authors of Genesis intended to convey. It is not at all what we normally understood. And if Cardinal Langton and that French printer Robert Stephens, had only noticed this we might have been saved major misunderstandings and distortions of the mission of Jesus that were based on incorrect divisions of the textual material in Genesis!

Let us look at the first three chapters of Genesis to detect what the profound issues were that faced those people twenty five or six centuries ago, and see how they went about resolving them. The texts can speak for themselves.

We Draw Our Major Paradigm of a Fallen World from the Genesis Creation Narratives

Let us take a closer look at Genesis 2.4 to Genesis 3:1-24.

The first two chapters of Genesis were constructed over the period from about the seventh to the fifth centuries BC, when the Jews were in exile, by amalgamating two already existing, but very different, stories of creation. One account is known as the Priestly text, Genesis 1:1-2:3. The other account, older probably by as much as three centuries, is called the Yahwistic account, which makes up our present-day Genesis 2:4-2:24.

The Yahwist creation story emphasizes that God is involved in all of humanity's day-to-day affairs, but in the Priestly story the opposite is true, God is transcendent and not very involved with the doings of the human race. In the Yahwist account humans are told to serve the Earth, but in the Priestly account they are supposed to subdue it.

If we look with a fair and objective mind at the text that came from a combination of these somewhat conflicting creation stories, it appears the authors of Genesis had another and bigger problem, trying to balance and reconcile what I will describe here as "Three Fundamental Convictions."

1. God is Good.
2. God is All-Powerful and Created the World.
3. The World is a Mixture of Good and Evil.

These three convictions cannot be held together because of one very obvious problem. A being who is all-goodness and all-powerful, could not have created a world, (at least as we understand "creating the world"), with as much suffering, evil and imperfection as this world has, and apparently always has had.

So let's see if we can go about resolving this dilemma. It looks like we have three options to choose from in trying to reconcile these three basic convictions that were obviously a problem for the redactors of Genesis. In these three options we will deny each of these three basic convictions in turn and see what the consequences would be.

OPTION ONE

1.	God is Good	Yes
2.	God is All-Powerful and Created the World	Yes
3.	The World is a Mixture of Good and Evil	NO

In short, if God is good, and also the Creator, how come there is so much undeniable evil, suffering and imperfection in the world? In our first option here, to get out of our dilemma, the world would have to be in a state of perfection, which it very obviously is not. We can't square a good God with this kind of "creation", so we have to reject number 3.

So let's go to Option Two: if God were NOT the creator of the world, then that would solve our dilemma.

OPTION TWO

1.	God is Good	Yes
2.	God Created the World	NO
3.	The World is a Mixture of Good and Evil	Yes

If God were not good, then it would be understandable that he might have created a world like the one we have.

All religious traditions have acknowledged the colossal amount of imperfection there is in the world. Earthly life is filled with suffering. It is alarming to realize that almost all species on Earth (with the exception of some creatures like the bees) can only live by killing something else. So most forms of life must consume each other in order to live. There is obviously something radically wrong with this situation.

Genesis, as we will see shortly, tries to blame this very obviously 'fallen' state of the world on the first humans, but some thinkers like the Gnostics said it was impossible to escape the view that the fault was God's.

To escape that blasphemous position, they suggested the cosmos was not created by God, but by some major being inferior to God. This being they called the "Demiurge," literally a cosmic craftsman or artisan who was responsible for the creation and maintenance of the physical universe. Given the kind of universe he produced the Demiurge must not be loving kind, or benevolent.

So if God is all powerful but <u>not</u> all loving, and did create the world, then our dilemma about evil and suffering in the world is resolved. This would be Option Three.

OPTION THREE

1.	God is Good	NO
2.	God Created the World	Yes
3.	The World is a Mixture of Good and Evil	Yes

But belief in a malign and vindictive creator is not an attractive belief system for us, and certainly was not acceptable to the authors of Genesis; they, just like us, still wanted to believe that universe comes from God. It was just as repugnant to them, as it would be to us, to accept that the Creator of the Universe, is not good, benign and loving.

If we want to maintain the belief that God is the Creator, and not some malign Demiurge, what are our options? How do we escape from this dilemma? This was exactly the major puzzle that faced the authors of Genesis, (and indeed faces all of us, even today). In trying to resolve this difficulty unfortunately they adopted a paradigm of how the state of affairs was at the beginning that was a gross misunderstanding. In the Christian period the mission and work of Jesus was interpreted within the framework of that misunderstood paradigm, which has made it impossible to properly understand what the work and mission of Jesus was really about. In fact, it helped to put in place these misunderstandings of his mission that for so long, paradoxically has kept the human race in the state of dis-empowerment which he had come to remove.

In short, the picture of the beginnings adopted by Genesis, as it is normally interpreted in the history of Christianity, is not what the authors of Genesis intended. They were putting in place a paradigm of a very different kind into which a proper understanding of the mission of Jesus would fit perfectly. It behooves us to lay out what that paradigm really was.

For more clarity we can now lay out the issues in chart form and divide up those early chapters of Genesis, as the authors themselves would have done, but not as Cardinal Stephen Langton did, for it is obvious he never really grasped what the early chapters of Genesis were about. We can look at the evidence now with an open mind and see how the authors of Genesis laid out their material in order to convey a profound message, which has largely escaped their readers for a very long time. This is what they would have done, had they been dividing up their text into chapters, which as pointed out earlier, did not happen for the best part of 2,000 years after Genesis was assembled.

As mentioned at the very start of this book, much of the actions of our mind belong in the realm of the unconscious, and it is there where all our programs operate, including the ones dis-empowering us spiritually, and most of those have to do with profound misunderstandings of Jesus and his mission. To remove these programs, as described at the beginning of this book, the only effective method is to re-build those programs from the ground up, by going back to where they originated. In that way we can see where the mistakes in interpretation were made about the significance of Jesus and his mission, and the historic molds and matrices into what he taught and did were constrained, so as to give them an utterly alien form from what he intended.

What was that? To see him against the traditional mis-interpretation of Genesis 2 and 3, as a Suffering Savior who came to undo the evil effects which the sinful actions of Adam and Eve had wrought on God's creation. The immediate effect of that misinterpretation of Genesis chapters 2 and 3, was to dis-empower both Jesus and all of us, instead of aiming at the goal he set out as the heart of his mission: how we should create reality, "Believe it is already yours and it shall be so," and to realize "You are all gods." This is really a very long way indeed from the Suffering Savior syndrome that has bedeviled Christianity for so long and left us all in a state of guilt, unworthiness, powerlessness and fear. The advice in some Christian circles today that this is the state that we should constantly keep in focus in order to be "saved" by Jesus, fundamentally undermines almost all of what Jesus really came to do and teach.

A Look at the Real Message of the Creation Narratives in Genesis, Chapters 2 and 3

It is not difficult to see that Genesis 2: 4-25 was intended as a unit by the individuals who assembled it. Cardinal Langton obviously did not spot that. If so, he might have made that section a chapter. If divisions are made in the wrong places they can completely change the messages of the ancient authors. One of the first examples is the first account of Genesis. The first account ends at Genesis 2:4a, not 1:31. By inserting the chapter break at 1:31 Cardinal Langton chopped off the ending of the account, the Seventh Day, and attached it to the second account. Why did he separate the last day of creation from the other six days? How does the chapter break affect the message and divide these texts differently than what the traditional division into chapters and verses has given us?

The authors of Genesis, in these twenty-one verses of Chapter 2, look at six sets of fundamental relationships that human beings have, ranging from their relationship to God, to the relationship between man and woman, right on down to the relationship with our work, and the relationship we have with life itself. Let us look at each relationship and the state in which that relationship happens to be.

Section One: Genesis 2.4-25

RELATIONSHIP	STATE OF THE RELATIONSHIP
God	Walking with God in the cool of the evening
Woman	Man and woman, two in one flesh: perfect equality
Animals	Named by the humans – indicates domination over them
Earth	Abundant fertility, 4 rivers for irrigation in Mesopotamia
Work	Very easy, looking after a garden
Life	They have eternal life

All six major relationships that humanity has, as described here, are in an ideal condition. Their relationship with God is obviously in a perfect state. The man and woman are walking with God in the cool of the evening – an image drawn from a custom in the ancient near East and which is still practised there even today in more remote areas. When the sun goes down and the temperature cools, the citizens of the town walk, often arm in arm, up and down the main thoroughfare, and relish being seen walking with the rich and powerful. Adam and Eve, in Genesis Chapter 2, in our own phrase "have it made."

The other relationships described are in an ideal state as well. The relationship between the man and woman is that of "two in one flesh." Unlike how that phrase of Genesis is often used in the marriage ceremony today, the primary purpose of that statement is not to signify that man and woman are united in some kind of indissoluble bond based on absolute identity, but to assert that they are of equal substance to each other. In short, absolute equality is the basis of their relationship. There is no superiority or inferiority between man and woman.

The animals are subject to the man and woman and are in harmony with them. That is conveyed by the man giving them their names. Work is easy, looking after a garden, and the earth is unimaginably fertile, conveyed by the image of the four rivers flowing in the one garden. The greatest boon of all is that they have the gift of eternal life in the human body.

Section two, Genesis 3: 8-24 was also obviously written as a unit, though Cardinal Langton did not spot that either.

We see that the same relationships as in Chapter 2 are also looked at in Chapter 3, except this time the same relationships are far indeed from being in an ideal state. Everything is in chaos and disorder.

Section Two: Genesis 3. 8-24

RELATIONSHIP	STATE
God	man and woman are hiding from God, naked.
Woman	is drawn to the man and is subjected to him.
Animals	The serpent now superior to the humans.
Earth	Is a cursed ground
Work	Is painful toil, "in the sweat of your brow you shall eat bread"
Life	Death – "dust you are and unto dust you shall return."

A seventh element is added: childbirth in pain. Since everlasting life is no longer a reality, the human race has to be replaced by new beings.

Childbirth: "...with pain you will give birth."

How did this happen? How did the glorious state of Chapter 2 become replaced by the misery of the state described in Chapter 3, the state we are all so familiar with today?

To help us with this, let us now look at the intervening portion of the text as divided by Cardinal Langton.

Section three, Chapter 3: 1-7, tries to explain how this catastrophe happened, within the framework of those three sets of options outlined earlier.

Section Three: Genesis 3: 1-7
The Explanation

God forbids them to eat of the fruit of the Tree of Knowledge of Good and Evil.

- A Serpent tempts them with a fruit of that tree (not an apple).
- He promises, if you eat this "You will not die" but will be like God.
- The woman desirous of gaining knowledge ate the fruit.
- She gave the fruit to her husband who ate it also

Their eyes were opened; they saw they were naked, and they lost in that moment all the glories of the Paradise State that were so beautifully described in the set of six perfect relationships described in Chapter 2.

So the humans wrecked God's creation. God is thus off the hook for creating an evil and imperfect world!

This is the option the authors of Genesis chose to resolve the dilemma of how a good and loving God could make a world like this. They felt compelled to say God made the world, but had to state that when God made the world it was in a perfect state. They could not say he made it as it now is, for then the charge of being evil and vindictive, like the Gnostic Demiurge, might attach to God. The 'blame' for the state of this world as we know it had to be placed somewhere else.

It was due to the disobedience of the first couple that matters were ruined. This was the solution to the dilemma which Genesis came up with.

But unfortunately, in this effort to explain things, the image of God has nevertheless suffered greatly, because he is portrayed as some kind of despot who is pleased as long as you obey, but takes away everything as a punishment if you do not. To get out of their dilemma the authors of Genesis chose to say the world was created in perfection but the humans ruined it. This is why the Gnostics were more realistic and authentic in realizing that the explanation of the creation being ruined by human sin could not hold water, so to protect their image of God the Gnostics had to take the creation out of God's hands altogether. Of course, looking back on all of this now with hindsight, and those three options they were grappling with, it is clear the dilemma would much more logically be resolved if the anthropomorphic images of God in Genesis, as some sort of human being greatly enlarged, were dropped, together with the anthropomorphic ways in which the creation was pictured as being accomplished.

To-day, with a better understanding of the physics of the physical universe, and of the realms that exist "above" us in frequency, the dilemma of a very imperfect creation emerging straight from the hand of the perfect Creator no longer presents the same difficulties. Instead, we can now see some alternative forms of explanation of the emergence of the physical universe, such as creation by the progressive lowering of frequency from Point Zero.

Replacing this image of an external and judgmental God with the teaching of the power of the Father within us all, is what Jesus came to announce. Unfortunately, his message was distorted into his being someone who took on the sinful burden of our First Parents and paid the price by his horrific passion and death that God extracted for our disobedience.

Did God Kill Jesus?

Of course, that leaves us with major questions about God.

How could a good and loving God demand the most painful death imaginable from his totally innocent Son? Even more importantly, what could that torture and death mean anyway to a parent who would ask, or indeed even permit such a sacrifice? How could the suffering and death of His innocent Son in some way make up for the alleged offenses offered by the human race to God since the beginning by the human race?

It looks like such a scenario would reduce God to the status of a vicious, vindictive, judgmental, and unmerciful despot. What sense could there be to such a system? Or could God be such a being? This understanding of Jesus as the Suffering Redeemer of the human race, so beloved of all Christian denominations today, now begins to look suspiciously like an atheistic belief of the highest order.

The issues we have facing us today far surpass the challenges the authors of Genesis faced in choosing between those three options I chose to illustrate their dilemma.

This is really what Jesus came to relieve; not by stepping into our place as a Suffering Savior, modeled on the sacrificial goat and lamb of Passover and Yom Kippur, but to do something entirely different. Unfortunately this has become almost entirely lost sight of in the Christian traditions that adhere to his name. Most of those traditions have always been based on profound misunderstandings of the early chapters of Genesis, and the paradigm they wanted to convey.

We end up in effect, having to save Jesus and his message from the plethora of misunderstandings that have upturned his glorious and empowering mission and message in order to focus on a sordid death in bloody gore to appease the anger of a vengeful God. Which means, in effect, no God, for there is absolutely no way in which such a being could be the Prime Creator of the Universe.

This is a great tragedy for Jesus. But it is even more tragic for us because all of those deeply entrenched beliefs about sin, guilt and the need to escape punishment before God, are functioning as extraordinarily powerful programs within the sub-conscious of everyone who has ever been taught these beliefs. This is a major reason why the human race is so dis-empowered, and why there is no sign today, in those groups that claim to revere his name, of what Jesus promised: that we would do all the great things that he did and greater. Something has obviously gone seriously wrong, and has been wrong for a long time.

So this is what the Genesis Creation Narratives really are about.

- They were not about telling us how everything began.
- But were about stating what kind of relationship existed between God and his Creation, according to the thought model of that era — and we still are not sure of that, and most have it badly wrong.

The mixture of good and evil we see in the world is a punishment of humankind by God for disobedience, and even today it seems we still need to suffer to pay for that disobedience (even though Jesus apparently has already paid for it).

There was no Fallen or Paradise State in the past. The Paradise State lies, not in our past, but as an ideal for our future and at which we must aim.

Laid out in Graphic Form

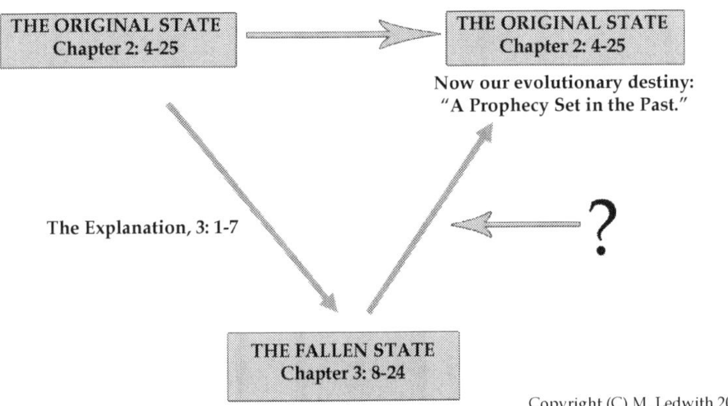

In other words, what is of significance for us in the teaching of Jesus is not the image of the gentle Jesus meek and mild, nor the Suffering Savior. What is significant is that he came to teach us how to draw forth the power that is within us all. As he said "You are all Gods." It was this which is indicated by the upward pointing arrow on the right side of the diagram. This is what he came to do: to show us how we could rise up from our present "fallen" state of guilt, fear, lack and dis-empowerment in so many forms, and evolve back to the ideal state. Of course, if you are back to the ideal state then these conundrums, with the three options that I described as facing the authors of Genesis, cease to exist because the world is the way it ought to be. But neither we or the world have evolved to where we should be. The mission of Jesus was to bring about that spiritual evolution. The sub-conscious religious programs react against our acceptance of such ideas.

The mistake of Genesis, if I can say that with all respect, was to assume that that Paradise or ideal state existed in the remote past of human history. Such a state never existed in the form described in Genesis chapters 2 and 3. The depiction of the Ideal State in Genesis 2 is a guide for us as to where we should be going. It is, in effect, a prophecy couched as if it had occurred in the past.

The "blame" for allegedly making such an imperfect world full of suffering and evil can only be thrown back on God if we imagine God as some type of enlarged version of ourselves, and if we imagine the creation of the universe as some enlarged version of a human style manufacture.

If it's the emanation of frequency 'down' from point zero that has created or brought everything into existence, then obviously, the whole paradigm of what creation is about must change radically. Likewise, must the understanding of how we envisage God to be in "himself," and in what way "he" was involved in the unfolding of Creation from Point Zero.

Nowadays many people are wakening up to the absurdity of calling God "He," as if "He" were some sort of enlarged human figure. So, they suggest alternative usages, such as 'She' or "It" or "The Universe" etc. Referring to God as "she" or 'it', is no doubt a welcome change from "he," but unfortunately those terms are no more accurate than 'he' when used to try to describe the being of God. I already mentioned an old story of an ant being interviewed about what ants believed about God, and whether it was appropriate to describe God as if he were an ant. In response to the interviewer the ant said that of course God is like an ant, but whereas ordinary ants have only one sting, God has two!

That is precisely what we are doing when we try to image God in his actions, whether at the creation of the universe, or at the opposite extreme, in his reaction to the behavior of individual humans, as being pleased, upset, angry or alienated. Fundamentally, this is turning God into a human being, with the weaker points of humanity removed, and the stronger points amplified. The God of the ants, after all has two stings! The way in which the average person imagines God to be is closer to seeing him as similar to the human form, rather than seeing God as the Prime Creator of the Universe. He puts people sitting at his right hand, (even though in some cultures the left-hand side is the position of honor); he is angry when we disobey his commandments, he is jealous of our attention paid to other 'gods,' he is upset by our sins and will severely punish us for them for all eternity. Does this sound like the Prime Creator of the Universe? Where did Jesus ever speak of this kind of God?

It is difficult for us to make the quantum leap to understand that God is not like any of those things, nor has God any of those human style characteristics.

We have to make the effort to realize that whatever God may be, the Prime Creator is not the folksy kind of individual as portrayed in the opening chapters of Genesis. The difference between the Prime Creator and human beings does not consist in whatever is the equivalent of God having two stings and his creatures having only one.

What Can We Know about God Anyway?

The name of God in Judaism is referred to as "The Tetragrammaton" ("Four Letters" in the Greek language) and is usually depicted as יהוה (YHWH). This name appears 6,828 times in the Hebrew Masoretic Text. It first appears at Genesis 2:4 and is normally rendered as "The LORD" in most English language Bible translations, although other versions use 'Yahweh' or 'Jehovah.'

I once noticed that if you take the four consonants of the name that it is forbidden to pronounce, "YHWH," and insert the vowels of the name that it is permissible to pronounce, "Adonai," you get the name "YeHoWaiH" — a spelling variant for "Jehovah." It was only much later that I discovered that the Masorites had inserted those vowels into the Tetragrammaton as a prompt to say "Adonai" when they came to read this section of scripture aloud.

Given the list of atrocities attributed to the Old Testament God, one can only wonder if this was the same being to whom Jesus referred as "The Father," or if those atrocities could be harmonized with other places where the God of compassion and love are so eloquently and movingly portrayed in other parts of the Hebrew Bible?

The Yahwist section uses the divine name 'Yahweh' from the very beginning. In contrast, the Elohist author is more historically accurate. In his account (as also in the Priestly account), the name 'Yahweh' was first revealed to Moses just before the Exodus. In his stories relating to before the time of Moses the author uses the divine name "Elohim," the more generic Hebrew way of referring to God.

Beginning with Exodus 3, however, it is especially difficult to tell the difference between Yahwist material and Elohist material. Beginning at that point both use the divine name 'Yahweh.' Usually, though, we can still identify them by their characteristic vocabularies, styles, and themes.

It is only if we imagine God as a human being enlarged that we run into that conundrum. So as human knowledge develops and progresses our vantage point improves.

If we start with the wrong presuppositions we cannot ever get a right answer. So, if one of the major wrong presumptions is to think that God made the world, then God obviously is pictured as similar to a human being in Genesis, which of course is what the God of the Hebrews was — Jehovah. Jehovah is a human being but not from this planet. So, it is perfectly understandable why those images of God should have held sway. So, if God decided on one particular busy week, to create the universe, and did it all in the space of six or seven days it was certainly a superhuman accomplishment, but entirely fictitious. The creation is something that occurs by the lowering of frequency from Point Zero.

So there is no being up there to carry the can for evil. Evil is a part of the stage we are at in this process.

What Jesus was coming to teach us, if we want to put it into the framework of the Hebrew documentation in Genesis, is how to convert the Fallen State to the Paradise State. In other words, if we want to put it contentiously, we are getting rid of everything to one side of the Fallen State, because those realities never existed in any recognizable sense for the human race. Our whole focus needs to center on getting back to a state in the future that never existed in the past. That's what Jesus came to teach us to do.

Given the molds, especially since the middle of the 19th century, in which Jesus is being understood, as "Gentle Jesus, Meek and Mild," or worse still as the "Suffering Savior," it should come as no surprise to us that those images certainly do not reflect what Jesus truly was and wanted to teach. Furthermore, these images such as portrayed in Mel Gibson's movie, "The Passion of the Christ," are actually powerful agents of dis-empowerment and directly contrary to what Jesus' message was. The 'good faith' dimensions of productions such as that, do not diminish their ability to cause profound harm to the sincere individual who wants to discover, know, and follow the teachings of Jesus Christ.

To revert to the diagram a few pages back, the history of humanity begins at the bottom rectangle in the chart, and our future course is to go back to a state where none of these things that Genesis laments in its depiction of the Fallen State will have a basis anymore, including physical mortality. This "Paradise" State can be accomplished by humanity, but the big question is: What are the techniques to do that; how do we ascend back to it?

Perhaps of even greater importance is, how do we get rid of the influence of the unconscious blocks that are keeping us in thralldom?

The first clue to discovering that is to look at the first humans and how they related to their Creators. That gives us a great clue how to go about attaining spiritual empowerment. Genesis, as we saw, was put in its present form about twenty-five or twenty-six centuries ago. The Hebrews main intent was to challenge the beliefs about God and God's creation of the world that they found in the culture all around them during the Babylonian Exile. The main sources that we know today that did that would be works such as the famous Mesopotamian epics from those far-off days, such as the Enuma Elish. the Epic of Gilgamesh, and the Epic of Athrahasis.

A dash of reality is needed badly here. All of the main actors in that fable woven by the authors of Genesis twenty-five hundred years ago referred to a scenario that actually took place possibly a quarter million years ago. And all those main participants that surrounded the original humans are still alive and well. They are not on social security, nor in a retirement home. They are doing well — every single one of them, including Jehovah, whose wings have been clipped a bit lately. But they are still alive.

So why aren't we still alive? How many incarnations have we, the members of the human race, gone through in the last quarter million years? And how many changes of roles have we had? And what do we understand of the significance of the process of these varied roles?

Consider a group of Jewish rabbis protesting today against the Germans of World War II. What we actually have, more than likely, is this group of Jewish rabbis, who were former heads of the SS, protesting against the Germans, who were the former Jewish people who were exterminated in the death camps. It is very hard for us to get our minds around these realities; that there is something called the Memory of the Soul which needs to be balanced. And the physics of the universe will make sure to magnetize us back to where our problem lay, if the aberration was too serious. It will magnetize us back into the best possible situation for us to rectify the balance of the soul. This is why protests about the past are usually directed at the wrong targets. For arguments sake let's say there is a protest being held nowadays against some Germans by individuals from Jerusalem. They are protesting against the Germans because of the atrocities committed during the Holocaust. But those modern Germans may well be the very Jewish victims of the Holocaust who have re-incarnated into the genetic line of those who perpetrated the atrocities. How odd if some protests are being perpetrated by the re-incarnation of those people who committed the atrocities, against those individuals who were the victims of the atrocities, who are now Germans.

To ponder deep facts such as this can give us a much better understanding, for example, of why Jesus taught us that we should not take revenge — the odds may very well be in peculiar situations like this, that the perpetrators of the atrocities are protesting against those who were their victims, not the other way round.

Does this give us any clue of where the world that we experience everyday comes from? It comes from the brain and the mind. Whatever we embrace and whatever we hold in the present is going to manifest out of the quantum field and the memory of the soul is a powerful agent in generating those mindsets.

If we have problems with our present world view, instead of kicking and screaming and blaming and shouting and weeping and gnashing our teeth, we should perhaps change our attitude. The reason why I am here is not about changing the world directly, it is about changing me first. And then everything will manifest accordingly. Jesus warned us that we will magnetize to us what we brood over.

Of course, there is an alarming realization looming not too far beneath the surface of all of this. If I can change the world by changing myself, is there really any such thing as an objective world at all? The answer to that has to be that there is not, in the sense of there being something entirely separate from my mind. That's the hardest thing of all for us to accept, because we sense an abyss opening up beneath our feet. At that stage, we may start to yearn for the old certitudes and draw back, and thus the cycle repeats itself.

SCROLL THREE THE CHEQUERED PAST OF THE HUMAN RACE

Chapter 11 The Wars of Gods and Men

To accurately understand what Jesus was about it is essential to be clear on the real circumstances in which our race came into existence. What we have learned from several researchers over recent years is that those circumstances were characterized by subservience, powerlessness and fear. However, it is important to note that these crippling mindsets had nothing at all to do with sinning against God.

The 'Paleocontact Hypothesis'

The second half of the 20th Century saw an explosion of investigations into the origins of our species, most of them now grouped rather condescendingly under the labels of 'Ancient Astronaut Theory' or the 'Paleocontact Hypothesis'. These investigators maintain that there is strong evidence that intelligent and highly advanced people from outside this Earth have visited us frequently since pre-historic times. Furthermore, this contact has had an enormous impact in the areas of human technology and religious viewpoints. Another point usually made is that the Gods of most, if not all, religions were actually extra-terrestrials, whose advanced technology convinced humans that the Visitors had divine status.

The Swiss researcher Erich Von Daniken is generally regarded as the father of the 'ancient astronaut' movement. Not surprisingly, the reception of his work has been highly controversial and, as is unfortunately often the case, many attempts have been made to discredit him on other grounds. He published 'Chariot of the Gods' in 1968, which became an instant best-seller. He is the author of eighteen other works on a variety of related topics.[135] However, the aspect of his work that aroused most interest was his assertion that we are physically descended from those ancient aliens.

There are several other authors in this genre as well, including David Icke, the author of twenty books in this field, the American-Italian author Peter Kolosimo, (author of seventeen books, only three of which have been translated from Italian into English), Zecharia Sitchin, Robert Temple, and most recently Gerald Clark's book – 'The Anunnaki of Nibiru: Mankind's Forgotten Creators, Enslavers, Saviors and Hidden Architects of the New World Order,' published in August 2013.

Temple is best known for his work 'The Sirius Mystery' (1976)[136] which contends that the Dogon people of Mali in West Africa had contact in ancient times with Aliens who came from the star system of Sirius. His work was based on the research of two distinguished anthropologists and ethnographers – Marcel Griaule (who worked with the Dogon in the 1930s), and Germaine Dieterlen (who lived with them for over twenty years, beginning in the early 1940s).

Giorgio A. Tsoukalos, Chairman and co-founder of 'Legendary Times' magazine, and consulting producer of the television series "Ancient Aliens," is probably the best-known figure today associated with bringing the fruits of all this historical research and many new findings to mass audiences.

This new 'alien' perspective came into its own with the deciphering of a massive collection of ancient Sumerian tablets, most notably by Zecharia Sitchin. In 1849 the British Archeologist

---

[135] The most recent of these are Twilight of the Gods: The Mayan Calendar and the Return of the Extraterrestrials, New Page Books, 2010, and Remnants of the Gods: A Visual Tour of Alien Influence in Egypt, Spain, France, Turkey, and Italy, New Page Books, 2013.

[136] Author also of The Genius of China, The Crystal Sun, The Sphinx Mystery, and Egyptian Dawn.

Sir Austen Henry Layard made a first discovery of cuneiform clay tablets in connection with his excavation of Nimrud and Nineveh, which was once the largest city in the world. Its ruins lie in north central Iraq, on the east bank of the Tigris River, across from the modern city of Mosul. The tablets are written in cuneiform script and are said to be one of the earliest known writing systems created by the Sumerians about 6,000 years ago.

In 1851, a massive collection of approximately 30,000 clay tablets from the 6th and 7th centuries BC, was discovered by Layard's team in the Palace of Ashurbanipal[137] the last great Assyrian King. The Collection has been named "The Library of Ashurbanipal.' The collection includes the Epic of Gilgamesh one of the finest specimens of ancient Babylonian poetry, and the Enuma Elish Creation Story. Most of Layard's cuneiform tablets are now in the British Museum.

It is recorded that when Alexander the Great saw Ashurbanipal's Library at Babylon he resolved to create a similar Library in his new city Alexandria, but he died at the age of 33 before he could realize his ambition. His friend and successor in Egypt, Ptolemy, built the Library and named it after Alexander. The stocking and arrangement of the Library was reputedly done by Demetrius of Phaleron, who had studied under Aristotle, during the reign of Ptolemy I Soter (c.323 BC – c.283 BC). It became one of the legendary libraries of the ancient world.

Scholars have spent decades trying to decipher these ancient Sumerian texts but more than half still remain untranslated. What has emerged so far is an uncanny resemblance to the main accounts in the Old Testament regarding the story of the creation of heaven and Earth from out of a watery abyss, stories of gods, an account of a devastating flood and a giant ark designed to save a remnant of the population.

Zecharia Sitchin spent more than 30 years translating these Sumerian Tablets. In his 1976 book, 'The 12th Planet', Sitchin claims that these cuneiform texts describe an alien race named the 'Anunnaki' who came to the Earth from an as yet undiscovered planet, called Nibiru, which enters our solar system every 3,500

[137] 668 – 627 BC.

years. Sitchin maintained that the Anunnaki evolved after the planet Nibiru entered our solar system and came first to Earth about 450,000 years ago. The Anunnaki were looking for minerals, especially for gold which they needed for the purifying of the air of their own planet. They discovered gold in South Africa and commenced elaborate operations to mine it there. Sitchin believed that these 'gods' were the working class of the expedition from Nibiru to Earth.

The reactions to Sitchin's proposal from established academics and archeologists have of course been predictable. In the same vein Michael Heiser[138] has attacked almost all of the 'ancient astronaut proponents', but none more vehemently than Zecharia Sitchin. Heiser alleged that Sitchin misinterpreted and mistranslated several crucial terms in the ancient astronaut scenario. His main accusation was that Sitchin should not have translated 'Nephilim' in the Book of Genesis as 'the fallen ones'. Instead, Heiser states, the word should have simply been translated as 'Giants'.

However new researchers such as Michael Tellinger[139] in particular, have come forward with very valuable research in more recent times. He claims to have discovered evidence in South Africa of gold mining in ancient times, and also believes that Sitchin's translation can be matched to landmarks and megalithic structures in the area.

The Anunna of Ki

While according to Sitchin's interpretations, the Anunna came to this Earth in the remote past, they only really got involved here about a quarter million years ago. Their name for this Earth was 'Ki'. They apparently fled here following a fierce conflict in their

[138] Bellingham, Washington State, The Unseen Realm: Recovering the Supernatural Worldview of the Bible, (July 2015).

[139] Slave Species of the Gods (2005); African Temples of the Anunnaki (2013); The Secret History of the Anunnaki, The Russell Scott Show.

own home region of the galaxy. They became known as the Annuna that belonged to this Earth...or in their language the 'Annuna-Ki'.

At the heart of their territory was a famous Garden, known in more recent folklore as the 'Garden of Eden'. It was the original Anunnaki settlement here and is located near Rashaya, El-Wadi, over 4,000 feet above sea level, in the south east of the Lebanon, near the Syrian border. It was apparently a wonderful area in which to live.

We have a lot of evidence about those times. I am emphasizing the reality of this evidence because, as we have learned, the subconscious programs are gatekeepers. They will not easily allow this information access into our minds since it threatens the picture of how the remote past and the origin of our race was traditionally understood.

The programs will tend to make us think that this is all just a web of fables that have no purpose other than to lead us astray about fundamental reality and our basic belief systems. For that reason, it's important to know that this information is well backed up by historical documentation. This evidence includes numerous ancient documents including the Nippur Tablets, the Epic of Atra-Hasis, the Epic of Gilgamesh, the Book of Enoch and certain parts of the Bible and the Qur'an.

The Sumerians, who were first recorded to have written about this region, called it Kharsag. The first inhabitants of Kharsag were led by three people: Anu, Enlil and Enki or Saam. The next in line was Ninhursag who, according to these tablets, was the female scientist who genetically combined the Anunnaki DNA with the DNA of an existing hominid on this planet. She had two other names: Nisgal and Mammi.

Recently Harvard scientist George Church[140] and his colleagues, following up on earlier efforts by scientists in Japan and Russia, spliced DNA from the extinct Hairy Mammoth into an elephant. They are attempting to bring back into existence this creature which has been extinct now for 3,600 years. In the light of proposals such as this, perhaps people's minds may be a little

[140] Robert Winthrop Professor of Genetics at Harvard Medical School and Professor of Health Sciences and Technology at Harvard and MIT.

more open to the possibility that the origin of our race might also have occurred through genetic manipulation.

The first inhabitants of Kharsag were led by:

- Anu
- Enlil
- Enki (Saam)
- Ninhursag (Nisgal, Mammi)
- Jehovah

Trying to unravel the relationships of those who were in charge when the Anunna first came is like trying to track the entire course of a single string of spaghetti in a bowl. It is messy, difficult, and in the end ... not all that very worthwhile. I am noting this in particular with respect to the last person on the list — Jehovah.

He is the person who really puts Jesus' role in much later times, into perspective. I don't know, and nobody else seems to know either, whether Jehovah was Nisgal's brother, her uncle, her nephew or her grandson. These are some of the more probable options. The bottom line is that Jehovah was very close to the powers that were in that time.

According to the Sumerian accounts we were genetically engineered as beasts of burden to dig gold, principally in South Africa. The run of the mill gods had gotten tired of being the laborers and demanded that they be replaced by slaves who would do their physical work. *"When the gods were many they did forced labor, they bore drudgery, great was the drudgery. So, the gods were digging water courses and canals — the life of the land. The Igigi gods were digging water courses. They dug the Tigris River; they dug the Euphrates River; they opened up springs from the depths ...Years of drudgery ... forced labor they bore, day and night."*[141] This was why they decided to create what we now call the human race ... and assigned the manufacture of the race to the female geneticist, Ninhursag.

[141] Quoted in Walter R. Mattfeld, The Garden of Eden Myth, Its Pre-Biblical Origins in Mesopotamian Myths (2010).

Recollect what I wrote earlier about how we inherit attitudes and characteristics through our DNA right back to our origins. If that is true, then the experiences of those ancient times are still with us in a very real sense to this day.

Despite our usefulness as beasts of burden, the Anunna eventually began to feel that we were too much trouble, no matter what benefits we conveyed. So they made five attempts to wipe out the humans. The first attempt was by causing a plague. It did horrific damage, but fundamentally didn't get their job done. The next attempt was a drought. The next was a famine and the salinization of the soil on which the human race needed to live. The next extermination attempt was the Deluge...in our terms, Noah's Flood. That apparently didn't work either because there wasn't enough water to do a thorough job. The last attempt was to make women infertile ... to induce stillbirths or to stop the birth of children.[142]

Why are we interested in Jehovah of the Anunna? Because it is Jehovah who makes perfect sense of what Jesus really was and why he came here. Jesus came to attack the program of that fearsome entity ... that God of the Old Testament whose threats and 'commandments' may cause us on our deathbeds to die in terror, irrespective of how noble a life we may have led. Do we find traces of these early people, the Anunna, in our own ancient documents in addition to the Atra-Hasis epic, the Barton Cylinder, the Nippur Tablets and all these other ancient Sumerian texts? Yes, we do have evidence in both the Old and the New Testament.

'In the Beginning...'

When we look to Genesis in the Old Testament, we read that *"In the beginning God created the heavens and the Earth ... and the spirit of God was brooding over the waters"*. This last part of the sentence is based on the Hebrew/Babylonian belief that water was the primordial substance from which everything else came.

---

[142] See The Epic of Atrahasis (I, 352 ff, II, 1-8)."

An interesting thing about this text occurred to me many years ago. In the Hebrew text of Genesis 1:1 we read:[143]

- "In the beginning God created the Heavens and the Earth..."
- Beresheet bara Elohim et hashamayim ve'et ha'aretz
- בראשית ברא אלהים את השמים ואת הארץ

'Beresheet' means 'In the beginning'. 'Bara' means 'created' — past tense. 'Elohim' is one of the words used for God in Hebrew. It is important to remember that the Hebrews were adamant that there was only one God. But we do have a slight problem, for in Hebrew the ending '...im' indicates a plural and <u>not</u> a singular noun. So what do we have here? The word for God in Genesis Chapter 1 is 'Eloh<u>im</u>' — a plural. Are we looking at a reference to 'gods' and not just one God? That's the first little problem. We'll explore others as we go along.

There is a reasonable consensus among scholars that the Book of Genesis was assembled into the form we know it today during the 5 to 6th Century BC while the Jewish people were in exile in Babylon.[144] Genesis is supposed to have been written by Moses. Indeed, according to conservative Jewish tradition, all five books of the Old Testament, called The Torah,[145] or the Pentateuch, were supposed to have been written by Moses. An obvious problem with that authorship, is that an account of the death of Moses is included in the Pentateuch.[146] At one stage some resourceful rabbis came up with the ingenious idea that God raised Moses from the dead for long enough to write the account of his own demise!

Moses is generally reckoned to have been born about 1393 BC and died about 1270 BC. He was born when the Israelites were slaves in Egypt and at a time when the authorities were gravely

[143] בראשית ברא אלהים את השמים ואת הארץ

[144] Babylon was the most famous city of ancient Mesopotamia. In modern Iraq, its ruins are about 60 miles southwest of Baghdad.

[145] Genesis, Exodus, Leviticus, Deuteronomy, Numbers.

[146] Deuteronomy 34.

concerned about the growth in numbers of the Hebrew people. About the time of Moses' birth (the third of three children) the Pharaoh issued a decree that all male Hebrew children should be drowned at birth. Moses' mother, Jochebed, concealed his birth, but eventually was forced to abandon him in a basket on the banks of the Nile. He was discovered by Bitya, a daughter of the Pharaoh, who raised him with the Royal Family. At about twenty years of age Moses fled from Egypt to Midian[147] after killing an Egyptian slave-master who was beating a Jew. In Midian he encountered the God of Israel speaking to him from a burning bush. The rest, as they say, is history.

Needless to say, the dates of all of these major historical figures and events are not possible to establish with precision at this point in time. We will work with the generally accepted dates.

Some authors have suggested that Moses grew up in the household of Pharaoh Akenaton, and was initiated into the mysteries by him. Akenaton reigned from 1352-1334 BC. But Moses had fled from Egypt to Midian, about the year 1373, after murdering the Egyptian guard. This was twenty years before Akenaton became Pharaoh. When Akenaton ascended the throne Moses would have been about forty years old. Working with the generally accepted dates, the Pharaoh on the throne when Moses was discovered in the basket would have been either Tutmoses IV[148] or Amenhotep III[149] Considering the dates as we know them, it was most likely Amenhotep III, father of Akenaton and grandfather of Tutankhamun, who reigned when Moses was taken into the Royal Family by Bitya.

To make things a little more complicated, however, the result of recent archeological excavations has some experts now suggesting that the date of the Exodus of the Jews from Egypt under Moses should be put two centuries further back — to the 15th Century BC. Apparently there is some archeological support for an exodus in that century. In contrast, there seems to be no archeological evidence to support an Exodus in the 13th Century BC.

[147] A territory on the eastern side of the Red Sea.

[148] 1400-1390 approx..

[149] 1388-1351 approx..

Coming back to Genesis, I knew many years ago that there was a convention in the 5th or 6th century BC that books dealing with fundamental topics, such the origin of the world or of the human race, always began with the first letter of the Hebrew alphabet. As mentioned earlier, the book of Genesis does not begin with the first letter of the Hebrew alphabet but with the second. So, I said to myself years ago as a student — *"What would happen if I put the first letter back from where, presumably, someone took it out long ago?"*

This is how things would go:

> Present Version: "Ba Rasheet bara Elohim…"
> then becomes
> Original Version: "A̲ba Rasheet bara Elohim…"

Now we have an "Ab," at the beginning of Genesis. To create the short 'a' sound after 'Ab' a second 'b' would be needed, which results in the Hebrew 'Abba,' or 'Father'. The text now reads *"The Father of the Beginnings created the Elohim (gods), the heavens and the Earth"*. This makes much more sense of Genesis, and solves the riddle of why a plural name seemed to be applied to God. It was not a name for God originally, but the name for a race of people. To cut a long story very short: 'God created the Anunna, the heavens and the Earth'.

Now, let us flash forward six chapters in Genesis to Chapter 6:4. Here it states — "In those days there were giants on the Earth, and also afterward, when the sons of God (that's the Anunna) came in to the daughters of men, they bore children to them. These were the mighty men that were of old, the men of renown

'The Nephilim', which is the word for 'giants' in Genesis 6, doesn't only mean giants according to Sitchin's view, it also means 'those that came down from above' — from the sky, though that interpretation is disputed. And "…when the sons of God came into the daughters of men…" that text, he says, should read instead… "…when the sons of the g̲o̲d̲s̲ came in to the daughters of men…" So, may we assume the gods were the Anunnaki? And the most prominent god was you know who … Jehovah.

According to the story the intermarriage of these 'giants' with the 'daughters of men' was the downfall of the human race. Why? Because the moral fiber of the humans was perceived to have become so corrupted that the chief God, Enlil, ordered that the humans be destroyed. They were not to be told of an impending disaster...a disaster in the form of colossal tsunamis and everything else that goes with that situation. We know that disaster as 'Noah's flood'. But Enlil's brother Enki ruined Enlil's plan to wipe out the human race. He broke confidence, according to the Sumerian texts,

So we're beginning to get Jesus a little bit more into focus now. Noah's flood is seen as a punishment for mankind both in the Sumerian tablets and in the Book of Genesis. Let's look a little more closely at how this message is portrayed. Hazazel was the first 'watcher' who came down to enjoy the Earth women. As a result, the moral fiber of the humans was 'corrupted'. In the Jewish faith, Hazazel is the demon of the Festival of Yom Kippur, the 'Day of Atonement' (literally translated). It is the day when worshippers conjure up how guilty they are before God and how they need to make up to him for all their sins.

One of the central ceremonies of Yom Kippur, in the days when there was still a Temple in Jerusalem, was the sacrifice of the lamb on the altar of the Temple and allowing its blood to flow down over the stone. This flowing blood symbolized the washing away of the sins of the human race through this annual sacrifice before God. The second ceremony consisted of loading up a spotless goat with symbolic baggage and driving it out into the wilderness of Judea – the abode of Hazazel. This ceremony symbolized the carrying away of the burdens of our sins. The goat and the lamb of Yom Kippur became the paradigms by which the message of Jesus was interpreted in the early communities who had heard his message during his ministry in Judea and Galilee.

So this is precisely the background against which the person and message of Jesus has been misunderstood. The symbolism of the lamb and the goat were skillfully combined in Jesus from very early on, but especially in the centuries that followed. He was the sacrificial lamb whose blood washed away our sins, and the goat who carried away on its back the burdens of our sins.

It's interesting to note what the first three Gospels of the New Testament — Matthew, Mark and Luke have to say in this regard. They are called the Synoptics, because fundamentally they repeat one another...which is a polite way of saying they copied each other wholesale. But the Gospel of John is different. An interesting thing about the Synoptics is that they regard the Last Supper of Jesus with his disciples as a Passover meal.

Every year the Jews celebrate Passover, the major Spring Festival, for a week beginning with the 15th day of the Jewish month, Nisan, to commemorate the time when they escaped from captivity in Egypt. In accordance with instructions from Jehovah, on a particular day, they slaughtered a lamb and smeared their door posts with its blood. The avenging Angel of the Lord passed over those doors that had been smeared, but killed the first-born child in the houses of everyone else in the land. So the feast of Passover is a commemoration of the Jews being spared the vengeance of God, a 'passing over without touching,' before they eventually escaped from Egypt, according to Exodus 12.

I have already noted that in the first three Gospels, Matthew, Mark and Luke, the Last Supper of Jesus with his disciples is indicated to be the Passover meal and that that cannot be historically accurate. If Jesus sat down with his disciples to eat the Passover Meal, then the day following that Passover Meal was one of the most sacred of all Jewish Festivals. There is absolutely no way that Jesus could have been hauled before the Sanhedrin and before Pontius Pilate and Caiphus, the High Priest, during such a solemn holiday. That would have been an absolutely flagrant violation of their own laws. The Gospel of John has a different take. It indicates that the Last Supper of Jesus with his disciples was held on the day before the day of the Passover Meal.

It is interesting that early in the second century there was a man still alive who had known John the Apostle in his old age. This man was Polycarp, Bishop of Smyrna, on the western coast of what is now Turkey. Polycarp testified that Easter is Passover...it's the same feast. But he also testified that the very early Christians, just after the time of Jesus, celebrated Easter on the first full moon after the Spring Equinox. In other words, Easter, according to the testimony of the tradition coming from John, was not necessarily celebrated on a Sunday, but on whatever day of the week the full moon appeared.

Reverting back to Genesis for the moment, it now appears the problem in the Garden of Eden was not a bad woman (Eve), but a bad god. All of the ancient mythologies of Greece, Canaan, Akad, Egypt, Assyria, Rome, the Hittites; all of them go back to the most ancient stories about gods and humanity that come from Genesis. And they all speak of the land called "Shinar" or "Shine'ar".

There was such a land. It's the land of the kingdom of Nimrod (Genesis 10:10) and of the Tower of Babel (Genesis 11:2). Up until just over 100 years ago nobody knew anything about Shine'ar apart from those two references. Archeologists then began to discover cities far more ancient than Nineveh and Babylon, such as Ur, Erech and Akkad. There was indeed a land called Shine'ar or, as we call it, 'Sumer'. It was the cradle of our civilization; the cradle of the human race. It is also the source of all our woes.

The reason why Jesus came here so many centuries later was to try to undo the malevolent effects of that ancient race of beings who were the creators of our physical bodies. And among those effects are some of the fundamental programs that prevent us from creating remarkable lives...programs that are alive and well in our sub-conscious minds to this day. We can't ever, as we well know, remove those programs unless we rebuild them from the ground up. And that is the reason why I am writing so much about the Anunna of Ki in the middle of a book about Jesus.

Scholars speak of the civilization of Sumer as coming 'out of nowhere'. Quite rightly so – it was unexpected, sudden and mysterious. All of a sudden literature, commerce, courts of justice, kings, priests, metallurgy, mathematics, irrigation and industry emerged. And it is the Sumerians that gave us our system of numbering. Did you ever wonder why there were 60 minutes in an hour and 60 seconds in a minute? Did you ever wonder why 12 was such a special number?

Did you ever wonder why we have a seven-day week? It is because the Sumerians were aware of only four planets which, with the Sun, the Earth and the Moon, made up a total of seven central heavenly bodies. And these bodies were of such supreme importance to them that they divided the days into groups of seven to honor them.

Napoleon Bonaparte, as you may probably remember, tried to base everything on the decimal system, as he did with such effect in other areas such as the monetary system in France. But his attempt to abolish the week and introduce a new decimalized ten day week, failed miserably. Those canny French were not going to trade in a day off every seven days, for a day off every ten. We owe all this family of systems to the Sumerians. Twelve hours, twelve months, twelve inches, twelve tribes, twelve Apostles and twelve houses of the Zodiac.

In the Bible 'Anakim' — Numbers 13:22;28;33, Deut.2:10;9:2

- Israelite heroes in Philistine wars slew 'Anakim': all people of gigantic size, 2 Sam. 21:16-22.
- Possibly the same name as 'ly-Anak' in Egyptian texts of 12-13th Dynasties, 1900-1700 BC.

The Sumerians say they got their knowledge from the Anunnaki. And just in case you think the Anunnaki are not mentioned in the Old Testament, they are, although the spelling is is somewhat different.

As noted earlier, Sitchin maintains that the Anunnaki first came here to Earth about 455,000 years ago. And that about 255,000 years ago they started the genetic manipulations that resulted in our race.

Voyager 2[150] was launched in 1977. As a result of its many years of research into our solar system, we now have information that confirms a lot of the early writings about the Anunnaki. It also answered questions about certain baffling phenomena in astronomy. For instance: Why is Uranus on its side? Why does Triton, the moon of Neptune, have a clockwise orbit while most

[150] Launched by NASA on August 20, 1977 to study the outer Solar System and eventually interstellar space. It is still operating after 40 years.

of the planets in this solar system have an anti-clockwise orbit? Why do the continents of the Earth all congregate on one side? And why does Earth have a moon that is too big for a planet the size of Earth?

From another perspective, 'The Chaldean Account of Genesis', written in 1876 by George Smith,[151] shows us how the Sumerian texts explain those same peculiar phenomena in our solar system, the existence of the asteroid belt, and also how the Earth and mankind were created.

For additional confirmation, we turn to Anton Parks, the author of many ground-breaking books. Two that are particularly relevant to our topic here were published in English at the end of 2013 – 'The Secret of the Dark Stars'[152] and 'Eden'[153]. Parks maintains that the opening chapters of Genesis are simply a greatly edited version of the tales about Eden and the Fall of Mankind, through the temptation by the Serpent, that had already been narrated centuries earlier in the ancient Sumerian Epics documented in the clay tablets found in Nippur. Parks also reveals his analyses of why the first man was named Adam, which means 'coming from the earth or the soil'.

Another author who has contributed a great deal of information about reptilian races is R.A. Boulay in his book 'Flying Serpents & Dragons, the Story of Mankind's Reptilian Past.'[154]

The Savage God of the Old Testament

Certain authors maintain that about twenty five thousand years ago a member of the Anunna took an unseemly interest in the group of people that we now refer to as the Hebrew nation. And he became what we have to agree is basically the savage

[151] Smith, (1840-1876) was an English Assyrologist, apprentice engraver, and was self-taught in cuneiform.

[152] The Secret of the Dark Stars (2013).

[153] Eden: The Truth about our Origins (2013).

[154] Published in English, April 2003.

God of the Old Testament. When he started to interact with the human race a lot of interesting things started to occur. But before we go into the specifics of that, let's look at a situation from more recent times.

The 'Cargo Cult' is the name given to a phenomenon that arose when indigenous peoples came into contact with Westerners for the first time. The most well-known form of it came from the Vanuatu area in the South Pacific at the end of World War II. American soldiers flying over a very remote area of Papua, New Guinea noticed communities of people living in the jungle who had apparently never been touched by contact with the outside world. The soldiers were dropping supplies by parachute to their own American troops in the jungles below. Occasionally they also dropped a container of supplies including food, candies and clothes to those native people in the jungle.

The war ended; all good things come to an end. There were no more crates of goodies dropping from the skies to the people in the wilderness. They were extremely distressed because their weekly 'supplies' were no longer coming in. So what did these people in the jungle do? To the best of their abilities they built an idol of what they had seen in the sky dropping down the goodies – an aeroplane. They then placed the model of the aeroplane in a shrine fashioned from the silk of the parachutes that had dropped the crates to them, and started to implore the 'gods' to return.

We might be tempted to judge the Hebrews of long ago as being very naïve when they believed Jehovah was the Creator God when he came down in vehicles with smoking engines and great noise. But is it so far-fetched? It is said that Jehovah never revealed himself to the people he was contacting. He discretely appeared in burning bushes and landed on tops of mountains and other remote areas, but always hid himself. We have great pity for the peoples of these remote areas in the Pacific in the days of World War II, for being so credulous that they regarded the American cargo planes as praeternatural and presumably their crews as 'gods'. But meanwhile you and I have been victims of the greatest 'Cargo Cult' of all time ourselves. Because we have been deluded into believing that Jehovah was the Creator God … and we still do.

So, who is this God of the Old Testament ... what kind of Being is he? I have referred to him several times as a 'savage god'. You may be wondering where that notion came from. Fortunately, we have a list of works that tell us how he was and still is as we saw earlier in this book. No one disputes this list. It is still current. This is not some dusty record dug up on an archeological site; this material is still on the books today. The Jews accept it as much as the Christians and Muslims.

When we asked some pages back,[155] to what kind of God did Jesus relate, we were able to produce a horrifying list of what this God had done according to certain Books of the Old Testament.

If you are thinking that this list could not possibly apply to the Creator God you are correct. Such a being could never be the Creator God. But it does apply to the God of the Old Testament ... the God we all believe to be 'the' Creator God. And I acknowledge that such a list as that is not easy reading. But since we are re-building programs here in order to free us from the dis-empowering fear of God, it is important for us to have this information in the forefront of our awareness.

We can even dare to ask was human sacrifice practiced in ancient Israel? Yes, up to about the 7th century BC. And when we review both the Old and the New Testament a lot more than that has been done, also allegedly in the name of 'God'.

---

[155] See "The Old Testament God" in Chapter 9: To What Kind of God did Jesus Relate?

Chapter 12
Addressing Crippling Religious Programs in the Sub-conscious Mind

Stretching the Mind

I stressed at the beginning of this book that unless we set about replacing those crippling programs in our sub-conscious mind we are going nowhere. No amount of information amassed, and no amount of research completed, will accomplish any fundamental change without us making this shift. Most people will find this immensely disturbing and unsettling. Consequently, they will unconsciously move towards rejecting any evidence that supports this new awareness. Unfortunately, when we do that, we obligingly do ourselves in. This is the quintessential example of the sub-conscious programs at work defending themselves and their positions, and we are not even consciously aware that it is going on. One of the saddest examples of this is if you try to convey to people that perhaps the version of Jesus and his message that they have been taught may not be the true picture. The average reaction is one of hostility and rejection, an infallible sign of the insecurity that lies behind such an instinctive response. It takes shape in the form of accusations that you are rejecting Jesus or God, whereas what you are doing is rejecting the caricatures of God and Jesus that unfortunately for so long we have been fed and blindly accepted, in place of the real thing.

The National Academy of Sciences was established by an Act of Congress, and signed by Abraham Lincoln in 1863. Members are elected by their peers for outstanding contributions to research. There are about 2,000 members today. Nearly 500 members of the NAS have won Nobel Prizes, and their publication, The Proceedings of the National Academy of Sciences, founded just over a century ago, is today one of the premier international journals publishing the results of original research.

I heard recently that a poll of the Members of the NAS revealed that 93% of the membership advised that they were "atheists." Is this a disturbing sign? Undoubtedly. It is of course true that most of those individuals do not possess the background to decide if they are atheist or not. They are going on the popular versions of belief systems with little knowledge of any deeper level in this field. In short, the declaration that "I am an atheist" may be based on a level of knowledge which the NAS itself would never accept within its own fields of inquiry.

All that being said, it is nevertheless a disturbing sign that the admittedly casual acquaintance these gifted individuals have with what are often blithely called "religious truths," are of this kind. Should we rush to assure them "Oh no, you've got things wrong? Not until we realize the sub-conscious programs that are present on both sides of the debate, and the barriers that exist — on both sides — to accepting objective knowledge. The whole paradigm that the members of the NAS are working with in terms of religion has to change, as has the paradigm of those on the 'religious' side of the potential debate. We all need to come to realize that the version of religious belief which we have been fed may not necessarily be the way things are. Will the representatives of religion have the will to face that inconvenient truth? Will the NAS Members have the will to face that same issue, and apply their own scientific credentials in, to them, the alien field of religion? It's probably too much to hope for, especially when they see so many individuals these days in the rather curious position of preaching and practicing hatred in the name of the God of Love.

Most of these current religious programs that plague us all, not just the distinguished NAS Members, originated centuries ago as a result of major defects in the understanding of what Jesus was, and said, and did. Instead of conveying what Jesus came to say and do, these negative and distorted programs totally undermine the basic intent of his message — which was to empower us to do all the things that he did and greater, by learning how to use the quantum field to create reality. Furthermore, if we hear some new and exciting insights about what Jesus came to do, insights that run contrary to our existing Jesus programs, then those old programs will block the new insights and information from acceptance…no matter how wonderful and accurate the new information may be. And, most surprisingly of all, no matter how eagerly we might want to embrace them consciously.

The paradigm of what we believe we know about the whole phenomenon of 'Jesus' establishes a further paradigm that will mold what we are able to accept about reality, about 'the beyond' and about our relationship with God. Unfortunately, these are the same patterns that cripple us spiritually.

To remove those programs and their dis-empowering influence, we have to begin by discovering where those programs originated, and then tediously re-build them from the ground up. It is only by doing this in a completely thorough fashion that we can make any progress. That's because if the sub-conscious mind detects any flaw in the logic of the argument designed to create new replacement programs, it will zero out the entire effort. As pointed out already, it is important to remember that the first business of the sub-conscious is to preserve its collection of programs and keep them intact.

With that said, I know it was not pleasant to look at that collection of texts from the Old Testament that I quoted earlier. A great number of sincere believers do not even realize that there are such horrific texts in what they regard as 'the inspired written word of God'.

But, it is precisely from these horrific texts that most of the fundamental attitudes of dis-empowerment that plague the human race originated. They inculcate fear of God, guilt, the sense of sin, the need to constantly express regret and repentance, and the hope that we will escape God's judgment at the end: the crippling attitudes that are precisely what Jesus came to teach us how to replace. What a travesty that those warped understandings of his message are now the central means used by the Church to convey exactly the opposite of what he taught: instead we are encouraged to have that sense of sin, shame, guilt and fear! And paradoxically the more we feel of this, the more righteous and close to God we are reckoned to be by the western religions.

The reason Jesus came was precisely to liberate us from these crippling programs that have been carefully insinuated by the religions for over two millennia. His mission most certainly was not to be a Suffering Savior who supposedly died the most horrible death imaginable to appease the vengeance of a Savage God.

In our crusade to replace the crippling programs in the sub-conscious, we have to be realistic. We can only go so far with any particular effort. This is why I will stop discussing a topic here before it is complete; repeat myself, and present ideas in different ways, from different vantage points. It is not a tidy and logical schema, but it is how the field of sub-conscious programs operate and if we ultimately want to make ourselves free of them this is the most effective way to proceed.

I like to use the image of an elastic band as a symbol of our mind-sets. We want to stretch the elastic band by re-forming our fundamental and deeply ingrained beliefs. But there is only so far we can go or the band will snap. That snapping means that we have reached our limit, the sub-conscious will not allow us to proceed any further. And if the 'elastic band' snaps the effort to replace the old programs with more enlightened and realistic ones will time out and the effort will be largely wasted.

So, we stretch the elastic band of our minds as far as it will go, and then we relax it before it snaps. Then we take a different but complimentary trajectory. This is the technique we are following in this book. We will look at the sources of where our central beliefs about Jesus originated, and then we will be able to see the distortions of history we have assimilated into our programs

The technique is to metaphorically stretch this elastic band of the mind until just before it snaps, and then you let it go. Then you start to stretch a different elastic band, and take that as far as it can tolerate on that particular occasion. As time goes on in this process, the elastic band will stretch further and further as we gradually extend the scope of the investigation. When we are dealing with the operations of the human mind at its deepest level these are the realities with which we must work. To recognize that these are the realities of the situation is what wisdom consists in, and in it we grasp the unfamiliar truth that this is the most effective method of creating change in those sub-conscious programs that dictate about 95% of our daily cognitive activity.

Translation: Often a Perilous Occupation

Even though no autograph copies of the New Testament documents survive, the original texts of the Gospels of the New Testament we have are in Greek.[156] This probably comes as a surprise since the mission of Jesus was conducted in Israel and, presumably, he used the ordinary languages of Israel at the time. Most of the ordinary people in Israel during his day no longer understood Hebrew – nor had they learned Greek, which had become the lingua franca of the Greek Empire at the time of Alexander. The day-to-day language of the people of Israel was generally Aramaic.[157] It was also the main language of the Talmud[158] and of significant portions of the Books of Ezra and Daniel.

Syriac is the major surviving dialectic of Aramaic today and is the liturgical language of Syriac Christianity. It's sad in many ways to realize that the closest language to what Jesus spoke is today the liturgical language of that devastated country. Syriac has also always been the liturgical language of the St. Thomas Christians in India.

The earliest manuscripts of many of the New Testament documents had no spaces between the words and no punctuation. The punctuation was added by other editors later, and they added it according to their own understanding of the texts, which was not always helpful or accurate.

The first major translation of the entire Bible was into Latin.

[156] However, it has been suggested that a now lost Gospel in Hebrew or Aramaic may lie behind the four Greek Gospels of the New Testament.

[157] In 132 AD Simon Bar Kokhba, as part of his briefly successful revolt against the Romans, tried to revive Hebrew and to make it the official language of the Jews.

[158] A record of rabbinic teachings from the first century to the sixth or seventh centuries of the Christian era.

It was completed by Saint Jerome in the 4th century.[159] Partial translations of the Bible into "English" did not begin until the seventh century and by the middle ages it had become a very perilous occupation. If translations of the New Testament were being made into English, the religious authorities often felt threatened as the bases for many of their positions did not seem to be supported by the texts of the New Testament.

John Wycliffe,[160] a Professor of Theology at Oxford University, supervised the making of a series of translations of the Biblical books, directly from the Latin Vulgate into English. He himself was the main translator, but it has been suggested that he was aided significantly by others such as Nicholas of Hereford,[161] John Purvey[162] and perhaps John Trevisa.[163] It should be remembered that Wycliff's translations were translations of a translation, not translations from the original tongues, so there were plenty of opportunities for misunderstandings and misinterpretations of the original version of the Bible.

Wycliffe's series appears to have been completed over the period 1384-1395. All of the translations of the Scriptures up to this point were made into Old and Middle English[164] and there was no "English" translation of the entire Bible before Wycliffe. The rapid spread of Wycliffe's Bible in England resulted in both Church and State promulgating a death sentence in England for possession of a copy of the Scriptures in English — "honor'd more in the breach than the observance,"[165] to borrow Shakespeare's phrase.

---

[159] He was commissioned by Pope Damasus I in 382 AD, to revise the collection of Latin texts of the Scriptures that the Church then used. These were known as the Vetus Latina (Old Latin) texts.

[160] c. 1331 — 31 December 1384.

[161] Chancellor of Oxford University in 1382.

[162] He lived with Wycliff until the latter's death in 1384.

[163] A fellow of Queen's College, Oxford from 1372-76, at the same time as Wycliff and Hereford.

[164] The term "Middle English" refers to the dialects of the English language spoken in parts of Britain from after the Norman Conquest under William the Conqueror (1066 AD), until the late 15th century.

[165] Hamlet, Act 1.

Wycliffe died on the last day of December 1384. The uproar and hatred he had caused by his assertion that the Church had drifted far from its foundations, as witnessed in the books of the New Testament, was enormous. We have only to remember that in 1428, forty-four years after his death, Pope Martin V decreed that Wycliffe's books be burned, his corpse dug up, the bones crushed, then burned again, and finally scattered into the River Swift that flows through Lutterworth, the city where he died.

One of the most interesting features of Wycliffe's philosophy, and a constant theme of his teaching, was his conviction that all reality pre-exists in the realm of thought and that it is by controlling thought that we manifest physical reality. Needless to say, such opinions did nothing to endear him to the status quo. Obviously, it's a theme curiously close to the heart of quantum mechanics and quantum physics, but six hundred years before the latter had emerged.

One hundred and ten years after Wycliffe's death, William Tyndale's[166] translation of most of the Bible into English began to appear. The Church was not happy with this translation either and Tyndale fled for his life from England to continental Europe because of the moves by the Church against him.

The main source that Wycliffe had had available to him from which to translate was the Latin Vulgate translation of St. Jerome, dating from the late fourth century. However, Tyndale's translation was the first English Bible able to draw directly from the original Hebrew and Greek texts as well.

In order for us to see the rapid development of the English language in the later Middle Ages, and the profound influence of Bible translations on it, it is interesting to compare a well-known text from the Scriptures and see how the text is rendered in the three translations I've just noted: firstly, Wycliffe's translation, then Tyndale's translation, and finally the version in the King James Bible — all three emerging in the space of just over two hundred years.

It is especially worth noting the major change in the style of the English language between Tyndale's translation (1536) and

[166] c. 1494—1536.

the King James Version that was published only 75 years later. However, in the more than 400 years since the publication of the King James Version the form of the English language has changed relatively little, which demonstrates one of the main effects that this translation had: it defined the form of modern English in use right down to today.

Take these two familiar verses from the beginning of Genesis:

Wycliffe's translation: 1382 to 1395.

[1]In the bigynnyng God made of nouyt heuene and erthe.

[2]Forsothe the erthe was idel and voide, and derknessis weren on the face of depthe; and the Spiryt of the Lord was borun on the watris.

Tyndale's Bible: 1525-1536.

[1]In the begynnynge God created heaven and erth.

[2]The erth was voyde and emptie ad darcknesse was vpon the depe and the spirite of god moved vpon the water

King James Version: 1611.

[1]In the beginning God created the heaven and the Earth.

[2]And the Earth was without form and void; and darkness was upon the face of the deep. And the Spirit of God moved upon the face of the waters.

Even though the phrase "Tyndale's Bible" is often used, it is not accurate, for Tyndale was never able to produce a complete Bible. By the time of his execution at the stake he had completed his translation of the New Testament in its entirety but only about half of the Old Testament.

Catholic Church authorities in England, including Sir Thomas More, denounced Tyndale's New Testament. It was banned and copies were publicly burned. The problem hinged on Tyndale's translation of some central Greek terms, three in particular: the terms that would normally be translated as 'Church,' 'Priest,' and 'Do penance'. Tyndale replaced the word 'Church' with 'Congregation' and replaced 'Priest' with 'Elder' or 'Senior'.

Instead of 'Do Penance', indicating acts of mortification and sacrifice to link us with the sufferings of Jesus for our sake, he substituted 'Repent'. This word essentially meant only a change of heart and the setting out on a new course in life without the necessity of any practical works of penance and reparation to God. These new translations of the teachings of Jesus in the New Testament, of course, challenged the very heart of several central tenets of the Church. Ironically where they caused most upset was where they seem to have caught the message of Jesus much more accurately than the traditional interpretations.

The Church maintained that it was an institution and that the word 'Church,' "*εκκλησία* (ekklesia)," referred to the visible organizational structure of the Church of the day. Tyndale's view, on the other hand, was that the Greek should not be translated as 'Church', but as 'Congregation,' so as to mean that it is the believers who constitute the Church, not the visible structure itself. By taking up this position Tyndale was undermining the entire way in which the Church had evolved to see itself, and in so doing gave an entirely different intent to the message of Jesus and to the manner of his connection to an organization in England in the sixteenth century.

Another consequence of translating 'ekklesia' as 'Congregation' meant that there was no room for the traditional view that the Church was a two-tier structure, composed of two classes of members, the clergy and the laity. The Church's view was that the clergy were of a higher order than the lay Christian and that each had quite different roles to play in the operations of the institution.

Tyndale's translation of the Greek term πρεσβύτερος *(presbuteros)* as 'Elder' rather than 'Priest,' further reinforced the idea that the clergy should not be regarded as above or separate from the so-called common believer. Thus, his translation undermined the basis of clerical power in the Church and opened up an entirely fresh way of seeing what the intent of Jesus was. Jesus did not come as a Suffering Savior, we have already asserted here many times, but neither did he establish a structure to succeed him based at its heart on the doing of penance and mortification, so as to make reparation to Jesus and God for what our sins have done.

For his pains, Tyndale was betrayed to the imperial authorities and was arrested in Antwerp in 1535. After a year's imprisonment at Vilvoorde, near Brussels, he joined the ranks of many others before and since who paid the same price for insisting on an accurate understanding of the New Testament: he was condemned to be burned alive at the stake for heresy – a sentence carried out sometime in late September or early October 1536. In the event, however, he was first strangled and then his dead body burned.[167] The man was gone; the influence of his translations lived on. It has been estimated that 76% of the text of the King James Old Testament was taken from Tyndale's translation, and 83% of the New Testament.

Can There Be Only One Version of Religious Truth?

In these days of religious extremism showing itself in so many parts of the world something needs to be said about the widespread conviction that there can be only one version of religious truth for all of humanity...and that the purity of that version has to be preserved at all costs. If there is only one version of the truth, then everyone who does not know or accept that version has to be brought to see the error of their ways. Basically, this means that you must believe what I believe. And you must be brought to justice if you don't. The mission then has to be to get as many people converted from outside the fold as you can.

Now that particular modus operandi, I have to say, only really began with the rise of Christianity. The second time that this trend showed itself was six centuries later with the rise of Islam. These are two of the three major religions of the West that feel it incumbent upon themselves to convert as many of the infidel (that would be you and me, in the eyes of Islam) as they can, to the true faith. But Christianity and Islam are just the second and the third attempts to establish a one world religion.

---

[167] Farris, Michael, From Tyndale to Madison (2007), p. 37.

The first attempt, somewhat surprisingly, was made by Buddhism in the 6th century BC. That attempt had enormous missionary success, except in southwest Asia. The Jews and the Persians were also convinced their religion was the only genuine brand, but they kept themselves to themselves and they didn't try to evangelize other people too forcibly. It's well to remember that the people of Iran/Persia today are not Arabs and, obviously, do not speak Arabic. They are Persian, and they speak Farsi.[168] A lot of people in the West do not realize that and a lot of mistakes can be made as a result.

Among the Religions of the Book, despite all appearances to the contrary, Christianity and Islam are actually sister religions. Is that good news or bad news? It is bad news, because there is nothing that can grate on your nerves more than a sibling.

There are a thousand affinities linking these two religions. To make matters even more intense, they both have their roots in Judaism, and in the cultures and religions of the ancient Middle East and ancient Greece.

The three great Western religions, Judaism, Christianity and Islam, in chronological order, have their roots in Abraham who, horror of horrors, even though the father of the Jewish faith, was not a Jew himself. Everyone admits he came from Ur of the Chaldees. Which is where? In present day southern Iraq, 220 miles south of Baghdad and 100 miles north of the Persian Gulf. Oh my God! Abraham was an Iraqi! How did all this go so wrong?

These three great Western religions that go back to Abraham are called the 'Religions of the Book' because of the major part sacred texts have played in these three religions, (in a way that texts don't play a part, for example, in Buddhism or Taoism or Hinduism).

But there are major differences between how Christianity regards its sacred texts, the New Testament, and how Judaism and Islam regard their sacred texts, the Hebrew Bible and the Qur'an. Both Judaism and Islam maintain that the central parts of their sacred texts, the Jewish Torah (the first five books of what Christians call the Old Testament) and the Muslim Qur'an, are

---

168 There are over sixty million native speakers of Farsi today, and perhaps up to forty million others who speak or understand it.

supposed to have been dictated personally by God.

Christianity has never made that claim for any of the books of the New Testament. Quite the contrary. The names of the distinguished human authors, Matthew, Mark, Luke and John have, for a long time, been proudly displayed at the beginning of these four documents that tell the story of the life of Christ – as they understood it. These are the human authors of the New Testament, not God.

I have already noted that it's also highly unlikely the individuals known as Matthew, Mark, Luke, and John actually wrote the documents that bear their names. Furthermore, it appears that there may not be a single word in the New Testament written by anyone who knew Jesus personally. Is that good news or bad news? We shall see.

The Book of Kells, a magnificent 8th century manuscript of the Four Gospels, is preserved in the Library of the University of Dublin at Trinity College.[169] The symbols of the Four Evangelists, or Gospel authors, Matthew, Mark, Luke and John, are portrayed on the front. Matthew is symbolized by a winged man or angel; Mark by a winged lion; Luke's symbol is a winged ox or bull; and John is symbolized by an eagle. Each symbol centers on wings: symbols of the desire of the human soul to reach a higher than human condition: in short, the works covered by those symbols are designed to empower such a transformation. Wings have to do with thought, imagination, freedom and victory, but have nothing to do with sin, penance, unworthiness and guilt. Obviously, the gifted scribes who set out the Gospels of the New Testament in the form of the Book of Kells were in an enlightened flow, far different from what is very common in modern times.

But even though Christians generally believe the Gospels were written by these four individuals Matthew, Mark, Luke and John, they don't believe the New Testament was dictated to those authors by God; at least not in the same way that God is supposed to have dictated their material to the writers of the Qur'an or the Jewish Torah. Nevertheless, Christians do believe that the New Testament was directly inspired by God. In fact, many of the members of the

---

[169] Kells is a town about fifteen miles north of Dublin.

Christian religions these days actually depart from the official position of their Churches on this matter. When they hear that the words of the New and Old Testaments are the inspired written words of God, they seem to understand by that that God sent these texts down by texting or email, or verbal audible dictation, directly from Heaven to those human authors.

No Original Versions of Any of the New Testament Documents Have Survived

Whatever may be said of the New Testament and whoever wrote it, and whether it was by the direct inspiration of God or not, unfortunately not one of the original copies of the books of the New Testament has survived. The earliest surviving manuscript fragment of the New Testament is the tiny Rylands Papyrus 52[170] dated somewhere between 125-175 AD, presumably well after the death of any of the writers of the New Testament books. It's also worth noting that, while there are officially twenty-seven 'Books' in the New Testament, some of these 'books' are only a page or two long.

We do not have the 'autograph' or original MSS of any of the books of the Bible, not even of the New Testament. Instead we have what several authors have described as multiple generations of error-ridden copies of the originals.

Within the context of those copies it's worth noting that Protestant Christian Churches and Catholics use the same New Testament. The Third Council of Carthage in 397 AD accepted 26 New Testament Books, and then, in 419 AD, added the Book of Revelation. Both Catholics and Protestants recognize 39 Books of the Old Testament, but Catholics include an additional seven;[171] a 66-book Old and New Testament "Protestant" Bible, versus a

[170] It contains a few verses of Chapter 18 of the Gospel of John.

[171] These seven books are found only in the Septuagint Greek MSS, not in the Hebrew, viz., Tobit, Judith, Wisdom of Solomon, Ecclesiasticus (Sirach), Baruch, and I and II Maccabees.

73-Book "Catholic" Bible.

The Muslim and Jewish people have always had the privilege of reading their own sacred texts in the original Arabic and Hebrew in which they were written. It is claimed that the Qur'an was delivered to Mohammed by the Angel Gabriel over a thirty-two year period that began on 22 December 609, and ended in 632 with Mohammed's death.

The Greek-speaking Christians in the East are known as the Orthodox. 'Orthodox' is the Greek language term for 'true teaching'. The Orthodox Churches so styled themselves because they believed they were the ones who preserved the truth, whereas the corrupt West drifted out of the fold and got most things wrong — about the New Testament in particular. The versions of the original texts of the New Testament, as we have them, were written in Greek. That means the Orthodox Christians of the East could always read the New Testament in their own language. But in the Middle Ages in the Western Churches few people could read that language. The first translation of the Scriptures for the West was Jerome's Latin version in the late fourth century, so for almost a thousand years the only people who could read the scriptures at all in the West, were the few (usually clerics) who understood Latin.

As I mentioned earlier, the first substantial English translation came with Wycliffe's Bible. Most of the trouble comes precisely from that. With the arrival of the new translations, it became apparent that the Church of those days had drifted far from what was outlined in its foundational documents in the New Testament, and now those who could read the scriptures for themselves, (especially the New Testament), could see that. An entirely different understanding of Jesus and what his message was, and how they related to the Church of those days, began to emerge. Obviously, the religious powers were far from pleased and made that very clear. Translation of the Scriptures was a risky business in those early days.

Unlike Judaism and Islam, during the first three centuries of its existence Christianity was a fugitive and prohibited religion. Being on the run from the authorities does not favor the careful preservation of historical documents. Whatever copying was done of the original texts of the New Testament in the early centuries, to put it mildly, was not done professionally, and the owners and copiers of the texts all too often were in fear of their lives from the powers that were. The surprise is not that we do not have the autograph, or original copies, of the books of the New Testament; the surprise is that we have any texts at all.

How Many Manuscripts?

Nowadays, once everything is set up, a printer can run off thousands of copies of a book, more or less at the press of a button, and it's done in a relatively short space of time. But in those olden days when the texts of the New Testament were copied by hand, it was a very different story. Obviously, there were no printers, publishers, bookshops or office supply stores, and it wasn't easy to even find someone who could read and write. The literacy level in the ancient world at the time of Jesus is optimistically reckoned at somewhere between 5-7% of the population, and some would put it as low as 3%.

After you had hunted down a person who could read and write, you then had to pay him. I have found it very interesting to do some approximate computations of what it would cost, for example, to make a copy of the Gospel of John in the late first or early second century. You would, of course, want to use parchment for such a distinguished piece of work.[172] The word 'parchment' refers to an animal skin (usually calf, sheep or goat) that has been prepared for writing. The preparation is quite involved. The raising of suitable animals, their slaughter, and the labor-intensive process of producing the parchment, meant it was extremely expensive. The term 'vellum' comes from the French word "veau" meaning a calf, and refers to parchment made from calf skin. Vellum was even more expensive than ordinary parchment. The skins of 40 to 50 animals would be needed.

[172] It is noteworthy that the U.S. Constitution, the Declaration of Independence, the Bill of Rights, and the Articles of Confederation are all written on parchment.

With an adequate supply of parchment and ink, you and your copyist are now ready to face the task. In the original Greek text of John, as we have it, there are 15,635 words. The cost of having the scribe you found make a copy of the Gospel would probably be about $2,500 – $3,000 in today's money, leaving aside entirely the cost of producing the parchment and ink. Today we press a button on our printer or computer and, lo and behold, after half an hour or so the whole document is there. Or it's copied electronically to a disc or computer in a matter of seconds at no cost at all. If we want to purchase a document online, I found several editions of the Gospel of John on sale at prices ranging from 49 cents to 99 cents for the entire Gospel – and obviously, you can buy as many copies as you wish.

I am pointing out the realities of copying skills and copying costs in the first or second century because it illustrates one of the fundamental difficulties we have with the New Testament record. Sometimes people, whose false reverence for the Scriptures almost borders on superstition, can forget these harsh realities surrounding the effort of producing copies of documents in ancient times. Because it was so difficult for so many centuries to access the written sources, it was very easy for various interpretations of the texts to flourish that may have had little value, or that were downright misleading.

Unprofessional copying of the New Testament was the normal situation in the early centuries of Christianity. This was very different from the situation in Judaism, and especially from the situation in the early years of Islam. When Islam emerged, it was in the ascendant politically as the established religion of Saudi Arabia. Christianity, by contrast, was a fugitive religion all throughout its formative centuries.

It is sad to reflect that Christianity does not possess the autograph of any of the twenty-seven books of the New Testament. The early Christians were normally poor and, as I've already noted, were probably also often on the run from the authorities. That situation didn't change for over three hundred years until Christianity became tolerated under the co-Emperors Constantine and Licinius.[173]

[173] February 313.

Consequently, it wasn't until the days of Constantine that copying of the manuscripts of the New Testament was done in any sort of professional manner.

Sometimes people who argue for the absolute reliability of the New Testament texts will say "We have 25,000 ancient manuscripts of the New Testament, which is far more manuscripts than we have of any other ancient work of those times." Homer's Iliad, the next best attested ancient text, has only 2,000 manuscripts. The Iliad is set during the Trojan War, which was fought around the time of Moses, 1260 to 1240 BC. It tells about the siege and destruction of the city of Troy, located in what is now North-Western Turkey.[174]

Or take the works of Julius Caesar[175] or Tacitus[176] or any of the classical authors close to the early years of Christianity. We have far fewer manuscripts of their works than we do of the New Testament. We have only about a dozen manuscripts of the works of Julius Caesar, Aristotle,[177] Pliny the Elder,[178] Tacitus, Herodotus[179] or Thucidides[180] — the famous Latin and Greek classical authors. So, one might be tempted to say, "Oh, by comparison with these classical authors, the text of the New Testament is on much more solid ground with 25,000 manuscripts, as opposed to a dozen or so for the works of a major author like Julius Caesar".

However, we must remember that the original version of every book of the New Testament that we know of was written in Greek. Three quarters of those 25,000 manuscripts that we now have of the New Testament are actually just translations from Greek into other languages.

---

174 Modern Hisarlik, Turkey. Just south of the Dardanelles Strait. A German archaeologist Heinrich Schliemann visited Frank Calvert, who owned the site, and secured permission to excavate Hisarlık. It is generally agreed nowadays, that the rough and uncouth methods used by Schliemann in the excavation, did irreparable damage to the site.

175 Died 15 March 44 BC.

176 Died about 117 AD.

177 Died 322 BC.

178 Died 79 BC.

179 Died 425 BC.

180 Died 296 BC.

Why do we need to be aware of all this kind of apparently recherché detail? You may be saying that this is tedious and boring. But remember, we are attacking the bases of very deep negative programs in our sub-conscious minds that have misconceptions about Jesus at their very root. If that is so, then we need to be very clear on the status and reliability of those basic documents that attest to him and his mission, so that we can assess whether those programs were soundly based or not on those sources, or was a lot of it based on what an illiterate populace was told to believe? To do that assessment effectively, and to remove effectively the crippling sub-conscious programs that depend on them, we need to be aware of all the details that went into the formation of those beliefs.

Let's concentrate on just the Greek manuscripts of the New Testament, of which at present we have 5,800. Some of these manuscripts are tiny fragments or only a couple of pages in length. It's somewhat disingenuous to call a two-page document a "Book" in the New Testament. Even to call each of those 25,000 documents 'manuscripts' is a bit of a stretch, because many contain only a fragment of text.

Only ten of those manuscripts contain the full text of the Bible. And what is even more significant is that only four of those ten manuscripts were written earlier than the 10th century. A thousand years had passed since the ministry of Jesus! And yet, in terms of a reliable witness to Jesus and his ministry, many seem to forget that we cannot just add up a total of manuscripts from widely separated periods of history and treat them as if they were all of equal value.

If I were to run off 100,000 copies of the New Testament tomorrow, it obviously would not affect in any way, shape or form, the reliability of the text of the New Testament as it was originally written. Obviously to have the original manuscript is infinitely superior to having multiple later copies, even if those copies may be from relatively ancient times. Since none at all of the original or autograph manuscripts of the New Testament have survived, what we are interested in is getting as close as we can to the date when the original book was written. Normally, the earlier the manuscript, the less likelihood there is of errors creeping in during copying multiple times.

A popular graphic on Wikipedia conveys the situation very well. The information in Wikipedia is not yet up to date as it states that 5,197 Greek MSS of the New Testament have been discovered, whereas the current total is 5,795. However, since the old adage still holds, "one picture is worth ten thousand words," I cite it here.

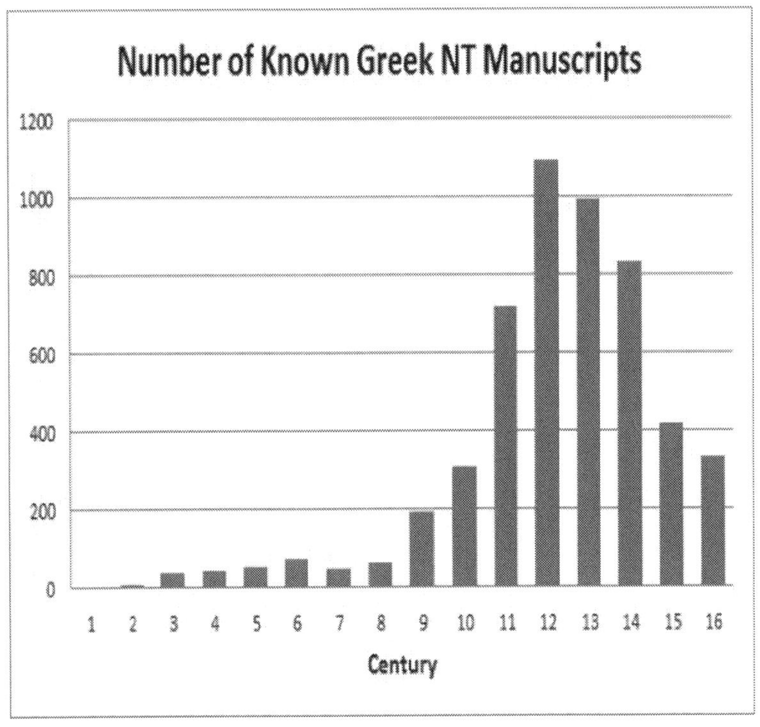

Diagram courtesy of Wikipedia

Look at the place for the first century at the bottom left side of the diagram. This is the period, according to most people, when most if not all of those New Testament books were written. How many manuscripts of the New Testament do we have from the first century? None.

How many manuscripts do we have in the 2nd century up to the year 300 AD? Eight.

Then the number gets better. We reach the climax about 1200 AD, when 1,090 manuscripts of the New Testament that we know of, were produced in that year. What is the difference in significance between 1,090 copies of the manuscripts produced by certain individuals in the year 1200 AD, and my printer producing 100,000 copies of the New Testament texts at the present day? Not that much.

You see on the diagram how the numbers of manuscript copies are decreasing as we pass into the 1400's. That is because of the invention of the printing press in the middle of the 16th century. Everybody knows, of course, that the man who invented the printing press was Johannes Gutenberg[181] from Mainz. It was a huge revolution, because for the first time you could print off multiple copies of books without tediously copying them by hand, and without risking the introduction of new copying errors each time, to which even the best scribal copiers were prone.

But the history of printing began a long, long time before Gutenberg. A set of block-printed documents was discovered in the Chinese North West, near Dunhaung, at the Caves of the Thousand Buddhas. The document was purchased in 1907 by the archaeologist Sir Marc Aurel Stein. This block printed document is dated 11 May 868, approximately 587 years before the Gutenberg Bible was first printed.

So nearly six hundred years before Gutenberg the Chinese Buddhist monks were setting ink to paper … to actual paper. The Chinese invented paper and ink and also the method known as block printing. Wooden blocks were carved out, a very laborious process in itself, and then they were damped with ink and then pressed onto a page. Obviously, the major part of the labor was in carving the wood blocks.

At the Caves of the Thousand Buddhas, in one of the earliest surviving books that was printed in this fashion, was discovered an old Buddhist text called "The Diamond Sutra". This text contains a collection of really significant documents; some of them religious – and giving a very different take on religion than is normally

[181] Gutenberg in 1439 was the first person in Europe to use moveable type and a mechanical printing press.

taken for granted, which is why I am devoting a little time to it here. These documents date from the 5th to the 11th centuries. There are works about a whole range of topics from history and mathematics, to folk song and dance. Most of the texts are Buddhist. But there are other religions represented in the collection as well such as Daoism, the Manicheans, and the Nestorian version of Christianity. Most of the manuscripts are in one of the Chinese languages or Tibetan. But there are other languages as well, that were completely unknown up to that discovery.[182]

I am spending some time here on the "Diamond Sutra" because there are striking parallels between the teachings of the Buddha Gautama as contained in the Diamond Sutra, and the teachings of Jesus. This is particularly true of the Sermon on the Mount, which was the quintessence of Jesus' teachings.

If we look at the Sermon on the Mount, we'll see that it corresponds point by point to the Buddha's teaching five hundred years earlier. Does that mean that Jesus was a plagiarist? No, it means that the Buddha and Jesus were heirs of a much more ancient source that lay behind both of them. Let's look at one of these teachings.

In the Diamond Sutra the Buddha has finished his daily walk. His monks gather together to have food and sit down and rest. One of the elders, a disciple, comes forward and he asks the Buddha a question. You always have to be suspicious of questions asked to masters by their disciples. Never second-guess a hierophant! It is not a career move! But anyway, the disciple asked the Buddha a question.

There is a dialog. The topic is very rarified ... the nature of perception. The Buddha often uses a lot of paradoxical phrases. When a Master Teacher uses a paradoxical phrase, of what is that a sign? That the topic can't be solved in the mindset of the physical or hertzian plane, because the reality being discussed exists too far above that plane of frequency.

We often refer to God having a right and a left hand. Right

---

[182] These include Khotanese, Sanskrit, Sogdian, Tangut, an Old Uyghur language, and even Hebrew. They are a major resource in the field of history, religious studies and manuscript studies.

hands and left hands belong in the hertzian or material plane, but not at Point Zero[183] which is presumably where the Creator 'resides' primarily. If we realize that the idea of God's right and left hands are an image, it is fine. But, if we take the analogy as literal truth, as so many religious people seem to do today, then we are in serious trouble.

The Buddha used to do this a lot. He said in answer to the question: "That which is called the Buddha Dharma is not the Buddha Dharma. Therefore, it is called the Buddha Dharma." This statement is in the Diamond Sutra. What is the Buddha trying to do there? He is trying to teach this disciple, whose name was Subhuti, to lay aside his previous limited notions of the nature of reality and enlightenment. And he is trying to convey that all forms, all thoughts, and all conceptions, are ultimately an illusion. Much as we may try to express them in the language of our reality, all these attempts are going to fail. Because those thoughts and forms do not have the root of their existence in our reality and therefore can't be thoroughly analyzed and explained in our level of reality.

So, a seeming absurdity, such as saying "the Buddha Dharma is not the Buddha Dharma which is why it's called the Buddha Dharma", makes perfect sense if you begin to understand it in that sense of opening you up to a far more ambitious horizon of reality. The realization that all of reality just does not occur to us as passive victims, but in reality is created by profoundly held thought: which was actually the core of the message of Jesus as well.

All forms, all thoughts, all conceptions are basically not accurate … that is what the Buddha is saying. In our terms today, he is saying that all reality comes from the quantum field. It's

---

[183] "The concept of God as creator, 'unmoved mover,' and 'first cause' that we find in Aristotle's philosophy and Thomas Aquinas's theology, is described by Ramtha in terms of the Void knowing itself and contemplating itself. This act of contemplation represents a unique movement in the Void that produced a point of awareness and knowingness of itself. This point of awareness is referred to as Point Zero, primary consciousness, consciousness and energy, the observer, and God." Jaime Leal-Anaya, "Introductory Essay to Ramtha's Teachings" In Ramtha, *A Beginner's Guide to Creating Reality,* Third ed. (JZK Publishing, 2004), p. 47.

not permanent and unchangeable. These forms, at which we are looking, are not solid, fixed and immutable. Painfully we have to eventually acknowledge that the type of reality that is confronting us is one that has been magnetized to us over a long period of time. Therefore, circumstances are all changeable by a significant change of the mind that produces them. But to do that effectively we have to bring ourselves through a process of removing those crippling programs. Usually we hold onto them, thereby affirming that this substance here in front of me is solid, real and unchangeable. The denial of that was the heart of the Buddha's teaching and it was also the heart of Jesus' teaching. In short, the true state of enlightenment is impossible to grasp or describe through the categories that we use to-day in interaction with our everyday physical world.

These teachings of the Buddha are not just very similar to the teachings of Jesus: the method the Buddha used was also very similar to the method that Jesus used. To see the number of parallels between the Sermon on the Mount, the quintessence of Jesus' teachings, and the Buddha's teachings, is extremely thought provoking, and we will look at that directly later.

Chapter 13
Jesus and Mary Magdalene: The Modern Turmoil

The Priory of Sion and Modern Secretive Religious Organizations

In 2003 Dan Brown published a book that became one of the world's best known novels. Though couched as fiction, the author has always insisted the book is based on sound historical fact. It has sold well over 80 million copies, making it, in terms of sales, one of the most successful publications of all time.

The novel portrays a battle between the Priory of Sion, an organization supposedly of medieval origin, and the modern secretive Opus Dei organization. The issue at stake is whether Jesus was married to Mary Magdalene.

Their children are said to have emigrated to what is now southern France. Through their intermarriage with local noble families what became the Merovingian Dynasty[184] was established, and they became the ancestors of a Royal Bloodline that provided the foundation for some of the most historic and prestigious of the European Monarchies.

Airing such ideas about Jesus is bound to be extremely controversial and Dan Brown even received some death threats during the turmoil caused by the book's publication.

I note here the very controversial claims of the Russian Aristocrat, Nicolas Notovitch. I note this only in passing, as I have already surveyed this matter in detail in my two-disc DVD set of more than a decade ago, "How Jesus Became a Christ." Notovitch claimed that he had broken his leg in India and recovered from the mishap at the Monastery of Hemis in Ladakh, in the extreme north of India-administered Kashmir. There he learned of a document kept in the Monastery which told the story of Jesus having travelled to India and Tibet during his so-called "lost years," before his public ministry in Israel. Notovitch published the document in 1894 in French under the title *La vie inconnue de Jesus Christ.*[185] In 1894 Notovitch published a book in French under the same title, now available as an ebook.[186] At the time of first publication it was translated into English, German, Spanish, and Italian.

According to the manuscript, Jesus left his homeland at an early age to travel with a caravan of merchants to India (Sindh), to study

---

[184] For nearly three hundred years the Merovingians ruled most of the territory corresponding to modern France and some neighboring regions, until their King was deposed by Pope Zachary in 752.

[185] "Life of Saint Issa, Best of the Sons of Men" — Isa being the Arabic name of Jesus in Islam.

[186] The Gutenberg Project has published the entire manuscript as a free ebook: *The Project Gutenberg eBook, The Unknown Life of Jesus Christ, by Nicolas Notovitch,* Translated by J. H. Connelly and L. Landsberg.

the laws of the great Buddhas. He is made welcome by the Jains, but he leaves them to spend time among the Buddhists. He spends six years there, learning Pali and studying their religious texts. At twenty-six he departs for home and arrives back in his own country at about the age of twenty-nine, after many adventures and risks to his life. Once he arrives in his own country he begins to preach.

Attempts were made to discredit Notovitch by several noted European Scholars such as the noted historian Max Müller, who wrote to the Abbot of Hemis inquiring about the manuscript, and was told that no such document existed and that no person called Notovitch had never visited their monastery. Other European scholars also investigated Notovitch's story, and the noted German Indologist, Leopold von Schroeder,[187] called Notovitch's story a "big fat lie."

Obviously at the height of power of the British Raj in India, the authorities of the Monastery of Hemis had learned something about not exposing the fundamental beliefs of the Europeans to any significant challenge. They continued to deny that the Notovitch document existed in their Archives or that any person called Notovitch had ever visited their Monastery.

However, in 1922 Swami Abhedananda visited the Hemis monastery to try to establish the veracity of the reports about Notovich that he had heard the previous year in the USA.

The lamas at Hemis told him that Notovitch had indeed been brought to their Monastery to recover from a broken leg at the time he indicated, and that he had been looked after there for six weeks. They also told him that the manuscript on Jesus Christ had been shown to Notovich and the contents interpreted so that he could translate them into Russian.

A substantial portion of the text he copied was later incorporated into *Swami Abhedananda's Journey into Kashmir & Tibet* published by the Ramakrishna Vedanta Math.[188] Swami Bharati Krishna Tirthe, head of the Monastery at Puri, publicly stated in 1952 that similar versions of the life of Jesus in India and Tibet were contained in many other collections held at the monasteries of the region.

---

187 Professor at Innsbruck and later at the University of Vienna.

188 Edition of 1 May 1987.

I wanted to have a brief reference to Abhedananda here as an indication from a reputable source, (which only came to light in relatively recent times), that indicates the real life of Jesus might be considerably different from the customary and familiar versions of it.

Allegations of Plagiarism

It's often thought that "The Da Vinci Code" or "Holy Blood, Holy Grail" were the places where such ideas about Jesus and Mary Magdalene were heard of for the first time, but in fact they were aired well over thirty years before the "Da Vinci Code" appeared, and over a decade before "Holy Blood, Holy Grail."

In his best-selling book, "The Jesus Scroll,"[189] published in 1972, the Australian writer Donovan Joyce, postulates that Jesus may have lived to the age of eighty years and died at Herod's fortress at Masada, the location of the last stand of the Jewish rebels against Rome in 73 AD.

Excavations were conducted at Masada from 1963-65. Joyce went to Israel to investigate reports of the recent discovery there of a document alleged to have been written by Jesus himself. However, he was denied permission to visit the digs at Masada by the official in charge, Yigael Yadin.[190]

Joyce maintains that in 1964 fifteen scrolls were discovered at Masada during the excavations. He claims to have seen one of them that was stolen, and revealed that he had been asked to help smuggle the stolen scroll out of Israel to a foreign buyer.

Joyce claims that that scroll was autobiographical and was signed by "Yeshua ben Ya'akob ben Gennesareth," which translates into English as "Jesus of Gennesareth, son of Jacob." Joyce identifies this person as Jesus of Nazareth.

In the scroll Yeshua ben Ya'akob describes himself as eighty years old and the last of the rightful Kings of Israel. Joyce suggests

[189] New American Library, 1972.

[190] Former politician and Chief of Staff of the Israeli Defence Forces.

that Yeshua had survived the crucifixion, and was present on Masada when it fell to the final Roman siege on April 16, in 73 or 74 AD.[191] He further asserts that Yeshua had married Mary Magdalene and had a child with her.

After his momentous visit to Israel, Joyce returned to Australia and published *The Jesus Scroll,* first in Sydney in 1972, and in London the following year. It quickly became an extremely controversial best-seller, and not surprisingly led to numerous death threats against Joyce himself. This was the first notable pronouncement in modern times of these themes about Jesus.

Ten years after "The Jesus Scroll" Michael Baigent, Richard Leigh and Henry Lincoln, published "Holy Blood, Holy Grail."[192] A further ten years later Lynn Picknett and Clive Prince published *The Templar Revelation.*[193]

In 2005 two of the authors of "Holy Blood, Holy Grail" sued Random House,[194] the publishers of "The Da Vinci Code," for breach of copyright, alleging that "The Da Vinci Code had "appropriated the architecture" of their book and that it had been "highjacked and exploited" by Dan Brown in the writing of his novel. It was obvious that Brown had used the material in "Holy Blood, Holy Grail" extensively, but apparently not in such a fashion that would sustain a copyright violation. Brown won the case in April 2006 after a three-week trial in London.

With regard to Dan Brown's use of another source, Clive Prince's "The Templar Revelation," it's been pointed out, among many other things, that one chapter of "The Templar Revelation" is titled "The Secret Code of Leonardo Da Vinci" which may have inspired Dan Brown's choice of title for "The Da Vinci Code."

---

[191] The calculation of the precise date is described on pp. 29 and 32 of "Ancient Warfare," by Duncan B. Campbell, (2010). "Capturing a desert fortress: Flavius Silva and the siege of Masada". Ancient Warfare, 4 (2): 28–35. 73 AD was the date traditionally assigned to the fall of the fortress, but during the excavations coins dating from 73 AD were discovered, which makes the earlier date almost impossible to sustain.

[192] Published 1982, Jonathan Cape.

[193] Published 1997, Transworld Publishers.

[194] Henry Lincoln did not join the suit.

Brown also borrows some historical and factual errors that are contained in "The Templar Revelation" which would tend to confirm his use of that book as a resource.

Margaret Starbird used the same themes in her novel "The Woman with the Alabaster Jar,"[195] published ten years before "The Da Vinci Code." Kathleen McGowan published her first novel, "The Expected One" in 1989, which also focused on Jesus and Mary Magdalene.[196]

In 2003 Lewis Perdue claimed "The Da Vinci Code" had plagiarized significant parts of two of his novels, "Daughter of God," published in 2000, and 1983's "The Da Vinci Legacy." Perdue was sued for his allegations by Random House which won a court ruling in New York against Perdue in 2005.

Muddying the Waters: Forgeries in France

One of the books that the authors of "Holy Blood, Holy Grail" claim to have influenced their project was *"L'Or de Rennes,"* a 1967 book by Gérard de Sède, with the collaboration of Pierre Plantard.

Gérard de Sède was the pen name of Gérard-Marie de Sède, who belonged to a noble family from the south west of France. His father was editor of the local Catholic newspaper which the family owned.

Gérard de Sède published more than twenty books, the best known of which was *"L'Or de Rennes,"* mentioned above, (later re-published as *"Le Trésor Maudit"*), "The Gold of Rennes, or the Strange Life of Bérenger Saunière, Priest of Rennes le Chateau," published in 1967. De Sède had led a very colorful life, from fighting in the French Resistance against the Nazis during World War II,

---

[195] Published 1993, Bear & Company.

[196] Followed by "The Book of Love," focusing on the life of Mathilda of Canossa, and "The Poet Prince," on the life of Lorenzo de Medici. "The Source of Miracles: Seven Steps to Transforming Your Life Through the Lord's Prayer," was published by Fireside in 2009.

to living in Nicaragua and Yugoslavia, and moving in Trotskyite circles in the hope of advancing the creation of a New World Order. Later in his life he moved back to France and abandoned a career in journalism in favor of becoming a farmer.

It was during this time he met Roger Lhomoy after the latter had drawn attention to himself by stating that there was a secret underground chamber beneath the Chateau de Gisors in Normandy, which he said contained nineteen stone sarcophagi and a collection of iron coffers, holding the lost treasure of the Knights Templar.

De Sède was enthralled by Lhomy's report and wrote an article about it which came to the attention of a certain Pierre Plantard.

Plantard and de Sède soon collaborated in writing an article "The Templars are Among Us," which was published in 1962. It contained a few references to "The Priory of Sion." It should be noted that an associate and friend of Plantard, Philipe de Chérisey, who like Roger Lhomoy, claimed the supposed underground chamber at Gisors contained "thirty iron coffers of the Archives of the Priory of Sion."

Lhomoy's claim of a subterranean chamber at Gisors was exposed as fraudulent by an official investigation in 1964.

Not put off by these developments, de Sède and Plantard produced "L'Or de Rennes" in 1967. The original manuscript was written by Plantard but was extensively revised and re-written by de Sède.

They invented a series of "facts" about the renowned priest of Rennes le Chateau, François-Bérenger Saunière,[197] in order to produce an account of the discovery of a fabled secret. Central to their book were two parchments allegedly discovered by Bérenger Saunière, but which were actually forgeries made by de Chérisey — to which forgery he confessed in 1977. The so-called manuscripts were forged by him in 1961 and deposited with a solicitor, Matthieu Boccon-Gibod at Paris.[198] Gérard de Sède only ever saw photocopies of those alleged historic parchments.

Le Trésor Maudit, was read by Henry Lincoln (whom I once

[197] 11 April 1852 — 22 January 1917.

[198] At 89 Quai d'Orsay, 75007 Paris 07 Palais-Bourbon.

was fortunate to meet in person at Rennes le Chateau), in 1969, and he persuaded BBC 2 to make a series of very successful documentaries on this topic in the 1970s. Lincoln then joined forces with Michael Baigent and Richard Leigh to investigate matters further. They eventually "found" the notorious *Dossiers Secrets*, a list of genealogies that had also been forged by Pierre Plantard, and deposited anonymously in the French National Library. The purpose was to create the impression of a close association between Plantard and the royal bloodlines of France. The documents allegedly described hundreds of years of medieval French and European history. However, they were also shown to be fakes that were generated by Plantard himself and Philippe de Chérisey, under the pseudonym "Philippe Toscan du Plantier".

Baigent, Leigh and Lincoln were unaware that the French documents were forgeries and used them as a major source for "Holy Blood, Holy Grail."

The response to "Holy Blood Holy Grail" from professional historians and scholars from many related fields was universally negative. They argued that most, if not all of the assertions, claims, ancient mysteries and conspiracy theories that were presented as facts, had no historical foundation.

In October 1993, in response to a judicial investigation that involved the searching of his house and the discovery of a large collection of forged documents, including some that proclaimed Plantard as the true King of France, and descendent of Jesus, Plantard admitted under oath that he had made everything up, especially with regard to the Priory of Sion.

On 3 February 2005, Channel 4 TV in the UK aired a program in which de Sede's son Arnaud stated emphatically that his father and Pierre Plantard had made up the whole story about the existence of a "Priory of Sion." To quote him verbatim on that program: "It is absolute piffle."

A Married Jesus: An Ancient Theme

However many controversies and lawsuits may have occurred between modern authors, and irrespective of how much shock was claimed to be caused in certain Christian quarters about the relationship of Jesus and Mary Magdalene after "The Da Vinci Code", the fact remains that this topic is in reality a very ancient one. It has been a consistent part of certain versions of dualistic Christianity from the earliest times, for example in Marcionism,[199] Manichaeism,[200] Paulicianism,[201] Bogomilism,[202] Albigensianism[203] and Catharism.[204]

All of these movements had elements of Dualism in them. Every person who has ever pondered fundamental things in even a modest fashion will have wrestled with the difficulty of how a God who is supposed to be all-powerful, all-loving, and who is the Creator of all that exists, could have left us with the kind of world we know, full of injustice, evil, hatred, suffering and lack. It is obvious that those three beliefs about God, all-powerful, all-loving, and the Creator, simply cannot be held together, but it is not so obvious that the solution to the problem lies in none of the familiar avenues of the past, but in abandoning entirely the old paradigm and forging a new one. My favorite example of this process at work, to which I have referred often here, was the move from the Earth-centered world view of Ptolemy,[205] to the sun centered view of Copernicus. As pointed out earlier, no amount of improving Ptolemy's system could ever have led us to Copernicus. The whole paradigm of Ptolemy had to be discarded and a new one forged. When the paradigm of Copernicus was adopted almost all of the

---

199 Mid 2nd century.

200 Mid 3rd century.

201 Mid 6th century.

202 10th century.

203 12th and 13th centuries.

204 12-14th centuries.

205 Claudius Ptolemy (c. 90 – c. 168 AD. Librarian at Alexandria.

many difficulties associated with Ptolemy's theories disappeared as if by magic.

The central lesson in this for all of us is that human knowledge does not just evolve and grow by the acquisition and addition of more information. Of even greater importance is the imaginative structure we endeavor to put on that knowledge and information: in short, substituting a new paradigm or framework for the old one. Many of the difficulties that have puzzled so many generations of religious believers, for instance, such as the example quoted above of an all-powerful and loving creator producing the grossly imperfect world such as we know,[206] has been pondered, written and spoken about by every major thinker of which we have records, with relatively little gain in insight at the end of it all. The shift comes when we realize that the old paradigm by which we pictured the relationship of the creator to the creation was inadequate, and that a new one is needed. The dualistic traditions listed above, such as Gnosticism pre-eminently, did their best with the old paradigms, but their results were never very satisfactory, particularly for the Gnostics. In fact, nowadays we would tend to regard many of them as bizarre.

As an example, the Gnostics realized that a perfectly good and all powerful creator could never have created the fully formed world such as we know it, so they postulated two gods, one a good god, the other evil. The good things in creation were attributed to the former, the imperfect to the latter. Since Jesus was central to God's work in the world a similar compromise had to be reached in his regard. The tradition seemed to indicate to them that there was an intimate relationship between Jesus and Mary Magdalene, but since for them sexuality was a necessary evil, and the material aspects of the world in general were viewed in the same light, then such a relationship of Jesus to Mary Magdalene had to have been done by a duplicate Jesus who got involved in the world of matter, while the other Jesus floated free above the contamination of the material world entirely.

One of the most thorough analyses of the entire set of dualistic interpretations of Christianity, was done by Peter of Vaux de

[206] Generally known in theological circles as "The Problem of Evil."

Cernay, in the early part of the 13th century. It particularly showed how the relationship between Jesus and Mary Magdalene was, as a consequence, viewed by them. Support in modern times for the idea that Jesus and Mary Magdalene were married seems to draw a lot of inspiration from this document, though unfortunately it seems, not at first hand. Laurence Gardner's *Bloodline of the Holy Grail* makes no mention of it. The authors of "Holy Blood, Holy Grail" give a summary of the text, but do not seem very familiar with it. When Scott Wolter, Alan Butler and, more lately, Janet Wolter,[207] allege that the Templars and Cathars were in league to protect the Bloodline descending from Jesus and Mary Magdalene, they do not seem to have given any weight to the testimony of Peter of Vaux de Cerney relating to the Cathar views of Jesus and Mary Magdalene.

Of course it has to be remembered that Peter's testimony about the Cathars comes from an exceedingly hostile source.

> "First it is to be known that the heretics held that there are two creators, viz., one of invisible things whom they call the benevolent God, and another of visible things whom they call the malevolent God...they also affirmed that all the Fathers of the Old Testament were damned, that John the Baptist was one of the greater demons. They also said in their secret doctrine that Christ who was born in the visible and terrestrial Bethlehem, and crucified in Jerusalem, was a bad man, and that Mary Magdalene was his concubine; and that she was the woman taken in adultery, of whom we read in the Gospel."

So in short, the Cathars are reported as believing that Jesus was evil, and that Mary Magdalene was his demonic concubine: it's difficult to imagine how an heroic dedication to protect their Bloodline could arise from such a belief system.

---

[207] TV Series, 'America Unearthed S02E01,' "Ark of the Covenant," March 2013, Before the Pyramids, with Christ Knight, 2011, Alan Butler and Janet Wolter, America: Nation of the Goddess, November 2015.

A Short Note on Rennes-le-Chateau

In 1999, an individual named Ben Hammott, actual name Bill Wilkinson, claimed to have found a Templar tomb near to Rennes-le-Château. The tale of how he found a series of clues that led him to a tomb near Rennes-le-Château in France strains all credulity. Nevertheless, Hammott's story attracted significant attention, especially after it was enshrined into a documentary called "Bloodline" in 2008, coupled with the assertion that the tomb allegedly discovered was that of Mary Magdalene.

Finally, in 2013, "Ben Hammott" confessed that the entire affair was a hoax. The filming of the interior of the alleged tomb of Mary Magdalene at Rennes le Chateau was apparently done on a makeshift set erected in a warehouse in the north of England.

Mary Magdalene and Jesus Could Not Have Been 'Married'

I referred earlier to a tiny fragment of the Greek New Testament preserved at the John Rylands Library in Manchester, England.[208] The front contains parts of some lines from the Gospel of John, chapters 18:31-33, in Greek. The back has parts of some lines from verses 37-38.

The content of the text itself is interesting. It is an account of the trial of Jesus before Pilate. Pilate said to the Jewish authorities about Jesus — "Take him yourself and judge him by your own law". But they said, "We have no right to execute anyone". And Pilate said, "So you want to execute him"? This took place, as the text said, to fulfill what Jesus had said about the kind of death he was going to meet. Pilate then went back inside the palace where

[208] This manuscript is named Papyrus 52 or P52. It dates from about 125 AD: the oldest surviving manuscript of the New Testament.

Jesus was imprisoned. He summoned Jesus to him and he said: "Are you the King of the Jews?"

"The King of the Jews." What has this to tell us about Jesus and his mission?

By descent, Jesus was heir to the Throne of Judea, since he was the heir of the Davidic line. To cause the plot to thicken even further Mary Magdalene was the heir of the Hasmonean line, the other royal house of Judea that descended from Judas Maccabeus.[209]

This is why Mary Magdalene and Jesus couldn't be married. They and their potential offspring, of which there were two, according to these sources, would be prime targets for the authorities, since their children would have united together the two Royal Houses of Judea. This would have created a deadly political alliance in a region of the Roman Empire that was extremely unsettled at that time. Bumping off of any offspring and their parents would be the order of the day for the powers that were.

Instead it appears Mary Magdalene and Jesus were joined in an arrangement that was much more familiar in the first century Judaism than it is anywhere today. It is called "Hotre" in the Coptic language of the Gospel of Philip[210] – an arrangement that is the same as marriage in every respect except one. That is that the heir(s) could not inherit. They could not inherit anything, whether money, property, titles or the Kingship of Judea. That measure, "Hotre", safeguarded their children from being a political threat to the heirs of Herod the Great and the Romans. Were Jesus and Mary Magdalene married in the technical legal sense current at the time and now? No. Were they married in a sense we all popularly understand? Yes.

---

[209] Died 160 BC. He was leader of the revolt against the Selucid Empire which was established in 312 BC after the dividing up of the Macedonian Empire of Alexander the Great, following his death in 323 BC.

[210] Dated to around the 3rd century but lost in modern times until rediscovered in a cave near Nag Hammadi, Egypt, in 1945.

Jesus and the Woman Taken in Adultery

Two of the oldest and almost complete MSS of the New Testament are the Codex Sinaiticus and Codex Vaticanus. The Codex Sinaiticus was found by Count Tischendorf in 1859 at the Monastery of St Catherine on Mount Sinai, and contains 400 leaves. The Codex Vaticanus was discovered in the Vatican Library. It has 759 leaves and contains almost all of the Old and New Testaments. No one knows when it came to the Vatican Library, but it is listed in a catalogue there dated 1475. The text itself has been dated to the mid 4th Century, and it may be one of the fifty bibles commissioned by Constantine[211] even though just in the texts of the Gospels alone there are 3,036 textual variations between Sinaiticus and Vaticanus.

Both MSS are written on parchment, and have a large number of corrections written over the original text. They are both dated to the mid-4th Century.

What is of great interest in the New Testament part of these two ancient texts is that in neither of them does the story of Jesus and the woman taken in adultery appear. However, in our modern versions of the New Testament the famous text appears in the Gospel of Saint John, Chapter 8, verses 3-11. In short, we have no option but conclude that it was inserted into the text of John only after the fourth century.

Jesus had come over to the Temple at dawn from spending the night on the Mount of Olives. He began to teach in the Temple Court.

The teachers of the Law and the Pharisees dragged before him a woman who was alleged to have been captured in adultery. We suspect this woman was Mary Magdalene. What she had actually been doing was arranging transport back to her own native area from Jerusalem. She was originally from Magdala on the northwestern side of the Sea of Galilee and was negotiating with a director of a camel train to take her there. His brother came in during the transaction, and he thought that she was trying to "lead

[211] McDonald & Sanders, The Canon Debate, pp. 414-415. Baker Publishing Group, December 2001.

his brother astray." So, he dragged her out into the public arena and accused her of trying to commit adultery. The punishment for adultery under Jewish law was death by stoning. It is still practiced in some of the Muslim areas of the world today.

This incident was far less about serving justice, however warped a form of justice it was, but about seeing what Jesus would say and especially to see if he would entrap himself. The Pharisees said to him: *"Teacher, this woman was caught in the act of adultery.[5] In the Law, Moses commanded us to stone such women. Now what do you say?"[6] They were using this question as a trap, in order to have a basis for accusing him."* If he said "Yes," that would have contradicted what he had just taught about the nature of forgiveness. Or if he said "No," he would be accused of blasphemy against the sacred text.

Where the incident took place was an open area, and there was a lot of dust on the ground. Jesus didn't answer their question. In fact, he did or said nothing for quite a long time. Meanwhile they were sitting themselves down comfortably, waiting to enjoy Jesus being roasted on the spit. Then after this very long silence Jesus stood up, went to the individuals leading the protest about the woman, and wrote something in the dust in front of each of the individuals who were sitting on the ground in the front line. What words was he writing? Their secret sins.

As we are told in the Gospels, one by one they faded away. Why? Because their mothers and their wives and their children were in the back row looking on, and they didn't want their shameful secrets to be exposed. Perhaps they feared the next thing Jesus would have done would be to speak their faults and failings out loud. He was good at chess moves.

Eventually everyone was gone and only the woman and Jesus remained. He said to her: "They are all gone, why don't you go?" She wasn't taking that for an answer. She said: "Who are you?" He didn't answer, but she followed him for the remainder of his days. The rest, as you well know, is history.

Someone once said that when we are trying to look at the life of Jesus through these ancient manuscripts it is like looking through a telescope the wrong way round.

Who Decided which Books Should Be in the Bible?

So what is the Bible anyway? A set of books accepted as Scripture? Not even the Christian Church is unified on this question. The Protestants accept fewer books than the Catholics. The Catholics add two additional books to the Old Testament – the Book of Maccabbes and the Book of Tobit. The Greek Orthodox accept these, plus the Prayer of Manasseh and the Book of Esdras. The Ethiopian Orthodox add on Enoch and Jubilees. The farther East you go, the more books in the Bible apparently.

As just mentioned, the story we know as Jesus and the woman taken in adultery was not in the New Testament until the fourth century. Furthermore, The Book of Revelation is the only Apocalypse in the New Testament and it wasn't accepted into the Bible until 419 AD. No surprise there, since it is a pretty bizarre book. But if it took Revelation and the story of Jesus and Magdalene four hundred years to make it into the New Testament, where does that leave the notion of "the inspired written word of God" let down from Heaven fully formed by some praeternatural form of texting or email? It is apparent, however way we may regard those works as inspired, the inspiration certainly did not take the form of God lowering down those books to us fully formed

There were also a lot of books that never got into the New Testament at all, but might have, and probably should have got there earlier than some who did make it. Good examples are "The Shepherd of Hermas,"[212] "The Epistle of Barnabas"[213] and the Didache, – a most sublime book. I don't know why the latter didn't ever get into the New Testament. "The Gospel of Thomas" is another that didn't make it, and of course we know why that didn't get into the New Testament: because it didn't go along with the views of Jesus held by the status quo.

[212] Late 1st to mid-2nd century.

[213] Cited in late 2nd century.

So back to translations ... we have dozens of versions. Our first step in trying to discover who Jesus was and what he did and said is to somehow get past the translations. In English, we have dozens and dozens of modern translations which are very well done – The New International Version, The American Standard Version, The Revised Standard Version, and so on. Some people prefer the King James Version; even to the point of saying it's the only inspired translation. Like Tyndale's Bible, the Kings James Version has contributed enormously to the English language. Nevertheless, we shouldn't forget that it was originally based on some of the most defective sets of Greek manuscripts texts that exist. Why? Because that was all they had to translate from in those days in Europe.

While it is based on manuscripts that are not the best, nevertheless, in terms of the English language that it uses to express those inaccuracies, it is sublime. People will take in a lot if the language is good. It is like taking a large glass of something tasty with a nasty pill.

Let's explore this issue a little deeper. Translation is really difficult with a dead language like New Testament Greek. It is quite different from Classical Greek, and the usual name given to it is "Koine Greek," which basically means "Street Greek" or "Slum Greek". The texts we have in this language are limited in range. And, of course, we have no living speakers of that language to consult now so as to be more clear on what was meant.

Take an example. Imagine that some thousands of years into the future all the English-speaking peoples of the world had perished – let's say in the year 7,000 AD. In 5,000 years time, let's say, they find some puzzling phrase in a text in the English language: "Having your cake and eating it". So is this something to do with picking up something that someone baked in an oven and masticating it? Is this what they are talking about? Obviously not. Or take other examples like "saving face", or someone "kicking the bucket" or "throwing in the towel". At present, we still have millions of people who speak the language so we can ask them what these idioms mean. But suppose there were no native speakers of English left, which is now the case with Koine Greek.

Do we really know what they meant by some of the metaphors or allusions in Koine Greek? We can make an informed guess, but we can't be sure.

In that collection of 5,800 Greek manuscripts that exist some scholars estimate that there are as many as 400,000 places where the manuscripts disagree with each other. Or, as one notable Biblical scholar famously expressed it — there are more variations in the text of the New Testament than there are words in the New Testament.[214]

So how are we going to escape from our program that these texts are the inspired written word of God let down directly in an elevator from heaven? Or sent by fax or email? I think we should have second thoughts on this, even if we do face, according to certain belief systems, bottomless perdition on our death bed as a result.

So in what sense can we claim to have in the scriptures "the inspired written words of God" when there is so much uncertainty about the words themselves? I am addressing this question to the fundamentalists. They claim we know everything that God meant in those very texts? In the King James translation there have been three major revisions since it was published first in 1611. These changes amount to over 100,000 alterations in the text. Were all these changes — or were none of them — inspired?

Are the texts also awash with readings altered by scribes who were overly zealous...? A notable case is the subject of the Christian Trinity. Most experts regard 1 John 5: 7-8 as one of the primary New Testament texts used to support belief in the Trinity. Most experts however also believe that the text was something added in by a scribe who was anxious to provide an explicit scriptural basis for a belief he was prone to accept: "For there are three that testify, the Spirit and the water and the blood, and these three are in agreement."[215]

We also know from early Christian references that there were several other letters written by the New Testament authors that did

---

[214] Bart Ehrman: Misquoting Jesus — The Story Behind Who Changed the Bible and Why. First paperback edition, Harper San Francisco, 2007.

[215] 1 John 5:7-8.

not survive, such as Paul's Third Letter to the Corinthians. There are at least another dozen documents like this that we know about, but they have not survived. We've been told time and time again that God took great care to ensure that the existing Gospels and Letters of the New Testament were preserved so as to come down to us intact. So what am I going to understand about these dozen letters that haven't survived? Was this carelessness on God's part since he allowed some of these other Letters to get lost? Or was it forgetfulness that delayed the recognition of the Book of Revelation as part of the New Testament for the best part of four hundred years? That's the only logical conclusion if we accept these premises. It shows you that you can't have black and white ideas about a topic unless you know very little about the subject, especially when discussing the formation and transmission of the New Testament.

Now some of these 400,000 variations in the various New Testament manuscripts are undoubtedly just the result of people having a bad morning and copying inaccurately. Obviously, we are not concerned with that. What we are much more concerned with are changes that were deliberately made in the text to accommodate different points of view theologically. To ensure, in other words, that sacred scripture corresponded to the teachings of the Church or is made to bolster up the teachings of the Church, instead of vice versa.

So do we have the Scriptures being tweaked to bolster up the Church's position, instead of the Church following the position of the Scriptures? I have in mind answers to questions such as, "Was Jesus divine or human or both?" What was the true status of women in the Church? Several other texts were twisted to bolster up views which the Church had already decided to adopt and then set about finding a reason to justify their position.

But all that being said about the King James Bible, we can never forget its major contribution to the evolution of the English language. Many of our everyday sayings first saw the light of day in the King James translation, some of which are listed below.

God forbid
A law unto themselves

Holier than thou
At their wits end
A man after his own heart
Honor your father and mother
Bottomless pit
How are the mighty fallen?
In the twinkling of an eye
A thorn in the flesh
The land of Nod
By their fruits you shall know them
A stumbling block
The land of milk and honey
Love your neighbor as yourself
Born again
Led as a sheep to the slaughter
Seek and you shall find
My name is legion
Let not your left hand know what your right hand does
Two-edged sword
Money is the root of all evil
Do not put new wine into old bottles
Am I my brother's keeper?
Charity covers a multitude of sins
Let my people go
Be all things to all men
Turn the other cheek
Suffer fools gladly
Set your own house in order
A wolf in sheep's clothing
Take root
A Dreamer of dreams
The last shall be first
The blind leading the blind
Death, where is your sting?
Will the leopard changes his spots
The lost sheep
The skin of my teeth

The powers that be
The spirit is willing the flesh is weak
They know not what they do
The signs of the times
Shall not bear false witness

And finally, adding to the above list, in the phrasing of the King James: "It is a better thing to give than to receive," — the only statement of Jesus that comes to us from outside the Gospels.

These phrases are all from the King James translation. But that translation, as already noted, for all its wonderful qualities as a classic of the English language, nevertheless is based upon some of the most defective texts of the Greek manuscripts of the New Testament.

A lot of people find it difficult to accept intellectually different interpretations of passages of scripture which they have always embraced emotionally: another sublime example of profound religious sub-conscious programming.

In the next section we will explore superstitions that disempower these sacred texts.

SCROLL FOUR
THE EVIDENCE FOR JESUS AND HISTORY'S IMPACT ON IT

Chapter 14
A Quasi-Superstitious Reverence for Sacred Texts only Dis-empowers Them

Musings on the Scriptures

The texts that are sacred to the three major religions of the West enshrine some of the most profound and uplifting material ever expressed in human history. Yet parts of these texts mirror some of the worst aspects of human nature as well. Unfortunately, we humans are all too prone to allow exaggerated and unjustifiable ideas to creep into our understanding of what these texts are and what they are meant to facilitate for us. The texts themselves are thereby radically dis-empowered and the evolution in spiritual terms, which they offer to us, is largely neutralized.

Sacred texts have always had a central place in the religious ceremonies and daily life of both Judaism and Christianity. It was normal in the synagogue services to have readings from what we now call the Old Testament. And from the earliest years the Christian communities also used Old Testament readings in their religious services.

The New Testament Letters, or "Epistles," as they are more commonly known today, began to appear about a generation after Jesus' ministry. The Gospels began to be written from about forty years onwards after the end of his public mission. These new writings, which came to be called "Gospels," then began to occupy a significant place in the early Christian religious services and in everyday veneration.

It is well to remind ourselves occasionally that many of the most cherished beliefs in Christianity, including some instances already cited here: for example, how we understand the divinity of Jesus; the nature of the Holy Trinity; what awaits us after death, and many of the central Bible stories have sometimes been at least partially influenced by scribal changes made in copying the Biblical texts, and can lead to significant alterations in understanding. And remember, sometimes the variations in the translation or copying were deliberately made to bolster up particular theological positions.

If we wish to assert that the texts of the New Testament are inspired by God, then what version of the sacred texts do we assert were inspired? Surely we would say it was the original, or autograph copies, written down by the four authors of the New Testament Gospels, and the authors of the other twenty-three documents that make up the New Testament Canon. Unfortunately, none of the autograph copies of any of these New Testament documents has survived.

The original language of the New Testament documents as we have them, is Greek, mostly in the Koine, or Alexandrian dialect of Greek — what we might perhaps today call 'street' Greek,[216] as already noted, rather than the classical form of the language. Is it only the original Koine Greek language versions of the texts that are inspired, or are the various translations from Koine Greek inspired as well — even when mistakes in copying or translation have been made?

If we want to replace these crippling religious programs, which come from sub-conscious areas in our minds, then we need to

[216] Greek was the common language of the Eastern Mediterranean from the time of Alexander the Great (335—323 BC) until the Muslim conquests in the 7th century AD. Koine Greek, or the Alexandrian Dialect of Greek, remained the court Language of the Eastern Roman Empire until the fall of Constantinople to the Muslims on 29 May 1453. Koine is also the language of the Septuagint, the 3rd-century BC Greek translation of the Hebrew Bible, and of most of the early Christian theological writing by the Fathers of the Church. It is still used today as the liturgical language of services in the Greek Orthodox Church.

seriously re-think what we assumed we knew about the Scriptures and how they were formed, and then re-build those programs from the ground up. We will be the winners in that process, but the Scriptures themselves even more so.

This is obviously not an attack on the Jewish and Christian Scriptures. People who may allege that have obviously not understood what it is I am conveying here. This is simply an attempt to arrive at an objective assessment of what the Scriptures truly are, how they came to be, and what belief in their divine inspiration implies — devoid of any positions based merely on historical sentiment or religious piety.

If We Don't Have the Original Documents, What Do We Have?

If we don't have the original texts of the documents of the New Testament, then what do we have? Bart Ehrman[217] puts it memorably, but somewhat misleadingly, when he states:

> "What good is it to say that the autographs (i.e., the originals) were inspired? We don't have the originals! We have only error-ridden copies, and the vast majority of these are centuries removed from the originals and different from them, evidently, in thousands of ways. There are more variations among our manuscripts than there are words in the New Testament."

There are approximately 130,000 words in an average modern English translation of the New Testament. Among the surviving hand-written manuscripts of the New Testament, according to Ehrman, there are over 400,000 places where the surviving manuscripts disagree. Ehrman makes a very thought-provoking point which certainly would make an impact in a lecture or book

[217] Misquoting Jesus. 7, 90.

aimed at a popular audience that was designed to wake people up to many aspects of their beliefs that they have never critically examined. However, in a more in depth look at the matter it is clear that the 400,000 variants is the total number that exists in all of the approximately five thousand manuscripts of the New Testament taken together. The erroneous and unfortunate impression often taken from that type of statement is that there are over 400,000 errors in the text of the New Testament.

For most of the renowned ancient documents in our culture, only a handful of manuscripts exist, some dating from 800-1,500 years or more after the original versions.

In the case of the works of "Homer" (if he was an historical individual, rather than a name applied to a group of writers functioning over a long period), the earliest manuscript has been dated to c. 730 BC. Six hundred and forty manuscripts of Homer's "Iliad" have come down to us, but all of them are separated from the original work by well over a thousand years. Eight manuscripts of the works of Thucydides (c. 460 - 395 AD) survive, but all of them date from more than fifteen hundred years after the originals. The historian Herodotus (484-425 BC) has eight manuscripts surviving, but all are separated by more than a thousand years from the original works. Seven manuscripts of the works of Plato (+384 BC) survive, but all of them are separated by more than a thousand years from the original text.

Ten manuscripts of the works of Julius Caesar (100-44 BC) survive, but all date from the Middle Ages. The works of Josephus (37-100 AD) have nine manuscripts, the earliest dating from the fifth century. Tacitus, (58-117 AD) was one of the greatest Roman Historians, from the Silver Age of Latin literature. The surviving portions of his major work—the *Annals of Imperial Rome*, examine the reigns of the Emperors Tiberius, Claudius, and Nero. His works span the history of the Roman Empire from the death of Augustus in AD 14 to the years of the First Jewish — Roman War in AD 70. However, the "Annals of Imperial Rome" survives in only two manuscripts, both from the middle ages, separated from the original work by more than a thousand years.

In this field quantity is certainly not quality, but scholars remain confident that they can still access the original text with a reasonable degree of certitude.

Compared with the major works of antiquity the textual evidence for the New Testament is extraordinary.[218] A recent assessment by Kostenberger and Kruger identifies 5,500 separate Greek manuscripts of the New Testament. These manuscripts fall into three categories: Uncials (texts written using Greek capital letters), Miniscules (texts written using lower case Greek letters, in cursive style), and Fragments.

The 2,795 Miniscule manuscripts date from the 9th to the 15th centuries, and contain 34 complete texts of the New Testament. The Uncial manuscripts contain almost complete texts of the New Testament and date back to the fourth century and in some cases even earlier. Three of the most notable Uncials are the Codex Vaticanus, dated 325-350 AD, which contains an almost complete text of the New Testament: the Codex Sinaiticus, dated to about 340 AD, which contains about half of the Old Testament and almost all of the New. Another Miniscule manuscript, the Codex Alexandrinus, has a complete text of the Old Testament and almost all of the New. It is dated to the middle of the fifth century.

The Fragments provide the most interesting information of all. The discovery of the Bodmer Papyri II collection was announced in 1956. It is dated to about 200 AD or earlier. It includes most of the first fourteen chapters of the Gospel of John and a lot of the last seven chapters.

The Chester Beatty Papyri are preserved at Dublin. Some of them used to be on long-term loan to Maynooth College where they were on display in the Pugin Library, and were viewed with great interest by the theological and Biblical students. The Chester Beatty Papyri contain most of the New Testament, and are dated to the mid-third century, a century or more earlier than the Codex Vaticanus and Codex Sinaiticus.

The most amazing fragment of all is the tiny John Rylands Papyrus, which is barely three inches square and contains the text of John 18:31-33, and John 18:37—38. Being dated between 117-133

[218] See Kostenberger and Kruger, The Heresy of Orthodoxy Crossway Books, Wheaton, IL:, 2010.

AD (though it may even be earlier). It is the earliest known copy of any part of the New Testament. This shows that the Gospel of John was in circulation in Egypt within 40 years of its composition.

In addition, 10,000 manuscripts of early translations of the New Testament into Latin exist today. By the 3rd and 4th centuries translations had also been made into Coptic and Syrian, Armenian and Georgian. There are also ancient references to almost every verse of the New Testament in the writings of the Church Fathers, so that if the text of the New Testament were to disappear entirely, it could be re-constructed from those quotations alone.

In the light of all this, in the final analysis what are we to make of Bart Ehrman's rather alarming statement in "Misquoting Jesus" that "there are more variations among our manuscripts than there are words in the New Testament" (p 90), and that the manuscripts "differ from one another in so many places that we don't even know how many differences there are" (p 10). He gives the misleading impression that there are so many variants in the New Testament manuscripts that we could never know what the New Testament authors originally wrote.

Well over half of the 400,000 variants to which Ehrman refers are spelling errors (200,000 of the errors are of this kind). Copying "ie" instead of 'ei,' is a common scribal error in copying the New Testament texts, (as common in Scripture as it is in our own writing today), or different choices of phonetic spelling (kreinai vs. krinai). There are a host of other differences in abbreviation or style that are really of no theological or doctrinal importance whatever. For example, a definite article appearing before a name—"the James"— is omitted in another version because it adds nothing to the meaning of the phrase.

Almost all the 400,000 variants are easy to spot and are fundamentally unimportant. A famous example is taken from some manuscripts of 1 Thess. 2:7 which read "We were *horses* among you" instead of "We were *gentle, or mild,* among you." The difference in Greek is small: *hippoi* vs. *nepioi*. Other manuscripts of 1 Thess. 2:7 have another variation; "We were *little children* among you" (*epioi*). It is easy in copying to confuse 'nepoi' "epioi" and 'hippoi.' Obviously no doctrinal or historical fact is at stake in those variations.

Needless to say, Ehrman's motives have been challenged by many conservative Christians who accuse him of trying to shock Christians about fundamental matters of belief. However, it has been pointed out that if some Christians are shocked by these kinds of statements the fault really lies with centuries of Christian theologians and pastors who have concealed the truth from their flocks. Luke Muehlhauser in *Common Sense Atheism* puts it bluntly:

"But if those facts shock Christians, that is not Ehrman's fault. It is the fault of Christian authors and pastors. Christian scholars have known these facts for centuries, but they have "protected" their flocks from the truth".

The Evangelical scholar Daniel Wallace sees the problem clearly: "The intentional dumbing down of the Church for the sake of filling more pews will ultimately lead to defection from Christ. Ehrman is to be thanked for giving us a wake-up call."[219]

Translations: Especially the King James

Nowadays we take for granted the availability of many different translations of the New and Old Testaments in our own language. But, to give some perspective, it's not all that awfully long ago in the history of England that the death penalty was attached to having an English translation of the Scriptures in your possession.

At the dawn of the twenty first century there were more than sixty different English translations of the New Testament Scriptures in print. It's difficult to decide whether an individual translation may be a modification of an earlier one or whether one should classify the translation of part of the Bible as a separate translation. Generally speaking, it's held that there have been about 900 translations of the scriptures into English since Tyndale's complete version of the New Testament appeared in 1526.[220]

[219] Article "Misquoting Jesus? Answering Bart Ehrman," in Bible.org, published July 3rd 2013. https://bible.org/article/gospel-according-bart

[220] William J. Chamberlin's "Catalogue of English Bible Translations," Greenfield, December 1991, 960 pp., is regarded as the standard reference work in the field.

As mentioned in an earlier chapter, the very earliest translations of the Greek New Testament were made into Latin in the middle to the late second century. St. Jerome produced a standard Latin translation which was completed in 406 AD. This version was called the "Versio Vulgata" or literally translated, the 'Common Version/Translation'. We now call it "The Vulgate". That Latin translation dominated Christianity in the West for over a thousand years and was the first major book printed.[221] It remains the official Bible of Catholicism today.

But let's look again at the English translations. The Stuarts came back to the throne of England in 1603 when James I succeeded Queen Elizabeth upon her death. You may recall that sixteen years earlier, on 8 February 1587, Queen Elizabeth had executed James' mother — Mary, Queen of Scots.

It was under the auspices of King James I that the first official translation of the Bible into English was embarked upon. It was necessary for someone of unparalleled stature, such as the King, to authorize such a venture since the first English translation of the New Testament published by William Tyndale seventy five years earlier[222] had ended with catastrophic results. Tyndale was hunted down and burned at the stake for blasphemy. The mere possession of an English translation of the Bible during those times in England merited the death sentence.

The Commission entrusted with the new task of translation by King James had it made very clear to them at the outset that certain key words in the texts should be translated in ways that were already familiar to generations of Church goers in England. The translations were not to disturb the simple faith of the people. They were told, for example, that there should be no translation of 'Church' as 'Congregation' and no translation of 'priest' as 'elder'. Neither should there be any blurring of the distinction between the clergy and the laity, and there should be no translation of 'charity' as 'love'.

We know Jesus could read and write. On one notable occasion, as told in Chapter 8 of St. John's Gospel, a woman accused of

---

221 By Johannes Gutenberg, at Mainz, in what is now Germany, in the 1450s.

222 1525-26.

adultery was hauled before Jesus so that they could challenge him to command she be stoned to death for her sin. After a tense and dreadful period of silence Jesus got up and bent down before each of the men in the front circle of accusers. Then he said, "He who is without sin among you cast the first stone". One by one they faded away in silence because before each accuser he had written their secret sins in the dust.

On another occasion Jesus came to visit Nazareth where he had been brought up. On the Sabbath Day he went to the Synagogue as was his normal practice. As a distinguished teacher he was invited to read the Scripture for the day, which was from the scroll of the Prophet Isaiah, Chapter 61, verses 1-2. The account is given in the Gospel of St. Luke, Chapter 4, verses 16-19: "The Spirit of the Lord is upon me, because he has anointed me to proclaim good news to the poor. He has sent me to proclaim freedom for the prisoners and recovery of sight for the blind, to set the oppressed free and proclaim the year of the Lord's favor."

This opens up a very interesting situation. For if we consult that text in Isaiah 61, the phrase underlined in the quotation above does not exist there. If the scriptures are supposed to be God's inspired written word, how can pieces be missing, or…did Jesus make a mistake in reading the Isaiah scroll?

Some help to resolve the difficulty may come when we realize that a famous Greek translation of the Old Testament, called the Septuagint, does have that phrase in its account of Isaiah. So, was Jesus reading at the Synagogue in Greek? Or was it the case that whoever was writing down the Gospel of Luke, some fifty years or more after that event took place in the Nazareth Synagogue, had the Greek Septuagint translation of Isaiah open before him and not the original Hebrew version? Did the writer of Luke's Gospel then use the Greek translation to provide the text Jesus had read out long before, but in Hebrew, not Greek?

However, to complicate matters further, the Hebrew text of Isaiah 61 contains a clause that is not in the Greek Septuagint of Isaiah; "to proclaim liberty to the captives, and "the opening of prison to them that are bound". So, to sum up, according to our short investigation here, the account of Jesus reading from Isaiah at the Nazareth Synagogue as told by Luke's Gospel includes a phrase that is not in the Hebrew text of Isaiah. And Luke's account also partially excludes or paraphrases another quotation which *is* in the Hebrew Isaiah – "the opening of prison to them that are bound" as a substitute for "to set at liberty them that are bruised". To be clear: Luke's Jesus reads a text that is not in the original version of Hebrew Isaiah and omits a second text that is.

Obviously neither of these textual differences are earth shattering in themselves. However, they certainly add more evidence to help disabuse us of any semi superstitious conviction that every individual word in the scriptures are verbally inspired, and come down from God directly without any loss, error or addition, something that the traditional understandings of the divine inspiration of the texts would have us believe. Convictions of this sort can do enormous damage to the proper understanding of the scriptural message.

Our Sources for Jesus outside the New Testament

There are brief and indirect references to Jesus in a few non-Christian sources:[223]

- Cornelius Tacitus, "Annals of Imperial Rome," published about 116 AD.
- Suetonius, in his "Life of Claudius," published in 121 AD.
- Pliny the Younger in a letter to Trajan about 112 AD, and
- Mara Bar-Serapion, a Syrian stoic philosopher who mentions Jesus in a letter to his son from prison, circa 70 AD.

---

[223] See Robert E. Van Voorst, Jesus outside the New Testament: an Introduction to the Ancient Evidence, Eerdmans, 2000.

However, the two most notable references to Jesus are in Books 18 and 20 of the "Antiquities" of the ancient Jewish historian, Josephus, written about 93-94 AD. The consensus among scholars today seems to be that, while there may have been an authentic nucleus in an original text of Book 18, Chapter 3, 3, (usually called the Testimonium Flavianum), which states that Jesus the Messiah was a wise teacher who was crucified by Pilate, the text as we have it is believed to have been embellished and elaborated on in the 4th century by a Christian copyist, and is therefore not fully authentic.

The reference in Book 18, Chapter 5, 2 to the imprisonment and death of John the Baptist is regarded as authentic, as is the reference in Book 20, Chapter 9, 1 to "the brother of Jesus who was called Christ, whose name was James".

a) Antiquities, 18.3.3

"Now there was about this time Jesus, a wise man, if it be lawful to call him a man, for he was a doer of wonderful works, a teacher of such men as receive the truth with pleasure. He drew over to him both many of the Jews, and many of the Gentiles. He was the Christ, and when Pilate, at the suggestion of the principal men among us, had condemned him to the cross, those that loved him at the first did not forsake him; for he appeared to them alive again the third day; as the divine prophets had foretold these and ten thousand other wonderful things concerning him. And the tribe of Christians so named from him are not extinct at this day."

b) Antiquities, 20.9.1

"But the younger Ananus who, as we said, received the high priesthood, was of a bold disposition and exceptionally daring; he followed the party of the Sadducees, who are severe in judgment above all the Jews, as we have already

> shown. As therefore Ananus was of such a disposition, he thought he had now a good opportunity, as Festus was now dead, and Albinus was still on the road; so he assembled a council of judges, and brought before it the brother of Jesus the so-called Christ, whose name was James, together with some others, and having accused them as law-breakers, he delivered them over to be stoned."

Whatever the verdict on the Josephus texts may eventually turn out to be, it is obvious that most of what we know about Jesus comes not from any secular source, but from the four Gospels of the New Testament.

Some information also comes from the fourteen Letters attributed to Paul in the New Testament. In terms of chronology, Paul is the first writer in the New Testament, issuing his first Letter to the Thessalonians about 50 AD. Paul's name is on fourteen books in the New Testament, however the Pauline authorship of six of them is believed to be forged.

How Close Were the New Testament Documents to the Time and Events They Were Describing?

Remember all of this discussion is about removing programs. Almost all the information we have on Jesus comes from the four Gospels, not from other contemporary secular or religious sources. Some pages back we looked at the potential for inaccuracies in the translations of the New Testament.

The next question we have to ask is: how close in time were those documents to the events they describe? If we take it that the ministry of Jesus came to an end about 30 AD, and we ask how close in date any of the four Gospels of the New Testament are to the historical events they claim to describe, we may be in for some surprises!

Can we begin our search by looking for a more accurate calculation of the birth date of Jesus?

The Date of the Birth of Jesus

We know from the two Infancy Narratives in the Gospels (Luke 2:1-39 and Matthew 1:18-2:23) that Herod the Great was still alive when Jesus was born. We are dependent on Josephus for the date when Herod died. He states in his *Antiquities*, 17.6.4, that there was an eclipse of the moon shortly before the death of Herod. That reference has usually been taken to refer to the eclipse of 13 March, 4 BC.

However, it has been pointed out[224] that this eclipse was only visible very late in the night in Judea, and besides was only a partial eclipse. Following that eclipse there were no further eclipses visible in Judea until the two eclipses that occurred on July 5 and December 29, 1 BC. Did Herod the Great die in 4 BC or 1 BC?

Josephus brackets Herod the Great's death "between a Fast and a Passover."

Some have identified the Fast with Yom Kippur, which normally occurs in the Gregorian Calendar around mid-September to mid-October. However, it would seem that the date of this Fast is too far from Passover, which occurs on the day after the first full moon after 21 March, in the northern hemisphere.

It's been pointed out[225] however, that there is another notable Jewish Fast that occurs a month before Passover, the Fast of Esther, which occurs on the day before the Festival of Purim. Purim fell on 12-13 March in 4 BC, a two-day period in which there was both a lunar eclipse and a Fast, one month before Passover.

There are three lines of argument that favor the year 4 BC, rather than 1 BC for the death of Herod. These were notably enunciated in the 19th Century by Emil Schürer in his *A History of the Jewish People in the Time of Jesus Christ.*

---

224 In the 19th Century by Édouard Caspari and Florian Riess.

225 By Suzanne Nadaf, Brookyn, New York.

Josephus tells us that Herod died shortly before Passover[226] which would make the lunar eclipse of March 4 BC, far more likely than a December eclipse.

Josephus also states that Herod reigned for 37 years from the time of his appointment in 40 BC, and 30 years from his conquest of Jerusalem,[227] which would also place death in 4 BC.

The reign of Herod's son and successor, Archelaus, began in 4 BC. Herod's other son, Herod Antipas, the Herod whom Jesus knew, also began his reign at latest by 4 BC, as witnessed by coinage of the time.

So, according to the evidence we have from Josephus, it appears Jesus was probably born shortly before March of 4 BC, and his mission ended somewhere in the period 26 to 30 AD, if his mission ended at about the age of 33 years, as tradition has it.

Now that we have established a date for the birth of Jesus, our next question is: how close are any of the four Gospels of Matthew, Mark, Luke, and John to the events of the life and mission of Jesus? The consensus of Biblical scholars nowadays is that Mark was the first Gospel not Matthew, which is the conventional arrangement. Most scholars agree that Mark was written in the late 60's or early 70's AD. Matthew came next about a decade later in the late 70's or the early 80's. And the so-called Luke's Gospel was written in the middle to the late 80's.

About 150 years ago scholars postulated that Matthew and Luke, in composing their Gospels, had access to another document in addition to Mark's Gospel. The scholars named this document "Q" from the German word 'quelle' meaning 'a source'. It is postulated that "Q" was composed about the year 50 AD. The existence of this other source was proposed to explain the material that is in both Matthew and Luke but not in Mark. The writer of Mark's Gospel was not aware of that source. Unfortunately, the hypothetical "Q" has not survived.

Scholars are divided as to when John's Gospel was written. It's likely it was composed in a number of segments — the main part probably being written in the late 90's. The epilogue at the end

226 Antiquities 17.9.3, The Jewish War 2.1.3.

227 Antiquities 17.8.1, War 1.33.8.

was possibly added in the early second century. And by that time undoubtedly John himself had long gone to the Planes of Bliss.

So what do we make of this? Jesus did do all those things that he is reputed to have done including healing the sick; walking on water; raising the dead; producing material things, such as bread, out of energy; and many other works of the same order. A lot of people who saw these things were obviously going to talk about what they saw. Wouldn't we all? But they did not write about them. Unfortunately, the four Gospels are our main source of information, not those gossiping people who witnessed a lot but left no records behind them.

But there is another class of testimony, which we will look at in more details at the end of this chapter: that Jesus apparently taught in poetic forms, and what he said was also memorized in poetic form and handed on. If so, even without written sources, we may be far more close to the originally spoken words than may have normally been realized hitherto when most of the emphasis was on written documentary sources.

But if the four Gospels are our main sources of information we have to realize, first of all, that they were written from the late 60's up to possibly the late 90's or maybe even a little bit later. They were composed over a range of three to four decades, and the earliest of them was separated from the events they described by a gap of about 40 years; the latest by about 70 years. But did they incorporate accurate memorized accounts of what Jesus said and did, which could be as close as you can get to eyewitness accounts?

What does all that mean? It's as if we today were putting down on paper a narrative of events that took place at the time of World War II, or at the end of the Vietnam War in 1975. That is exactly the span of time by which the Gospel texts in the New Testament are separated from the events they describe. Between 40 to 70 years is a long time to wait before putting your thoughts down on paper, especially if they are someone else's thoughts. But if at the time of World War II someone wrote a highly accurate poem or song about some crucial event, would that not be passed down unaltered?

As far as I can tell there have been more books written about Jesus than any other single individual in human history. The next biggest total belongs to Napoleon Bonaparte. But all of the Jesus books that have ever been written, all of those tens of thousands of books, depend ultimately on the four Gospels of the New Testament. Unfortunately, none of these Gospels are contemporary with Jesus in the customary sense of that term as we use it in Western culture.

The day-to-day language of Jesus and the Apostles was likely Aramaic, which was part of the northwestern group of Semitic languages which includes Hebrew and Phoenician. Syriac is the major Aramaic dialect and is still used as their liturgical language by the St. Thomas Christians in India, the Syriac Orthodox Church, the Syriac Catholic Church and the Ancient Church of the East.

Hebrew had almost died out in Israel by the time of Jesus, and reading the texts in the Synagogue in Hebrew had to be followed by a reading of a translation into Aramaic. The Gospels as we have them were written in neither of these languages, but in Greek. And most likely these four books were not written in Israel but in territories far away from the center of Jesus' ministry and, as we saw, many decades after his time.

Were the Four Gospels Written by the People Whose Names They Bear ... Matthew, Mark, Luke and John?

People often defend the view that the Gospels were written by the people whose names are associated with them today. The justification is that the early theologians in the Church, called "The Fathers of the Church,"[228] didn't ever speculate about who wrote the Gospels but accepted the names of the authors they traditionally bore.

However, that notion is true only of the Church Fathers from about the middle of the second century onwards. The early Fathers of the Church do not refer to the four Gospels by the names they have today. They treat them as anonymous documents with no

[228] Eminent theologians who laid the scholarly foundations of Christianity in the early centuries. That title is normally applied to individuals who lived befoe about 700 AD.

authors' names attached to them. It looks like the names of the authors began to be associated with particular Gospel texts only about the middle of the second century.

The standard belief, according to Church tradition, is that the four Gospels were written by Matthew, Mark, Luke and John. Matthew was a tax collector. Mark was the secretary of Peter and was with him in Rome before Peter was executed. Luke was a disciple of Paul. Only Matthew and John were two of the twelve Apostles. Luke never met Jesus. Paul never met Jesus, *pace* that incident on the road to Damascus. Unfortunately, the evidence just doesn't support the view that these four named individuals wrote the Gospels.

When trying to discover who is the author of a book like any of the New Testament writings, the most obvious place to look is within the texts themselves. Does the author of any Gospel refer to himself by name? Does he refer to some incidents or events that he witnessed that would tie his name to the Gospel as its author? The answer to both questions is "No."

Secondly, we could look at what evidence comes from outside the texts. Do other contemporary authors refer to the author of the work? And what information can we gather about the alleged author's life from other sources?

The first thing to note about the four Gospels of the New Testament, which are our primary witnesses for what Jesus actually was and said and did, as opposed to the Jesus we have been traditionally served up, is that they do not claim Matthew, Mark, Luke and John to be their authors. The term they use is "Kata…" Kata Matthaion, Kata Iōannēn, etc.

"Kata" is a Greek term which denotes "handed down from" or "according to". In other words, what the phrase means is: "The Gospel according to Matthew, according to John, etc." The very titles themselves are saying unequivocally that these four named people did not themselves write the documents. It was their tradition that was picked up and revered, and put down in writing by others.

We need to be clear that whoever placed these titles on the Gospels in the middle of the second century was not trying to convey that Matthew, Mark, Luke and John were the authors. Instead, by their choice of phrasing, they were intending to convey that Mathew, Mark, Luke and John were NOT the authors. The actual authors of the Four Gospels most likely had never witnessed the life of Jesus or any of the incidents that were described in their texts.

As already noted, the original autograph copy of none of the Gospels of the New Testament has survived, so we can't go there for help. In fact, it is not even clear that there was any single recognized title for any of the four Gospels originally. What we find is that in thousands of manuscripts there is a wide variety of titles given to them. Scholars have therefore concluded that there wasn't any single original title on any of the Gospels but that the names were added by later scribes.

Was It Even Possible That the Gospels Could Have Been Written by the People Whose Names Were Put on Them Later?

It is highly unlikely. The literacy rate in Israel towards the close of the Biblical period is variously reckoned to have been about 1.5% to perhaps about 3%. It's hard for us to grasp the significance of this today since we have grown accustomed to literacy rates of about 95%. Even in the days of Roman rule the literacy rate was unlikely to have gone above 3% so only very few could read, and even fewer could write well. Only very few could write complex works of prose like the Gospels of the New Testament.

People who attain that standard of literacy were certainly the elite, and you can rest assured that none of them were people who eked out a living by fishing on the shores of the Lake of Galilee.

John, the Son of Zededee, the disciple of Jesus and alleged author of the Fourth Gospel, lived for a long, long time. He lived long enough to know Polycarp,[229] Bishop of Smyrna, (a town on the west coast of modern Turkey). Polycarp and the Christians

---

[229] Bishop of Smyrna. Died 155 AD.

at Smyrna followed the custom of John of celebrating Easter on the day after the Spring Equinox, whether it fell on a weekday or not. In contrast, most early Christians celebrated Easter on the first Sunday after the first full moon after the Spring Equinox.

This calculation of Easter is tied in with the question of whether the Last Supper of Jesus with his disciples was a Passover meal, celebrated the night before Passover. The witness of John would imply it was not. If the Last Supper had been a Passover Meal, then the events of the next day, Passover itself, which included the hauling of Jesus before the various assemblies such as the Sanhedrin, could never have taken place. Passover was a sacred festival on which no work was permitted.

But whatever John was he was certainly poor — a peasant. His ordinary language would have been Aramaic, not Greek, and certainly not the eloquent Greek of the Gospel that bears his name. The Greek of the Gospel of John is a beautiful, sophisticated and eloquent language. The opening verse reads: "In the beginning was the word, the word was with God, and the word was God."[230] Many consider the first chapter of the Gospel to have been an ancient Christian hymn.

Furthermore, to add insult to injury, in the Acts of the Apostles both John and Peter are described as 'agrammatos' in Greek. You'll find that tactfully translated in modern versions of Acts as 'unschooled'. However, a more blunt translation would say that Peter and John were 'illiterate' — the correct translation of 'agrammatos'. Peter, the first Pope, was illiterate. The Greek of the Gospel of John is a sublime form of Greek, and most assuredly, whoever wrote it was not an illiterate person.

Papias (AD 70—c. 163) was Bishop of Hierapolis, modern Pamukkale, a town just south of present-day Istanbul. He was a contemporary of Polycarp and is an important source of early Christian oral tradition. Papias says that John Mark wrote his Gospel in Rome, based upon the preaching of Peter. Mark was not a disciple of Jesus, in fact he had never met Jesus, and obviously therefore wasn't an eye witness to the events of his mission.

---

[230] John 1:1: Ἐν ἀρχῇ ἦν ὁ Λόγος, καὶ ὁ Λόγος ἦν πρὸς τὸν Θεόν, καὶ Θεὸς ἦν ὁ Λόγος.

Let's look back at those three Synoptic Gospels, Matthew, Mark and Luke, and let's accept, as we saw earlier, that Mark is the first Gospel. The next Gospel in chronological order is Matthew, supposedly written by Matthew who was an Apostle of Jesus. And what we find is that Matthew copies close to 90% of the actual text of Mark into his own Gospel. "Luke" in turn copies about 65% of Mark into his own Gospel. This is why it is impossible to deny that Mark, not Matthew, was the first Gospel.

It is noteworthy that Mark never calls Jesus 'God'. Nor does he claim that Jesus existed as a divine being within the Godhead before his earthly life. Furthermore, Mark has no account of the birth of Jesus, miraculous or otherwise. And he has no account of any appearances of Jesus after he rose from the dead.

It was at least ten years after Mark that Matthew's Gospel appeared. This means that the two elements that the later Church tradition began to emphasize as the very foundations of the Christian faith – the virgin birth and the post-resurrection appearances – do not appear at all in the original Gospel of the New Testament, which raises the question: are those two elements part of the original Christian message?

What if Matthew the Apostle was actually the author of the Gospel that bears his name? It is clear that the Apostle Matthew was a disciple of Jesus, and an eyewitness of all that transpired during the ministry of Jesus. If Matthew's Gospel were written by Matthew the Apostle, why would he need to borrow 80% of his stuff from someone else (Mark) who was not an eye witness to the mission of Jesus?

The 'Matthew' Gospel adds in or corrects Jewish elements which Mark had omitted. An example is Mark (3:4) where Elijah is named before Moses. But Matthew (17:3), in his revised version of Mark's Gospel text, puts Moses before Elijah, because Moses was far more important to the Jews than Elijah. Mark (11:10) refers to the "Kingdom of our Father," "Father" meaning David. No Jew would refer to David as "our Father," because it was Abraham who was the Father of the Jews. So it appears that "Matthew" altered his source (Mark) to bring it more into line with the traditional Jewish belief about the status of Abraham.

To put all this into perspective let's look at Matthew the Apostle again. He was a tax collector by profession, who of course was looked down upon and despised by the Jews. He would have been an outcast from the Jewish religious community. Why would he be supporting that community in a Gospel?

Peter was a confidante of Jesus obviously. But Peter was illiterate. Why would Matthew alter the recollections of Peter? To make Peter's view more consistent with Jewish teachings. So if it seems to be the case that Matthew copied most of his Gospel from Mark, and most of the rest from other sources, it would suggest that Matthew didn't have any personal connection with Jesus and did not witness his life and his teachings. We can conclude then that the author of the second Gospel was not Matthew the Apostle.

Most scholars now suspect that the anonymous author of Matthew's Gospel was very likely to have been a Greek-speaking Jew who lived outside of Palestine in the Jewish Diaspora. He corrected many of the non-Jewish statements in Mark. It is also noteworthy that when Matthew quotes from the Old Testament he uses the Greek Septuagint and not the Hebrew text. This gives further weight to the conviction that the author of the Gospel of Matthew was a Greek speaking Jew.

Mark also makes mistakes about Jewish geography. For example, in Mark Chapter 7:31 it is stated that Jesus travelled out of Tyre through Sidon (north of Tyre) to the Sea of Galilee which is south of Tyre. In other words, if would be the equivalent of saying that someone drove from New York to Chicago through Los Angeles. In short, whoever wrote this narrative of Mark's Gospel was not familiar with the geography of Israel and did not know where those towns were. Those errors could hardly have been made if the author really was Mark the travelling companion of Peter, who was a native of the area.

If the author of the Greek text of Matthew actually was Matthew the tax collector, his work would have made him an outcast from the Jewish religious family. Furthermore, he was Aramaic speaking. The Gospel that we have under his name doesn't seem to be a translation from Aramaic, because if you know both languages it would be easy to detect an Aramaic origin for the document.

In short, it appears that attributing the authorship of these two Gospels to Mark, the disciple of Peter, and to Matthew, the tax collector who was one of the Twelve apostles of Jesus, is impossible to sustain.

So, If the evidence doesn't support Mark and Matthew as the authors of the Gospels that bear their names, what about Luke? Luke also borrows heavily from Mark. As I mentioned, 65% of the Gospel of St. Mark is transferred in a beautiful act of sacred plagiarism into the Gospel of St. Luke.

Most experts agree that Luke wrote the Acts of the Apostles as well as the Gospel that bears his name. In the Acts of the Apostles, Luke refers to John Mark who was the secretary of Peter at Rome. But he never identifies John Mark, the associate of Peter, as one of his major sources, which would be strange if Luke believed that John Mark wrote the Gospel that has his name.

It seems then that the effort to construe John Mark as the author of Mark's Gospel was an attempt that had not yet been made in the time of Luke. In short, Luke changed Mark, which was written by an anonymous author, to suit his own purposes. For example, Luke gives an entirely different slant to the Passion Narratives of Jesus. Mark talks about Jesus being oppressed and suffering and being cast out. Whereas in Luke, Jesus is absolutely unaffected by any of these external things that were happening to him.

The Acts of the Apostles, as I already stated, is customarily attributed to Luke. Luke was a travelling companion of Paul. So if Luke wrote the Acts of the Apostles, and was travelling all around the place with Paul, then what Luke says about Paul's doings should harmonize with what Paul says about his own doings? But this is also not so.

The author of the Acts of the Apostles says in the first chapter (1:21) that he is not going to call anyone an 'Apostle' unless they were disciples of Jesus during his ministry. Fair enough. Paul obviously was not one of the disciples of Jesus. He never even met Jesus, apart from that awkward encounter on the road to Damascus. But despite never having met Jesus, Paul himself insists several times in his letters that he is a fully paid-up, card-carrying Apostle (1 Cor.9,1-2). He is contradicting the account of Luke, who was supposed to be his travelling companion, and if he was, then he should know everything about Paul.

Paul is stated by the author of Acts (Acts 13:31) to recognize the higher authority of the 'original' Apostles who had witnessed what Jesus did and said during his ministry. But Paul himself in effect says: "I am as good as any of those guys, even though I wasn't there." That's stated in the Letter to the Galatians, 2.6. This translation is admittedly free, but the heart of the matter is unaltered. In fact, I think that on the occasion when Paul wrote that Letter to the Galatians, he was having a bad day. When he was referring to the original Apostles, the twelve who were with Jesus, he says of them; "those who seem to be important". And he says: "whatever they were makes no difference to me ... they added nothing to my message."

So later in the same chapter, when Peter, the head of the Apostles, comes to Antioch in Syria, Paul tells us about Peter: "I opposed him face to face because he was wrong, and I chastised him for his hypocrisy". Even though Paul had never met Jesus, apparently he interpreted his mystical encounter with Jesus on the road to Damascus as equivalently conferring on him the status of Apostle. In fact, however, that mystical encounter, far from that being an apostolic mandate, was the direct opposite, a chastisement for Paul's persecution of the early Christians.

Paul's name has traditionally been attached to fourteen of the Books of the New Testament as we have it today. In short more than half the New Testament is supposed to have been written by him. But doubts have been raised for a very long time about whether Paul was really the author of seven of these documents that bear his name: to wit, the Letter to the Ephesians, the Letter to the Colossians, the Letter to the Hebrews, the second Letter to the Thessalonians, and 1 Timothy, 2 Timothy and Titus.[231] Scholars don't believe that Paul was the author of those works, but that they were forged in his name.

Certainly, in the case of four of these Letters it seems clear that Paul's name was simply tagged on. Why? Apparently the use of

---

[231] For example see, Sanders, E. P; *Paul and Palestinian Judaism,* 1977, and Just, Felix, S.J., Ph.D: *The Deutero-Pauline Letters.*

his name was to gain acceptance and status for the documents. The authenticity of Thessalonians and Colossians is also in doubt. But, generally, scholars accept that the other seven letters are written by Paul. We also know of four other genuine letters of Paul that didn't survive … they have been lost. If Scripture is supposed to be preserved and inspired by God, how did these letters get lost?

Concentrating on the Letters of Paul that are accepted as genuine, we can contrast Paul with what the author of Acts (attributed to Luke) says about the same matters. For example, the author of Acts in Chapter 9 states that Paul consulted Ananias, and preached in the synagogue in Damascus after his conversion. After a few days he travelled down from Damascus to Jerusalem. There Barnabas introduced Paul to quite a range of the original Apostles. But Paul himself says he "did not consult anyone" after his conversion, but travelled into Arabia. He says he didn't go down to Jerusalem for three years after his conversion. And when he did he only met two Apostles, Peter and James, the brother of Jesus (Galatians 1:16-19).

Paul's journey to Arabia is not mentioned at all by the author of the Acts of the Apostles. That journey was a major undertaking in those days. You couldn't just buy a plane ticket and hop on board, and a short while later you are there.

In Acts, Chapter 16, we are told of Paul's visit to Lystra, located about half way along the southern coast of modern Turkey. There he met Timothy, who was a well-respected young disciple. His mother was Jewish, so technically he was a Jew, since Jewish descent is very sensibly reckoned through the female line.

Timothy's father was a Greek. Paul wanted to take Timothy with him to help out. But according to the Acts of the Apostles, Paul insisted on Timothy first being circumcised. He was in his middle 20's, so circumcision was not a pleasant prospect. Why did Paul request this? Because they were going to speak to people who were Jewish, so Timothy needed to be circumcised to prove he was an authentic Jew.

However, when we move from Acts to Paul's Letter to the Galatians, 7:19, which was written about 50 AD, Paul says: "Circumcision is nothing, and uncircumcision is nothing. Keeping

God's commandments is what counts. Let each one remain in the situation he was in when God called him…each man should remain in the situation God called him to." In other words: "No circumcision, thank you." This might indicate that The Epistle to the Galatians witnesses to Paul having changed his mind on the importance of circumcision and, therefore, that Galatians came later than Acts.

Given all of these inconsistencies between the author of the Acts of the Apostles, allegedly Luke, who was a daily travelling companion of Paul, and Paul himself, it seems highly unlikely that whoever wrote the Acts was an associate of Paul. The view among Biblical scholars today is that the author of Luke/Acts was likely someone from the area Paul traversed in his missionary journeys. Perhaps as much as a generation later the author addressed the issues that were being faced by Christians in very different circumstances than were there when Paul was preaching his message.

Jesus the Poet

Did Jesus Teach in Poetry?

It comes as a surprise to most people to hear that most of the quotations from Jesus in the Gospels of the New Testament are actually in the form of poetry not prose.

As has already been mentioned several times here, the prevailing view among scholars today is that the four New Testament Gospels were originally written in Koine Greek,[232] which had become the common language of the eastern Mediterranean since the conquests of Alexander. However, and with good reason, some have maintained the Gospels were originally written in Aramaic or Hebrew, and only later translated into Greek. That is the view of the Assyrian Church which traces its origins back to

[232] ἡ κοινὴ διάλεκτος, "the common dialect."

Thomas the Apostle. In its liturgy, it still uses the Eastern Aramaic language. The headquarters of the Church is in Ebril, northern Iraq, and its members are found from south-eastern Turkey to north western Iran, and all across eastern Syria.

Jesus presumably spoke and taught in Aramaic as it was the common language of Judea in the first century, though we know he could also read, and presumably understand, Hebrew. Aramaic remained the common language right up to the rebellion of the Jewish leader, Simon Bar Kokhba (132 AD to 135 AD), who wanted to restore Hebrew as the official language of the country. The prevailing wisdom is that in the time of Jesus Hebrew would probably have been known only by the educated, or the religiously devout classes in Galilea and Judea, but would probably also have been used for more official-style documentation, as it was for most of the books of the Hebrew Bible. However, others have asserted it is not possible to sustain such a case, and say Hebrew was known in Judea and Galilee in the time of Jesus to a much wider extent than is currently assumed.

Obviously at this juncture it will never be possible to answer such questions definitively. However, it is not correct to assume that Aramaic was some popular variation or dialect form of Hebrew. While they use the same alphabet, Hebrew and Aramaic are as different from each other as German is from English. Aramaic (also known as Chaldean or Syrian) is an ancient Semitic language that has been documented as far back as the 9th century BC. It was the common language of ancient Mesopotamia and was used extensively all over south-west Asia in commercial and governmental affairs. During the years 597-539 BC, approximately, the Hebrews learned it when they were imprisoned in Babylon, and they brought it back with them on their return to Israel. However, they preserved Hebrew as the language of the Synagogue to read the Scriptures, which necessitated translating the texts afterwards into Aramaic, the everyday language of the people.

To add to the confusion, by the time of Jesus, Aramaic had become so identified with the Jewish people that it was normally referred to as "Hebrew." This is how the term is used in the New Testament itself.

For example, the familiar King James version of John 19:13 reads:

> "When Pilate therefore heard that saying, he brought Jesus forth, and sat down in the judgment seat in a place that is called the Pavement, but in the Hebrew, Gabbatha."

Verse 17 reads:

> "And he bearing his cross went forth into a place called the place of a skull, which is called in the Hebrew Golgotha."

Both "Gabbatha" and 'Golgotha' are Aramaic words, but John refers to them as "Hebrew," which would have been the normal usage of the term "Hebrew" at the time.

Other examples of Aramaic phrases surviving into the Greek translation of the New Testament are well known:

> Mark 5:41: Talitha cum: "Little girl, get up!"
> Mark 7: 34: Ephphatha: "Be opened."
> Mark 11: Hosanna: "O Lord, save us."
> Mark 14:36: Abba: "Father."
> Matt. 5:22: Raca: "fool."
> Matt. 27:46: Eli lema sabachthani: "My God, my God, why have you forsaken me?"
> John 20:16: Rabbouni: "teacher"

If we inspect the Greek manuscripts of the New Testament carefully we will soon see that every supposed reference to "Aramaic" there actually uses some version of the word Εβραιστι (Ebraisti) which means "Hebrew," and there is no use of Συριστι, (Suristi) which means "Aramaic," the reason being, as explained above, that in contemporary usage the term "Hebrew" had become used to describe 'Aramaic' by that time.

A Poetic Gospel?

Leaving aside for the moment the question of what the original language of the four Gospels was, it cannot be disputed that if the Gospel quotations of Jesus are looked at in an Aramaic translation of the New Testament,[233] their poetic form is clearly seen. That poetic structure is usually lost in the Greek versions, which would incline one to the view that an Aramaic text may well have been the original.

In English literature, we are accustomed to find rhyme in poetry as well as rhythm, but normally Hebrew or Aramaic poetry does not rhyme. Instead it uses a variety of other well-known poetic techniques. In his research almost a century ago, Charles Burney was astonished to find that when he translated the sayings of Jesus from Greek back into Aramaic, the statements of Jesus in the first three Gospels were actually in poetry, with familiar poetic forms and rhythms.

This Rev. Charles F. Burney,[234] discoverer of the poetry of Jesus, was an extremely interesting individual in his own right. He was appointed Oriel Professor of the Interpretation of Holy Scripture at Oxford University in June 1914, and five years later was elected a Fellow of Oriel College. He published several severely disturbing works on Biblical history. In "Israel's Settlement in Canaan", he applied many discoveries from Babylonian sources to explain Israel's early history in Canaan, and one of his most disturbing conclusions for conventional believers had to do with who the God of Israel really was.

Burney claimed that the first people known to have worshiped 'Yahweh,' or "Jehovah," as the one God, were a tribe of Amorite Kenite Arabs called the Rechabites. More recent archeological evidence has now reinforced his view that it was the Kenites, an

---

[233] The Aramaic version of the New Testament exists in two forms: firstly, in the classic Syrian New Testament, part of the Peshitta Bible or "Peshitta;" and secondly in a modern translation made from Koine Greek in 1997, and published by the Bible Society in Lebanon in the same year.

[234] 4 November 1868 — 15 April 1925.

Arab tribe that pre-dates Abraham and Ishmael, who were the first to call upon God by the name of "Yahweh," or 'Jehovah,' and to worship him as the one true God. It was they, he claims, who introduced the Israelites to the worship of Yahweh-God or Jehovah. So by Charles Burney's account, the God of the Jews was originally an Amorite Deity.

The rise of the Amorite kingdoms, from the 21st Century BC to the end of the 17th Century BC, in southern Mesopotamia especially, brought about many profound changes in every aspect of daily life. The people, the cattle and the land, that had belonged to the Gods, the King and the Priests since the days of the Anunnaki, were now liberated, and restored to the people by the Ammorite Monarchs. A new and long-lasting society composed of free people, prosperous merchants, and powerful farmers began to emerge. The priests continued to serve the gods but the economic affairs of the country were no longer in their hands.

Charles Burney ignited another bombshell in his work "The Aramaic Origin of the Fourth Gospel."[235] Conventional scholarship these days places the writing of John no earlier than the 90s. But Burney claimed that the Gospel of John was a literal Greek translation of a Gospel originally written in Aramaic by a Jewish disciple of Jesus. He maintained that the first chapter of John was an early Christian hymn which John copied into his Gospel. He also maintained that it was clear that the author of John thought in Aramaic, and this inevitably inclined one to the belief that the author of John was an eyewitness to the teachings and deeds of Jesus, not someone who perhaps had never known Jesus personally, or who wrote his account more than sixty years after the facts. So much for the stir caused by the renowned Charles Burney regarding the most sacred tenets of Judaism and of the New Testament itself!

If Burney discovered that Jesus delivered his message in poetic form, and maintained that it cannot be understand in its fullness unless we understand the poetic forms and techniques that he used, then surely it behooves us to find out something that will

[235] Clarendon Press, 1922. Re-published March 1st, 2004, by Wipf & Stock Publishers.

help us to appreciate the significance of those poetic devices in ancient Hebrew poetry.

Prominent Features of Hebrew and Aramaic Poetry

a) Parallelism

Experts[236] point out that the most prominent feature in Hebrew and Aramaic poetry is parallelism. Juxtaposing two or more phrases that are similar in meaning but different in form, is the most common form of parallelism, and the usual form of it is known as 'synonymous parallelism.' A good example from the Old Testament is Psalm 38:1:

> "O Lord, rebuke me not in your wrath,
> Nor chasten me in your hot displeasure."

Another common form of Biblical parallelism, which for convenience we can call "contrary parallelism," puts two clauses together that are a contrast of ideas.

Psalm 1:6 says:

> The Lord knows the way of the righteous,
> But the way of the ungodly will perish.

A third form of parallelism places two clauses together, with the second clause completing the sense of the first. We can refer to this as "amplifying parallelism."

Psalm 3:4:

> "I cried out to the Lord with my voice, and he heard me out of his holy mountain."

[236] Burney, C.F., The Poetry of Our Lord: An Examination of the Formal Elements of Hebrew Poetry in the Discourses of Jesus Christ, 1924, Dalman, Gustaf: The Words of Jesus Considered in the Light of Post-Biblical Jewish Writings and the Aramaic language,1997, Potkay, Adam. The Story of Joy: from the Bible to Late Romanticism, 2009, S.A. Missick: Christ's Words as Hebrew Poetry, 2011.

Good examples of synonymous parallelism are found all through the teachings of Jesus:

Luke 21:10, Mark 10:14, Matthew. 24:7:
Suffer the little children
And forbid them not to come to me.
Love your enemies,
Do good to those who hate you.
Bless those who curse you,
Pray for those who persecute you.

Matthew 25:29:
The sun shall be darkened
And the moon shall not give her light.
The stars will fall from heaven
And the powers of heaven shall be shaken.

Luke 6: 37-38:
Judge not and you will not be judged
Condemn not and you will not be condemned

The renowned New Testament scholar, Joachim Jeremias, states that in the three Synoptic Gospels contrary parallelisms occur more than one hundred times in the teachings of Jesus. He concludes that the frequency with which this occurs indicates that this must have been the way in which Jesus actually spoke, and it is most unlikely to be something that was invented by the editors.

It's well to realize in this investigation that we are not embarking on some form of esoteric or recherché investigation into ancient Hebrew and Aramaic poetry, just for its own sake. If it is indeed the case that the words of Jesus were delivered in poetic form and memorized, then we can assume with a great deal of confidence that we are dealing with the words and techniques that Jesus actually used, so some form of an understanding of those techniques is essential to understanding the true import of what he taught.

b) Rhythm

Another striking feature of the teachings of Jesus when read in Aramaic or Hebrew is the use of rhythm. Jeremias detected three main forms of rhythm used for different purposes by Jesus: a four-beat, three-beat, and two-beat rhythm, plus a fourth form called the "Kiva Rhythm" which was traditionally used to express strong emotion in Hebrew poetry.

The four-beat rhythm conveys repose. It often was used for giving instruction and sometimes, but not always, was used to bring consolation. It was pre-eminently the one used when Jesus instructed the disciples.

Mark 4: 25:
For whoever has, to him will be given,
But whoever does not have,
Even what he has will be taken from him.

Matthew 10: 24-25:
A disciple is not above his teacher,
Nor a servant above his master,
It is enough for a disciple to be like his teacher,
And a servant like his master.

The three-beat rhythm is typical of the Wisdom literature of the Old Testament, and is favored for the communication of wisdom. It was the most typical rhythm used by Jesus, and is most notably found in the Beatitudes.

Luke 8:20:
The foxes have holes,
And the birds of the air have nests,
But the Son of Man has nowhere to lay his head.

The Kiva rhythm was used for mourning, using two-beat, three-beat and four-beat structures. It was used to express strong inner emotion, especially admonitions, warnings and threats.

Matthew 7:6:
Do not give what is holy to dogs,
And do not cast your pearls before swine.

Matthew 11:17:
We piped for you and you did not dance,
We sang a dirge and you did not weep.

Luke 23:31:
If they do this when the tree is green,
What will they do when it is dry?

The Lord's Prayer in the New Testament has both rhyme and rhythm when translated back into Aramaic. So do the Beatitudes, which enshrine the central tenets of Christian discipleship. Jeremias noted with regard to the Beatitudes that only with the petitions in the first-person plural do they go over to the four-beat rhythm, and then they revert to the two-beat rhythm in the final petition.

c) Word Play

We call it punning, but working with the sounds of language, or playing on the similarity in sounds of different words, is another prominent technique in Hebrew and Aramaic poetry, and one that was used extensively by Jesus, as has been pointed out notably by William Sanford La Sor.[237]

Matthew 3:9: And do not think you can say to yourselves, 'We have Abraham as our father.' I tell you that out of these stones God can raise up sons for Abraham.

Banim = sons, and Abnim = stones.

[237] William Sanford LaSor (1911-1991) was the Professor of Old Testament at Fuller Theological Seminary in Pasadena, California, and published *Old Testament Survey: The Message, Form, and Background of the Old Testament,* in 1982.

Matthew 27:6

[6] The chief priests picked up the coins and said, "It is against the law to put this into the treasury, since it is blood money."

Shdamy = Value in money blood=dam

John 8:34

[34]Jesus replied, "Very truly I tell you, everyone who does sin is a slave to sin.

Abed = a slave; Ahbdah = a doer

As Stephen Missick[238] points out:" Every serious reader of the Bible needs to know how Hebrew poetry works. Everyone who wants to intelligently read the Bible needs to understand certain basic facts about how it is written. One of these basic facts is Hebrew poetry." Since poetry was used so extensively by Jesus, knowing the significance of the techniques he used will help us to acquire a deeper level of understanding and emphasis in what he actually said, as opposed to what we have been told he said.

---

238 *Christ's Words as Hebrew Poetry,* 2011. Also, author of *Treasures of the Language of Jesus: the Aramaic Source of Christ's Teachings,* Xlibris, 2000, *The Words of Jesus in the Original Aramaic: Discovering the Semitic Roots of Christianity,* Xulon Press, 2006, and *Mary of Magdala: Magdalene, the Forgotten Aramaic Prophetess of Christianity,* Xlibris, 2006.

Three Gospels, One Source: Oral or Written?

The Gospels of Matthew, Mark and Luke are strikingly similar in content. For that reason, since the 1780's, they have been called "the Synoptic Gospels," "synoptic" being a term that derives from two Greek words, "syn," meaning "together with," and "optic," related to "seeing." The combined words, "synoptic," literally means "seeing together." Matthew, Mark, and Luke are all recording, more or less, the same events in the life of Jesus and from the same point of view.

Good examples of these parallel accounts in the Synoptics are the following narratives:

Prediction of the Messiah	Mt. 3: 11-12	Mk. 1.7-8	Lk 3: 15-18
Calming of the Storm at Sea	Mt. 8: 23-27	Mk. 4: 35-41	Lk. 8:22-26
Parable of Mustard Seed	Mt. 13:31-32	Mk. 4: 30-32	Lk. 13:18-19
Healing of the Leper	Mt 8:1-4	Mk. 1: 40-45	Lk. 5: 12-16
Healing of Daughter of Jairus	Mt 9: 18-26	Mk.5: 21-43	Lk. 8: 40-56
Parable of the Sower	Mt 13: 1-9	Mk. 4: 1-9	Lk.. 8: 40-56
New Wine and Old Wineskins	Mt. 9:14		

When one lays out the corresponding sections of these three Gospel side by side in parallel columns, the really remarkable thing is not just that they are obviously narrating the same event, but that the words used in all three accounts usually correspond verbatim. What does this tell us?

A particularly good illustration of this can be seen in the three accounts of the call of Matthew, or Levi,[239] the tax collector, in Matthew 9, Mark 2, and Luke 5.

Matthew 9:9-13	Mark 2:14-17	Luke 5: 27-32
He saw a man called Matthew sitting at the tax booth, and he said to him: "Follow me." And he got up and followed him.	He saw Levi, son of Alpheus, sitting at the tax booth, and he said to him "Follow me." And he got up and followed him.	..he saw a tax collector named Levi sitting at the tax booth, and he said to him, "Follow me." And he got up, left everything and followed him.
Matthew 9:11	**Mark 2:16**	**Luke 5:30**
..they said to his disciples, "Why does your Teacher eat with tax collectors and sinners?"	.. they said to his disciples, "Why does he eat with tax collectors and sinners?"	.. were complaining to his disciples, saying, "Why do you eat and drink with tax collectors and sinners?"
Matthew 9:12	**Mark 2:17**	**Luke 5:31**
"But when he heard this, he said, "Those who are well have no need of a physician, but those who are sick."	"When Jesus heard this, he said, "Those who are well have no need of a physician, but those who are sick."	"Jesus answered, 'Those who are well have no need of a physician, but those who are sick.'"

[239] Matthew the Apostle was also known as Levi.

Another good illustration can be found in the Parable of the Sower in Matthew 13:3-9, Mark 4: 3-9, and Luke 8: 5-8.

Matthew 13: 3-9	Mark 4: 3-9	Luke 8: 5-8
A farmer went out to sow his seed. [4] As he was scattering the seed, some fell along the path, and the birds came and ate it up.	A farmer went out to sow his seed. [4] As he was scattering the seed, some fell along the path, and the birds came and ate it up.	[5] "A farmer went out to sow his seed. As he was scattering the seed, some fell along the path; it was trampled on, and the birds ate it up.
[5] Some fell on rocky places, where it did not have much soil. It sprang up quickly, because the soil was shallow. [6] But when the sun came up, the plants were scorched, and they withered because they had no root.	[5] Some fell on rocky places, where it did not have much soil. It sprang up quickly, because the soil was shallow. [6] But when the sun came up, the plants were scorched, and they withered because they had no root.	[6] Some fell on rocky ground, and when it came up, the plants withered because they had no moisture.
[7] Other seed fell among thorns, which grew up and choked the plants.	[7] Other seed fell among thorns, which grew up and choked the plants, so that they did not bear grain.	[7] Other seed fell among thorns, which grew up with it and choked the plants.
[8] Still other seed fell on good soil, where it produced a crop—a hundred, sixty or thirty times what was sown. [9] Whoever has ears, let them hear."	[8] Still other seed fell on good soil. It came up, grew and produced a crop, some multiplying thirty, some sixty, some a hundred times." [9] Then Jesus said, "Whoever has ears to hear, let them hear."	[8] Still other seed fell on good soil. It came up and yielded a crop, a hundred times more than was sown." When he said this, he called out, "Whoever has ears to hear, let them hear."

Parallels that are almost verbatim, such as in these two examples above, can be found in many sections of the Synoptic Gospels, most notably in the seven close parallels I listed above. This is remarkable when we consider that the Synoptic Gospels as we have them were probably written down in regions separated by great distances, and at widely differing times. What do these facts tell us about the origin and formation of the Gospels? And how reliable is their testimony to Jesus?

Jesus and his disciples were all Torah-observant Jews, and as a matter of course they would have studied and memorized at least parts of the Torah when growing up. Poetry helps memorization. But it was not extraordinarily unusual, then or now, for Rabbis and others to have committed all 79,976 of the Hebrew words of the Torah to memory. Such memorization is also found in Islam, with 'Hafiz' or "Hafiza" referring to a man or woman who has memorized the entire Qu'ran. Such memory feats were far more common when the literacy rate was much lower than it is now. As already noted, at the time of Jesus, it is estimated that the literacy rate among Jewish people in Galilee and Judea would have probably been, optimistically, somewhere between 3-4 % of the population.

Is it possible that the poetic proclamations of Jesus were committed to memory by those who heard them, and that they were recited frequently, as it was customary to do with at least parts of the Torah? Were the authors of the three Synoptic Gospels aware of those memorized accounts, and does this explain the nearly verbatim accounts which they wrote describing the same incidents? It seems to me that this may be a far more likely reason for the agreements between the Synoptics, rather than the suggestion that there may have been an earlier written text or texts which they used, but which have not survived. Scholars of the New Testament naturally look for written sources, but, especially in the times we are speaking of, oral sources are equally important and may well have preceded all the written ones. Why look for an extraordinary explanation when an obvious one is staring us in the face?

If we look at the texts I used in the illustrations above, you can see another very interesting fact: the three accounts of the same incident occur in quite different places in the three Gospels; in the first example, the Call of Levi is found in Chapter 9 in Matthew, Chapter 2 in Mark, and Chapter 5 in Luke. In the second example, the Parable of the Sower is found in Chapter 13 in Matthew, Chapter 4 in Mark, and Chapter 8 in Luke.

This could hardly be the case if they were all using an earlier written account as a source.

Scholars of the New Testament sometimes make factually correct statements such as "76% of Mark is found almost verbatim in both Matthew and Luke," or that "97% of Mark is found in Matthew and Luke combined." Only 3% of the content of Mark is unique to Mark himself. It is also a fact that 18% of Mark is in Matthew but not in Luke.

Maybe most significant of all, is that Matthew and Luke do not always narrate events in the same sequence, but when they do, the sequence they follow is the sequence found in Mark.

As already mentioned, according to most modern scholars the most likely scenario is that Mark was the first Gospel. It is only fair to point out that it was not until the 19th century that this was first suggested. It is also when modern scholars also began to postulate that Mark was a source used by both Matthew and Luke.

Of course, it needs to be remembered that none of the synoptic gospels name their author or authors. The naming that we use today dates only from the second century AD.

The brute facts are that, in terms of Greek words, 46% of Matthew is borrowed from Mark, and 41% of Luke comes from Mark. A little over a third of Luke is not borrowed from Mark, and a fifth of Matthew is not borrowed from Mark either. About 25% of Matthew and Luke are identical, but that identical section is not found in Mark at all. If they were using Mark as a source, as most of the modern scholars maintain, then the only conclusion must be that they acquired that 25% from somewhere else. Or is it possible that Mark was not the first Gospel, but perhaps Matthew, and that, since that 25% is in Matthew, it was copied by Luke?

Or is there another explanation entirely?

There are significant historical difficulties attaching to the modern scholars' view about which of our Gospels came first. The earliest testimony comes from Papias, Bishop of Hierapolis, in the south west of modern Turkey, beside the city of Pamukkale. About the year 130 AD, he wrote: "Matthew compiled the sayings of the Lord in the Aramaic language and everyone translated them as well as he could."

The next earliest evidence we have comes from Iraeneus of Lyon, writing about the year 180 AD. He says: Matthew wrote his Gospel for the Hebrews "in their own tongue" and this was done "while Peter and Paul were preaching in Rome." According to some significant recent research, it seems likely that Paul arrived in Rome early in the year 66 and Peter came there later in the same year. It seems likely that Paul was executed in January 67, and Peter in February of the following year.

If we are interpreting Iraeneus correctly, he is saying that it was after the deaths of Peter and Paul that Mark wrote his Gospel for the Christians in Rome, and that Matthew had been written before that, presumably therefore, before 67 or 68.

About 244 AD Origen (185-254) also testified that the first Gospel was written in "Hebrew" by Matthew.

As noted above, it was only in the nineteenth century that it began to be postulated that Mark was the first Gospel written. From the time of Jesus up to Desiderius Erasmus[240] in the 16th Century, it had been universally accepted that Matthew was the first Gospel and that it had been written first in Hebrew or Aramaic. Erasmus maintained that it was futile to maintain the original Gospel was in Aramaic or Hebrew since there is no evidence of any original Hebrew or Aramaic manuscript of Matthew's Gospel. But that argument does not carry much weight since we do not have the autograph copies of any of the Greek Gospels either.

Hints of an Aramaic/Hebrew Original?

There are some intriguing facts, including some hints in the texts of the New Testament itself, that indicate the original version of the Gospel texts, whether in the form of a document or

240 1469-1536.

not, was likely in Hebrew/Aramaic, and not in Koine Greek as we have them.

Josephus states explicitly that his country did not encourage the learning of Greek, and the implication is that a Greek-speaking Jew would have been a rarity in the time of Jesus.

There are also some striking examples of obvious mis-translations from Aramaic in some of the Greek texts of the New Testament.

a) Seeing All the Kingdoms of the World from the Top of a High Mountain?

One passage of logical improbability is in the Greek text of Matthew 4: 8, recounting the temptation of Jesus by the Devil.

> "Again, the devil took him to a very high mountain and showed him all the kingdoms of the world and their splendor."

In Ibn Shaprut's medieval translation of the Greek text of Matthew the Hebrew word found is "eretz," which can mean either 'earth' or "land." It may have been possible that all the kingdoms of the land of Israel could be seen from a tall mountain, such as Mt. Tabor, but most interpreters long ago gave up trying to square the circle and regard the whole episode as some form of mystical experience. And of course, if we want to take this text literally, we have to note that seeing all the kingdoms of the world from a high vantage point could only be done if the Earth were flat.

Another interesting mis-translation from Syriac/Aramaic into the New Testament Greek text occurs in Matthew 24 and Luke 12.

b) "Cut to Pieces"?

Matthew 24:50-51:

> The master of that servant will come on a day he does not anticipate and at an hour he does not expect. [51]Then he will

cut him to pieces and assign him a place with the hypocrites, where there will be weeping and gnashing of teeth.

Luke 12:46

46The master of that servant will come on a day when he does not expect him, and at an hour of which he is unaware. Then He will cut him to pieces and assign him a place with the unbelievers.

It is difficult to assess the usefulness, or indeed probability, of being 'cut to pieces,' as this Greek text says, before being assigned to the unbelievers, or to anyone else! Indeed, down the years, rivers of ink have been spent by scholars trying to find all sort of mystical interpretations of how being cut to pieces might symbolize the presence of Christ in all the members of his Church, and many other even less credible interpretations.

Almost a century ago, Agnes Smith Lewis discovered the Sinaitic Palimpsest, (with her sister Margaret Dunlop Gibson), at St. Catherine's Monastery in the Sinai. It is the oldest known text of the Gospels in Syriac, dating to the 4th century, and was the most important manuscript discovery since the Codex Sinaiticus was discovered by Constantin Von Tischendorf in 1859.

Agnes Smith pointed out that the verb "palleg" used in all the Aramaic/Syriac versions of these texts, has two meanings: the first means "to cut in pieces," and the second means "to assign to someone their portion."

Agnes Smith contends that whoever translated Matthew and Luke into Greek misunderstood the Aramaic/Syriac idiom and the sense in which the Aramaic word "palleg" was being used. She maintained the correct translation should be: "shall allot his portion and place him with the unbelievers," instead of: "shall cut him to pieces and place him with the unbelievers."

From our perspective, the importance of the discovery lies in the fact that the mistranslation indicates an Aramaic/Syriac original which preceded the Greek New Testament.

c) A Camel and the Eye of a Needle

Those who maintain the original text of Matthew was in Aramaic not Greek, often cite the well-known New Testament translation:" It is easier for a camel (καμηλος) to pass through the eye of a needle, than for a rich man to enter the Kingdom of Heaven." (Mark 10:25, Matthew 19:24, Luke 18:25).

In Aramaic, the word for "camel" (גמלא) is spelled identically to the word for "rope" (גמלא), so the correct translation in this case then becomes: "It is easier for "a rope to pass through the eye of a needle…" which obviously makes a lot more sense than the former translation, and also forges a connection with the passage on removing a beam from your eye, as quoted in Matthew 7:5 and Luke 6:41-42.

Again, the mistranslation indicates that an Aramaic text preceded the Greek version.

Is Looking for a Written Source of the Synoptic Gospels Misguided?

What do we make of all these interesting myriad details – before they start to make our heads spin too much? It is fascinating to learn all of these intricate details, but our over-all intent on researching them is far deeper than merely satisfying some antiquarian interest.

Earlier in this book we looked at how dis-empowering negative sub-conscious programs can be, especially when they bear on how we understand Jesus to have been. We saw that to effectively change those programs a certain technique is needed. Assailing a program head-on is completely counter-productive and only makes the last state worse than the first. The only effective way to escape the dis-empowering influence of those programs is to go back and thoroughly re-examine the sources from which they grew, and begin to see them in an entirely fresh perspective. In this way, new and empowering programs are formed, while the old programs fade away of their own accord. It's precisely for this reason that we need to go into such detail concerning matters such as whether Jesus taught in poetry, and in what language, and especially with what techniques, was his message handed on before it was enshrined in the Gospels.

All these statistics concerning the possible methods of formation of the Gospels are very interesting, but what do they really tell us about how faithfully all of these various accounts captured the message of Jesus? If the discovery that Jesus communicated his teachings in poetic form means anything, it means that we are dealing with the written accounts of eyewitnesses who heard those teachings and committed them to memory — as was the custom. Needless to say, that would have enormous implications.

Why are we so interested in finding out if the original text was in Aramaic or Greek and which Gospel was written first? Because once we translate the Greek texts into Aramaic we find that they rhyme. If they rhyme, it is highly likely that we now have the original words Jesus spoke to eyewitnesses.

These words in Aramaic can also tell us a lot about what Jesus emphasized as the heart of his message, which is so different from the forms in which it is conventionally presented. We looked at the poetic forms in which Jesus delivered his message, and the particular structures such as parallelisms and word play that characterized his more pastoral teachings and encouragements, as opposed to the dire warnings and general instructions that he also gave. When looked at in Aramaic these poetic features are so prominent and unmistakable that it seems beyond any realistic doubt that this is the form in which Jesus actually spoke. The Hebrew tradition at the time of Jesus of committing crucially important texts to accurate memory lends credence to this position. Where such a small percentage of the population was literate it seems the rhythmic passages and parallelisms we've seen here were key features in committing those sayings very accurately into memory.

Thus, the picture with which we emerge from this investigation, with a leaning towards the radical, is not the conventional one that's often put forward by Biblical scholars. "What we have a set of

Gospels written, at best, 30-60 years after the events they describe, and perhaps not a word in them is written by anyone who knew Jesus personally." That sort of conclusion can only come when we impose on other times and circumstances realities and paradigms that originated only in much later times and circumstances.

The discovery that Jesus spoke in poetry in the original language versions of the New Testament Gospels, needless to say, has enormous ramifications. What it now appears we have in general in the Gospels, is the later commitment to writing of accounts that came from eyewitnesses and that were then accurately memorized, as was the custom. Scholars who tend to fascinate on written evidence must be open to also respect the oral tradition, and come around to the very distinct possibility that the original "sources" of the message of Jesus were not an original document or documents, whether Aramaic Matthew or the legendary "Q"[241] document of the Biblical scholars.

Having discovered the poetic structures that characterize the teachings of Jesus we now acknowledge the great likelihood that the sources used by the Gospel writers were not an earlier document or documents, but those magnificently and accurately memorized teachings, couched in poetic form to aid memory.

I pointed out above one puzzling fact that bears this out. When the Synoptic writers are putting their texts together we saw that they narrate the same events, but not just that, they narrate them almost verbatim, word for word. However, what is interesting is that they include these accounts in radically differing parts of their Gospels, which is puzzling at first, but much more likely to have happened if they were recording many separate memorized units, or episodes in the teachings of Jesus, rather than copying earlier written sources

To put it in a nutshell, once we detect a section of Hebrew poetry in the written versions of the sayings of Jesus, then it seems we can be morally certain that these poetic sections bear the mark of an eyewitness testimony.

[241] "Q," standing for "Quelle" meaning 'Source'," was first postulated by Biblical Scholars in 1900, as an hypothetical written source used by the authors of the Synoptics in composing their own works.

"You are all Gods," or "I died for your sins": Will the Real Jesus Please Stand Up?

Why did our Savior have to die? Very significant difficulties indeed attend the conviction that Jesus came here to suffer and die for our sins. If God is all powerful and omniscient, were there not other possibilities rather than have Jesus die a bloody and cruel death on the cross? And above all, how could his death have been so effective that it could remove every stain of sin ever committed at any point in past, present or future history? John gives a very different perspective.

It is well attested[242] that the Gospel of John was the last of the New Testament Gospels to be written, the consensus these days being for a date in the 90s.

Like the Synoptics, the Gospel of John is anonymous, but the author of John claims to be an eyewitness of the public ministry of Jesus, "This is the disciple who is testifying to these things and wrote these things, and we know that his testimony is true."[243] John is the only author of a Gospel who claims to be an eyewitness of what he narrates. While the identity of the author has been the subject of a great deal of controversy, the consensus nowadays is that the author was indeed John the Apostle, who was also the author of the Book of Revelation. But whoever wrote down the words of the Gospel, most assuredly it was not John himself, since we know from elsewhere in the New Testament[244] that, like most of the Apostles, he was illiterate.

Irenaeus[245] claims that John lived on into the reign of the Emperor Trajan (AD 98-117). For about eighteen months he

---

[242] Eusebius, *Historia Ecclesiastica,* 3.24.7, Iraeneus, *Adversus. Haereses.* iii.1.1, and Clement as testified by Eusebius, in *Historia Ecclesiastica*, 4.14.7.

[243] John 21:24.

[244] Acts 4:13.

[245] *Adversus Haereses.*

was imprisoned on Patmos, an island close to the western shore of Turkey. It was common for the Roman authorities to punish by banishment offenses such as sorcery, magic, and prophecy, especially prophecy with a political dimension. John's Book of Revelation would have provided plenty of the latter sort to upset the powers that were. Patmos is less than a hundred miles offshore from the city of Ephesus, near the modern village of Selcuk. Ephesus is where John is believed to have spent his final days, and where he had had a house built for the mother of Jesus. It is believed that John composed the Book of Revelation as a result of visions he had while a prisoner on Patmos. Jerome places John's death "in the 68th year after Our Lord's Passion,"[246] which would be 97 AD, assuming the crucifixion occurred in the year 30 AD.

John's Gospel has four obvious divisions: a Prologue, (1:1-18), a Book of Signs (1:19-12:50), a Book of Glory (13: 1 – 20:31), and an Epilogue, (Chapter 21). The structure John has given to his work is obvious: there are 'seven signs,' and seven matching "I am" sayings and discourses, which culminate with Thomas's proclamation of Jesus as Lord and God.

In addition to being an eyewitness of the events he narrates, given the time and place of writing, it is almost certain that the author of John would have been familiar with the contents of the Synoptic Gospels. This is borne out by the fact that the author of the John clearly intended to supplement the material in the Synoptics. Given that John says nothing about so many significant topics and events narrated in the Synoptics, and given how he transposes so many of their major themes, it seems very likely the changes John made to the Synoptics' structure were deliberate. If that is so, the reasons for the changes would be of enormous interest to us.

John's Gospel is generally recognized as a more reflective account of the teachings of Jesus than the three Synoptics. In that sense, John's intent is to present the events of the life of Jesus, not as they occurred, or when he first heard of them. The elements in the Synoptic accounts that John omits from his own narrative are very noteworthy. For instance, there is no mention of the Lord's Prayer, no mention of the casting out of demons by Jesus, (to isolate Satan

[246] *De vir.* ill. 9

as the chief protagonist), no mention of the Sermon on the Mount, the Last Super (transformed into the Bread of Life Discourse), or any of the parables of Jesus. Nor does John include anything to do with the period when Jesus was growing up (to emphasize pre-existence of the Word before this life).

Of equal significance are the elements that John does narrate but that are not given in the Synoptics; the raising of Lazarus from the dead (after four days in the tomb in a warm climate,[247] the climax of John's Seven Signs), the farewell discourse at the Last Supper, as well as the mention of other visits of Jesus and the Apostles to Jerusalem before the final one. Finally, he emphasizes the Roman trial of Jesus, not the Jewish trial. All these are missing from the Synoptics.

It is worth noting that when Jesus was told that his friend Lazarus was seriously ill, he deliberately delayed a few days before going to see him. When he eventually arrived at the home of Lazarus at Bethany, two miles outside Jerusalem, Lazarus was already dead. The people who were gathered there to console his two mourning sisters would have all held one particular belief in common about death and the spirit of the dead person: "For three days (after death) the soul keeps on returning to the grave, thinking that it will go back (into the body), but when it sees that the facial features have become disfigured, it departs and abandons it (the body).[248] "Jesus delayed his arrival at Bethany deliberately until all hope for Lazarus was definitively gone among those who held those central beliefs. It was another sign that he was preaching an entirely new order of things.

The additions and omissions in John begin to make great sense if we understand that John's intent is to present the events of the life of Jesus, not as they occurred, or when he first heard of or witnessed them, but in terms of the profound significance which

[247] When Jesus asked that the stone sealing the tomb be rolled back, Lazarus's sister, Martha, objects that there will be a smell. *John* 11:39: "But, Lord," said Martha, the sister of the dead man, "by this time there is a bad odor, for he has been there four days."

[248] *Ecclesiastes Rabbah* 12:6, *Genesis Rabbah*, 100:7, *Leviticus Rabbah* 18:1. The *Rabbah* were early commentaries on the written Torah.

he came to realize they had after a lifetime of contemplating them. He stood back to assess that central significance of Jesus' mission.

Absent in John are the heart-warming and inspirational stories of the Synoptics. John wanted to convey that Jesus intended to set up an entirely new dispensation on this Earth for those who wanted to implement his message. He was not here to simply deliver an inspirational encouragement to right living, which is precisely how his mission is so frequently misunderstood.

However, what is most striking of all are the tantalizing and mind-boggling statements of Jesus that John records for the first time; "You are all Gods;" (10:34); "You will do all of the things I did, and greater than these will you do." (14:12). And finally, the same message that is also in Matthew 21:22 and Mark 11:24: 'When you want something, believe it is already yours and it shall be so.' (1 John 5: 14-15).

It would be hard to find a more explicit expression than this, of how to create reality through the action of the mind on the quantum field.

It is a whole new way of life that John understands Jesus to be proclaiming. The parameters have changed, the whole paradigm has altered. Why we are in this world at all is to clean up our act. Our purpose here is not to learn how to create in the quantum field. The problem is precisely that we are already creating in the quantum field all the time, but creating the wrong stuff!

This is where our biggest problem resides and it was to deal with this that Jesus taught what he did. What we manifest from the quantum field is, infallibly, not what we say or shout about at God, but what we profoundly accept at our deepest level. This is what Jesus meant by "having faith."

One of the sternest warnings of Jesus was not to put new wine into old wineskins: in short not to try to cram his teachings into world views that were utterly alien to the teachings.

I came across a rather amusing example of this recently. One of the cornerstones of the new dispensation Jesus proclaimed was: "Whatever you ask for in prayer, believe it is already yours and it shall be so." It's so easy to see that some forms of preaching these days expound this new and unfamiliar teaching but they do it within the old mindset., The so-called "Health and Wealth" preachers do it. It's also been called the 'Name it and Claim it' Gospel, or the 'Blab it and Grab it' Gospel, or even more solemnly, 'Positive Confession Theology' or, simply, the 'Prosperity Gospel.'

There is no doubt that all these sorts of movements are a very welcome change indeed from the 'hell fire and brimstone, doom and gloom, put up with your suffering and lack, bear your sufferings with Jesus,' style of preaching, which is now fortunately mostly on the wane. Nevertheless, the health and wealth preachers are trying to put a square peg into a round hole. They tell people to "name it and claim it in prayer," because "Jesus said it would be ours if we ask."

"Heal my cancer," "Make me enormously wealthy," etc. But when it doesn't work like the preacher said it would, then they tell us that it's our fault because we didn't "ask in faith."

This is not a faithful interpretation of what Jesus taught as narrated by John. We saw that John was concerned to convey that what Jesus was doing was setting up an entirely new dispensation on this Earth. A basic stage in this was all to do with getting rid of our crippling underlying attitudes of lack, dis-empowerment, guilt and fear.

"Praying for something and knowing it is already ours," is an exercise in the physics of the quantum field, not the request of a supplicant to a supervising Deity, who may or may not be disposed to grant the request. That's new wine into old wineskins with a vengeance.

As explained earlier, our dis-empowering attitudes have been solidified in us over years of negative programming since our most impressionable years, and further, such programs are even inherited by us through our DNA. This is what we are projecting on to the quantum field, and it is what is manifesting into our lives whether we realize it or not. Our major task in this life is not to learn how to create in the quantum field, but to learn how to change what it is we are already creating. The heart of the task facing us is to learn how to deal with the host of negative sub-conscious programs that we have inherited, and are adding to all the time.

When John says that when we pray we should believe that we already possess what it is we are praying for, we are faced with an entirely new scenario than what is traditionally understood by praying. In short, the traditional attitudes that accompany praying: the begging, imploring, asking, beseeching, wishing, hoping and desiring, are a recipe for disaster. I've referred to these and similar terms as 'the vocabulary of doom'.[249] If the "Prosperity Gospel" preaches that we can have what we pray for, the way to go about it is not by shouting louder and louder, or more desperately to God, asking or demanding of him to grant our request, but rather to isolate what crippling sub-conscious program within us is already preventing that reality from manifesting from the quantum field without even having to ask. Then we will have stopped putting new wine into old wineskins. The 'old wineskin' is the image of a superintending Deity, "up there" whose will it may be to grant us prosperity, or happiness, or whatever, and who will judge if we are worthy to receive it. There is no such process at work in this matter, and the sooner we realize that the better. Then we can start to apply our energies where they will yield better results than trying to prove our worthiness to receive some request before some human-style image of "God."

We need to take the advice of Jesus very seriously, and already be what it is we desire to manifest, as opposed to merely playing a role. To do that we need to root out those crippling sub-conscious programs, because while they are there we can never truly begin to imagine that "I am wealthy" or happy or successful, or whatever else it is for which I "pray." If you can truly believe "it is already mine," then you have succeeded in removing the crippling program in that field. But we know that can only be done by going back to the sources where those crippling programs first originated, seeing how the facts really were, and then re-building a new program. There is a little more attached to removing a new program of this kind, than simply addressing God in a loud voice, or insisting you have faith.

Needless to say, this goes directly counter to what we now call "common sense," but it is how the quantum field functions. In

[249] See Miceal Ledwith, DVD Series, Vol. 1: *The Hamburger Universe.*

many ways, the quantum field is like a giant frequency mirror, that reflects back to us only what we present to it.

This is the new dispensation of life on Earth that dictated what John chose to emphasize, and why he omitted what he did.

"We are all Gods." Some have tried to tone down this statement and say that what John meant is that we would all become 'judges,' or have some other exalted role, but not 'Gods.' But the word in the "Greek text of John is 'theoi," "gods." There is no mention of "judges" or anything equivalent to that word. The intent of Jesus was that we learn to do all that he did and greater. It was in interaction with the quantum field that he did his extraordinary feats we still call miracles. We have all descended from the Zero Point and are all endeavoring to master that vast and varied landscape of the various densities of creation that we have traversed during our descent into the material realm.

What Jesus did was extraordinary in the extreme, but they were not "miracles." They were effects that came from a sublime mastery of the physics of the quantum field.

When we have mastered that we will have fulfilled our purpose and become God-man and God-woman realized into the material plane. That is when we will begin to do all that Jesus did and more. That is when we will have fulfilled the purpose with which we embarked on this grand adventure into descending frequency aeons ago.

Jesus' instruction on what to do and what to avoid in our thoughts and actions was never intended to be a list of virtues to practice and sins to avoid. It was all about teaching us how to live in a way that would bring about a state of mastery of the material plane within us, through the interaction with the quantum field of those deepest levels of acceptance within us. If we can live as he taught we are setting up a field which will maximize the focus of our intent. Nothing could be further removed from a list of sins to avoid because of fear of punishment, or a list of virtues to practice, in anticipation of a post-mortem reward. But this is precisely what the teachings of Jesus have been turned into.

The key is to be able to 'pray' from the deepest level of acceptance within us. When our work to accomplish that is achieved, then truly John's vision for us will be realized.

We are not here to work out our salvation in fear and trembling before a judgmental God, nor are we here to save our souls. We are here to do incomparably more than that. We are not here to earn the right to the joys of Heaven in beatitude, or to escape the fearsome punishments of Hell for all eternity. However wonderful that may appear superficially, we are here to achieve something far more wonderful than that.

For the vast majority of people, what we are here to do will take quite a shift to grasp and accept since we have grown so accustomed to hearing the matter couched in an entirely different and antiquated paradigm. The terminology used to describe this 'new' state will obviously vary from age to age as humanity struggles to come to grasp with the fundamental nature of reality. In our terms in the twenty first century, we express it as being here to learn how to create out of the quantum field, and when we have done that all these dimensions of existence, so charmingly, comfortingly and naively described as "Heaven," will lie open to us in this life, and all that goes with it.

A major step in this process is to recognize that most of the ways in which we imagine "God" are childish and off the mark. However we may choose to imagine how the Creator and Source of all that exists actually is, that Creator is most certainly not some kind of human being enlarged, which is, (when all is said and done), the way most human beings imagine God to be.

Nor can such a Being, who is not some kind of human being enlarged, be pleased, placated or angered by anything humans can perpetrate. The joy and fulfillment that accompany mastery of the quantum field are incomparably greater than anything that could possibly ever come from sitting on a damp cloud playing a harp for all eternity. Likewise, the misuse of our creative abilities brings its own retribution, again way beyond anything that our childish images of hell and purgatory could ever convey.

In John's Gospel, once we realized the sayings of Jesus were in poetic form in the original tongues, and that we can therefore rest assured that we have the actual terms in which he spoke, we realize with certainty that Jesus came not to improve our behavior or to suffer and die for our sins, but to inaugurate a whole new dispensation on Earth. Now it's up to us to begin to implement what his teachings really were about, instead of insisting on putting that new wine once again into old wineskins.

Techniques for the Quantum World: Love Is Not a Virtue to Be Practised, but an Energy Field in which to Live

Let me reiterate, the relatively recent discovery that Jesus' teachings are in poetic form assures us that we are most likely dealing with the very words he uttered that were handed down from eyewitnesses, not just with accounts put together at a later date.

Nowhere is this more important than when we come to what the Gospels indisputably convey was the central reality about which he spoke. That central reality the Greek texts translated as "Agape." Our poor English equivalent has always haplessly translated that as 'love,' whereas in fact it is so much more. John states, in 1 John 4:8, and 4:16b, that "God is Love." There is a vast difference in being a loving being, compared to being an entity whose very essence is Agape.

If God is love, and we are exhorted to be God-like, then we too are being encouraged to acquire a state of being, not just to practice a virtue. In several places in this book I've used the analogy of what took place when the world view of Ptolemy, that the Earth was at the center of the universe, was replaced by that of Copernicus. No amount of improvement of Ptolemy would ever have led to Copernicus. The whole paradigm of Ptolemy had to be jettisoned and replaced with an entirely different paradigm. This is in fact the process by which human knowledge, in every field, has always made revolutionary advances.

Jesus introduced a Copernican revolution into how the relationship of human beings to the Creator ought to be understood, and Agape is at the very heart of that.

'Agape' or "love," then is not just, as we always assume, a virtue to be practiced, even the highest of all the virtues. Rather it is an energy field, a state of being, in which to live.

When we look at the poetic structures of Jesus' teachings, we find him conveying in the homely terms that his audiences could grasp, the mindset, the attitudes, and ways of thinking that would keep us in that empowered state of being that he had come to teach. In homely terms and in practical stories Jesus conveys a complex and profound teaching on the ways of thought and behavior that we would be wise to practice. Do not take any moral short cuts, he is saying, as we are often tempted to do when we feel we need to teach someone a lesson or take revenge for some real, or most likely imagined, wrongs. What we deeply accept and feel is what we are projecting for manifestation into the quantum field, not what we say or think. Manifesting from the quantum field does not require us to say anything, for our most powerful "prayer" is what we are.

If we look at even the few examples it has been possible to give in this section, we can see that all his teachings were about attaining and empowering that state. The poetry, the rhythm, the parables and the parallelisms all endeavored to convey in a memorable fashion the truths that would manifest that state and enable us to remain in it. They were not given in the abstract form of how to create reality through the mind, for such an approach would inevitably have fallen on deaf ears to the types of audience he was addressing: every day he was faced with a new place, new people and new situations, mostly in very humble and illiterate settings. Instead the message was given by illustrating from ordinary life the way in which we should think and act. It was 'fake it till you make it." If we consistently live in the way he taught we will soon come into realization that what we deeply accept is what reality manifests before us. His message was a rich discourse on how everyday life should be lived in order to accomplish radical empowerment.

This is the direct opposite of wishing and praying, or practicing virtue, and whether we accomplish it or not has nothing to do with 'faith' or its absence. It is all about profound acceptance, and that is the key to manifestation.

We will search in vain in the poetry and imagery of Jesus for any hint or suggestion that he came here to suffer and die for our sins to appease the anger of a vengeful God. Instead we see nothing except the techniques of attaining and preserving us in a state of empowerment, so that what we declare to be, actually is. Fear, unworthiness or doubt he tells us, destroys that state.

Paradoxically, and most unfortunately, it is precisely fear, unworthiness, guilt and doubt, that form the core of the warped versions of his teachings that have been retailed to us. Down through so many centuries these have distorted beyond recognition a supremely liberating and empowering message, and replaced it with the world view of a single life, based on fear of God and the potential of losing our eternal destiny.

"Believing it is already ours" has nothing whatsoever to do with begging, asking or praying. In fact, these are the very attitudes that block manifestation. It's ironic that these mindsets are so often presented as the attitudes to be cultivated when we pray.

Profound acceptance is the key to manifestation, and to be able to reach that level requires the transcending of our extensive array of sub-conscious programs. As explained earlier, that simply cannot be accomplished by any conscious act or decision, and those who believe that have profoundly misunderstood what is taking place here.

Chapter 15
Deciding the Canon of Scripture

If we believe the New Testament was inspired by God, what versions of those texts were inspired? Most people would say the original texts. Since almost every scholar admits that we do not have the original of any document in the New Testament is it then a legitimate question to ask whether we can speak of God inspiring the texts at all?

What about the 400,000 places specified by Bart Ehrman, for example, where the texts disagree with each other? Further, if we don't have any inspired text, what is to be said of religious institutions that are supposed to be founded on those texts?

It is enlightening to spend a little time contemplating the number of books in the Bible, and then begin to realize that apparently the number of books in the Bible depends on the religion to which you belong.

The early Christians held at least five councils where they attempted to decide on what books should be in the Bible, or, in short, fix the canon of the Bible. However, it was not until 28 August 397 AD, at the Third Council of Carthage, that the Christians finally felt able to decide on what books should be included in the Bible. That Bible had 73 books, 46 in the Old Testament and 27 in the New Testament. Those books were written by forty different authors in three different languages over a space of more than fifteen hundred years, and on three different continents — Africa, Asia and Europe.

During the Protestant Reformation, 1,100 years after the Council of Carthage, Martin Luther had doubts about the validity of seven books traditionally included in the Canon of the Old Testament. He removed them from the Canon, thus reducing the number of books in the Protestant Old Testament to 66. The Protestant churches have followed this practice ever since. The Catholic Church however, retained all 73 books which the Council of Carthage had decided to include in the Canon in 397 AD.

This raises some interesting problems for the Lutheran Churches. If seven books of the Bible were regard by the Christian Church as part of the inspired written word of God for well over 1,000 years, do those books now suddenly become uninspired as a result of Luther's actions? Of were Christians deluded in believing they were ever inspired in the first place? It looks like the Lutherans, as a consequence of their actions at the Reformation, would have to opt for one or other of these position, neither of which is particularly palatable for belief in the divine inspiration of the Biblical texts.

Corruption of the Scripture texts obviously can be a serious problem and is certainly at the very heart of any attempt to remove those religious programs that may be crippling us spiritually. I'm not saying it's an insoluble problem, but the difficulty is certainly increased when we realize that unfortunately most people who subscribe to the Christian faith today are often completely oblivious to the fact that such a major problem even exists.

There is an allied problem here as well – the belief that the Biblical texts, as they were written, communicate in the same way that we find normal and usual today. So we assume when we are reading some of the earlier books of the Bible, such as the first three chapters of Genesis, in a good modern translation, that we can read them with the same level of understanding as reading a copy of the New York Times or the Washington Post. Not so.

Their way of communication was entirely different from what we take for granted today. As is detailed in another part of this book, a good example of this is how we assume instinctively that the message we get from reading the first three chapters of Genesis is actually what the authors of Genesis meant to convey. In fact, their message is radically different from how we instinctively interpret them.

"The Inspired, Written Word of God"

In assessing the contribution of the Scriptures to spiritual evolution, one of the most controversial aspects is the belief, expressed in many different forms, that these scriptures are "inspired" by God. Generally speaking, there have been three main ways in which the belief that the Bible is inspired has been spelled out:

a) God dictated the books of both Old and New Testaments, word for word, and the authors of those books wrote down those words.

b) The "inspiration" of God moved the writers, who then choose the exact words that God wished to have express his message.

c) The ideas contained in the Bible are "inspired," but the words to express those ideas were left to the individual authors to select.

In the Catholic Church, the belief in scriptural inspiration has been classically worded as: "the inspired, written word of God as contained in the Old and New Testaments".

Four major pronouncements on this subject have been made in modern historical times. The first pronouncement was at Vatican Council I.[250] Two decades later the second came in the classical Encyclical of Pope Leo XIII, "Providentissimus Deus".[251] The third was in the encyclical "Divino Afflante Spiritu" of Pius XII.[252] These three documents largely shaped the discussion of Biblical inspiration right up to the Second Vatican Council which made its contribution about this issue in one of the central documents of the Council, "Dei Verbum".[253]

The Catholic understanding of divine inspiration of the Bible, as expressed in all four of these documents, largely falls into category b) above. This position is very hard to maintain in the light of remarks such as made by Bart Ehrman – that, as a matter of fact, there are more discrepancies in the manuscripts of the Biblical texts than there are words in the Biblical texts.

Once again, the root of the problem may lie in simple mis-translation. When Jerome did the first translation of the New Testament, it was made from the original Greek into Latin. The main text of the New Testament that sheds light on the "inspiration of the Biblical books by God" is in Paul's Second Letter to Timothy, Chapter 3, vv. 16-17. The King James translation of these two verses reads: "All Scripture is given by inspiration of God."

"Inspiration" is a tricky word in English, and as we apply it to the New Testament it implies some form of brooding presence of God over the sacred texts. But when we look a little closer we see that the original Greek word that Jerome translated as 'inspired' was 'theopneustos'. That Greek word does not mean 'inspired', it means "breathed out by God".

[250] "Dogmatic Constitution on the Catholic Faith," session 3, Chapter 2. Issued 24 April 1870.

[251] 18 November 1893.

[252] 30 September 1943.

[253] *Dogmatic Constitution on Divine Revelation,* promulgated by Pope Paul VI on November 18, 1965.

"Inspiration" is a bad choice of words not merely because it suggests this brooding presence of God over each word of text, but also because the Latin word from which 'inspiration' comes is 'inspirare'. 'Inspirare' in Latin means to 'breathe in'. It does not mean to 'breathe out'...which is what the Greek word it is supposed to translate is actually saying. The Greek text does not say "God took a deep breath" but the contrary: "God breathed out". Jerome's translation and its adoption by the King James version as 'inspired' has created a new meaning for the word, which we now use every day. Examples include: "That was an inspired piece of music;" "I was inspired by what he said". At the same time, the original usage of 'breathing in' still persists in the English language today. In medical circles 'inspired' means 'to breathe in'. For example, "Inspired air must be humidified".

Aware of this mistake, most modern translations of the New Testament avoid the word 'inspired' entirely because it has those connotations of breathing in, not out, which is contrary to the meaning of the major Biblical text explaining God's role in the formation of the texts of the New Testament. The realization of this true meaning of 2 Timothy 3.16-17 helps move us away from a quasi-superstitious understanding of what 'Biblical inspiration' actually is, which is frequently found in right-wing fundamentalist branches of Christianity. That better understanding facilitates the real purpose which the scriptures can fulfill in our development.

Realizing the level of misunderstanding that exists regarding the concept of divine inspiration of the scripture led the erudite, but extremely conservative German theologian, Josef Ratzinger to say in exasperation about "Dei Verbum" (the major text on scriptural revelation and inspiration from Vatican II) when it was issued in November 1965:

"The brief form of the Preface and the barely concealed illogicalities that it contains betray clearly the confusion from which it has emerged." "We need a thorough overhaul of the whole understanding of how the Bible is understood to be inspired."[254]

[254] Joseph Ratzinger, 'Dogmatic Constitution on Divine Revelation, Origin and Background' in: Herbert Vorgrimler (ed.), *Commentary on the Documents of Vatican II*, 5 volumes (New York: Herder and Herder, 1967-1969.

Chapter 16
Genesis: The Struggle to Believe Contradictory Things about God

What Tasks Faced the Authors of Genesis?

We can begin to see without much effort that even if the familiar emphasis on suffering, guilt, and the fear of God's vengeance didn't originate with Genesis, the structure and message of Genesis nevertheless gave such a mindset a major boost.

This mindset is a black hole from which to try to escape. If Jesus is to be seen as a redeemer, then there has to be something from which he redeems the human race. That 'something' has usually been described as the 'Fall of Mankind'. In other words, if there was no 'Fall' then there would have been no need of a redemption; there would be no need to be 'saved'.

The whole idea of the "Fall of Mankind" is based on an acceptance of three central beliefs. Firstly, that there is a God who made the whole of creation. Secondly, that God is all-powerful, and thirdly, that God is all-loving.

But if God is all-loving, and all-powerful, and is also the Creator of everything that exists, how come there is so much suffering, evil and injustice in the world? It just doesn't add up, does it?

This is a major difficulty in traditional belief. And this is exactly what the authors of Genesis were trying to address. How can a good God, who is all powerful, and the creator of all, exist side by side with such massive evil and suffering? This is what this narrative in Genesis tried to clarify. We will explore this narrative in the following sections.

According to Judaic tradition the first five books of the Old Testament — Genesis, Exodus, Leviticus, Deuteronomy and Numbers — were all supposed to have been written by Moses. But the scholarly consensus is that the Book of Genesis was written five or six hundred years after Moses had died. But of course, when considering great issues that is a relatively small matter!

However, if you open the Book of Genesis and look at this account of the 'Fall of Mankind', you will discover that in the first three chapters we don't have one account of this hypothesis about the Fall of Mankind. Instead we have two accounts that have been cut and pasted together, without editing them so as to fit together into one cohesive narrative of how the creation occurred. Consequently, it is no surprise that the result is not very streamlined.

So why did the authors of Genesis put this book together? Because they wanted to oppose the beliefs about the origin of the universe and the current situation of the human race that were prevalent in Babylon at the time they were imprisoned there.

The two accounts that were clobbered together are called respectively the 'Priestly Account' and the 'Account from Jehovah' or "The Yahwist Account." They appear to have been written about two or three hundred years apart. The 'Priestly Account' is the newer of these two, written about the 5th century BC. In the text of Genesis as we have it, the 'Priestly Account' begins with the start of Genesis — Genesis 1.1, down to the third verse of Chapter 2. The 'Jehovah Account' begins in Chapter 2 verse four, and runs through to the end of that chapter. That Account is dated by scholars to the 7th or 8th century BC.

The Yahwist account of ancient history is deeply pessimistic. There is increasing violence, disobedience of God and widespread corruption. Mankind has been cursed and condemned to an Earth that has been cursed along with him. The first human brothers are embroiled in a drama of fratricide, and the violence and corruption of all mortals is vividly portrayed. Things become so bad that God sent a Flood to destroy mankind, but it achieves nothing as the heart of mankind remains as corrupt as before. The Canaanites have been cursed, the mighty Babylonian Empire emerges to punish them, and the people are dispersed and divided into different language groups. The Yahwist negative impression of humanity is never in doubt; prone to violence, war, disobedience and strife of all kinds. This pessimistic view of humanity is projected backwards by the writer of the Yahwist tradition as he ponders the mystery of the origin of the human race.

On the other hand, the Priestly Account is overwhelmingly positive and upbeat. The creation is not cursed, but is created good, as is humanity. Both male and female are created in God's image. The genealogy from Adam to Noah goes against the Yahwist Genealogy of constantly increasing violence down through history, and instead tells of how the earliest generations of humans all proceed from "the image and likeness of God." The Flood is included in the Priestly Account, but it results in the first Covenant between God and his people.

It is not hard to see that there are major contradictions between these two accounts. This is a good thing to be aware of if we are inclined to believe that the entire Bible is the inspired written word of God that came down by email, text or fax from Heaven.

It seems that the later Priestly Writer was dissatisfied with the earlier Yahwist pessimism, and set out to produce a narrative of a much more positive character that reflected his own theological agenda. It seems very likely that the Priestly Account was produced to entirely replace the earlier pessimistic Yahwist Account, but instead what happened is that someone came along later and tried to preserve both accounts, even though they contained many very basic flat-out contradictions. The Priestly Account was inserted into the Yahwist Account

Looking more closely at the first three chapters of Genesis, six major contradictions between these two accounts become immediately obvious. These contradictions are reviewed in the box below. It is customary to use 'P' to designate the newer Priestly version and 'Y' to designate the Jehovah or the Yahwist Account.

The Contradictions in Genesis between the Priestly (P) and Jehovah or Yahwist (Y) Accounts

P – The world comes from water.
Y – The world is a desert, dry and barren.
These contradictions occur in the same chapter.

P — The birds and the beasts are created before mankind.
Y —The human race is created before the birds and the beasts.

So which were created first? Why didn't they leave these contradictions out altogether or go with just one or the other of them?

P — The fowl are made from water.
Y — The fowl are made out of the earth.

The next contradiction is much closer to home:
P — Man is made in the image of God.
Y — Mankind is made out of the slime of the earth.
A distinct disimprovement!!

P — Man is Lord of the Earth.
Y — Man is just hired help. We are here to look after a garden — to be caretakers.
P — Man and woman are created together.
Y — Man is created first and then the birds and the beasts, and then finally, as an afterthought, woman is created from man's rib.
So, she is just a rib woman!

There are fifty chapters in the Book of Genesis, but in the short space of just these first three, there are these six obvious and irreconcilable contradictions. This can appear to be very tedious material, so why am I pointing all this out? Because we are trying to figure out from where the program of Jesus as a 'Suffering Savior' came.

When we can personally see and understand that program's roots, we can then dis-empower it from controlling our thoughts and manifestations about why we are here in this world in the first place. The old program will fade away of its own accord in the face of indisputable historical fact and information. Psychologically, a crippling sub-conscious program will only alter if the mind clearly, and as a personal experience, sees all of the historic detail and roots from which such a mistaken belief originally sprang. The basis of that most crippling of all programs relating to Jesus lies in this section of Genesis. So, first we note these contradictions.

Let's place ourselves in the position of the authors of Genesis in about the 5th Century BC. Our goal is to reconcile these two contradictory accounts of how creation happened which were already part of their belief system. They wanted to include them in a new Book which would come to be named, as was the convention, after its opening phrase, "In the beginnings…" or in modern terms, 'Genesis'. The challenge is made worse if the authors of Genesis believe that these two accounts in some sense or other came down from God directly and remain untouchable.

If you and I were trying to put these two narratives together twenty-five hundred years ago, we'd probably be inclined to opt for one of them and discard the other, rather than state six blatant contradictions in the opening chapters of our new Book. That I think actually was the intent of the Priestly Author. But here we are discussing this quandary that faced the authors of Genesis, as a consequence of believing that something 'came down directly from God'. If that is someone's belief, then the content of what has 'come down' is sacrosanct and cannot be altered in any way. In modern terms, we can cut and paste, but we can't delete. Even though the consequence of that policy is that we produce a massively contradictory account of the origins of things, we would see that as a lesser problem than daring to alter a revelation from God. Apparently, it is better to appear as a fool, than to let go of something that you (mistakenly) believe, came directly from God.

This issue is a big block in all of us, even today. I am emphasizing this because it's a powerful example of how even the authors of Genesis weren't able to get beyond their blocks. They did everything except jettison what common sense dictated they should.

Finally, as a footnote, the Book of Genesis does not shed any light on the origins of the human race, nor was that its intention, even though attempts have often been made to use it in this way, in fundamentalist circles especially. As has so often been expressed by various authors, on both side of the evolution versus creation debate: "The Bible is not a textbook of Science." In any event, we now know a lot more about the origins of the world and of our race than they did two and a half thousand years ago when these two narratives were combined.

As we saw the original text of Genesis (or any Old Testament texts) did not have any chapter or verse divisions. The chapter divisions[255] were devised by Stephen Langton, Archbishop of Canterbury in 1227, and some of the divisions were unfortunate and misleading. This is especially true of the early chapters of Genesis, where his divisions clearly indicate he did not understand what Genesis was attempting to convey, and his divisions significantly obscure what the authors of Genesis were attempting to do. When we can see beyond these unfortunate and misleading division of Genesis into the present system of chapters, we begin to see better what they real intent of the authors of Genesis was: to figure out an answer as to how an all-good and powerful God could have created a world that contains so much imperfection and evil.

Reliance of Genesis on Ancient Myths

But worse is still to come. Why? Because myths about the origin of our race were known in cultures all over the world long, long, before the Book of Genesis, or the earlier individual Yahwist and Priestly traditions, were ever even thought of.

At the Temple of Abu Simbel, at the bottom of the Nile in Egypt, there is a representation of a man and a woman in a garden with a serpent coiled around a tree behind them. And in an Indian cave temple, there is an ancient sculptured column with what is apparently intended to represent the first man and woman at the foot of a tree, with a serpent in the branches above them. The serpent is offering them a fruit of the tree from its mouth.

---

[255] A Jewish Rabbi named Nathan divided the Hebrew Bible into verses in 1448. Robert Estienne, (also known as Stephanus), divided the New Testament into verses in 1555.

These two examples, from India and from Egypt, as well as many other historical examples, predate the Book of Genesis, not by a small margin, but by thousands of years. What are we going to make of this? Was this information a direct revelation by God, that at the beginning of time we were sitting in a garden, in unwise company...with a snake and a rib woman?

In the Babylonian city of Nimrod, the ruins of which have been dated to 1500-2000 BC, there is a famous collection of terra cotta tablets that tell the story of the creation of humanity, the story of the Deluge – Noah's flood, and the Story of the Tower of Babel. They predate Genesis by at least a thousand years. So, were the first three chapters of Genesis news when they appeared? By no means...they were very ancient stuff. Were they copied by the authors of Genesis? It appears so. And worse still, the information was apparently copied from a heathen, pagan source. Was Jehovah sleeping that he allowed all this to go on?

It has often been suggested that the reason we have so many myths about the origin of the human race is because of our longing to overcome death and achieve immortality. Longing to become immortal is, I suppose, the fundamental wish we all have...a wish disguised in many different forms. But since we are already immortal at the level that is most deep in us, I assume this longing is about achieving physical immortality. But how and why should we go about trying to achieve physical immortality, when we are already immortal in the sense that really counts? After we cast off the physical body at death we still continue to exist. But if we have to lose most, if not all, of the memories of each life as we re-incarnate into a new physical body that just sucks. So, it seems the heart of the matter that is a burden to us, is not so much that we die, but that we lose all memory of the previous incarnation. If we did not lose the memories, would physical death then appear much less of a direful fate to us? So, is physical immortality the real dream, or is it the retention of memories?

Surely if what we really are lies beyond this plane, is there not some way we can draw down some power or influence from that plane...from the depths of what we really are, so that we at least can assure physical longevity way beyond the customary human lifespan? How to accomplish that was at the core of what Jesus came to teach, and that was his purpose. He would be highly amused to hear he came here to die for our sins.

This urge to achieve immortality is spread across all human cultures ancient and modern, and they center on the brutal fact of the mortality of the physical body in death, and our desire to avoid that fate.

Let's look at this a little more closely. When somebody near and dear to us dies, we have to face the awful prospect that they are gone, and they are gone for good. Take an example. A dearly loved member of your family dies. Some years later you may happen to recognize that dear departed one when he or she re-incarnates. But while you recognize that the child is hauntingly similar in many ways to the loved one you lost, you also recognize that the child and the departed one are not the same person that you knew so well. Why is that? What happens?

It's the physicality of an individual and the physical persona that perishes with death, and that is normally the only level at which we came to know, perhaps even those nearest and dearest to us. That superficial level is the level at which we knew them and interacted in all spheres of life with them; that level is not immortal. When the personality is gone, that person we may have known only at that relatively superficial level is also gone, and what's more, is gone for good. What re-incarnates is the essence of what made that person a person. To the extent that we knew them at a deeper level than the physical is the extent that we will recognize them, and they us, in reincarnation.

That person that we knew and lost to death is not sitting up there somewhere on a cloud waiting for us in Heaven. That is a comforting notion that helps us bear the deep pain of the loss of a loved one. (There should be a Spiritual Surgeon General's warning about beliefs that give comfort, for usually they only pander to our self-deceptions). But that beloved person, as we knew him or her in such a superficial, physical way, has ceased to exist permanently. That is the painful tragedy revealed in all of these ancient myths, and the reason why so many of these myths have been painfully elaborated over the millennia.

For the most part the individual that you and I know is the personality, not the spirit and the soul of that person who was your mother or your father or beloved spouse or child. You knew the personality, you loved the personality...but it is the body and the personality that die at death. We are not going to see that person again. We will come to know their essence or spirit, who they really were again, but we will not know the superficial dimensions by which we knew them in the past. In other words, their body and personality are gone. This is why there is such a thirst for 'immortality'. The goal of that 'immortality' is that the individual we knew and loved somehow doesn't perish but remains, and that is a major self-deception.

This goes back into the mists of time...the longing to live on physically. Snakes periodically shed their skins. That fact gave rise to the belief in very, very ancient times that snakes were being reborn, that they continued to live on in a new body. It was only a short stretch for the snake to then become the symbol of immortality. In other words, if we could only become snakes we could continue to live by shedding the worn-out body and still keep everything that mattered consciously intact.

This is where the myths began. They are older than Genesis and way, way older than the Jewish tradition, and way, way older than Jehovah. The belief came into existence that God had intended humanity to have eternal life. But how did that situation change? Because the wily serpent stole that gift. By that set of mental gymnastics, God was acquitted for the obviously poor job he had made of creation.

It is blatantly obvious that whoever designed this creation designed it on a slim budget, and many shortcuts, were taken in the process that should not have been taken. Alternatively, the view can be taken that the creation is still relatively in its infancy. In effect, the creation has not yet been designed, but is still unfolding into a design, and hopefully the very obvious deficiencies that exist in it now will gradually be filtered out and transcended over the passage of the aeons.

Genesis: Sloppy Work?

When you compare the narratives that we have in Genesis today with some of the other creation myths that are far, far older, it becomes obvious that Genesis did some sloppy work.

Genesis doesn't spell out the full details of the significance of the serpent, or the significance of the Tree of Life. But the older cultures do. To emphasize the reality once again, the Genesis account appears to describe a creation that was obviously put together on a very slim budget, and in which a lot of short cuts were taken that should not have been taken because taking them has set us out on the wrong trajectory.

In the original versions of the 'Fall of Mankind' epics, summing up the dozen or so of them that are still around, God placed the first man and woman in a Garden of Delights. There were two main trees in the Garden...the Tree of Life and the Tree of Death. In Genesis, however, this arrangement was altered — the Tree of Death became the Tree of Knowledge. We interpret this to mean that knowledge brings death. So, the message is: stop probing, don't inquire, and don't even ask if two and two make four, because if you do you are going to burn: a very old program. As Lord Tennyson wrote of the Charge of the Light Brigade at the Battle of Balaclava[256] on October 25, 1854:

Not tho' the soldier knew
Some one had blunder'd:
Theirs not to make reply,
Theirs not to reason why,
Theirs but to do & die,
Into the valley of Death
Rode the six hundred.

[256] Battle of Balaclava (Ukraine) in the Crimean War (1854-56). eerily reminiscent of today's crises in the same area. Russia's only warm water ports lay on the Black Sea. The Dardanelles was the long narrow strait of water that controlled entrance to the Black Sea.

"Ours not to reason why.
Ours but to do and die."

Or as so often equivalently stated in religious terms:

"Ours to worship and obey:
Ours not to ask the reason why."

In the older versions of the creation myths, God sent the immortal serpent with a message for the first human pair. The message was overwhelmingly positive: to eat the fruit of the Tree of Life and become immortal. He warned them on no account to eat the fruit of the Tree of Death, because if they did they would die and so would all their descendants. It was a make or break situation, God told the serpent.

But the wily serpent, of course, saw his chance, and he reversed the message. He said in essence – Permit me to introduce myself, I'm the guy that sheds his skin, so obviously, I have mastered the art of physical immortality. I have a message from God specifically for you. You are to eat the fruit of this tree, (which he did not tell them was the Tree of Death) and you will become immortal. Do not eat the fruit of the other tree. The humans ate the fruit of the Tree of Death. As a result they became mortal, but they were also expelled for their disobedience from the Garden of Delights. Meanwhile the reptile ate the fruit of the Tree of Life and achieved immortality for himself and his descendants. The lesson here is: Never send a message through a serpent.

This scenario just described is really crucial to grasp if we are going to escape from these crippling sub-conscious programs. We need to thoroughly understand where all of this preoccupation with suffering, death and mortality came from originally.

To make matters worse, it's thought that the ultimate origin of all of these stories, including the supposed immortality of serpents, actually came from Africa, where legends of immortal serpents have survived in a lot of forms to this day.

Now let's look at all this from another perspective. Horrific things were done to the Jews and several other categories of people during the Holocaust of World War II. If the quantum field is a reality and means anything, we can surmise that if a certain level of atrocity is perpetrated by someone, or some class of people, against another person or class of people, the only really effective way to balance the souls' memory may be for the entities who were the oppressed in the previous life, to come back into the genetic line of the people who oppressed them, and vice versa.

In terms of the World War II Holocaust what would that mean? That many of the Nazi perpetrators of the atrocities in the death camps in Europe may potentially now be Jewish Rabbis in Jerusalem? And many of the Jews who suffered in the death camps may now be incarnated into the genetic line of the Nazis. A chilling dose of reality can often shed light on profound matters.

How this process works is extraordinary. But what does it show? It potentially shows the ultimate absurdly of protests about the horrors of the past. We are most likely protesting against the wrong people, most likely expressing our anger against the very individuals who suffered, and we who are expressing this anger may well have been the very perpetrators of the injustices against which we now protest.

Learning the lessons of the past need to be centered on change, not vengeance. It all comes back to 'presence' in the quantum field. This I'm sure was one of the reasons why Jesus taught us not to seek vengeance for the past wrongs we have endured. The wrong may have been so horrific that the only way to balance and heal the soul's memory was to enter the genetic line of the perpetrators and in that context vengeance becomes absurd.

I noted earlier, that this paradigm came out of Africa long ago. That is the ultimate horror…that the inspired written word of God given to Moses on Mount Sinai turns out to have been a rather late arrival on the scene. And that the actual origins of this creation story came from, of all places, Africa, from whence our race began.

Let's return to the subject of suffering: If I am suffering, does the conviction that suffering has a value help me to bear my suffering? It does, of course. But does it really have a value, or have we been misled? We know that when people suffer and go through ordeals, it sometimes brings out the best in them. That is an entirely different matter from what we are talking about here.

Just as gold comes out of a crucible, very often heroism comes out of suffering, but this way of producing heroism is far from the ideal condition of things. Rather we are asking: did God give an edict that I should suffer and that it was a thing to be pursued deliberately? No, God did not. Can we go beyond that and say it is God's will that we bear our suffering, or that God or Jesus looks favorably on us in that kind of situation? No, we cannot.

Can we still now say that Jesus was a Suffering Savior who came here to die for our sins to appease the vengeance of a savage God? No, I'm afraid not. Was this somehow rooted in the tradition of Genesis? It was not.

Fear Based Religion and an External God

Among the many alien races that exist, the Anunna of Ki have had a profound connection with the people of this Earth ("Ki" is their term for this Earth). An immensely long period of time after their arrival here on Earth, it is said our race was genetically engineered by a female member of the Annuna, called Ninhursag, Nisgal or Mammi. It is ironic that the female geneticist who engineered our species has the same name we now apply to our mothers – "Mammi." Apparently, that was how it happened. She was our Mama, and still is.

Why Do Men Have Nipples and Breasts?

People who dismiss the 'ancient alien' hypothesis out of hand, or our origins from Mammi, might well spend a little while pondering the odd fact that men have nipples and breasts.

According to the biologists, apparently, we all start out as female. Its only after six weeks of gestation in the womb that the outlines of what will become arms, legs, faces – and tails – begin to appear. Its only at about the same period that the rudiments of gender begin to manifest. If the fetus has a Y chromosome, testosterone will start to turn the buds for sexual organs into testes, which then pump out more testosterone. Individuals who remain female do not have this input of testosterone, and they stay with the original human blueprint, which is female.

So, men have nipples and breasts because they already had them at the beginning before they became male. You might ask why evolution didn't remove the breasts and nipples in males that so blatantly betray our origin from Mammi? Evolution apparently only eliminates features of the body that threaten survival and reproduction, so because there's no biological cost to men having boobs and nipples, there they remain to testify to the circumstances of our origin, for everyone who has an eye to see and a mind to understand.

The Emergence of Jehovah

A long time after the origins of the human race, to wit about 25,000 years ago, the entity Jehovah emerged into prominence. He is the entity who largely has shaped the whole mindset of the religions of the West — Judaism, Christianity and Islam. The three main features of the changes that Jehovah instituted are:

- The subjugation of women.
- The establishment of a patriarchal society that's designed to control the masses.
- The establishment of a fear-based religion, founded on belief in an external God.

About 25,000 years ago this colossal triple burden was placed on the human race and it has persisted since. This was the same scenario that certain enlightened individuals contemplated much later — 2,000 years ago. They decided that once again it was time to try to do something to alter the situation. They formed a plan focused on confronting these three matters listed above. The solution was centered on the entity that would come to be known as Jesus, who would incarnate into the human race and teach us how to change the existing situation by reclaiming the power that we had lost through so many centuries of fear, unworthiness and guilt. As we have already seen, after his mission his empowering message became disastrously distorted, and was turned into something entirely different.

Not alone has all this dis-information been disseminated about these three major issues, but it's also now imbedded in our DNA and in our neuronets. That gives us another insight into how difficult it is to accomplish profound personal change. But the difference is that now we know why. The process of accomplishing profound personal change is not based just on amassing information, however wonderful, for that is only a first step. We have to move on dis-empowering those sub-conscious programs of old, which is a delicate and tricky task, since the primary duty of the sub-conscious programs is to ensure their own survival. We have gained some clues as to how to approach this delicate task by engaging in a sort of case history — by looking at Genesis itself.

An all-powerful and good Creator, could not have made the kind of world we have ...everyone who has an open mind agrees on that. If God is all-good, is the Creator of the universes, is all-powerful, and loves us, how could he permit this kind of world that we have, to exist?

There are a number of options we can take in trying to answer that question. None of them are very palatable. And the more palatable ones are self-contradictory. So maybe, like Genesis, we may have to settle for second best.

The Clue from the Missing First Letter

Let's look at another informative clue hidden at the very beginning of Genesis. Stan Tenen[257] told me once that if you take

[257] *The Alphabet That Changed the World: How Genesis Preserves a Science of Consciousness in Geometry and Gesture*, 2011.

the numerical value of the first 28 letters in the first sentence of Genesis, and plot them on a graph, it gives the form of a Triad. This is intriguing.

In most languages, there is no numerical value attached to the letters of the alphabet, but there is in Hebrew, because the Hebrews didn't have a number system. Neither did the Romans, who indicated numbers by letters of the alphabet; as we know, V stood for five, X for 10, C for 100, and M for 1,000. Fortunately, that system perished: think of trying to use a Tablet, Phone or laptop computer without numbers or the decimal system!

Between the first and fourth centuries Indian mathematicians invented what is now known as the Hindu-Arabic numeral system, the same 1-9 system that we use today. In the original form of the numbers the number of angles in each figure stood for the number it represented. It is easy to see this in the original form of number 4, for example. The symbol for zero, introduced by Indian mathematicians about the year 500 AD, was the major advance which contributed to the efficiency of the system. The zero was adopted by Arabian mathematicians in the ninth century, and the Hindu-Arabic numeral system is now the most widely used system for indicating numbers.

Many years ago, when I was studying Biblical Hebrew, I happened to notice that the written text of the Book of Genesis didn't follow the customary system. The tradition in Judaism at that time was that when writing about matters of fundamental concern, such as the origin of all things, you began with the first letter of the alphabet. Oddly, however, Genesis begins with the second letter of the Hebrew alphabet.

The opening sentence of Genesis is:

"Ba Rasheet bara Elohim — בראשית ברא אלהים

Usually this is translated as: "In the beginning, God made the heavens and the Earth..."

This puzzled me. When I was about 20 years old, my Professor of Classical Hebrew wasn't the kind of person to whom you could pose a question like this without risk of serious academic repercussions! But of course, I could still ponder these questions privately. The word for God, "Elohim," in the Priestly Tradition in Genesis, ends with – 'im' which is puzzling since 'im' is the plural form in Hebrew. I knew that the Hebrew tradition always insisted emphatically that there was one God and one God only…in spite of the fact that they were surrounded by polytheists in all their neighboring regions. Because of that I felt it was extremely odd that their name for God was a plural – 'Gods' not 'God'.

Having noticed that the first line of Genesis didn't begin with an 'Aleph', the first letter of the Hebrew alphabet, I decided one day to put in the missing Aleph and discovered that instead of the traditional meaning…" In the beginning God made the heavens and the Earth…" the whole meaning of the sentence was altered – just by the addition of that one letter.

With the addition of that change, Genesis 1:1 now says: "Abba rasheet bara Elohim…". In translation, "The Father, (Abba), of the Beginnings, created the Elohim, the heavens and the Earth." So, the puzzle of the plural reference to God is now gone, and we see instead that the word did not refer to God at all, but to a race known as the "Elohim." Who were these Elohim? The Anunnaki.

The Father of the Beginnings and the Description of the Original State in Genesis ... The Paradise State

In this section, Genesis 2.4-25, courtesy of the divisions made by Langton and Stephens, we have the following elements:

1. God

What is God doing? Taking a break. He is walking in the cool of the evening. In Mediterranean countries before the advent of air conditioning people used to walk up and down in the streets of their village to cool off at dusk.

2. The woman and the man

The woman is related to the man as "two in one flesh". What does that mean? Does that mean they are stuck together? No. It means they are of the same substance. The phrase is meant to express that they are perfectly equal.

3. The animals

The animals are brought before the first man and woman and they are given names by them. In the Hebrew tradition of old, if you could name somebody you were their Lord. So, this is sending a message which says that the animals are at an inferior level to the humans.

4. The earth itself

This garden had excellent topsoil and is abundantly fertile. There was no need to water the lawn during the summer because there were four rivers running through it. The Tigris (Hiddekei), the Euphrates (Perat), the Pishon and the Gihon are mentioned in Genesis. There is an abundance of water for irrigation. The work itself consequently was absolutely easy. Looking after a garden...you could do it easily in the afternoon. The man could eat the fruit of any tree in the Garden except one – the fruit of the Tree of Knowledge of Good and Evil. If he eats that fruit God tells the man he will die (Genesis 2: 16-17).

5. Life

There was no death in the Garden, life continued without end.

That's the picture of the Original State. No awkward questions are posed about God. He has done everything well.

Now, let's look at the contrasting state as described in Genesis, 3:8-24. What picture do we have here? The opposite condition to "The Paradise" State. 'The Fallen State' is how we name the disastrous situation after the serpent had done his work. The same six elements that were examined in Chapter 2, describing the

Original State, are now taken up for examination once again, but this time in their Fallen or damaged state. There is, however, the addition of a sixth significant element to the Fallen State, childbirth, which needed to be added to ensure survival of the human species, since mankind no longer enjoyed eternal life.

The Fallen State

1. God

How is God pictured now in the Fallen State? Remember God and the first couple were walking in the cool of the evening in the Paradise State of Genesis, told in Chapter 2. Now, in the Fallen State, God is marauding around the garden looking for victims. The man and the woman are hiding from Him. They are naked and embarrassed. Things have gone to pot.

2. The Woman and Man

Remember that in the Paradise State the woman was absolutely equal to the man: "two in one flesh". But what's the situation now in the Fallen State? According to Genesis 3, the woman is drawn towards the man and cannot help it…she is subjugated to the man by that attraction. She is no longer free and no longer equal.

3. The animals

Because the humans had named the animals in the Paradise Account, the animals were subject to the humans. Now, however, the animals have the upper hand over the humans and, apparently, the serpent is in charge.

4. The earth

It was an abundantly fertile place in Chapter 2. But now in Chapter 3 the earth is a cursed ground. And while the work was very easy in the Paradise State, and could be done at leisure after lunch, now it is painful toil. "In the sweat of your brow you shall eat bread."

5. Life

In the Paradise State of Chapter 2 life was eternal. But what is it like in the Fallen State? Death. "Dust you are. Unto dust you shall return."

6. Childbirth

Now there is a new, sixth element added, that was not in the Paradise description. If you are not going to live forever you need to replicate the species. So, childbirth is introduced as part of the condition of the Fallen State. In that way people will have new bodies to return to. In addition, Genesis says that childbirth will be a painful process, caused to be so by the disobedience of our first parents in Eden.

With this background, the authors struggle to rationalize those irreconcilable three concepts with the three options with which they had to juggle. This was the best that they could do.

Now we begin to see more of the background to Jesus as the Suffering Savior, because this story of the Fall of the humans in Genesis is the very state that later generations of Christians alleged was the reason that caused Jesus to come into this world 2,000 years ago. Since the Fall, as described in Genesis 3, the prevailing dogma is that God and humanity have been in a state of alienation and enmity. Jesus was tasked with restoring relations with God and making up to him for all of the offenses humans have committed, since the creation of the human race.

This is the distorted version of Genesis chapters 2 and 3 and the distorted version of the mission of Jesus that we all still live with today.

As explained earlier, the authors of Genesis had three options before them. What did they do? To justify how the Paradise State (the version of affairs in Genesis Chapter 2) was replaced by the Fallen State (the Genesis Chapter 3 version), they went for an explanation which they spelled out in Genesis 3:1-7, according to

Langton's divisions of the text.

What's the Explanation there? Temptation by the Serpent. It is important to note that this is the background of how a mindset was created that, to this day, is crippling the message of Jesus and his mission. And it is the major contributing factor to our programs about Jesus being the Suffering Savior.

Langton and Stephens would have done much better if they had known something more about what they were doing. They did not realize that the authors of Genesis were trying to reconcile three major beliefs about God. The way they tried to reconcile them was to postulate that God had originally made the world in a perfect state, without any pain, suffering or lack. So, God is off the hook for evil in the world. But the world is full of evil. How did that happen? The fault was due to the serpent who tempted the first human couple to go against God's commands and bring down disaster on themselves.

Had Stephen Langton known his stuff he would have made divisions in the text vastly different from the chapter divisions he actually made. The Paradise State should have been one division. The section dealing with who was at fault, would be another section, and the Fallen State that resulted, would have been the third division. Then it would have been far easier to see the message of these first three chapters of Genesis clearly. The authors are contrasting the condition in which humanity was created by God, with the condition of Humanity after they had sinned against God. Within the limits of their understanding, this was the only way in which the authors of Genesis could preserve their two central beliefs, that God was good, and that he was the creator of the world.

We have already seen how, by contrast, the ancient 'pagan' creation narratives, far older than Genesis, couched matters. In those accounts the serpent sold them a dummy and ate the fruit of immortality himself. In the newer Genesis account, the serpent is still the deceiver. He tells the first human couple that if they eat the fruit God forbade them to eat then they will become like the Gods. The woman who wanted to gain knowledge, (the forbidden tree was the Tree of Knowledge), ate the fruit, and she gave it to her husband who also ate it. Once they did "their eyes were opened" and they saw they were naked.

As noted earlier, none of these three options we outlined works satisfactorily for us, or for Genesis.

What did Genesis do? It introduced a fourth option: *The world was made good by God.* Thereby, God is off the hook for creating the massive amount of evil and imperfection that is so obvious in our world. Genesis says that God did create the world, but he made it in a perfect state. Someone else messed it up. That's Option number four. That is the origin of the Fall narratives in Genesis, whose primary purpose was to avoid blaming God for the existence of evil.

We see now that the Genesis Creation Narratives are not talking about how everything began. Genesis is not about beginnings. It's about a relationship that exists between God and his or her creation. We are still not sure of that relationship. But in Genesis it is portrayed that the mixture of good and evil in our world is a punishment of humankind by God for disobedience.

The familiar corruptions of the teachings of Jesus say that it was this "fallen" condition he came to rectify. Jesus is the archetypal anti-Serpent. Instead of that, what Jesus came to do was set up an entirely new dispensation, based on learning to create by mastery of the quantum field.

A Prophecy Set in the Past?

Our destiny in evolution for the future is to recover the Paradise condition. This is what Jesus came to teach, they say. However, the real question here, of course, is was there actually ever a Paradise State, or was it just a device that had to be used in order to protect God from the charge of creating an imperfect world? The authors of Genesis had to postulate a Paradise State at the beginning of things. Not from any privileged knowledge of the remote beginnings of things, but as a postulate, in their world view, that was necessary to get God off the hook for evil. Given what we know today of the origins and progress of things, is it not much more likely that the Paradise State of Genesis 2, is rather a prophecy of a potential for the present and future of humanity, than an account of some blissful condition at the start of things? Unfortunately, accounting for why we have a Fallen State instead of a Paradise, can be accomplished only by blaming the original sin of humanity, hence the ultimate root of all dis-empowering programs. As we saw already on page 234:

Laid out in Graphic Form

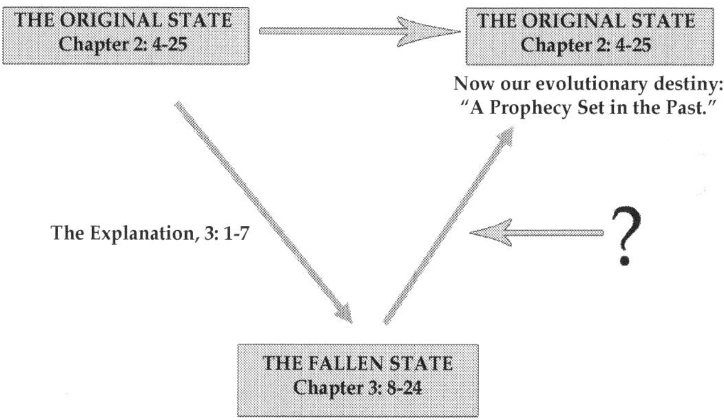

Jesus came to break the stranglehold of Jehovah. But this message has been dis-empowered, hijacked, and derailed. If we venerate the customary models of Jesus, such as 'the gentle Jesus, meek and mild', the 'suffering savior' or any of the other popular models of him, we are never going to ascend back to, or rise to, the Paradise State. Unfortunately, this is the form in which the message of Jesus is presented today by those who claim to have been mandated to carry on his mission. And this message infallibly ensures the perpetuation of a state of victimization, powerlessness, unworthiness, guilt and fear.

Most people have a physical visceral reaction to what is being pointed out here. If some people of a fundamentalist mindset especially hear such discussion they tend to react blindly, as if we have committed the ultimate offense. And they proceed accordingly, often finding themselves, as pointed out earlier, in the odd position of preaching and practicing hatred in the name of the God of Love.

Why do we feel this visceral reaction? Because that reaction is what our sub-conscious programs generate. As mentioned above, the basic task of these programs is first of all to ensure their own survival. So, we get distinctly uncomfortable when this sort of material is mentioned. This is an indication of one thing: that our crippling sub-conscious programs are feeling threatened. It does not mean that we have to stand up and defend Jesus against impious and heretical criticism.

If we feel distinctly uncomfortable about all this then that's a good sign that we are on the road to de-programming. But like riding that backwards bicycle, it is inevitably going to take time. These programs do have to fade away of their own accord once new ones based on more accurate facts and assessments are constructed. Let's trust we have enough persistence to go through with it.

Why did God make people? Was it so he could torture most of them by burning in Hell forever? Why did he do that, goes that line of reasoning? Because he wants us all to love his son. Who is his son? He is his own son. The quintessential 'Do it yourself.'

And last, George Bernard Shaw – "Most people don't pray; they only beg." As I stated earlier, that is the most effective way of ensuring you never get what you want. If we want something and we start to pray, beg, implore, beseech or wish for it, we can never get it. Why, because the only thing that interacts with the quantum field is presence. And if we are longing for something, then what is present for me is the longing. If I am trying to heal an incurable cancer, and I am racked by pain, and nausea, I have to step entirely out of all of that to feel completely well. Without that there can never be any hope of a positive result from my initiative, and it is I who have decreed that that be so.

For this reason, most people, when they pray to be healed from illness, only increase the depth of their illness. That is because they don't realize that in Jesus' teaching the law of cause and effect is reversed. In other words, it is not something that causes something. You have to first *be* the something for it to appear. You have to manifest the effect before it can become a reality. The law of cause and effect is reversed in interaction with the quantum field. The effect in a very real sense, is the cause. That is a much more realistic picture of how reality actually is. Unfortunately Jesus' message was contorted into an ignoring of that reality.

Condition of the Humans at the Beginning of Their History: Source of the Great Diseases of the Mind

What were the conditions of the original humans, say a quarter million years ago? ... not all that long ago in the perspective of history. What were the main characteristics of our unfortunate emergence, in terms of physicality?

1. Terrific inferiority and insecurity
2. Ignorance about reality. We hadn't a clue about what was what.
3. Mortality and sickness. The Anunnaki, our creators, as I said earlier, are still alive and well today as they were then. But the human race was plagued with illness, sickness and death.
4. And then eventually when the Anunnaki packed up and left, about 4000 years ago, we experienced a major sense of abandonment that we were left behind, we were abandoned. One thing insecure people fear above all, is being "dumped." We were dumped. But the ultimate fear in all of us is not about betrayal or being dumped by other human beings. Our ultimate fear that's way down there in the dark, dark depths is the fear of abandonment by God. Or the fear that maybe the afterlife, the world of spirits or whatever, is not as we thought it was, where everything was hunky dory and beautiful. Maybe it's not that way there. Maybe its uncannily similar to what we experience here, as some form of dim reflection of it in lowered frequency. That's a great discouragement.

We need to deal as a priority with those relics of our abandonment by the Anunnaki that have come down to us through the aeons. I call them — "The Four Great Diseases of the Mind." If the mind is what creates reality, as quantum physics tell us, then obviously unless we heal these 'diseases' of the mind first, we are on a hiding to nothing.

The need for approval or disapproval is our first big problem. The lack of self-knowledge, and the tendency to blame, are the next two, and fourthly, the religious mindset, an ingenious construction manufactured out of those first three.

The picture of a hamburger is on the cover of my first DVD named "The Hamburger Universe." I was speaking about this tropic about fifteen or twenty years ago and was attempting to depict our mindset with a sketch on a whiteboard. I drew a flat Earth in the middle, and above it I drew the vault of the Heavens. After all, whenever we are praying to God, thinking about God, cursing God or asking God — where do we look? Up. This is why I was so always so worried about people in the southern hemisphere, because I didn't know where they were looking when they looked up!

God, and the angels and the saints, and our dear departed who have gone before us, are up there on the top floor. But if you draw another arc beneath the flat Earth, then in that lower arc is represented the realm of Satan and all those who have lost their salvation and are condemned by God to spend an eternity in punishment.

In our tradition, there are a variety of Hells on offer: the hot hell and the cold hell, for example. Thanks for this insight to Dante Alighieri.[258] He realized that no matter how awful something is, with the passage of time we somewhat get partially used to it. If there is a gauge in Hell registering the amount of suffering of the damned, then for achieving the maximum effect of God's intent, the suffering has to be kept at 100%. However, if we are in a burning pit of fire for a very long time, say one million years or so, maybe we can begin to get somewhat used to it, and the needle

---

[258] 1265-1321.

on the suffering indicator scale may down from 100% to perhaps 98% or even 95%. In Dante's Hell, once this happens, we are then immediately switched from the hot Hell to the cold Hell to get the suffering level back up to 100%. We are endlessly switching back and forth between Hells, according to the Dante's "Divine Comedy," even if the topic is not very comic. Both of these hells were registered on the bottom floor of the sketch I had drawn on the white board one day when I was teaching years ago. The old Master Teacher came in a few hours later after I had drawn this sketch on the board, and he said "This looks like a hamburger," and proceeded to add lettuce and tomatoes etc., to the sketch. That is how the "Hamburger Universe" image came into existence.

The Hamburger Universe is a mindset, and is unfortunately how we normally think about human destiny. God is up there, and the Devil is down there. In between the two we are here on Earth. We're here trying to work out the repercussions of these Four Great Diseases of the Mind in the middle layer of the hamburger.

Let's have a look at those four great 'diseases' of the mind:

1. *The need for approval or disapproval* is the first disease of the mind. It is obviously a sign that a conviction of profound lack lives within me, because I am constantly looking outside of myself for affirmation. That means I don't believe in myself. That is then a 'present state' in me. What does that state do when it is constantly being radiated from me into the quantum field? It creates more of the same problem I already have. That is not a good place to be. That is the first thing we've got to address, and it was the first thing that the message of Jesus Christ addressed when he came to direct us from the Fallen State back to the Original Paradise or Future State, which never was a past state for humanity. We did not begin in a Paradise condition from which we fell to where we now are. That explanation was devised, as I have explained already, as a device within a static world-view, to get God off the hook for evil. We no longer need that explanation.

2. *The second 'disease' is lack of self-knowledge.* We don't know who we are. If I don't know who I am, and the fundamental element of that knowing is, as Jesus said, to realize we are all Gods, then we have crippled ourselves. We have hamstrung ourselves and we crave more of the subjugation and inferiority with which we have already deeply wounded ourselves, for victimization is akin to a drug addiction.

3. *The third great disease of the mind is the tendency to blame.* Everything is always someone else's fault. Remember the old adage that said when you point the finger of accusation at somebody there is one finger pointing at them, and the other four are pointing back at you. We have remorse, and we have guilt, and we have fear when we are in this mindset, and we are always blaming that on someone else. In the quantum field this mindset obviously generates more of the same.

4. *The fourth great disease is a combination of the first three, and it produces what I call "the religious attitude."* At the heart of this attitude lie guilt, victimization, pain, and suffering, and these are, paradoxically, the very qualities that many traditional religious institutions today characterize as pre-eminently praiseworthy.

What did these diseases of the mind do? They put us on a non-stop roller coaster of emotion. Emotion is at once our greatest weapon and our greatest tool, because unless we can engage what we wish to create with emotion, (but not in a polarized emotion), we are not going anywhere.

Emotion can also be our worst enemy, and usually is if uncontrolled. All these blocks are enormous barriers to our greatness. However, once we are alerted to them we can see the way opening up to a wonderful life. This is what happens if we can get the message of Jesus straight and not lose ourselves in the salvation matrix.

It is really important to remember that when the Anunnaki, or Annuna of Ki, ruled over the Middle East after the Deluge, the humans were very dependent upon them for technical assistance and knowledge. When the Annuna withdrew, the humans felt deserted and lost. They became psychologically susceptible to manipulation by those who had been given authority as priests and kings by the Annuna before their departure. Not long after the gods left those who were administering their realms for them, the managers who were human, took over. They are the ancestors of the royal bloodlines of today and the prototypes of ancient religious leadership.

Because they so missed the Annuna, one segment of the managers devoted themselves to an enterprise to persuade the Annuna to return. So, came the expectation of return, which evolved into, for example, the Rapture, or the "Second Coming," and the many other forms for the hope of the return of the gods, into which this longing has evolved over thousands of years. That was the principal factor in the origin of the form of religion we now take for granted. It was focused on the top floor of the Hamburger Universe in the hope that the gods would return. The other managers administered the system. These cults led to the modern institutions of royalty and religion.

The main religions fomented the idea of etheric beings who lived in the sky. They manipulated us so we were no longer talking about flesh and blood gods, which the Anunna were. We are now talking about a new area entirely which we call the supernatural. There is actually no supernatural in the traditional sense, but something far more wonderful. There are just different levels of frequency. But the supernatural is one of the most direful elements of superstition that has kept our minds in prison.

It is important not to confuse representatives of a more advanced species with the consciousness and energy that's the source of creation, which is what we call God. That's what happens when people project human-style ideas into the unknown where they don't belong. If and when the existence of alien life should be proven beyond doubt, that proof will likely come from confrontation with a species far more advanced than ours, else they would never have got here to confront us. The instinctive tendency of humanity in such a situation, due to so many centuries of programming in the Hamburger-universe mindset, would be once again to bow down, worship and obey, and the whole thing starts over again, one more time.

The Illuminati and the Bloodline Groups

The history of our race has been skillfully deformed over a long time in order to protect those who imposed themselves on the Earth and their descendants. At the time of writing we see the cult of the feminine has been deliberately suppressed and subjugated to a dominant patriarchy.

To what did that lead us? The Illuminati and the Bloodline Groups. The Illuminati developed from the religious groups after the gods left and the bloodlines were the ones who took over the practical management of affairs.

One of the mandates that was given to Jesus was to establish a new bloodline that would permeate and re-vivify the old. To the best of our knowledge that descent has come down through the Merovingian Kings of part of modern France, who ruled from around 481 AD to 752 AD. The Merovingians claimed to have direct bloodline links to Mary Magdalene and Jesus. Dagobert II, was the king of Austrasia from 676 to 679, and is the most notable of the Merovingian Kings. Those kings were deposed by the Pope in 751 because he feared their power. He replaced them with what we now know as the Carolingian Dynasty, of which Charlemagne was probably the most distinguished member.

Constantine built a huge Basilica in Rome over the tomb of St. Peter in Nero's Circus, where he had been crucified, beginning about the year 320. It took thirty years to complete.

Four hundred and fifty years later, in the year 800, at the Christmas Eve Mass in Constantine's Basilica, Charlemagne, King of the Franks, was in a place of honor in front of the High Altar.

During the Mass that night, to Charlemagne's great surprise, the Pope, Leo III, approached him, and placed a crown on his head. In effect, the Pope was saying "You are now the Emperor of the Romans, and you are acting on my behalf (the Pope's) to rule Europe." The Holy Roman Emperors had in effect replaced the Merovingian Kings in the eyes of the Papacy.

That laid the foundations for the Holy Roman Empire. Charlemagne had united most of Western Europe for the first time since the Roman Empire. It embraced modern Germany, Austria, Belgium, Croatia, the Czech Republic, Denmark, France, Italy, Liechtenstein, Luxemburg, Morocco, the Netherlands, Poland, San Marino, Slovenia, Slovakia and Switzerland. This Empire lasted right up to the time of Napoleon and was finally dissolved only in 1806. I can't resist quoting Voltaire: "This conglomeration which calls itself the 'Holy Roman Empire,' was neither holy, or Roman or an Empire."

The House of Bourbon produced the French Kings, who also claim ancestry from the Merovingians, and, while royalty in France is gone, the Bourbons have been restored and are now Kings of Spain.

The House of Stuart eventually came to be the most direct line of the Royal bloodlines.

There have been all sorts of plots by people to subvert that bloodline. But I don't know if the bloodline needs subversion, since it has subverted itself a long time ago.

The Move towards Constantine

We can't assume that everything that is in Christianity today goes back to the time of Jesus. Within two decades of his Passion, problems of major proportions were already showing themselves in the Christian communities.

The earliest followers of Jesus were Jewish, and they continued to frequent the Temple and the Synagogues as long as they were permitted, which was for the best part of fifty years. It was inevitable that the sacrifices of the lambs in the Temple, especially at Passover and Yom Kippur, exerted a profound influence on how Jesus came to be perceived as the sacrificial lamb who was slain for us because of our sins.

But by the end of the first century a very different version of the Christian message had appeared, which included a lot of ideas and customs that had their roots in the pagan philosophies of Greece and Rome rather than in Jesus himself. Indeed, by about the year 120 AD, several historians point out that the Christian Church was undeniably, in many important ways, very different indeed in terms of belief from the group that had existed in the days of the Apostles.

One of the main features in this process of change was how they envisaged Jesus himself. What kind of a being was he? Was he an inspired and enlightened teacher or was he more? Was Jesus just an ordinary man, who by his own struggle and effort became God, or was he adopted by God as a reward for his efforts? Or was he God who came down into human form? Our own "efforts" to attain what Jesus meant when he said we could do all he did and greater, have a lot to learn from these tortured discussions of the second and third centuries.

This debate in the early Fourth Century formed most of those crippling programs we are now battling against in order to attain real spiritual power. Is the Father the one true God? Or is the Father, the Son and the Holy Spirit the one true God? How do we fit these three into one? Most of the struggles the Christian theologians had in those far-off days seventeen hundred years ago, was to try to show by an extremely inventive vocabulary that they were not asserting a mathematical absurdity when speaking about God being three in one.

One prominent view of Jesus said he was a human being who worked his way up into Godhead. You and I are badly mistaken in our more enlightened modern spiritual endeavors, if we are trying to work our way up into Godhead, for that was not the teaching Jesus came to give us. Instead we should be focused on taking out the garbage from our consciousness, so as to reveal the Godhead that already exists there. That is what Jesus did teach. That's a big job but also a very different one.

Constantine became the sole Roman Emperor in 324 AD, having defeated his co-Emperor and brother-in-law Licinius in a military struggle that had lasted for ten years. The Roman Empire was in its twilight. It couldn't afford the major religious and social strife that existed, and most of the divisions were based on serious differences about Jesus' teachings and differing convictions about who or what he really was. Constantine saw that he had to do something about bringing this strife to an end as he sat on a very troubled and insecure throne. The restoration of civil and religious order was of paramount importance for him to consolidate his rule, and it was obvious that most of the sources of disorder in the Empire were now religious.

Twelve years before, Constantine and his co-Emperor, Licinius, met in the year 312 at Milan and issued a Decree, normally called the Edict of Milan (although I don't think there was ever a formal Edict), which tolerated the practice of all religions, including Christianity. Contrary to what's often believed, the Edict of Milan did not outlaw the traditional religions, nor did it establish Christianity as the state religion.

At that stage Constantine had just overcome a major revolt against him. The Horse Guard in the Emperor's retinue in Rome had sided with his rival. The Horse Guard's quarters were beside what's now the Lateran Palace. Constantine flattened the Horse Guard's stables, which were vast, and the Horse Guards Palace beside the stables he gave to Pope Miltiades to use as a residence, about the year 313. Miltiades was a Berber from North Africa, and the last North African Pope.

The Vatican has become almost synonymous with the Popes and the Catholic Church, but in fact the Popes have lived a relatively short span of years at the Vatican. The Lateran Palace became the Papal Residence for over a thousand years in 313. It was the headquarters of the Catholic Church and is the Cathedral of the Diocese of Rome since 324 AD.

Even though Constantine and his Co-Emperor had legitimized Christianity, Constantine did not become a Christian until he was on his deathbed. There was a belief current in Christianity then that once you received Baptism all the sins you had committed up to that moment, no matter how serious, would be wiped out. I assume Constantine wanted to get the maximum value out of the system, and then hope his timing was right so that he didn't expire before someone had an opportunity to pour water on his head.

It's interesting in itself, to see how baptism became so significant. Like the Eucharist, it's a very, very ancient ceremony. The period from the time of Jesus up to the present is nothing compared to the length of time prior to Jesus when the Eucharist was celebrated.

What did it represent? It was a feast — a scared feast of bread, wine and water. The bread represented the physical body in the Hertzian plane. The wine represented the spirit that came from Point Zero. And the water represented the human soul that kept the memory of that journey. These three sacred elements were a celebration of the reality of human existence and of the whole panorama of creation. That's what Jesus celebrated with his disciples at the Last Supper, not on the Passover, but on the previous day.

Likewise, the ceremony of baptism also had its origins long before the time of Jesus. As pointed out earlier, in the Priestly tradition of Genesis, it was believed that everything came from water. If everything came from water, how does this knowledge enable me to accomplish monumental personal change? The ancients thought it would be accomplished by going back into the primeval substance out of which everything emerged — submersion in water. Over time that procedure was streamlined because it wasn't practical to have so much water sloshing around. It evolved into simply pouring water on the head, and eventually with some Christian groups it became simply the sprinkling water on your forehead. Whatever the form was, it was supposed to signify, or even cause, a profound re-birth, by joining oneself with the primeval substance of creation. Later the belief took the form that the ceremony caused the forgiveness of all sins up to the time it was administered.

It wasn't about that at all. The earlier, pre-Christian, baptism was a sign that you had understood where you were in creation and that you were leaving behind the old stuff, going back down into the primeval substance from which everything had emerged, and then emerging as a new creation. In a metaphorical sense you were "born again".

By the time of Constantine the understanding of Baptism had degenerated to the belief that if you receive baptism, all your sins committed prior to that moment were remitted in the sight of God.

Secure in this belief Constantine postponed baptism until someone poured some water on his head as he was dying. Constantine went to his maker believing everything would thereby be made be okay, including the murder of his eldest son, the murder of his wife and of numerous political rivals.

Chapter 17
The Jesus of Constantine

Constantine and Nicaea: Jesus Becomes a Stranger

To understand Constantine's major involvement with the Catholic Church we have to go back to about the year 318 AD. St. Mark, the individual who is traditionally regarded as the author of the Gospel of Mark, is believed to have evangelized the city of Alexandria. The early Christians built a church for him there in a suburb of the city called Baucalis. On Easter Sunday in 68 AD Mark was attacked in his Church by a mob, dragged through the streets and murdered. The Christians buried his body under the High Altar.

In 311, a priest of Alexandria, Arius, son of Ammonius, was excommunicated for his theological views by Bishop Peter of Alexandria. The excommunication was later lifted, and Arius was then assigned to St. Mark's Church in Baucalis, possibly so that he might learn something from what had happened to St. Mark there, two hundred and fifty years before. The reconciliation between Arius and his bishop did not last long however, and in the same year that Christianity was legitimized Arius began to publicly oppose the views of the new bishop of Alexandria, Alexander, and caused an enormous uproar by promulgating his novel views about Jesus. Specifically, he disagreed with Alexander's teaching that Jesus, the Son of God, had existed eternally, being "generated" eternally by the Father. Instead, Arius insisted that "there was a time when the Son was not." Jesus Christ therefore must be numbered among the created beings, and however great in dignity, he was still a human being.

Matters reached the tipping point when Bishop Alexander called a meeting at which more than one hundred bishops from Egypt and Libya assembled. At their assembly in 321 they condemned Arius as a heretic and castigated his views. Despite the condemnation, Arius nevertheless continued to preach his views, and what was even more alarming to the bishops, he was gaining ever larger amounts of followers sympathetic to his views.

Eventually the Bishop of Alexandria took Arius's pension away and banished him. Arius went to live in the Holy Land. Bishop Alexander published his "Epistle Against the Arians," a five thousand-word document condemning the views of Arius, and any other views that were sympathetic to him. Arius responded with another document refuting the Bishop's position. This firing of theological fusillades at each other continued for quite a long time and people were getting extremely worked up about the whole matter.

Constantine wrote to the bishop of Alexandria and to Arius, who was now back in Africa, and he lamented the fact that they had stirred up such chaos over matters which he described in the letter as of no practical importance: issues such as who or what God or Jesus was. Constantine was obviously no theologian! He advised them to be sensible and asked them to come to an agreement without delay. What hope was there of that? Somewhat even less than a snowball's chance in hell.

Since there was going to be no satisfactory resolution it was suggested to Constantine that the only thing to do was call all the bishops of the world together and to try to knock some sense into their heads.

There were approximately eighteen hundred bishops in the world at that time. The center of world power in the West was in northwestern Turkey, at Constantinople, now Istanbul. The Emperor undertook the mammoth task of writing very respectful letters to all the bishops of the Christian world. He invited them to a meeting with the view to resolving these disruptive controversies once and for all.

The bishops were asked to assemble by the 20th of May in the year 325 AD at Constantine's Summer Palace at Nicaea, about 60 miles as the crow flies from his main residence at Constantinople, a distance of about 140 miles by road today. In a customary act of humility Constantine was to name the city after himself, in the year 330. It retained that name for a long time. In 1923, in the 1600th anniversary of its foundation, the name of the city was changed from Constantinople to Istanbul at the instigation of Mustafa Kemal Atatürk, first President of Turkey, and the capital was moved from Istanbul to Ankara.

Constantine offered the 1,800 bishops of the world free travel and lodgings for themselves and a small retinue of retainers. They were allowed to bring three people to fold their garments and do the ironing and washing. It's generally accepted that 318 bishops showed up. They began their meeting on 20th of May, 325. Most of the attendees were Greeks. There were only seven bishops from the Latin Church, including two priests Victor and Vincentius, who represented the Pope, Sylvester I.

They were given a rather intimidating agenda: deciding what was it that was correct to believe about God. I am sure many of the great philosophers of the past who had labored over these questions for lifetimes would have been appalled at this new method of discovering truth by a vote.

Pause for a little perspective! One of history's greatest theologians, Augustine, Bishop in Hippo Regius, on the Mediterranean coast of present day Northeastern Algeria, spent 30 years, (this is not a good sign!), working on his major Treatise. What was it about? The Holy Trinity. He was trying to figure out how three could be made equal to one and how Jesus related to the Father and Holy Spirit within that scheme. He had worked on this problem for 30 years with no great result.

This is the same topic that had been before the Council of Nicaea a century before Augustine. But Augustine wasn't doing well with his project. One day he decided he needed a breath of fresh air so he went out for a walk on the beach to refresh his brain, and hopefully produce some new insights.

As he was walking along the beach he saw a little boy who had dug a hole in the sand about a foot wide. The little boy had a shell in his hand and he was running backwards and forwards to the ocean and putting a shell full of water into the hole each time. Augustine said: 'Little boy what the heck are you doing?' The child gave him a very sweet smile and said: 'I am emptying all the water in the ocean into this hole with a sea shell'. Augustine wasn't in a very good mood that day because he was finding his theological writing so difficult, so he said: 'You can't do that child; have sense. There is no way that little hole could ever contain all the water in the ocean, even if you could transfer it with a sea shell. It's completely impossible'.

The little child looked up at him, gave him a beautiful smile, and said: 'It's no more impossible than what you are trying to do' – and vanished. You have to admit, that was the ultimate grand exit!

The bishops a hundred years prior to Augustine's time who were assembled for Constantine's Council at Nicaea didn't appear to have any such qualms. In view of the damage they did to the message of Jesus it would have been a great benefit to the human race if a few visits from a miraculous child could have been arranged at Nicaea.

Constantine, and his brother-in-law and Co-Emperor Licinus, issued The Edict of Milan in February 313 AD, which tolerated the practice of Christianity, it also gave back all property of Christians which had been confiscated, especially in the most savage of the many persecutions against the Christians by Diocletian, which only ended with his death in 311.

Constantine was extremely superstitious, and absolutely

paranoid about offending the gods worshipped in the Empire at that time. He was not converted to Christianity, but he regarded the god of Christianity as the most powerful of the many gods, and certainly didn't want to upset him.

In this light it's easy to understand that the Edict of Milan, was more an indication of Roman obsession with pacifying a multitude of gods than it was any indication of what Constantine or Licinius actually believed. Above all, it was a political move to try to bring to an end the many fractious religious differences within the Empire.

Homesickness As a Source of Doctrine

For a long time the Christians had had their property confiscated and had been pursued and persecuted in a multitude of ways by the predecessors of Constantine and Licinius. As the 318 bishops processed into the main hall of Constantine's Summer Palace at Nicaea on the solemn opening day of the Council, the scars and the mutilations of those persecutions were very evident.

According to the historian Theodoret of Cyrus, Bishop Paphnutius from Egypt walked with very great difficulty. He had been tortured by being tied up and having his knees crushed by enormous weights. As if that were not enough, he had one of his eyes gouged out by a Roman soldier.

There is a tradition that Constantine embraced Bishop Paphnutius on the opening day and kissed his eyeless cheeks. Both tortures had been inflicted on Paphnutius because he refused to deny that Jesus was the Son of God.

The hands of Bishop Paul of Neocaesaria were paralyzed and bore terrible scars from burning with red hot irons. Why? For the same reason. The list goes on and on. Large numbers of the bishops at Nicaea were crippled in varying degrees from various tortures and from having undergone penal servitude in the stone quarries of the Roman Empire at the behest of the predecessors of Constantine and Licinius. Now they are sitting down to dinner with the Emperor himself. They would have signed almost anything... and unfortunately they did.

For this reason Thoedoret called the entry procession to the Council of Nicaea 'A Procession of Martyrs' because that was the reality. None of the theological issues before the Council of Nicaea were abstract issues for these men. They had all paid dearly for what they believed. The question was, how justified an interpretation of the teachings of Jesus was what they believed, and how justified was what the Council of Nicaea decided to impose on the world's Christians in matters of belief?

It should also be obvious, given those same circumstances of the time, that most of these bishops had little in the way of learning or education. If John the Apostle was called unlettered and illiterate, then certainly most of these bishops were illiterate or very, very poorly educated. Most of them had only a very slight acquaintance with Christian theology, and basically knew squat about the major theological issues before them.

The bishops assembled on the 20th of May at Nicaea and had three weeks of discussion until the Emperor arrived on June 14th.

The sessions were held in the principal Church and in the Great Hall of Constantine's Imperial Palace. All the guests were superbly taken care of, and since there were over 300 bishops with some retainers each, it's reasonably easy to calculate the number of people Constantine was entertaining to dinner each evening: approximately 2,000 individuals — a figure which one later Arabic manuscript actually quotes.

It was in Constantine's political interest to have the church vigorous and united. Constantine, as I stated earlier, was no theologian. He knew very little, and cared less, about the niceties of the theological issues before that Council. As long as the bishops agreed on something, he didn't care much what it was they agreed on. He just wanted to bring the disruptive and draining religious controversies to a close.

Why is it necessary to stress this? Because it shows the desperate situation in which most of the huge blocks to our spiritual empowerment grew up. Unfortunately, most of them grew to maturity in that hall at Nicaea.

For the opening ceremony Constantine was magnificently dressed, wearing an outer cloak glistening with gold and precious stones. When all the bishops were assembled, he made his grand entrance. A chair of solid gold awaited him at the end of the Great Hall. He conducted the Council along the lines of meetings of the Roman Senate, with which he was very familiar.

He opened the proceedings with a speech in Latin. He besought the bishops to bring order and harmony to the Church. He stated they had better things to do with their time and energy than indulging in these personal quarrels and bitter recriminations about stuff that doesn't matter a hoot — like the relationships between God and Jesus! Having made his case, he removed himself from most of the subsequent deliberations.

It's amusing sometimes to leaf through the long list of accusations of what the Council of Nicaea and Constantine himself are supposed to have done to the Church. *The Da Vinci Code* is a marvelous example of the kind of pseudo-historical accusations levelled at Nicaea, but far from the only one. It is said there, for example, that Constantine called the Council so he could impose the Christian faith on the Empire. Unlikely, since he wasn't even a Christian himself at the time!

It's alleged he decided what books should be part of the Bible by throwing all the sacred writings that existed at that time on to a big table. The ones that stayed on top were included in the Bible. The ones that fell on the floor were out, and became the apocryphal documents.

Furthermore, it was said that the dogma of the Trinity — the Father, Son and Spirit, co-equal and co-eternal — was settled by a very small majority vote. And that Constantine made sure that the dogma of the Trinity would be passed by assassinating some uncooperative bishops prior to the vote in order to get a majority. Not so.

It was even alleged by Shirley McLaine in "Out on a Limb" that the Church suppressed all of its original teachings about reincarnation at the Council of Nicaea. Shirley is actually referring to the Council of Constantinople, held in 381 AD, 56 years after Nicaea, but she calls it the Council of Nicaea. Like Constantine,

Shirley is apparently no theologian either, for neither the Council of Nicaea or of Constantinople, devoted more than one sentence to reincarnation, and that only indirectly. It wasn't even on the agenda and certainly wasn't a major issue at either of these Councils.

False and Real Problems at Nicaea

There are lots of problems with the transactions of the Council of Nicaea, but:

1. There were no assassinations of bishops — though I can imagine circumstances in which such a course of action would have proven very attractive!

2. It was Constantine together with Pope Sylvester who called the Council.

3. Reincarnation, or its condemnation, was not on the agenda

4. The main Christian dogmas proposed at Nicaea passed with a vote of more than 99% in favor. Why? Basically, because the bishops wanted to go home.

5. The issue of what books should be in the Bible was never raised at Nicaea — with all due apologies to a vast amount of New Age literature.

6. The Canon of the Old and New Testament was not decided at Nicaea, whether by Constantine throwing books on the table in a fit of pique, or by a vote of the bishops. The matter never came up there at all.

There are enough real problems relating to the Council of Nicaea without inventing false ones.

The Council was focused in the main on the controversy that is known by Arius's name, the priest of Alexandria who had been assigned to the Church where St. Mark was murdered. Arius said, very sensibly, that if Jesus is the Son of God he must have had a beginning like all sons. So, he must have been a special creation of God. If Jesus was the Son, then the Father must be older than the Son. They couldn't be co-eternal. That is sensible enough.

Now Arius was described by one of his enemies as "tall and lean, of distinguished appearance and polished address. Woman doted on him. They were charmed by his beautiful manners and touched by his appearance. He looked very ascetic. He was obviously a holy man as he was thin. And men were impressed by his aura of intellectual superiority and knowledge.

If the Father begat the Son, the Son must have had a beginning when he was begotten. From this it should follow that there was a time when the Son was not. It therefore necessarily follows that He (the Son) had his substance from nothing. He didn't exist from all eternity. That sums up the essence of Arius' doctrine. And however strange you and I may find it today, this was an issue that divided the world at that time.

A very conservative body of churchmen believed that Arius was too liberal in his views. They believed his views were heretical, and yet others thought he was too conservative, and that he should have gone even further.

Arius felt that the beliefs about Jesus, as he actually was, had become contaminated by importing quite different understandings of God from Greek and other philosophies. He was quite right. Arius based his views on Jesus by appealing to two verses in the New Testament.

John 14:28:

"the Father is greater than I."

And a letter of Saint Paul in Colossians 1:15:

"(Jesus) the first-born of all creation."

But Arius insisted that these texts showed that the godhead of the Father was greater than the godhead of the Son and that, therefore, they were not co-equal and not co-eternal. Which, of course, seems perfectly logical.

But what is false in it is the image of God as a human being enlarged, who had a Son just as an earthly father might have a son. It is helpful if we can see that by using these human style images we have in effect turned God into a creature. It's important to realize that what we are talking about here is Point Zero, from which all of the creation descends in frequency. *The Prime Creator, the Father, is Point Zero.* It is in that being that we live and move and have our being. None of the categories of Nicaea are in any way helpful in this context because they began with the wrong assumptions. In so doing they exacerbate the difficulties enormously.

The opposing view to Arius was held by Athanasius, who was also from Alexandria. He said the Father, Son and Spirit were one, but at the same time they were distinct from each other. No one could get their heads around this. Most of the bishops who were there had no knowledge of anything much in the line of philosophy or theology.

To sum up the two opposing views: Arius said that Jesus was a human being, a perfect human being, but a man nevertheless. Arius never said that Jesus was just an ordinary man. His view, on the contrary, was that Jesus was a very, very extraordinary man, but a man nevertheless. If Jesus was born a human being and attained what he did, obviously the message is that you and I can do it as well. That is what Jesus came to teach us, and saying that is what got Arius into serious trouble.

But Athanasius, on the other hand, said that Jesus was the Godhead incarnate. How can we possibly in any way, shape or form relate to that? It is from this gathering in this hall at Nicaea that most of the modern blocks to our spiritual power emerged. We are still holding on to them grimly.

Instead it needs some courage to recognize that this was a clumsy solution, with a political motivation, that was cobbled together hastily, and never really worked.

But we still feel we have no alternative but to hang on to those conceptions of Jesus that came from Nicaea, even though we can see that these are among our biggest barriers to attaining to spiritual empowerment. To get rid of those programs and their crippling effect on us, we have to understand from whence they came, which is why we need to do all of these detailed historical investigations to ascertain, in simple terms, what really happened.

Constantine presided at some of the sessions at Nicaea. Needless to say, given their history of persecution by his predecessors, that "Procession of Martyrs" as the Bishops at Nicaea were so aptly called, were overawed by the Emperor's presence.

They held daily sessions. Arius was heard several times, so was Athanasius. And there was serious discussion. But eventually an extraordinary thing happened. The Emperor obviously was paying the bill for 2,000 people for dinner every night and wanted them to agree on something, preferably sooner rather than later, and didn't really care much on what they agreed, as long as they agreed.

A lot of people didn't like the view of Arius which they understood to say that Jesus was a man who worked his way up to become God. But they had nothing adequate with which to replace it. The only other view before the Council was Athanasius's view which had nothing much to recommend it, and was espoused by only a minority. But what did the Bishops of Nicaea do? They said if we are ever going to get out of here we better agree on something. They wanted to go home. So, they voted in Athanasius's formula, which nobody really liked.

This is how the most sublime truths about Jesus Christ as the incarnation of the Eternal Word all came to be. The Bishops were anxious to get home. Is it any wonder the mission and message of Jesus was lost by the Church?

The session ended on 25th August. It was the 20th anniversary of Constantine becoming co-Emperor. He held a splendid dinner in the main hall and he gave very generous gifts to all the participants. Then he asked for a final session to wrap up and he exhorted all the bishops to work for peace. He asked for their prayers and he gave them permission to go home, which is really what they all wanted more than anything else by that stage.

So, what did the Council of Nicaea do for the Church? It left it in the rather odd position of putting the seal of approval on a view that was held by only a minority. Basically, that view had little to recommend it. But with the Emperor breathing down their necks they accepted the views of Athanasius about God, and God's relation to Jesus. Why? Because they all wanted to get out of there.

Constantine was very pleased. He felt the result justified all the expense and trouble. He wasn't a Christian himself. In fact, the following year he had both his wife and his eldest son Crispus killed. Crispus had been a major military success in the region now known as France. Constantine's wife Fausta, step-mother of Crispus, was insanely jealous of him, and told Constantine that Crispus had tried to rape her. True to his impetuous nature Constantine had his favorite son executed. Some months later he discovered the truth, that the allegation of attempted rape had been totally the invention of Fausta so as to undermine the influence of Crispus with his father. Constantine was more merciful to his wife than he had been to his son. She used to take steam baths. One day he locked the door, turned up the heat and left her there until she died.

This is the man who prescribed over the Council of Nicaea and is the one responsible for us believing that Jesus was co-eternal with the Father and is the incarnation of the Logos from whom all creation began.

If Jesus was ever unapproachable before, he was certainly way out of reach now. The promise of Jesus that we would do all the wonders he did and greater, fades into impossibility. We have been saddled with that dis-empowerment because of these doings at Nicaea

The only real unanimity at Nicaea was that the bishops wanted to go home. The Council summed up its views on Jesus and the Holy Trinity in the famous creed or symbol of Nicaea, a document of 150 words. We all know them:

"I believe in one God the Father Almighty, Maker of all things visible and invisible, and in one Lord Jesus Christ the only begotten Son of the Father, of the substance of the Father. God from God, light from light, true God from true God, begotten not made, of one being with the Father through whom all things are made both in Heaven and on Earth. Who for us men and for our salvation descended (notice here, no women), was incarnate, and was made man, suffered, died and rose again on the third day, ascended into Heaven and comes to judge the living and the dead…"

Why were we are saddled with that formula that so profoundly dis-empowers us? Because Constantine wanted unanimity and the bishops wanted to go home.

So, what did the Creed of Nicaea do for Jesus and his message? Was Jesus approachable or could he be imitated? Did he came to show us the way, to show us the technique, or method, by which we might imitate him and become like him? If there was ever any doubt whether he could be imitated, it was now gone forever, because Jesus has now been placed on this absolutely inaccessible pedestal. His mission on Earth was reduced to being a Suffering Savior atoning to the Father for our sins, instead of teaching us how we could regain the exercise of the godhead that we already had.

Nicaea was the beginning of the death knell for the marvelous message of liberation which Jesus had taught three hundred years before. For almost two millennia now the human being has been portrayed in Christianity as a victim and an unworthy sinner. Our main role is to unceasingly thank Jesus for all he did and make reparation to him for his suffering on our behalf, (and in extreme cases to wear hair shirts under our clothes and tie sharp objects to hurt our skin, so we can suffer to the maximum, as some rather sinister organizations in the Church have started to do today). But never dare to try to imitate what Jesus was, or take heed of what he taught us about how to do that.

Nicaea was the beginning of the death of that marvelous message. And when the bishops went home what did they do? They kept on doing what they had always done before the Council.

The disagreements got worse and often turned bloody and violent. Many Christians were killed and maimed over their differing views about God and Jesus. In the years 342-43, at the height of this turmoil, it is estimated that more Christians were slaughtered by Christians than in all of the horrible persecutions of Christians under the Roman Empire, put together. It's a curious position to find yourself in: preaching and practicing hatred in the name of a God of Love.

The disagreements began to focus on another issue very soon – the Holy Spirit. Nicaea had simply said "We believe in the Holy Spirit." But what is the Holy Spirit? Is it another name for God, or is it an attribute of God, like God's Mercy or God's Justice? Or is the Holy Spirit just something God does when he is bored?

After Constantine, the Controversy Continues

Constantine died in 337. Forty four years after his death, the Emperor Theodosius called another Council in 381, which was held close to Nicaea, at Constantinople. The new Archbishop of Constantinople, Gregory Nanzianzen, pressed the bishops to adopt his view of the Holy Spirit, which was that the Holy Spirit was consubstantial with the Father. That is, they are the same being.

Before the Council even got off the ground, a huge amount of the bishops left and refused to take any part because they didn't believe the Holy Spirit was God. Very few will ever tell you that. Archbishop Gregory Nanzianzen got into a major tantrum and had a fit of apoplexy because the bishops would not accept his views about the Holy Spirit. He became seriously ill.

Consequently, a replacement for Archbishop Gregory to preside over the Council had to be found. They nominated Nectarius, who was a retired city senator in Constantinople – a layman, who wasn't even a Christian. The Emperor Justinian himself had only been baptized one year previously. The whole proceedings are in the hands of a non-Christian and the Emperor is a neophyte. But nevertheless, these two people put in place a major dogma that has created intractable problems about God and human destiny ever since. And neither of the two of them had the foggiest clue about what they were doing.

Probably Jesus Christ would have been the most surprised of all to hear such a fuss being made of his being consubstantial with the Father, because as he had taught clearly, we are all consubstantial with the Father and the Holy Spirit. Jesus would never have recognized that there were two such beings in the form Nicaea described.

Jesus had often referred to the fact that the "Father and I are one". But it wasn't the "Father" in the sense of Nicaea. Nor was the Spirit understood in the way that the Council of Constantinople understood it in the year 381 either. So, it was that the teaching for which there is no obvious basis in scripture, and which was the view only of the minority of bishops, was locked into place, and anyone who opposed it then or thereafter was branded as a heretic, and punished accordingly.

We have an extraordinary situation from Nicaea in which a belief about God and the relationship of Jesus to God, and our relationship to God and Jesus, was a view the majority didn't accept. They just voted it in to get things finished. It's no wonder the 'agreement' at Nicaea didn't work.

Nicaea's Trinity – Not Exclusively Christian?

It's often supposed that belief in the Trinity is an exclusively, refined, purified major Christian doctrine that only started to bloom at Nicaea and was completed at Constantinople in 381. The truth is that almost every nation in antiquity, thousands of years before Nicaea, held similar views. In Babylonia, Sumeria, India, Greece, and Egypt, all of the deities were in triads.

According to the most ancient beliefs in Sumer of which we have records, the universe is divided into three sections. Each section belonged to a god. The sky belonged to Anu, the Earth to Enlil, and Ea dominated the waters. All together they made up the Triad of Great Gods. In Babylon, they worshiped a god with three heads. You've heard that two heads are better than one. Three, I suppose, must be better still.

They used the equilateral triangle as a symbol of a trinity in unity, which was a revered symbol in almost all the ancient religions. In India, the three gods Brahma, Vishnu and Shiva, have no distinction between them. A single being appears in three forms by the act of creation, the act of preservation, and the act of destruction. Three functions, but the three gods are one.

In the fourth century BC Aristotle said: "All things are three and thrice is all; and let us use this number in the worship of the gods, for as the Pythagoreans say, everything and all things are bounded by three's, for the end, the middle and the beginning have this number in everything, and these compose the number of the trinity."

In Egypt, it was believed that all gods were in three's. No god came into being before Amun, and the Hymn to Amun says: "All gods are three, Amun, Ra and Ptah. Hidden is his name as Amun, he is Ra in face and his body is Ptah." This came very close to the Christian belief in Trinitarian monotheism. Ancient Rome worshipped three gods, Jupiter, Neptune and Pluto. The Germans worshipped three gods, Wodan, Thor and Fricco.

It is clear that the idea of God as Trinity comes from the ancient pagan religions. Jesus never mentioned such an idea and the word Trinity does not appear at all in the text of the New Testament.

So was that in the late fourth century the Doctrine of the Three in One, with Jesus understood as the incarnation of the Second, became the paramount doctrine of Christianity. But not without enormous resistance, culminating in widespread riots and bloodshed.

Nor was it treated as an esoteric, abstract area of Christian belief suitable only for pondering by philosophers and theologians. Joan Bocher was burned to death in England in 1550 AD. Her crime? The Encyclopaedia Britannica (1964) says: "She was condemned for open blasphemy in denying the Trinity, the one offense which all the church had regarded as unforgivable ever since the struggle with Arianism."

On October 27th, 1553, Michael Servetus, a medical practitioner, was burned at the stake at Geneva, Switzerland, for denying the doctrine of the Trinity. *In 1693, a pamphlet attacking the Trinity was burned by order of the House of Lords in the British Parliament, and the following year its printer and author were prosecuted.

Was the Jesus meek and mild picture an obstacle to our empowerment? Yes. Was the suffering savior an obstacle to our belief? Absolutely. But it was nothing compared to what the

Councils of Nicaea and Constantinople set up. These Councils established the quintessential blocks to our understanding of Jesus and to our attainment of empowerment.

The idea of the Trinity was pagan in origin, and it wasn't adopted by the Church until three hundred years after the passion of Jesus. By the Trinity proclamation he was made even more remote, even more inaccessible. He could never be imitated now, which was, after all, the primary purpose for which he came. It looks as if this was specifically designed to frustrate the spread of the true message of Jesus.

It needs some courage to recognize that Nicaea was a clumsy solution with a political motivation that was cobbled together and never really worked.

What did the council of Nicaea do? Much of the fundamental beliefs about Jesus Christ came from that Conference room at Nicaea nearly seventeen hundred years ago. It set the stage for our massive dis-empowerment which has lasted right down to this present day. It corrupts the understandings of what Jesus was doing to bring us from the "Fallen State" of Genesis up to where we can start to create the Paradise State. There never was a perfect state in the past succeeded by the Fall. We are in the "Fallen State" and have always been since our origin. However, our destiny is to manifest what Genesis describes in terms of "the Paradise State." How to accomplish that transition is what Jesus came to teach. Instead, the massive distortions of his message that have come down to us, set the stage for dis-empowerment on a massive scale. We grimly hold onto those dis-empowering ideas for dear life because we think it's demanded by God that we do. We are in the curious position of believing the will of God for us consists precisely in insuring that we can never imitate what Jesus told us we should.

How then do we remove these crippling programs that we have taken from Nicaea? By first of all understanding the weird circumstances at Nicaea that produced them. Once that program has been nailed, then we move on to replace the old programs with better ones, because we have taken the trouble to inform ourselves of what actually occurred at Nicaea when those beliefs were proclaimed.

Remember the primary duty of any sub-conscious program in our minds is to ensure its own survival. The only way that obstacle can be by-passed is to thoroughly and objectively discover what the facts were that allowed the formation of that program to be developed in the first place. When we discover what the facts actually were, we are on our way to building a new program and the old one will fall away of its own accord. It is only in the building of the new program that the old and defective one will be replaced. As I have emphasized already, there is no way to directly expel a negative program from our sub-conscious mind. The only path forward is to investigate what the historical circumstances were and see if they support our negative programs. Sub-conscious programs won't disappear of their own accord, they have to be replaced by more accurate and positive programs. If we begin with the wrong presuppositions we will never get the right answer. If we understand what the Creator is, as Point Zero, rather than picturing the Creator as some form of human being enlarged, then we have begun the shift of the entire paradigm relating to God as Trinity, and how Jesus related to this concept.

As noted earlier, if we look at the history of astronomy we can now see that there was no way that improving the views of Ptolemy would ever lead to the position of Copernicus. It doesn't matter how many improvements you add. Someone once calculated that in the days just before Nicolas Copernicus there were about 1,486 problems with the theories of Ptolemy, because the planets and the stars weren't turning up where they should be, if you believed the Sun and all the planets were orbiting the Earth. All those 1,486 problems vanished overnight when Copernicus said you got it all wrong and produced his new model. What was needed was not more and more details, information or insights. What was needed was an abandonment of the old paradigm and the taking up of an entirely new one: everything in the solar system doesn't revolve around the Earth, but around the Sun.

When are we going to get a Copernican revolution of our fundamental spiritual beliefs? There are far, far, more than 1,486 problems with our systems of belief currently. Maybe we need to adopt a new paradigm entirely, and then might not all or at least most of the difficulties with belief vanish instantaneously when we start to view things from a different perspective? That is one potential to which all the major religious leaders of the world seem irrevocably opposed.

The Names of God

The great works of literature of Mesopotamia were completely unknown in the West until the middle of the 19th century: the Epic of Gilgamesh, the Epic of Athrahasis, the Enuma Elish, the Descent of Innana and the Myth of Etana. They were written in cuneiform, which began to be deciphered by brilliant scholars such as George Smith and Henry Rawlinson. In 1846 the Library of Ashurbanipal was discovered at Nineveh. It is calculated that at present the total number of clay tablets from Sumer that have been recovered is over one million. George Smith was responsible for deciphering The Epic of Gilgamesh, and in 1872, famously, the Mesopotamian version of the Flood Story, which until then were thought to be original to the Biblical Book of Genesis

In fact, all the significant accounts in the Hebrew Bible, the creation of humanity, the creation of the Earth, the Great Flood, the destruction of humanity, and the Tower of Babel, are all paralled in these ancient secular collections.

The story of the Flood in Genesis and the Flood story from "The Epic of Gilgamesh" have twenty major points in common. The only realistic explanation has to be one of the following:

a) Genesis was copied from Gilgamesh.
b) Gilgamesh was copied from Genesis.
c) They both were copied from an earlier source.

For obvious reasons, the first option is the most likely.

Many of the 'gods' in these accounts are named, and accounts survive of how they helped the humans learn about agriculture, the care of agricultural animals, astronomy, the creation of calendars and the science of irrigation. The Sumerian rulers never claimed to be discoverers of this knowledge themselves, instead attributing it to their Gods, the Anunnaki, meaning "Those who from Heaven to Earth Came."

Zecharia Sitchin tells us: "It is that the Sumerian people, (later on the Akkadian, Assyrian and Babylonians) carved on clay tablets, (three quarters of a million texts, most of the tablets are contracts for goods & services and administrative tablets), that tell a story that is both familiar and fantastic. The tablets, which have never changed from the date of creating them, have been found in digs all over the Middle East."

"The oldest stories of the Bible including the creation of Earth, the creation of man, the flood and the destruction of mankind, the Tower of Babel all are contained in these tablets."

"The tablets talk of multiple gods with different names that helped the people learn about harvesting, shepherding, astronomy, the calendar, irrigation, etc. Sitchin has shown that the level of understanding and advanced thinking could not have been by accident and chance. The Sumerian kings and priests never claimed credit for this knowledge; the tablets always attributed the information to their gods."

Many of the tablets discuss the eating and dietary habits of these gods that inhabited the temples, who were cared for by the humans with reverence. This is no fantasy, the tablets contain bills of sale for the materials delivered to the temples, and foods that were consumed and paid for.

Some of the gods would not eat meat before Mid-day, or if they were served in anything but gold bowls or gold cups would throw it back to the humans.

Many authors and scholars have shown that the Bible writers picked up many of these ancient stories and influences and wrote them down the best they could at the time, not having direct access to the tablets, but only hearing them repeated publicly at festivals. But later on, the mistranslations appeared because of the different languages, influences of individual authors, and scribes and translators that placed their own stamp and belief systems on them.

Sitchin has shown certain words have an older origin than the Hebrew language and it is a known fact that Hebrew borrows words from Aramaic, Canaanite, Akkadian, etc. These words are clues to cultures which preceded the Hebrews. Sitchin never stated that the grammar would be perfect to match the plurality of the word gods/Elohim.

He stated that certain words contain evidence and history with them that show the older influence from those previous cultures.

While the Hebrew Bible seems monotheistic in general terms all throughout, nevertheless there is considerable evidence that the people of Israel, as a whole, were not monotheists before they were taken into exile in Babylon in the 6th Century BC. The Bible itself tells us that many of the people chose to worship idols and foreign gods instead of the God of the Bible. In the 8th Century BC the monotheistic worship of the God of the Bible was in competition with several other cults that were not monotheistic. In fact, some have asserted that their religion at that early period consisted of the recognition of many gods, but with the regular worship of only one divinity. It's been pointed out that even the First Commandment may reflect such a belief system: "Thou shalt have no other gods before me." The oldest books of the Bible such as the Book of Hosea and the Book of Nahum, portray a similar situation, probably from the 7th Century BC, where the people of Israel are upbraided for their worship of many gods. Some Jewish believers recoil in horror at the mere suggestion that their ancestors in the Jewish tradition could ever have wasted their time on false gods, but the evidence is abundant, and the evidence is from the Bible itself.

Among those alien gods cherished by the ancient Jewish people were Amon, the chief god of Egypt (Jeremiah 46:25), Tammuz, the Babylonian fertility god (Ezechiel 8:14), Baal-Zebub, a popular deity of the Philistines, referred to in 2 Kings 1:1-6,16-17, Matthew 12:24, Mark 3:22 (and Luke 11:15: "By Beelzebub, the prince of demons, he casts out demons"). "Beelzebub" was the Greek form of the Hebrew name "Baal-Zebub", meaning "Lord of the Flies."

Bel, the chief deity of Babylon (Isaiah 46:1) was another name for the sun god, Marduk. Nebo, the god of learning and writing was the son of Marduk. (Jeremiah. 50:2; Jeremiah 51:44).

Baal, was the Canaanite and Phoenician god of fertility and rain, usually pictured as standing on a bull, (Judges 2:10-13). Baal was popularly associated with Asherah and Ashtoreth, goddesses of fertility.

Ashtoreth, a goddess of war and fertility (Judges 2:12-13) was the consort of Baal, and was associated with the evening star. She was known as Ishtar in Babylon, in Greece as Aphrodite, and in Rome as Venus. (Judges 10:6; 1 Samuel. 7:3-4; 1 Samuel. 12:10; 1 Samuel. 31:10; 1 Kings 11:5,33).

Molech, the chief deity of Ammon was another prominent pagan god. (1 Kings 11:4-5, Lev 18:21). The practice of sacrificing children to Molech was common in Phoenicia and the region nearby; (Leviticus 20:2-5; 1 Kings 11:7,33; 2 Kings 23:10). Josiah destroyed the area where the altars for child sacrifice were located; (2 Kings 23:13; Isaiah 57:9; Jeremiah 32:35; Jeremiah 49:1,3; Zepaniah 1:5;).

Asherah, (Exodus 34:13-14) a Canaanite goddess, was the consort of El, the chief Canaanite god. Wooden poles, that often had her image carved on them, were often erected to worship her. (Deuteronomy. 7:5; Judges 6:25-30). We hear of Gideon destroying an Asherah pole; 1Kings 14:15,23; 15:13; 16:33; and 18:19. Elijah summons 400 prophets of Asherah to Mount Carmel.[259]

There are also instances in the Old Testament where "Élohim" refers to deities that are not related to Israel.

It has also been suggested that angels are what became of the false gods once monotheism became established in Israel.

Deadly Models of Jesus

Let us ponder a few facts before we proceed:

1. Jesus is probably the most influential person who ever lived.

[259] See also King Josiah's reforms: 2 Kings 23:4-7,13-16, Isaiah 27:9; Jeremiah 17:2; Micah 5:14.

2. The well-intentioned misunderstandings about what he said and did have contributed to a set of very powerful and controlling programs that are based in our sub-conscious minds.

3. If we're trying to address these programs we first need to discover the sources of information which led to their creation in our minds. What are our sources? The main sources are the Gospels of the New Testament and there are enormous problems with the ways in which those Gospels have been understood and interpreted. Then we need to look at how these understandings were further shaped by the Church down the centuries, to meet very many other agendas.

And having looked at those and assessed them we will now look at the models of Jesus, the molds, the ways of understanding Jesus that arose in our tradition. Probably at the top of the list stands the image of Jesus as Suffering Savior and its mindset: an excellent presentation of which was Mel Gibson's movie, "The Passion of the Christ."

Arising from what Jesus was believed to have endured during his passion, we have had a major emphasis all down through Christian history on the redemptive value of suffering. So, if I am suffering I should put up with it. And in a sense, the more I have to suffer the gladder I should be. Why? Because I am imitating Christ Jesus and am going to be spared the pains of Hell in the Life of the World to Come as a result. Basically, we have a set of accusations levelled at us that Jesus suffered a lot for us, and now he is saying: 'You owe me'.

So, what are we supposed to do? We have to imitate him. Apparently, that means we have to suffer. But where in the New Testament did Jesus ever ask us to suffer? The several other ways in which Jesus said we should imitate him seem to have been lost in the shuffle, so that suffering seems to be the only career path. Where does all this pre-occupation with sin and suffering come from? It comes from much more ancient roots than a mis-characterization of Jesus: as we saw earlier, it came from the particular shape that was given to the story of the Fall of Mankind.

The story has been spun in the old familiar ways of the circular arguments. Jesus wouldn't have had to come and suffer and die for us unless people had done something catastrophically bad in the past. Therefore, there must have been a Fall somewhere in the remote past of the human race, otherwise there would be no need for a Redeemer to come and suffer for us.

As detailed earlier in this book, the notion of the Fall of the human race served a convenient and fundamental purpose for the authors of the early chapters of Genesis: getting God off the hook for creating a world filled with so much suffering, injustice and lack, the world such as we have it, despite all its beauty.

A lot of the people who believe this, believe also that the universe was created in the year 4004 BC on the 23rd of September at 9:00 in the morning. These are the figures quoted by James Ussher, Anglican Archbishop of Armagh, in present-day Northern Ireland. His book was published in 1650 AD.[260]

According to Ussher, from his careful compilation of the various historical references quoted in the Old Testament, God created the world in that particular year and at that particular time. The first 4,000 years apparently didn't go well, because the first human couple didn't behave themselves. God was greatly displeased and a line was drawn in the sand about 2,000 years ago when God decided then that someone had to make up to him for all the sins and insults down the course of those four millenia. He figured out a plan, we are told. I will send down my only Son, totally innocent and without blame, to suffer the most cruel death imaginable. After my Son goes through all that I will be made happy again. But unless the human race makes up for all the suffering – which I imposed on my only Son – they may go to Hell and burn for all eternity

What a travesty of the teachings of Jesus Christ! What would Jesus make of this version of what he came to teach?

To what image of God are we subscribing here? Of what kind of entity are we speaking? What parent would want or allow

[260] Ussher, James: *Annales Veteris Testamenti,* 1650.

their children to suffer greatly, however guilty? What does this say about God? I assure you, nothing God would like to have said about him. But if you ponder the list of atrocities which we are told that same God, the Jehovah of the Old Testament, perpetrated thirteen or fourteen hundred years before the time of Jesus, you would not be in the least surprised to find that this interpretation of why Jesus had to suffer might just fit right in.

I pointed out earlier that there are six major contradictions in the account of the creation in the first few chapters of the Book of Genesis. Earlier accounts dealing with the origin of things, known by Biblical scholars as the Priestly Tradition and the Yahwist Tradition, (one of them about three hundred years older than the other) were believed in the 19th century to be the sources out of which our account of creation was made.

The Pentateuch or Torah, (the Greek and Hebrew titles respectively for what we call the first five books of the Hebrew Bible (The Christian "Old Testament"): Genesis, Exodus, Leviticus, Deuteronomy and Numbers), contain many inconsistencies, varying styles, and repetitions and different names for God.

For example, there are two different accounts of the creation, two covenants with Abraham and two revelations by God to Jacob at Bethel, two calls to Moses to rescue the Israelites from Egypt, two genealogies of Seth and two of Shem, two sets of laws at Sinai, and two accounts of the Tabernacle or Tent of Meeting. Scholars up to the 19th Century had concluded that at least four separate sources lay behind the Pentateuch, but the situation radically changed in Biblical research in the 20th Century. That described a much more complex set of circumstances surrounding the emergence of the Pentateuch, including denying that the Priestly and Yahwist 'sources' had actually ever existed as independent documents, but were collections of fragmentary stories, hymns and other traditions of varying kinds.[261]

---

[261] See, Frank Moore Cross, *Canaanite Myth and Hebrew Epic*, 1973, Hans Heinrich Schmid, *The So-called Jahwist*, 1976, the Swiss theologian, Martin Rose, *Une Herméneutique de l'Ancien Testament, Comprendre, se Comprendre, Faire Comprendre*, 2003. John Van Seters, *Abraham in History and Tradition*, 2004, Rolf Rendtorff, *The Problem of the Process of Transmission in the Pentateuch*, 1989.

As pointed out earlier, accounts of the origins of the human race existed all over the world thousands of years before any of the five books of the Torah were written. I've noted already that there is one at the Temple of Abu Simbel at the bottom of the Nile. There is a depiction of a man and woman in a garden with a serpent coiled around a tree. Another comes from a Cave Temple in India: a sculptured column with the first man and woman at the foot of a tree with a serpent entwined in its branches above them offering them some of the fruit of the tree from its mouth.

But in the account of the original or Paradise State in Genesis, God had put the man and woman in a Garden of Delights. There were two trees in the ancient accounts. The Tree of Life, and the Tree of Death, were the older titles, but in the Genesis account, the Tree of Death of the older accounts was re-named the Tree of Knowledge.

In the older versions, and I mean older than Genesis by 1,000, 2,000, or even 3,000 years, God had sent the serpent to tell the first human pair to eat the fruit of the Tree of Life and become immortal. But they were not to eat the fruit of the Tree of Death, because if they did they would die and so would all their descendants.

The wily serpent reversed the message. He told them to eat the fruit of the Tree of Death and they did. They were expelled from the Garden and became mortal. The reptile ate the fruit of the Tree of Life and achieved immortality for himself and his descendants. It was from the fact, it was said, that serpents shed their skins, and were assumed to take on a fresh new body, that the whole idea that the serpent was immortal arose. This is the explanation in those ancient depictions as to why the serpent is considered immortal but not us humans.

In the older sources God administered no test to the early humans. He simply sent word to the humans to eat the fruit of the Tree of Life. Needless to say, in these older sources there was no subsequent punishment for eating from the wrong tree either. But when the authors of Genesis come along they have a large task: to explain how an all-just and all-powerful God could create the amount of evil that there is in the world? A key ingredient in that was to be able to shift the blame for evil from God to the first humans. To achieve that, the humans had to be blamed, not God, and so we see where we have arrived today.

Can we then say that it's God's will that we bear our suffering, or that God looks favorably on us in that situation? There is not a shred of evidence anywhere to justify that belief.

Consequently, was Jesus a suffering savior who came here to die for our sins to appease the vengeance of a savage God? I am afraid he was not.

But by the time of Jesus there was a second problem facing those who wrote the sacred texts. If Jesus was God's only Son how could he have been subjected to all of these atrocities? The New Testament writers neatly combined the reflections of Genesis on God the Creator, and Evil, with the need to make up to God for the sinfulness of the human race, which explained to them why Jesus had to suffer and die.

I have several times already quoted Ludwig Feuerbach, the great German philosopher, who said in the middle of the 1800's, "it is not that God made man in his own image. It is that mankind has made God in their own image"[262]

And the biggest problem that you and I have is that there is a massive program in all of us that believes fervently, thanks to 250,000 years of programming in our DNA, that God actually is some type of human being enlarged, and all of the Old Testament texts assume that background paradigm. To emphasize this again, however God may be, most assuredly he is not that.

Chapter 18
Five Processes: The Brain and Mind Warping Reality

If we are engaged in a project to rid ourselves of the unwelcome effects of the effects of sub-conscious programs, particularly in the religious parts of our make-up, we have to pick our endeavors

[262] Ludwig Feuerbach, *The Essence of Christianity*, (*Das Wesen des Christentums*), 1841.

carefully. As mentioned earlier, the primary purpose of all the mind's sub-conscious programs, is to ensure their own survival. Consequently, if we embark on a course which may be perceived as threatening to the sub-conscious program, it is highly likely that our efforts against it will be neutralized, again without our conscious awareness of it happening. It is essential then that we embark on a course of improvement that seems non-threatening to the existing programs.

The day, of course, is long gone when we think of any particular area of the brain as being solely responsible for a brain function.[263] That view of things belonged to a time when our knowledge of the brain largely came from the effects of brain lesions in specific areas. Now we see the functions of the brain more in terms of mutually interacting systems, rather than in terms of specific areas dedicated to a function.

The occipital lobe at the rear of the brain is entirely devoted to vision: so, it is at the heart of the systems in the brain where optical illusions are processed.[264] It is interesting to note also that sub-conscious brain programs related to anxiety and fear appear to have their home in the rear part of the brain, as well as in its neighbor, the two amygdalae, almond-shaped groups of nuclei deeply buried in the mid-lower regions of the brain.

"Amygdala hijack"

'Amygdala hijack' was a phrase coined by Daniel Goleman[265] and it has become a well-known term in sessions that deal with how to handle difficult people or situations. The term was coined

---

[263] See Dr. Joseph E LeDoux, *Separating Findings from Conclusions*, **in** "Psychology Today," August 10, 2015.

264 Expert in *Cognitive Psychology,* Dr. Pascale Michelon, SharpBrains' Manager for Educational Projects. Contributor to The SharpBrains Guide to Brain Fitness: How to Optimize Brain Health and Performance at Any Age," SharpBrains, 2013.

[265] *Emotional Intelligence: Why it Can Matter More than IQ,* Bantam Books, 1995.

to describe an overwhelming emotional response in the brain, out of all proportion to the stimulus that had been applied. The reason for this is because the stimulus triggered a much more significant sub-conscious emotional threat. Dr. Coleman coined the term because during an "Amygdala Hijack," the amygdalae highjack the neocortex — the area of conscious thought.

Any stimulus that comes in through the eyes or ears or any of the bodily senses goes directly to the thalamus, and on to the amygdalae before any signal reaches the neocortex. It is a primitive survival mechanism. In short, all of this takes place sub-consciously. In experiments with animals it was discovered that their amygdalae can respond to a perception in as little as twelve thousandths of a second. This a survival mechanism that is hard-wired, and allows us to respond to any input of emergency information before the conscious brain is even aware of it, much less able to assess the options. Hence the phrase "Amygdalae Hijack," because the amygdalae have taken charge of affairs before there can be any conscious input.[266]

Of all the primordial fears besetting human beings who subscribe to some religious belief system in the West, the fear of eternal punishment for sin must surely rank at the top. Perhaps in our analyses of the mechanisms that facilitate optical illusions in the rear of the brain, coupled with the contribution of the amygdalae in mental states of fear or stress, we may also gain some useful insights and relief in dealing with deeply entrenched sub-conscious religious programs that are misleading.

According to recent research, the pre-frontal cortex normally exercises a moderating influence on the automatic, unconscious and impulsive structures of the amygdalae and other parts of the limbic system. Applying this to the religious field it is apparent that most members of religious congregations normally could not have the necessary education and information to assess the true standing of matters of belief or religious practice that are proposed for their acceptance, so that sort of contribution from their pre-frontal cortex is almost inevitably lacking. In addition, there is

---

[266] See also Paul Whalen and Justin Kim of Dartmouth College, in the September 2016 issue of *The Journal of Neuroscience*.

also, the deeply ingrained conviction, especially among those of fundamentalist leanings, that it would be impious to even try to assess the standing of what they believe, for fear of incurring God's anger. Here we are back again to the realms of fear in the brain.

For the reasons stated above, we are going to investigate this area by using a non-threatening example, optical illusions, which may reveal to us how the mind and brain work in interpreting, or even altering reality, especially under conditions of fear or anxiety.

It's been stated that the brain and mind in many ways operate like a code-cracking machine.

Let us take five samples of this process at work and observe how the sub-conscious functions of the brain and mind work in the perception of optical illusions. It will give us an excellent insight into how the brain can influence our perception of any reality, illusory or not, largely depending on the type of sub-conscious programs that are already resident in my mind.

If You Can Raed Tihs, You Msut Be Raelly Smrat

First Example:

Can we read what's in the following paragraph, made famous by Natalie Wolchover? At first glance it baffles us, but then the sub-conscious mind gets to work to interpret the text, and then we find we can read it without too much difficulty.

It deson't mttaer in waht oredr the ltteers in a wrod aepapr, the olny iprmoatnt tihng is taht the frist and lsat ltteer are in the rghit pcale. The rset can be a toatl mses and you can sitll raed it wouthit pobelrm.[267]

This phenomenon has been labeled Typoglycemia, and it has attracted a lot of debate and controversy in the study of the cognitive processes behind reading written text. Many of the aspects of those controversies fortunately do not relate to the aspects of the matter

[267] Natalie Wolchover: "Breaking the Code: Why Yuor Barin Can Raed This," Live Science, February 2012.

which we are examining here.

> You culod witre a
> wlhoe sentnece
> with msot wrosd msplseleid, just as lnog as the frist
> and lsat ltteer rieman the same, the human bairn
> can siltl detremnie what is bineg wirtetn

The author of If You Can Raed Tihs, You Msut Be Raelly Smrat,[268] was Dr. Graham Rawlinson.[269]

As he said in his essay "Reibadailty" in New Scientist:[270]

"This reminds me of my PhD at Nottingham University (1976), which showed that randomizing letters in the middle of words had little or no effect on the ability of skilled readers to understand the text. Indeed, one rapid reader noticed only four or five errors in an A4 page of muddled text.

This is easy to denmtrasote. In a puiltacibon of New Scnieitst youcould ramdinose all the letetrs, keipeng the first two and last two the same,and reibadailty would hadrly be aftcfeed. My ansaylis did not come to much beucase the thoery at the time was for shape and senqeuce retigcionon.

The resaon for this is suerly that idnetiyfing coentnt by paarllel prseocsing speeds up regnicoiton. We only need the first and last two letetrs to spot chganes in meniang."

If the brain is a code cracker that works without us being conscious of the process, what else is the brain and mind doing unconsciously?

Does an unconscious part of us control most things without our suspecting it? And how crucial it is that we get to the stage where we are able to consciously alter what's in that controlling sub-conscious element that's part of our makeup?

---

268 Published by Fox News, March 31, 2008.

269 Graham Rawlinson, *The Significance of Letter Position in Word Recognition,* Ph.D Thesis, 1976, Nottingham University.

270 *New Scientist*, 29 May 1999.

Second Example:

"All men know the
benefit of useful things,
but nobody knows the benefit of futility.
Where can I find a man
who has forgotten words
so that I can have a
word with him?" [271]

How many F's are there in the document?[272] Take time to count them carefully.

Most people count six; that's the average. But there are actually eight "f's." Even if I go over that document really carefully, and even if I already know there are eight, it is still very hard to find all eight "f"s. Why? Because when we're reading anything the subconscious aspect of the mind glazes over the f's in words like the preposition 'of'. The mind automatically processes small words like 'and' and 'from' and 'of' and 'if,' and this process is totally unconscious, so as a result we find it hard to discern the 'f's in small words.

Here are the eight words, that contain the eight "f"s, italicized and underlined.

All men know the
benefit *of* *useful* things,
but nobody knows the
benefit *of* *futility*.
Where can I *find* a man
who has *forgotten* words
so that I can have a
word with him?

What am I attempting to show by these examples? To alert

[271] From Chuang Tzu, (399 – 295 B.C.), one of the greatest of the ancient Chinese Philosophers.

[272] *The Wisdom of China: A Collection of Chinese Sayings,* Collected and translated by *Yu Wu* Song.

ourselves to the existence of powerful programs in our minds by illustrating, through the very ordinary and simple examples offered by these texts, that the programs are very real. Unless we see this personally in practice the message does not really sink in. We may say "Oh yes; I accept that there are programs in my mind, — in the sub conscious or super conscious" — but I know nevertheless, that irrespective of what I say in the abstract, I don't really believe it.

I have to see the program in action in practice, (and preferably see it in many different situations), to really see and accept that a program exists, in order to make any progress in our efforts to no longer be subject to these automatic programs. It is easy to see this in the case of these carefully selected pieces of text and the six types of optical illusions I am using here. What is not quite so easy is to see how these same processes of the mind are also at work in every deep-seated conviction that we have long ago admitted into our sub-conscious — and most of which serve very positive functions. In the religious realm unfortunately that is not the case.

Third Example:

Picture the gateway as A. In the well-known illustration below, by how much is the line AC coming from the gateway down to the right of the picture longer than the line coming from A to B on the left of the picture? Is the line A to C a quarter longer, or even more long than the line A to B?

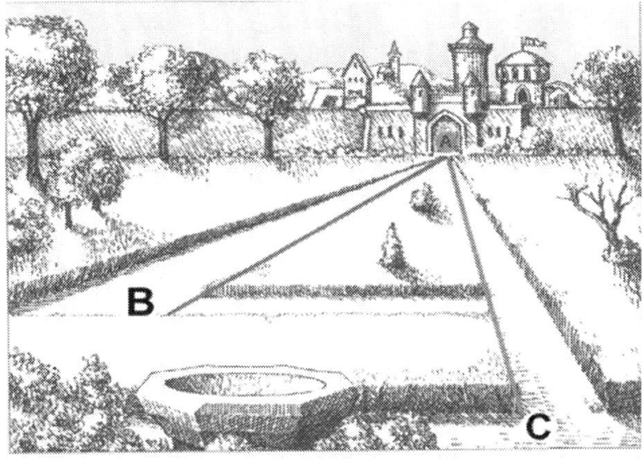

In fact, A to B is longer than A to C. The line A to B is 6 units long and A to C is 5 1/2 units long.

Looking at the picture we find it hard to accept that, but if we physically measure it we find that the line A to B is longer.

But we are here simply trying to bring home to ourselves that there is something, of which we are not conscious, working powerfully in us. This bringing home to ourselves is an essential first step in the dissolving of any sub-conscious program.

Fourth Example:

In another example, The Kanizsa Triangle,[273] which has been discussed earlier in this book, the white triad in the image below, does not exist. In fact, there are no triads in this image, just three "v's" and what look like three Pac Men. But because of the way our mind functions it creates these shapes that actually do not exist in physical form, by extrapolation from the images that we do see. But no matter how hard we try, we cannot *not* see the outline of the white triangle. In short, once having seen it I can never again un-see it.

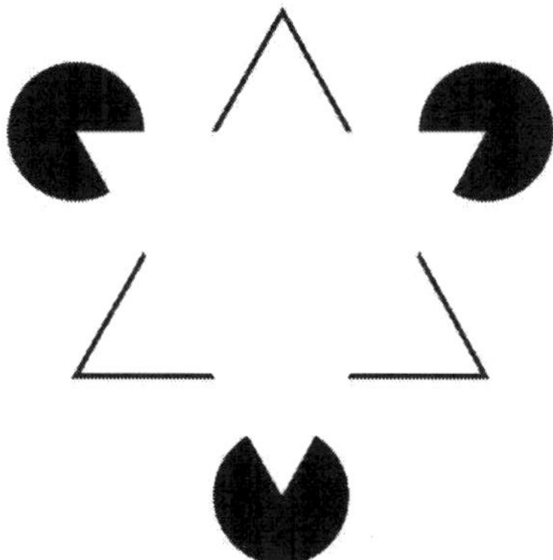

[273] See chapter one of this book.

Fifth Example:

And another excellent example of this same form of illusion at work is the next illustration. Are these five individuals chatting to each other or are we just looking at white chess pieces?[274]

We are doing both. Observe the way the image alters? Which one do we see first? People. Why is that? Because they're a darker shade, which is easier for the eye and the mind to pick up than a lighter shade.

From this short investigation of five forms of optical illusion, we have seen different aspects of the brain/mind's sub-conscious activity affecting our perception without us being aware of it.

1. Words with inside letters jumbled.

> The first lesson we learned is that the brain/mind strives to make meaningful what is not meaningful, by manipulating the visual data. The brain/mind is always looking for meaning.

What is the application of this for our purposes here? If Jesus is presented to us from an early age as suffering, abused and covered with blood, we'll try to make sense out of that. And, by golly, our mind is going to make sense of it whether the result adds up or not. In short, the mind will make sense of it, whether the result is true or not.

[274] Courtesy of Blaze Press, 2014.

2. Counting the occurrences of the letter 'f.'

When you find out how many f's are in this document it shows us how the brain processes some information, and skips stages in that processing, without us ever being consciously aware of it happening.

3. Two lines drawn from Gateway.

Our brain tells us that the first line is shorter than the other, even though the reverse is the case. There is nothing we can do about that, even after we know which line is longer, because what is estimating the distances in our minds is sub-conscious, and therefore. by definition, not under conscious control. Applying this to the religious sphere, we may have our inaccurate beliefs about Jesus corrected, but we may be unable to escape the emotional power of the old programs that see him in an entirely different way.

4. The Kaniza Triangle

This illusion shows we can perceive things that are not there at all: no matter what perspective we use we cannot NOT see what we know does not exist. This bears an uncanny resemblance to the processes active in some forms of religious belief, especially in the fundamentalist traditions.

5. Chess Pieces or People?

The fourth one is that we can perceive things in two completely different ways, yet both interpretations are equally valid. The religious right finds it hard to accept that there can be two interpretations that are contradictory, yet both are right. Religious movements in general find it very difficult to admit that there can be more than one valid way of viewing the same thing.

To have some personal experience of this kind of process at work in the brain/mind is crucial, if I am trying to effectively unravel the programs of negative religious belief systems. To see them at work, to recognize they are there, through viewing these unthreatening optical illusions is a very powerful influence in getting us to see that these processes exist and what it is advisable for us to do in dealing with them.

These are examples of the main processes of the brain/mind at work. If we are going to affect reality through the quantum field, these are the main types of program in the mind that we have to deal with, but they cannot be confronted, since the primary duty of any sub-conscious program is to shut down anything that might threaten its existence. As already noted, there is no point at all in that, because the more you confront them the stronger the sub-conscious programs become. A different method has to be used. That method consists of replacing the old program with a new one constructed from the ground up, but this time constructed from facts, not prejudice or misapprehensions.

This is why earlier in this book we had to go through all the torturous process of looking at what Constantine did at the Council of Nicaea? Why? Because those beliefs about the Holy Trinity and about "Jesus as God's only begotten Son who pre-existed for all eternity" came from that Council. And if you understand how it originated, and all the hanky-panky that went on before it, and how only a minority of the Fathers of the Council of Nicaea were in favor of it, then you have begun to take the foundations from under the old programs, that were based on inaccuracies, and they will start to fade away of their own accord.

If I believe, as Nicaea taught, that Jesus is God's only Son who pre-existed from all eternity, and if I also believe from St. John's Gospel that the heart of the message of Jesus was to exhort us to imitate what he did, and to do the wonders he did, there obviously isn't any hope whatever that I could ever attain to being the kind of being described in the lofty and ethereal terms of Nicaea. Therefore, I am doomed to a life of powerlessness, lack, worthlessness and inequality, in short, the direct opposite to the state of imitating Jesus. Ironically this is caused by my being loyal to what I have been taught is divinely inspired truth about the reality of Jesus.

Forgetting As a Tool of Reform

Research shows that under certain circumstances we can train ourselves to forget details about a particular memory.

Forgetting memories can be a very negative thing, especially in the tragic circumstances of certain illnesses. But maybe it can be a very healthful thing when we are working to remove the negative influence of sub-conscious programs. It's at least good to be aware that such a phenomenon is well recognized. Most of what we know in this sphere came from the researches of Dr. Malcolm David MacLeod, then Professor at Saint Andrews University[275] in Scotland.

"People with conditions like PTSD and depression have intrusive, uncontrollable negative thoughts that make them unable to move on with their lives" states McCloud's student, Dr. Saima Noreen,[276] who became interested in the process of intentional forgetting

With regard to many of the beliefs we hold about Jesus, in particular the Suffering Savior, we have to rebuild that program. To help that process along we may have to intentionally forget what we were taught in grade school about the Suffering Savior and what Jesus did to make up for our sins. The situation is not too different from the basics of PTSD.

Saima Noreen says "our research shows that we can actually change or reduce the accessibility of certain details". With her colleague, Professor Malcolm MacLeod, she decided to investigate measures that might help individuals who had been held hostage. There are a lot of unfortunate cases in this situation that stem from the conflicts in Iraq and Afghanistan, especially. MacLeod and Noreen wanted to help such individuals who had developed severe physiological disorders. They discovered that memories in such individuals are so vivid and striking that it's very difficult

[275] Located in Fife, Scotland. St. Andrews, after Oxford and Cambridge, is the third oldest University in the English-speaking world. Founded 1410.

[276] Goldsmiths, University of London.

to keep out of the mind the recollection of all sorts of horrible events that were personally experienced. This phenomenon bears striking resemblances to deeply buried religious programming. In this process, MacLeod and Noreen realized that the last thing they wanted to do was to try to stuff down and suppress those memories, because then they fester like a cyst, and the last case becomes worse than the first.

In 2001 a scientist named Michael Anderson published a study where he taught his volunteers pairs of unrelated words. Like apple and desk. And then, through a procedure which he called the "think/no think" technique, he taught them to forget the pairings that they had learned. He showed the subjects sets of words like 'barbecue', 'theater', 'occasion', 'rapid,' and then they were asked to generate one specific memory in response to each word. Their experiment used 24 words and the subjects described their memories of those terms in a scientific environment. Then they were dismissed and asked to return a week later.

What the participants had said was typed out during the week, and when they returned they were presented with a transcript of each of the memories they had shared, and the specific word that had sparked off the memory. Then they were asked to revive their memories of the memories, and review which word went with which. At that stage, they were put before a computer and told they would see each of these words flash on the computer screen in front of them. If the word appeared in green they were supposed to repeat out loud the memory that they had associated with that word. But if the word appeared in red font it was crucial that they not even think about the memory associated with that word.

What did the experiment show? MacLeod and Noreen showed the subjects 16 of the 24 words over and over and over. Each time the person who was volunteering either repeated the memory, or blocked the memory, depending on the color of the font.

Some people apparently pictured a blank, that was their way of forgetting, and some people distracted themselves by thinking about a mocha latte or a milkshake. But there was a significant forgetting effect – about a 12% drop in the level of details recalled, which is a very significant effect.

However, what is most interesting for us is the parts of the memories that were forgotten. There was the original memory, but after the original memory was blocked again and again, certain details began to fall away. For one particular lady, it was not what she had forgotten that was interesting, but the personal meaning associated with that memory. The blocking caused that lady to lose the sense that it was emotionally painful. That's what the researchers found generally. People don't forget the facts. What they forget is how they felt about the facts. And of course, that's the point of all this exercise: it is not the facts of the past that cause us trouble but the memories of those facts. Our aim is to forget the memories (or belief systems) that are causing the damage.

What a memory really means is usually realized only sometime after the event has taken place.

People who compete in memory competitions practice techniques about how to remember, and they accomplish prodigious feats of memory that nobody thought was even remotely possible.

At the March 2012 USA Memory Championships, the champion, Nelson Dellis, had memorized 303 random numbers in the correct order, and 162 unknown names and faces. And 24 lines of poetry. All this in a couple of hours.

If we had these kinds of technologies could we expand a person's ability to forget, which is fundamentally what we're trying to do with Jesus, or more accurately the distortions about Jesus? Could we expand the ability to forget in the same way that memory competitors expanded their ability to remember? If we could do that, would that then remove a sub-conscious program that is blocking my relationship with the quantum field, so that the next time I try to heal myself, I may dare to hope that I am at least well on the way not just to saying that it is so, but that it will be?

How did Nelson Dellis remember, in the correct order, 303 random numbers, read out to him over the space of 5 minutes? He did it by association.

What is association? Remember the story of the little boy who was sent to his bedroom for doing something horrendous. And when he went into his bedroom there was a burst of lightening and a thunderbolt. He really felt that he had angered God for spilling the cat's milk.

This little Scottish boy refused to eat two nasty shriveled prunes that were part of his dinner. His mother begs him, tells him they're very good for him, and when that doesn't work, she said, as she had said so often before: 'If you don't obey, God will be angry.' Usually that tactic worked, but this time the child held out, shouted 'No,' and stamped the floor. The mother sent him straight to bed.

But shortly afterwards a thunderstorm comes. The mother felt sad that she said such things to her child, and she goes in to comfort him because of the lightning storm. She sneaks down to his bedroom and opens the door, expecting to find him burrowed under the covers. But he is at the window peering out. As she watches, the little boy shakes his head and says in an incredulous, reproving tone — "Such a fuss to make over two prunes!"

Chapter 19
The Heart of the Matter

The Supremely Awkward Question: "Do You Love Me?"

Franz Uri Boas, "the Father of American Anthropology," had strong connections with the Pacific North West. In 1881 he earned a doctorate in Physics from the University of Kiel in Germany. For most of his life, including his long tenure as Professor of Anthropology at Columbia, he did field work with the cultures of the indigenous cultures of the Pacific Northwest. I am referring to him here because of a famous study he did in relation to the culture and language of the Baffin Island Inuit[277] peoples in Canada. The

[277] Baffin Island is the largest island in Canada and the fifth largest in the world, with an area of almost 196,000 sq miles. It is characterized by long winters and short summers. Snow falls most of the year and the average annual temperature is 17 degrees F.

insights he gained are extremely useful in pondering the meaning and implications of words and terms that have long been central to the interpretations of the teachings of Jesus.

In 1897 Dr. Boas organized the Jesup North Pacific Expedition, (1897—1902). This was a major anthropological expedition to Siberia, Alaska, and the northwest coast of Canada. Its intent was to investigate the relationships among the peoples at each side of the Bering Strait.

Boas spent five years studying the peoples of the Pacific Northwest,[278] whose ancestors had come across the Bering Strait from what is now North Eastern Russia. In his landmark book, "Race: The History of an Idea in America," Thomas Gossett[279] said about the work of Boas, "It is possible that Boas did more to combat race prejudice than any other person in history."

In September 2008, an investigation led by Dr. Patricia Sutherland[280] found artifacts on Baffin Island that may be evidence of contact with Europeans several centuries even before the Vikings' arrival in Greenland around 990 AD.

Boas got credit for making a claim that the Eskimos have dozens or even hundreds of words for snow. David Robson in New Scientist, at the end of December 2012, said 'although the idea continues to capture public imagination most linguists consider it an urban legend, born of sloppy scholarship and journalistic exaggeration'. Laura Martin wrote in the same vein in 1986.[281] In a humorous article, Geoffrey K. Pullum went so far as to call it the "Great Eskimo Vocabulary Hoax."[282] But a similar vein of research in other geographical areas bolsters up the Boas findings, especially a study of the Sami peoples of Northern Scandinavia.

---

[278] The multi-year expedition was sponsored by American industrialist-philanthropist Morris Jesup (President of the American Museum of Natural History).

[279] Thomas Gossett, *"Race: The History of an Idea in America,"* 1963; reprinted 1997, Oxford University Press.

[280] In Edmund Carpenter (Editor), *Upside Down: Arctic Realities,* 2011.

[281] Laura Martin: *Eskimo Words for Snow,* in "American Anthropologist," Vol. 88, no. 2, June 1986.

[282] July 1991, University of Chicago Press.

We've all heard these claims, that the Eskimos, or the Sami peoples of northern Scandinavia[283] have some outrageous number of words for snow. And the Pygmies in the rainforest in Central Africa, it is said, have 500 or more words for different shades of green — and all that sort of thing.

Whatever way the argument going back to Boas may eventually resolve, it still appears to be a sound principle in modern anthropology, that anything that is regarded as of intense interest to the people of a particular culture will generate a myriad of words designed to explore its every nuance. In short, the importance that something has for a particular group is reflected in the number of words they have to describe that reality. I refer to Boas here because he did most of the pioneering work in explaining how this process works, and how what is nearest and dearest to the hearts of a people infallibly manifests itself in terms of vocabulary.

We are interested in the process by which this works, not the geographical locations per se, for there is nothing unique to be learned from the alleged proliferation of Eskimo words for snow, or darkest African Pygmies being able to speak of sixty-four or even five hundred different shades of green. These phenomena exist in some form in all cultures, not just in these. All that's required is for the topic to be of sufficient interest, and then the detailed vocabulary will appear — whether it's among Arctic Eskimos, Pygmies of darkest Africa or the Eskimos of Rainier, Tenino and Tumwater, Washington.

Types of snow or shades of green obviously are not our biggest problems in the Pacific North West, and unlike the Eskimos and far north Scandinavians, we have a very limited vocabulary to describe these things. By contrast, to take just a random example from our own culture, communication or typing text really seems to be a huge deal for us in the Western world these days, especially

[283] Studies of the Sami languages of Norway, Sweden and Finland, conclude that the languages have anywhere from 180 snow- and ice-related words, and as many as 300 different words for types of snow, tracks in snow, and conditions of the use of snow. See Ole Henrik Magga, "*Diversity in Saami terminology for reindeer, snow, and ice,*" International Social Science Journal, Volume 58, Issue 187, pages 25—34, March 2006.

when you see two teenagers texting each other, while sitting three feet apart on a park bench. I was surprised recently when a young friend of mine told me some of her classmates, immersed in the world of tablets, I Phones and thumb drives, did not really know what a CD or DVD was. If this is so then I assume VHS and Super 8 etc., must have long ago been relegated to the Stone Age of the digital world. The world of technology is changing very rapidly, we all know; but that very statement itself is now in danger of becoming the greatest cliché of all time.

I grew weary once of counting on my desktop how many fonts are now available for typing on a tablet or computer. It turned out to be a far worse situation than the Eskimo snow vocabulary! Late one night I eventually stopped, but only after I had counted more than 300 fonts. Yet I've seen advertisements that claim to have over 160,000 fonts for sale. There are categories that include Bold fonts, Calligraphic fonts, Cursive fonts, Script fonts, Celtic fonts, Fun fonts and all the other individual families of fonts or old boring friends like Garamond, Helvetica, Arial, Arial Bold, Empty Round and so on, and so on.

Granted we don't have a large snow vocabulary, and have only a few words for green in the English language. But obviously typing must be of paramount importance to us in the West in the early 21st. Century, since there seems to be more than 160,000 different fonts for typing available? So, based on the insights of Boas, that the more important or central something is to a culture, the more words and verbal echoes the culture will have to describe its every nuance. That insight is now a tool of research for us in our investigation of a term that is at the heart of this book: the word "love."

Sanskrit we are told has ninety-six words for love. Ancient Persian has eighty. English has only one. What conclusions may we draw from a people whose language has only one word for "love"? Or, to couch it more poignantly, if richness of vocabulary reveals what really matters to a people, what does it say about the culture and values of a people who have only one term for love? I think it speaks volumes, especially about our ability in this culture to really understand what the message of Jesus was all about.

Robert Johnson wrote a wonderful essay on this topic two

decades ago: "The Fisher King and the Handless Maiden."[284] Johnson says the problem he's analyzing is:

"...indicative of the poverty of awareness or emphasis that we give to that tremendously important realm of feeling. Eskimos have thirty words for snow, because it's a life and death matter to them to have exact information about the element with which they live so intimately.

If we had a vocabulary of thirty words for love...we would immediately be richer and more intelligent in this human element that's so close to our hearts. An Eskimo probably would die of clumsiness if he had only one word to describe snow; we are close to dying (here) of loneliness because we have only one word for 'love.' Of all the Western languages, English may be the most lacking when it comes to feeling".

It wasn't for nothing that the British needed a stiff upper lip to conquer a significant part of the world in the days of Queen Victoria.

In 1989 Alan Soble published a landmark book "Eros, Agape and Philia: Readings in the Philosophy of Love," grappling with the intellectual problem of what "love" really is, and apparently not really aware of the inappropriateness of an intellectual investigation of a reality that is not at all intellectual in nature. He structured his investigation around the three major traditions that focus on the main Greek words for love: Eros, Agape and Philia.[285]

What relevance has all this to properly understanding the message of Jesus? Enormous implications.

You may remember that the Apostle Peter is generally regarded as having been the chief of the Apostles. All four Gospels of the New Testament tell us that at the private meal with his disciples in

[284] Robert A. Johnson, "*The Fisher King and the Handless Maiden: Understanding the Wounded Feeling Function in Masculine and Feminine Psychology.*" HarperCollins, 1993.

[285] "Eros is acquisitive, egocentric or even selfish; agape is a giving love. Eros is an unconstant, unfaithful love, while agape is unwavering and continues to give despite ingratitude. Eros is a love that responds to the merit or value of its object; while agape creates value in its object as a result of loving it ... Finally, eros is an ascending love, the human's route to God; agape is a descending love, God's route to humans ... Philia is caught between eros and agape."

the final hours of his public ministry, Jesus had said to his Apostles that one of them would betray him.[286] In his typically arrogant and braggadocio style, Peter blurted out in unprintable words: "XXX***!!!!! !!!!," I will never betray you"[287]. But Jesus said to him, soberly, "I tell you, before the cock crows tomorrow morning you will have denied me three times." Peter cursed, and swore and denied it again. But within a few hours, around a charcoal fire where he was warming himself, he three times denied that he ever knew Jesus. Once something is repeated three times in ancient Jewish law, it is considered permanent. It's called a "chazakah."[288] It's now the status quo.

The narrative of John 21, one of the richest passages in the entire New Testament, is obviously constructed as a parallel to the scene of Peter's denial of Jesus a few days before at the Court of the High Priest. It recounts a meeting of Jesus with his apostles shortly after the passion. They had been fishing all night out in their boats, but caught nothing. At dawn, they saw a man standing on the shore, and while they did not recognize him, they knew nevertheless that it was Jesus. He shouted to ask if they had caught anything. They had to admit they had not. He called out to them to drop their nets on the right-hand side of the boat. When they did, their nets were filled to the brim. We are told there were 153 large fish in the net. (I've often wondered who was sufficiently distracted at such a dramatic moment to count them!). As already noted, St. Jerome says it was thought at that time in history that there were only 153 species of fish known, so the number may signify absolute abundance rather than a tally of how many fish they had actually caught. Jerome refers to Oppian's poem on fishing, "Halieutica,[289]

---

286 Matthew 26:33-35, Mark 14:29-31, Luke 22:33-34 and John 13:36-38. The most striking account is in the Gospel of Matthew.

287 "Peter replied, 'Even if all fall away on account of you, I never will.' 'I tell you the truth,' Jesus answered, 'This very night, before the rooster crows, you will disown me three times.' But Peter declared, 'Even if I have to die with you, I will never disown you.' And all the other disciples said the same." Matthew 26.33-35.

288 Hebrew: חזקה — *khazakah.*

289 Written 177-180 AD.

but Oppian gives no list of fish species that would add up to 153, and besides the Gospel was written long before the poem. At that time, casting into the right side of the ocean depths was a symbol of accessing Sub-conscious Mind, so Jesus' instruction might have contained a hidden message?

Laboring, trying, for hours on end, yielded nothing. But when trust was placed in the powers of the Sub-conscious Mind, absolute abundance resulted, as signified by the number 153. Effort yields nothing; approaching through the realm of the sub-conscious yields abundance, not just abundance, but the maximum, especially if 153 symbolized all the types of fish that were then known to exist.

Jesus awaited them while they came to shore. He had prepared for them a charcoal fire with some fish and bread. Remember that it was while Peter was warming himself around another charcoal fire on the day Jesus was arrested, that he denied him three times – less than a week before this meeting on the beach. On that chilly early morning around a charcoal fire by the Sea of Tiberias, the meeting was bound to have been tense, with a very touchy subject not yet mentioned.

Is what we're looking at in this incident, the rehabilitation of Peter; so crucial, so symbolic, and so often referred to, in order to bolster up the headship of the Christian Church over the last twenty centuries? That much is true, as far as it goes, but the meaning and implications of this incident go far deeper than that. There was much more going on than traditional Church interpretations manage to get.

In the Greek language scholars tell us that there are thirty-three different words for "love." In translation, something is always lost in the process especially if the original is dealing with complex realities and shades of meaning.

I want to focus on a few words from this passage towards the end of the Gospel. These words tell us about something that was at the very heart of the message of Jesus. A lot of space in this book was taken up earlier in pointing out the difficulties in properly understanding that message and what the consequences of that has been right down to our own time. We want to become more clear on what the message actually was, and on precisely why it's so difficult for us to understand properly. That's in large part due to the crippling programs we have been fed about Jesus and his message down the centuries.

Philia versus Agape

As we know, the original New Testament texts that we have were written in Greek. In our day, in the twenty first century, it is never very enticing or appealing to be invited to look at the original Greek of a text to discover what was really meant! But you are being invited to do this here, not for any reasons of pseudo-scholarship, but for reasons deeply buried in the psychology of the sub-conscious programs that rule us in terms of belief. Ponder the effect that even glancing briefly at the original words, will have on the programs of the sub-conscious mind? It will have an extremely powerful impact, psychologically and sub-consciously, to know you have seen with your own eyes, and engaged, the original text of what was written, and have not just relied on one of the thousands of more or less accurate translations of the accounts of what Jesus said and did – not to mention the second and third hand accounts, and countless interpretations down the ages, that we have been fed.

The first word to look at in the Greek original of John 21 is the noun "Philia" (φιλία), and its verb, "Philo" (φιλῶ). Since English has only one word for "love," we can translate the noun 'Philia' into English only in some approximate way. For want of a better term in English, we'll translate it as "the love between friends." Likewise, the verb "Philo" means "to love," in the same sense of "a love between friends." If we were to look for a single term in English to translate both "Philo" and 'Philia,' "affection" probably would not be too far off the mark.

The other Greek word of note in this passage from John 21, is the noun "Agape" (ἀγάπη). Again, we have no single term in English to translate it. It means spiritual love, unconditional love, pure love, the love of God, the love that God (not Jehovah) has for the creation, etc. When all is said and done, Agape cannot be adequately translated into any other language. Our phrases "unconditional love," or "Divine love," perhaps come closest, but 'Agape' has far more depth than either of these phrases manages to convey.

Take Philia, and Agape, the two nouns, and their related verbs, 'Philo' and 'Agapeis'? How do these Greek terms in the New Testament translate into our language, and what do they tell us about the message of Jesus?

I came across a passage once which I think helps to understand the difference.

> 1. A "Friend" would ask "May I come over to see you at some convenient time next week?"
>
> 2. "Real friends" would say, "I'm coming over right now, dammit."
>
> 3. And "Best Friends," – they would say nothing – they just appear on the doorstep.

If we were trying to express in Greek these three categories of friendship in the three sentences above,' "Friends, "Real Friends," and "Best Friends?" – which word would you say best describes the relationship that each of these three categories of friends had with you? Obviously Agape goes best with number 3.

Keeping these terms in mind I want to look at this classic exchange between Jesus and Peter – which has had a profound influence in shaping the Christian Church, and Christian teaching about "love" for almost 2,000 years.

"When they had finished eating Jesus said to Simon Peter, "Simon son of John, do you love me more than these?" Simon Peter said, "Yes, Lord; you know that I love you." And Jesus said, "Feed my lambs."

A few minutes later Jesus asked him a second time: "Simon, son of John, do you love me?" And Peter must have felt that perhaps the Passion had affected Jesus' mind a little bit. He's asking me a second time what I've already clearly answered. Nevertheless, Simon Peter said, "Yes, Lord, you know that I love you." Jesus said, "Take care of my sheep."

Then to cap it all, ten minutes later, Jesus said to him again, "Simon, son of John, do you love me?" And Peter now felt very hurt because he had been asked this a third time. He said, "Lord, you know all things; you know that I love you." And Jesus said, "Feed my sheep."

When you and I today look at that text in English we are puzzled at the repetition. The English translation of the passage makes it look like a rather boring and pedestrian exchange. Why did Jesus ask the same question three times over? Or did he? Around this charcoal fire on the beach is Jesus just trying to sock it to Peter three times for what he did the previous week around a charcoal fire when he betrayed him three times, even after having been warned in advance just a few hours beforehand?

But when we look at the text, not in an English translation, but in the Koine Greek[290] language in which it was written, we see clearly that here we are not looking at the same question being asked three times at all. Obviously, you can't see that in English, since the English language has only one word for 'love.' But if you look at the Greek original, the triple repetition makes perfect sense and is very enlightening. Why? Because in the first two questions he asks Peter, Jesus is using a different word for "love," with a profoundly different meaning than the word for "love" used by Peter. But Peter, in each of his three replies, uses the same word, and it is not the same word that Jesus uses in the first two questions.

What is of even more importance here is that when we understand what this triple exchange conveys, we now also understand very clearly, that this is portraying an antidote to those very dubious and crippling images of God that we cherish so much: the sinner-victim relationships, the programs of submission rituals, sin, penance, suffering, worthlessness, redemption, reparation, being saved, etc. These three questions are aimed at bringing to awareness what is at the very heart of the message of Jesus. You will notice that this crucial exchange in John 21 has nothing remotely to say about being a Dying Savior. If Jesus had been that, this would have been a prime time to express it.

[290] The common language of the Mediterranean region and the Middle East from the time of Alexander the Great onwards. It was a dialect of Classical Greek.

Let's now look at the text again, but this time in the Greek original, and see more clearly what Jesus was really asking.

We'll compare what the Greek original says and what the English translation is able to convey rather poorly. The Greek word for the second person singular form of the verb "to love," is "Do you love" ("Agapas?" ἀγαπᾷς), and the response of Peter, in the first person singular form of the verb, is "Philo," (φιλῶ, "I have a soft spot for you," or "I have an affection for you"). These words are underlined.

For people who are not used to declined languages, such as Latin and Classical Greek, all this requires a little effort to understand, but when we contemplate the magnitude of what this tiny clarification lends to understanding the heart of the message of Jesus, it must surely be worth the modest effort it requires.

> 15 So when they had dined, Jesus said to Simon Peter,
> Simon, son of John, do you love me more than these? He
> said unto him, Yes, Lord; you know that I love you. He said
> to him, Feed my lambs.
>
> 15 Ὅτε οὖν ἠρίστησαν, λέγει τῷ Σίμωνι Πέτρῳ ὁ Ἰησοῦς·
> Σίμων Ἰωνᾶ, ἀγαπᾷς με πλεῖον τούτων; λέγει αὐτῷ· ναί, Κύριε,
> σὺ οἶδας ὅτι φιλῶ σε. λέγει αὐτῷ· βόσκε τὰ ἀρνία μου.

In his question Jesus uses 'Agapas?' "(Do you love me with the most profound form of love, Agape"?), but Peter replies with "Philo" (Literally, "Yes, I do have an affection for you").

> 16 He said to him again the second time, Simon, son of
> John, do you love me? He said to him, Yes, Lord; you know
> that I love you. He said to him, Shepherd my sheep.
>
> 16 λέγει αὐτῷ πάλιν δεύτερον· Σίμων Ἰωνᾶ, ἀγαπᾷς με;
> λέγει αὐτῷ· ναί, Κύριε, σὺ οἶδας ὅτι φιλῶ σε. λέγει αὐτῷ·
> ποίμαινε τὰ πρόβατά μου.

Here you notice that in the second question Jesus again uses 'Agapas?' But Peter replies again using "Philo." Jesus says, "Simon, son of John, do you love me with "Agape"? (the most profound form of love that can exist). And Peter again replies, "Lord you know that I "Philo" you, i.e. "You know I have a soft spot for you."

It doesn't cut it, but Peter doesn't get it.

For the second time we see that Peter does not answer what Jesus asked him. Instead Peter responds using "Philo:" "Yes, we're friends. I have an affection for you. Why can't you get it Jesus? I've told you twice now!"

> [17]"He said to him the third time, "Simon, son of John, do you love me?"
>
> [17]λέγει αὐτῷ τὸ τρίτον· Σίμων Ἰωνᾶ, φιλεῖς με;
>
> "Peter was grieved because he said to him the third time, "Do you love me?"
>
> ἐλυπήθη ὁ Πέτρος ὅτι εἶπεν αὐτῷ τὸ τρίτον, φιλεῖς με,
>
> 'And he said to him, "Lord, you know all things; you know that I love you." Jesus said to him, "Feed my sheep." '

Looking at the above text in the Greek original:

> καὶ εἶπεν αὐτῷ· Κύριε, σὺ πάντα οἶδας, σὺ γινώσκεις ὅτι φιλῶ σε. λέγει αὐτῷ ὁ Ἰησοῦς· βόσκε τὰ πρόβατά μου.

Note that in this third question above, in verse 17, Jesus now uses the verb "Philo" for the first time.

Jesus asks in the Greek text "Phileis me? (Do you have an affection for me?) and Peter replies using the same verb: "Philo se" — "I do have an affection for you.

When you see the Greek terms used in the original you begin to realize that this is not a going-over of the same thing three times; a repetition of a question which has already been answered. There is a very great difference.

The third time Jesus says, "Simon, son of John, do you love me?" Jesus is no longer using the word "Agape." Jesus has been disappointed twice, and is now lowering the standard. He realized that Peter just couldn't measure up.

Equivalently, the third time he asks Peter the question, Jesus is giving up, and simply asks: "Simon, do you at least have an affection for me?" Peter was upset and he says for the third time: "I do have an affection for you."

Jesus was actually asking Peter, "Do you love me with an unconditional love?" That was something that had been at the very heart of the teaching of Jesus and was the very foundation for us ever being able to do all the wonders he did and greater. What did Peter do? He dodged the question three times. In fact, it seems more likely he never got the question at all. So, Peter flunked.

At the end, Jesus said, "Feed my sheep." In short "I know you are doing the best you can, but you have not been able to attain to what I asked." "You can't measure up to what I asked."

Note the three different instructions with regard to the "sheep" given by Jesus to Peter. The three different instructions also have a profound significance related to the forms of "love" being used in the narrative. The three different instructions about the "sheep" in the three answers of Jesus are themselves of great interest.

The three different instructions illustrate the roles that Jesus sees Peter as capable of fulfilling, based on the answers he gave. His first instruction was "Take care of my little lambs grazing;" (Boske (be grazing) ta agnia (the little lambs) mou (of me), something with which a young child would have been entrusted in ancient Israel.

The second instruction of Jesus to Peter was "Take care of my sheep grazing." (ποιμένας τα προβατα μου; "Poimaine ta probata mou.") "Poimaine" means to act as a shepherd. "Probata" means adult sheep. This second instruction is not assigning Peter a role of major significance, but the word does indicate a supervisory role. It's a slight promotion from being a child shepherd.

The third instruction does not use "Poimaine" but "Boske." Peter didn't make the grade, so he was relegated again to overseeing the flock while it was grazing, ("Boske") this time including both sheep and lambs, but again a relatively minor role in the imagery of pastoral life in first century Judaism.

This is the principal New Testament text that is adduced to support the position of the Headship of the Christian Church(es). In this endeavor down the centuries some commentators have equated the lambs with the laity in the church and the sheep with the clergy.

Some scholars maintain that there is not any great significance in the use of the different terms, and that Jesus was trying to rehabilitate Peter for the three times he had denied him. It is certainly true that the language used during this awkward early morning encounter on the beach, was probably Aramaic, not koine

Greek, the language in which the Gospel of John was written.

In Mel Gibson's "The Passion of the Christ," the entire dialogue is done in Aramaic, with English subtitles. The suggestion is that Aramaic was the language of Jesus and his disciples and of the entire land of Palestine at the time.

But the land of Palestine then, like the same region of the world today, was multilingual. In any town one would have heard at least Aramaic, Koine Greek, and undoubtedly some of the Persian languages as well as Egyptian and Latin.

The second chapter of the Acts of the Apostles[291] describes the situation well:

> "Now there were dwelling in Jerusalem Jews, devout men from every nation under heaven. … Parthians and Medes and Elamites and residents of Mesopotamia, Judea and Cappadocia, Pontus and Asia, Phrygia and Pamphylia, Egypt and the parts of Libya belonging to Cyrene, and visitors from Rome, both Jews and proselytes, Cretans and Arabians."

It is equally true that the Aramaic vocabulary for 'love' is not as rich as the Greek. However, irrespective of whichever language the original dialogue was conducted in, it seems difficult to deny that whoever wrote down these accounts for John in Greek, and selected these Greek terms deliberately, was acutely aware of the levels Jesus was probing with Peter. He conveyed by the choice of terms that Jesus had to reluctantly conclude that Peter was not able at that time to make the grade: to understand what was at the heart of the message of Jesus, the access to true spiritual power through what we now know as the quantum field.

Power Consists in Being in the Flow of What God Is

"Agape," as Jesus used it in his teachings, wasn't just about affection or unconditional love between people. If Peter had been

291 Acts 2:5-11.

able to reach the state of agape when thinking of Jesus, then he would have had agape for all people and for all things, for this is a state to which we attain, and when we have attained it, it embraces all things. It is not an emotional, sentimental or emotional feeling we have for others, which is often the way 'agape' is interpreted.

If we attain to agape for even one person, then it is impossible to have less than agape for other people. We can't love someone with agape, while holding a grudge, or hating, or wishing for vengeance on someone or something else.

Agape is much more close to being an expression in physics than it is to being a reference to the most profound of human feelings or emotions. When we use it, we are expressing a state to which we have attained. It is much more than a feeling we are experiencing, or an emotion that we are having. What we are discussing here are not characteristics of deep human feelings and emotions, but rather fundamental attitudes towards everything that exists, to which Jesus taught we could aspire by a profound examination of reality. Agape has nothing to do with a fuzzy warm feeling towards others. The teaching of Jesus was not focused on enabling us how to be "nice" people; though obviously that would follow, if within ourselves we really had accomplished the state of agape.

We are not really interested here in the ins and outs of the meaning of agape as an end in itself. What we are really interested in here is finding out what state did Jesus wish us to be in so that we could accomplished all the wonderful things that he did and more?[292]

In short, what kind of state do I need to be in to really and effectively create reality in the quantum field? That is what Jesus was asking of Peter on that cold morning by the lake.

Is it easy to attain that state? Earlier in this book I spent some time conveying how easy it is in theory, but how hard it is in practice. Why is that? Basically because of all the inbuilt programs that are working against our attaining that state.

If agape is really a state, then when I ask someone whether they love me, and use the word "agape," I'm really asking them if

[292] John 14:12.

they are in this state with regard to me, or whether they are even able to access this state? I am not acting as an insecure individual who wants to know if "You love me" in some sort of mawkish or sentimental and reassuring way. It is something entirely different, just as it was with Jesus and Peter on the shore of the lake.

Being in the state of agape is the quintessential state for being able to alter reality through the mind. It was the very heart of the message of Jesus. To teach this was his central purpose when he came. He did not come to be a Suffering Savior, who would avert from us the anger of a vengeful God, but to teach us to be Masters of Creation in the Quantum Field. This was the center of his message, not an interesting footnote. It is hard to get this, given the age-old versions of it that have been retailed to the contrary for most of two thousand years. When we are in agape we are in a state of power, because we are in the flow of what God is.

Negativity and the Quantum Field

We are burdened with a host of dis-empowering programs based on profound misconceptions about both God and Jesus. But it's not just that we have understood God and Jesus wrongly; neither do we understand the whole process we are attempting to transact here in this world, often referred to as "working out our salvation." We are confronted with the prospect of a vengeful Creator, and the various images that have been used to spell that out down the centuries: Jesus as the Suffering Savior who takes the burdens of our sins on his back, as the goat of Yom Kippur did, representing us in the Temple ceremony in Jerusalem long ago. Jesus is also pictured as the Sacrificial Lamb of Yom Kippur or Passover, whose blood, flowing down the stone altar of the Temple after the sacrifice, was supposed to wash away our sins and guilt before a vengeful and offended God. What are we supposed to be doing here in this world? It is commonly expressed as "working out our salvation" or "being saved."

If Jesus, instead of all this, came to teach us how to be Masters of Creation in the Quantum Field, then we have to ask what do all these traditional images of blood, suffering, reparation, lack, guilt and unworthiness, have to do with becoming a Master of the Quantum Reality, and therefore of all that exists? And what has "Being Saved," whatever that means, got to do with anything?

The panorama of a vengeful God's creation has produced images of a direful kind that have had a powerful negative influence down the ages. What chance have we of attaining the state of agape in that consciousness? Minus zero. Most of the big struggles that we encounter when aiming at becoming spiritually empowered, are usually matters of physics masquerading as religious programs. The sooner we realize that, the more powerful we will become spiritually.

To be able to do the wonderful, as Jesus promised we could do, we have to access the state of mind in which we can affect the quantum field most effectively. When we accomplish that then the wonderful can begin to occur. But if we are all slaves to the many sub-conscious programs to the contrary that we looked at in the earlier part of this book, what happens then? Our chances of affecting the quantum field *in a positive way* are almost non-existent.

If, in my heart of hearts, I fully accept that I am a worthless sinner, believing that in some warped way this might attract the favorable attention of an offended and vengeful God, then the quantum field will mirror precisely that state of worthlessness back to me. That unfortunately is the state in which many of those who claim to follow Jesus and his message are in today. It should be obvious that following the unfortunate advice delivered by so many preachers and teachers, that we should ceaselessly acknowledge our worthlessness and sinfulness, can never accomplish anything positive, but instead deepens the problems in which we already are.

The fact of the matter is that most normal people are always in a state that can access the quantum field most effectively. What state is that? Where we totally and completely accept what we are. If I utterly accept that I am worthless, powerless and wretched, that is a state of clarity within me, and it is the clarity within me that has a direct connection to the quantum field. In that condition it is my declared acceptance of worthlessness and lack that is constantly broadcasting to the quantum field, so it constantly worsens that state of lack. Would any sane person consciously and knowingly agree to such a state, much less agree to it being presented as the ideal state or the state that best represents the message of Jesus?

Or do I try to create, and then wonder why nothing is happening — or worse — do I wonder why things have become worse instead of getting better as a result of my "prayer" or my effort at creating reality? Why should I wonder at that, since that is precisely what I have myself presented for manifestation to the quantum field. That is how I really am at my deepest level. As I have stressed so often in this book, we have forgotten the heart of Jesus' message about manifestation. The way we have grown to understand prayer in the religious tradition is asking God to grant us something that we do *not* already have. Jesus' form of prayer was the contrary of that: it requires us to "Believe it is already yours."[293]

In short, our everyday understanding of what prayer is, will not find a support in the New Testament. We look on prayer as a way of getting things, usually being doled out by a supervising God. Instead it is a process by which we alter reality, as I've pointed out earlier. Unfortunately, our serious misunderstanding of the process by which it works, very often results in "getting" the opposite of what our expressed intentions were. If Jesus' teaching is valid, then it is what we deeply believe that we already are, that is constantly manifesting out of the quantum field. What we believe we already are will manifest for us out of the quantum field, not what we may be happening to speak in words at that same time. I am obviously not consciously asking, hoping, wishing or imploring with regard to my state of worthlessness: I am doing worse than that, for I am fully accepting at my deepest level that that is how I am.

The bottom line is that while I may be *asking* for positive and wonderful things in "prayer," which I do <u>no</u>t believe are already mine, it is that state of worthlessness and lack which <u>I do believe I already am</u>, and which I am now presenting to the quantum field, that will manifest into my reality. Since the wonderful things are

---

[293] Mark 11:24.

not believed to be already mine, I have thereby prevented them from manifesting. Worse, I may have caused the lack of them in my life to manifest, since what I projected to the quantum field was my lack of those things by asking, praying or wishing for them. The only thing "asking", etc., will manifest in the quantum field is an intensification of "asking for," which I would not be doing unless I lacked what I asked for.

The quantum field manifests what we, at the deepest and most profound level of our acceptance, declare to be so, and only that. It has no judgment on what or how we ask, but simply causes to occur what we have accepted at the deepest level of our being. The quantum field does not assess what we have presented to it as "more difficult" or less easy. There is no such judgment in the quantum field. There is no thing easier or harder to manifest in the quantum field. The 'easier' or 'harder' component in manifestation is solely a revelation of our ability, or lack of it, to accept what we wish to create. Ease or difficulty is meaningless in the quantum field. However, it is all-relevant to the mind needed to create reality. An advanced accomplishment of this skill was how Jesus performed his extraordinary feats of healing.

If I want to improve my situation, whether it be related to health, wealth or happiness, it is necessary to first approach the quantum field in a state of agape, not in a state of victimhood, alienation, enmity or worthlessness. When I successfully realize a condition of agape in my consciousness, it is then that positive manifestation will begin to occur, for I have cleaned house before I present my declaration of what I believe I already am. It is then that I am clear; it is then that my power is not sidetracked or distracted from the task in hand, and will not be diverted to accomplish what deep down I have already accepted that I am. That would be an unfortunate state of affairs. When we hate, wish for vengeance, or hold grudges, it is ourselves that we sabotage, not the person at whom we aim the grudges. Jesus taught us to root out such attitudes from who we are. That was not because those attitudes were sins. It was because of the fact that as long as we hold on to this kind of attitude, it takes us over and then what we manifest out of the quantum field will mirror those attitudes. What we are uttering as empty platitudes from our mouths will have no effect. While we hold on to these attitudes we completely sabotage our ability to create positive realities out of the quantum field. This is why Jesus insisted so much on forgiveness, for unless we do forgive, the grudges we hold will form an impenetrable barrier to us emerging into the state of Agape, and from there into the manifestation of enormous spiritual power.

Manifestation and Forgiveness

It is all too easy to lapse into understanding "forgiveness" as some sort of favor we do to spiritually lesser beings, from our lofty perch of moral rectitude. We may feel these creatures do not really deserve to be forgiven, nor can they really grasp the magnitude of the favor I am doing them, but I am doing it anyway as Jesus said we should! In short, our trap is that forgiveness can so easily become an exercise in moral superiority: the polar opposite of what Jesus taught.

Whether anyone deserves forgiveness or not should be the last and least of our worries. Forgiveness has little to do with those we forgive: it has all to do with me. Forgiveness opens up the floodgates of power in you and me when we exercise it in the way Jesus taught, for forgiveness releases all the blocks to our empowerment and puts us in the flow of what God is, Agape. I see everyone and everything with the same attitude as their Creator. Does that make me a 'nice' person? Absolutely, but 'niceness' is very much a side issue here, not the heart of the matter. What we want to do is clear the path to where I have power to manifest reality at will.

To attain the state of true forgiveness it's also very helpful to realize that ultimately everyone has magnetized to him or herself what they themselves are in their deepest depths, and also have magnetized the circumstances in which they operate every day. As Shakespeare expressed it:" The fault, dear Brutus, is not in our stars, but in ourselves that we are underlings."[294] It was expressed

[294] Julius Caesar, Act 1, Scene 2.

less succinctly by John Green in his 2012 novel centered on a teenage cancer patient, "The Fault in Our Stars."[295]

From that perspective, there is never any blame to be cast at others. There will of course be a need of reparation for damage done, but not for blame. Khalil Gibran had a poignant expression: "One day you will ask me, which is more important? My life or yours? I will say mine, and you will walk away, not knowing that you are my life."

Allocation of blame is a prime indicator that we just haven't got what Jesus meant. This is one of the harshest and least comforting of all lessons to come home to us when we embark on the so called "spiritual path," i.e., the path based on the truths of physics, or on how this universe actually works. The teachings of Jesus were all about that higher form of physics that we normally refer to as a "spiritual path." If this perspective is found strange we perhaps should remember that it's not so long ago since classical physics found it hard to accept into its wisdom, what quantum mechanics was indicating about the deepest levels of all reality.

The answers Peter gave to Jesus in this section of the Gospel of John showed he was not able to reach that state at all, and probably did not even understand what the question was all about.

"Agape," this intriguing word in the Greek language, is obviously extraordinarily profound. It's not describing an emotional quality in relationships. It's a state of being, actually the fundamental state of all reality. The fundamental reality in physics which created the universe is this frequency of agape. How can we work with the physical universe in terms of interaction with the quantum field? By getting into the state of consciousness which accompanied the emergence of the creation from the Creator. 'Agape' is the state where a profound interaction can occur with physical reality. It is the state in which we are in a very basic sense imitating and entering as Gods.

We are getting down now to the physics of the message of Jesus. I'm using that term to be provocative deliberately. In this perspective, we can begin to see that the message of Jesus, in a profound sense, really wasn't a "religious" message at all. It

[295] Dutton Books.

was a message about the structure of material reality and how you and I can interact with it to our advantage. It was a message about empowerment. When I say it was not a religious message I mean to imply that it was from the stance of believing in a God outside, whom we had to obey and from whom we asked favors, that the religious attitude came. If we don't learn to create reality as masters of reality we are condemned to the wheel of someone else's creation.

Jesus wanted us to realize the kind of reality in which we all live. When we realize that then we can ask what are we really here to do? To explore. What are we here to accomplish? A meaningful radical change, but of course only if we want to. We start with a change in ourselves, and once we have accomplished that then we can change what's external to us.

Why does it have to be that way? Because if I don't change myself first, I am constantly broadcasting to the quantum field the boring reality of what I already am myself at my deepest level. I never suspect that what I am at my deepest level is magnetizing to me more of the same, and will continue to do so until I introduce that monumental personal change in myself which begins my journey to become a Master of the Quantum Field. That is the very kernel of the Christian message.

If I exist in a consciousness of unworthiness, sin, lack, guilt or fear, then I am broadcasting that to the quantum field. It does not matter what words emerge from my mouth, nor with what force they may emerge. What matters is what it is that I am at my deepest level, and it is that that will manifest. My first step is to clean house, and do it profoundly. My first step is not to make reparation for sin to God.

As pointed out earlier, such an action would in any case actually be an atheistic position for it proposes an image of God that is needy and vindictive. This is not how the Creator of the Universe is, and such a concept of the Creator, (or "the Father," as Jesus used to refer to the Creator), never had any place in the teachings of Jesus.

The Unfortunate Character of Most Religious Terms

The familiar religious terms we use are a major problem when we try to manifest something. Fundamentally, they make it impossible to manifest what it is we desire. Once we begin to pray, hope, desire, beseech, beg or implore God, or some revered saint or angel, for something, our effort is doomed to failure, because we have forgotten the fundamental instruction of Jesus. I call this 'wishing list' list "the vocabulary of doom."

When we express a wish for something, we are saying it is not already ours. If we cannot reach a level of acceptance that it is ours, then we would be really better off not asking, begging or praying at all, for the quantum field will respond to our basic attitude. If that basic attitude in us is asking, begging, praying, hoping or imploring, we need to recognize that these are all fundamentally states of lack, and by operating from these states as my fundamental condition, it is lack which will inevitably manifest back to me.

If I am unfortunately stricken by a catastrophic disease, it is usually direfully nauseating and painful. I may I feel I am the most wretched being on the face of the earth. In such a state of illness it is enormously difficult to lift ourselves into the state that I am already radiantly healthy. However, that is the only way in which so called "miraculous healing," can be accomplished in the quantum field, and when it is accomplished, the result is profound and mind boggling.

By now it should be apparent that "praying" to be healed, in the conventional sense, is only inviting disaster, because, as already stated, "healed" is not how I know I am, and it is precisely because it is not how I am that I am asking for help to reach it. The fact that some enlightened beings may intervene surreptitiously to help us from time to time when we are stricken, does not invalidate the truth of the mechanics of this process if we wish to accomplish the healing ourselves.

If we understand that we are now accessing a higher form of physics than is customarily understood, we will also soon realize that the sooner we stop using the term "miraculous" the sooner we will be in touch with how reality actually functions, and the more powerful we will be in utilizing the knowledge of these processes to accomplish the wonderful. "Miraculous" implies the existence of a state of affairs beyond this realm from which we might be relieved of sickness, poverty or lack. The "miraculous" implies an intervention that goes against the laws of nature and it certainly goes against the teaching of Jesus.

The truth is that "a miracle" does not go against the laws of nature, but only against the level of knowledge and understanding that we have of the realities behind those laws. "Miraculous" is a term that belongs to a previous stage of our spiritual evolution. There is nothing "miraculous" about miracles. These extraordinary phenomena are actually a normal part of the higher physics of the universe, which will work for us if we know how to activate that physics. Abandoning the term 'miraculous' and all the paraphernalia that goes with it, would be a good start.

First, let us change ourselves, then we won't need to change the world, because the world will mold automatically to what we are. We've got the methodology backwards.

In accordance with the message of Jesus, what happens if I have managed to realize that the power is in me when I attain the state of Agape, which is to look upon myself, and everyone, or every single thing, with the same attitude with which the Creator looks upon them? Well then, "The Kingdom of Heaven" will have come to pass. Is the Kingdom of Heaven a religious phrase? No. Is Heaven a religious place where in order to gain admittance you need a Visa obtained on grounds of good behavior? No. It also is a state of physics, just like Agape.

Agape, Forgiveness and "The Kingdom of God"

This is another place where a look at the original text won't do us any harm: in fact it'll do an awful lot of harm to our crippling programs. If we rant and rave at our crippling programs we only further empower them, as we saw earlier in this book.

In response to a question, Jesus said that the Kingdom of God is not something that you can find by looking around you: it's about something entirely different – a state within ourselves. He said that a lot! Unfortunately, for the most part, no one got it.

If people sometimes start to have doubts, it does not mean that they may be steering close to putting their eternal salvation in peril. It may simply be that they have started to think. Similarly, it would be well to realize that we should not first think of praying when all else fails, but should do it before we do anything else, and above all to make sure our form of 'prayer' is actually a form of declaration that the state I wish to see manifest is already a reality. "Fake it till you make it," could be a realistic summary of Jesus' teaching.

The phrases "The Kingdom of God," and "Kingdom of Heaven," are not found at all in the Old Testament, and the first Old Testament reference to God as King does not appear until the 8th Century BC.[296] Nevertheless Israel had a strong expectation of some form of Savior who would re-establish justice, destroy the enemies of Israel, and restore the quality of life. The expectation was of a human deliverer; perhaps a warrior figure, such as David had been. Jesus taught that the Kingdom is something very different from those age-old expectations about it which the Jewish people had adopted, and which had a strong strain of the apocalyptic.

Jesus is quoted as using two phrases, "The Kingdom of God" and the "Kingdom of Heaven." Are these different Kingdoms or does the difference have any meaning for us? There are seventy places in the New Testament where the phrase "Kingdom of God" occurs. The phrase "The Kingdom of Heaven" is only found thirty-three times, and only in the Gospel of St. Matthew. Matthew also has four places where the phrase "Kingdom of God" is used.[297] When you compare the references it seems likely that the two phrases are being used interchangeably. If Mark is the oldest Gospel then most scholars believe that the older form "Kingdom of God" is the form Jesus himself probably used.

---

[296] Isaiah 8.

[297] Matthew 12:28; 19:34; 21:31, and 43.

It becomes obvious Jesus is not referring to any sort of external regime established by a Savior/Messiah figure. He says the Kingdom is not something you can find by observing outside of yourself. In modern times we could not even see it with a telescope or a microscope, nor can we find it by looking up or down. It's not an object in the physical universe at all. It's a state. How do you get in to that state that constitutes the "Kingdom of God"? By first getting into another state called' Agape.' The heart of the Kingdom of God, the center of the secret of human empowerment, is the state of Agape.

As already stated, when we cling grimly to our resentments, or our thirst for vengeance, or our grudges, we are actually doing ourselves in. This is why Jesus so often stressed the crucial importance of forgiveness; without it we can only create what our resentment, or sense of worthlessness or lack, automatically brings about in the quantum field. Forgiveness is not, as it often portrayed, the prerogative of the weak and timid; it is an essential prerequisite for living in an empowered state.

In the Luke's Gospel, 17:20 it states: "The Pharisees asked Jesus when the Kingdom of God would come." It was something they were looking forward to, when Jehovah would return and bash in the heads of all the infidels, and they themselves, the Pharisees, would be shown to have been right all along. Jesus said very calmly "People can't observe the coming of the kingdom of God." Why? Because it is already within you. Its arrival is an internal developmental process.

The adverb translated "within" is the Greek term "entos" (εντός) which means "inside," 'within me.' 'Entos' can only mean 'within me,' or "inside me," it most definitively does not mean "among us," which unfortunately is the sense in which it is often rendered in several modern major translations of the Bible. Of course, some branches of Christianity today, and some that are on the fringes of Christianity today, believe the Kingdom of God is something that is going to occur in the future, when the experiment of Jesus is finished up. It will involve all sorts of manifestations of a public nature. And all the malefactors will have their heads bashed in and the playing field will be levelled. This apocalyptic sense is all that the "Kingdom of God" has come to mean to a lot of people in our times.

What's the manifestation of the coming of the Kingdom of God? According to Jesus it is not something that is coming at all. Why? Because it is already here. It's not something for the future that you can observe arriving, as if it were an object or a manifestation or an occurrence in the physical world, no. It's a state, and it's a state that's central to the present not to the future.

In the Gospel of Thomas, there is a famous addition to the information about the Kingdom given in the Gospels of the New Testament. Jesus is quoted as saying: "The Kingdom of Heaven is within you and all around you." The original of the Gospel of Thomas, as we have it, is in Coptic, not Greek. The same emphasis is in this Gospel as is in the New Testament; but there are different terms for "within you" and for "all around you." According to the Gospel of Thomas, those who are in this state of Agape resonate, and are sustained and supported by everyone else who is in that same state all around them. It's within everyone and is a field that unites everyone who is of the same mindset. The manifesting ability in the quantum field is at its height when groups unite their energies while in the state of Agape.

Can we find some examples that are not cliché, to illustrate what might happen, if any of us reached in some significant, if not permanent way, that state of Agape? For various reasons, mainly to break the mold, perhaps a good example would be Ram Dass. His former name was Richard Alpert before he joined his religious movement that lies in the general tradition of Hinduism.

He is author of the book "Be Here Now."[298] In that book there is a story about an Indian guru, Neen Karoli Baba meeting with Ram Dass. At the time, Alpert/Ram Dass was big into drugs, especially LSD. Neen Karoli Baba was about to become his teacher, and he liked Alpert's major drug addiction even less than Alpert himself.

So Karoli Baba decided to teach Alpert a lesson. Showing he was an advanced being, he did not go down the futile path of ordering him to give up LSD as a condition of accepting him as a

[298] Published by the Lama Foundation, San Cristobal, New Mexico, 1971.

disciple, for he knew where that would end. Alpert might manage to give it up, but would almost inevitably feel resentment later for having done it. Instead, Karoli Baba stretched out his hand and asked Alpert to give him some of his LSD. Apparently, Alpert gave him a dose that would have kept him on a high for twelve hours or more. But even though Alpert had put such a substantial dose into Karoli Baba's hand, Baba still kept his hand stretched out. To make a very long story very short, he was eventually given, not just another helping, and another helping; he was given four or five times what would normally be regarded as a fatal dose of LSD.

Richard Alpert tells us that he felt really badly that he was going to risk killing this very special and highly enlightened being, for he felt the world would be a lot worse off without him. When Baba had received into his hand four or five times the fatal dose, to Alpert's horror, he swallowed it all down and just sat there smiling. Apparently, it takes about an hour for LSD to take effect. So they sat there for an hour. Richard Alpert was now wondering how the heck he was going to explain all this to the authorities after Karoli Baba had kicked the bucket. They sat for another hour, and another hour, and Baba was still smiling away. They sat for four hours and on to five. Nothing happened. Baba just sat there smiling normally. He was not telling or advising Alpert to give up LSD, he was teaching in such a way as to remove a program relating to hallucinogenics from Richard Alpert's subconscious mind.

What was he teaching? That the way to expanded consciousness, Agape, was not through the use of mind-altering drugs. That nearly always ends badly. All they do, even marijuana, is create a 'high' by destroying the cells of the body, particularly of the brain. And the demonstration by Karoli Baba that the drugs were under his conscious control within the body, changed Richard Alpert/Ram Dass profoundly from that day forward, and led him to see there was an entirely different and empowering way of achieving the 'highs' he sought, without the significant side effects of drug taking.

The three great Western religions that have their root in Abraham teach us how to <u>relate</u> to God. They teach us how to search and find out what God's will supposedly is for us. And they teach that we will be glad when we do it, especially when this life is over. Because after death you then go up rather than down. Of course, this is not the message Jesus taught. But it is the version of it with which we are familiar – the version incidentally that has given us all these crippling programs. From these perspectives, God is seen basically as just a human being enlarged, with the same virtues and the same failings as humans – vindictive, offended, demanding retribution for individuals who sin against his dictates.

As I stated earlier, this book is not directly about Jesus and his life at all. It's about the crippling set of programs that we have been left with because of the distortions of the message of Jesus, and the distortions of his teachings about the Father that have been served up to us down the centuries. This book is about escaping from the mess of dis-empowerment that those distortions have inflicted on us. Normally we haven't even the slightest clue that these beliefs are distortions, much less do we have any clue as to how we might start to emerge from their crippling influence on us.

The drug culture of the sixties and seventies was fascinated by the Eastern Religions. Instead of what the Western religions had been doing for so long, the Eastern religions that became so well known in the West, did not teach a maze of details about God, and about us, and how we should relate to or "please" God, (forgive the term), or do God's will – whatever that might mean – usually something we figure out ourselves which mirrors our own deficiencies and proclivities. Instead the Eastern religions taught about attaining the consciousness of God and making it our own.

You will remember that awful incident in Paris a few years ago, the assassination of the editors of the magazine "Charlie Hebdo," (as well as all the other terrorist atrocities perpetrated since then?).[299] One of the cartoons "Charlie Hebdo" had on the cover had an inscription that said it all. "God can take care of Mohammed on his own, he doesn't need your help."

Likewise, if we can stop regarding God as some sort of super-human creature enlarged, (which is how most of the religions view

---

[299] On 7 January 2015.

God), then we will realize that God the Creator of the Universes must be amazingly different from the homely images in which we are accustomed to caricature "Him." Realistically, God, in any recognizable sense, cannot need our attention, our devotion, our obedience, our placating, and our absolving. If God is infinite in every respect then it should be obvious there is nothing we can add to God, or subtract from God's greatness, or from God's being in any other sense either.

Instead, it's all about us in our relation to quantum states.

But if the image of God to which we relate is that of a human being enlarged, then we should realize that we can no longer be a believing Christian, Muslim or Jew. People may claim that they are religious while relating to this type of understanding of God that sees him as just a human being enlarged, with all the familiar human characteristics, such as being offended, or wanting to settle scores, either here and now or in the hereafter.

If I relate to a conception of God such as this, based on a world view that parts of the human race had several millennia ago, then I am no longer a believer but an atheist, even though I may still claim that I am a religious person. The fact is I am believing in an idol, a type of God who does not exist. Indeed, if truth be told, many of the actions attributed to "God" in the religious traditions would show that such an entity could never be God the Creator. We cannot add or subtract anything from the Creator. If we raise our sights and envisage what the Creator might truly be like, then in reality the whole panorama of this family of beliefs, such as God's displeasure at sin, or his forgiveness of sin, or rewards or punishments being meted out now or later, and the whole web of complex issues that go with these beliefs, will be seen to have no basis whatever on which to stand.

Knowing what even now we know about the vastness of the universe, how could we ever apply such terms to the Being that is behind it all, in which we are supposed "to live, move and have our being.?" We need to raise our sights. It's what Jesus came to do two thousand years ago, but look what was made of his efforts: a system of teachings and insights that was designed to uplift and empower humanity as a whole, was turned into a sectarian collection of beliefs whose primary and inevitable result was to sink humanity even deeper into an already critical state of worthlessness, powerlessness guilt and unworthiness.

Early in his Pontificate Pope Francis visited the United States. People of all religions and none responded positively to this wonderful man. Some say the crime rate in New York went down dramatically at the time of his visit, and some even went so far as to say that people were more pleasant to each other in the city. No doubt we are waiting for some cynic to say that anything that makes New Yorkers more pleasant to each other, even for a day, is certainly a force to be reckoned with.

But I was struck by the number of times people on television were expressing their desire to find out "What God wants from me," or what God's will in my life is, etc.. This is a wonderful thing to behold, but I am concerned that it is based on an illusion: a mistaken conception of how God is, and how God relates to us. However we may imagine the Creator of the Universe to be, that being is certainly not this kind of human being enlarged. And while people may derive great comfort and inspiration from feeling they are close to such an imagined entity, in the long term the effects of carrying such a mindset is far from a positive thing.

If I am finding problems here with this apparent cosy-ing up to an all-too-familiar and human-style God, I am not doing so because I want to make God into some distant, abstract, remote type of philosophical Being, in some inaccessible frequency of the universe. My problem with these attitudes expressed in the framework of emotion sparked by the Pope's visit, is that despite the apparent impression of intimacy with God, realistically such people are actually making God more distant from them than ever.

The reality is that it is in the frequency of the Creator that we all exist, and if we can get over the age-old tabu against acknowledging that we all have the divine life within us, which Jesus taught as a cornerstone of his message, then we may some day come to realize that God can in no sense be "out-there," but that it is in the life of the Creator that we ourselves always live, move and have our being, even as "sinners." If we once ceased from this state we would cease to exist, and every historical trace of our existence up to that point would vanish. This means that it is within ourselves that we must figure out "what God wants for me," for in relation to me that is where the Creator resides, and not as some Old Man with a Beard in the Clouds.

In short, there is no way in which the intimacy of our relationship with the Creator can ever be increased or decreased. If decreased, it would result in our annihilation. Thinking and acting against the state of Agape has its own very serious consequences, but to couch those consequences as being punished by an eternity of Hell fire is, firstly, based on utterly false conceptions of reality, but even more importantly, prevents those counter movements to the force of Agape being effectively addressed and resolved.

I want to stress one more time, that, unfortunately, the ways in which the religions mostly picture God today, and picture human destiny in relation to God which they market, are fundamentally atheistic. The type of Being envisaged as behind such belief systems could never be the Creator.

The Eastern religions teach about attaining God-consciousness. And for many of the drug generation of course that was about attaining a personal relationship with God, which, obviously, the Western religions either ignored completely or managed to accomplish only in a few rare and precious individuals down through the centuries. But what the drug cultures of the sixties and the seventies didn't realize was that attaining God consciousness was existing in a state of Agape. And that was not about any relationship at all of an external kind, with anything or anyone. As Jesus put it so well, "The Kingdom of God is inside you."

What did the anecdote about Ram Dass tell us? If we are in a state of Agape, we may decide to be affected or not be affected by physical reality, because we're in the frequency that creates reality, not receives it. Creating, not receiving, is the key. This is the very opposite of the prospect of a wretched sinner proclaiming worthlessness and begging for forgiveness, so often put forth as an ideal by the western religions. Creating, not receiving, was the very cornerstone of Jesus' teaching. Receiving, not creating, has become the cornerstone of the historical religions.

Chapter 20
New Religious Stirrings in the Mid-20th Century: The Beatles, the Buddha, TM and the Rest

While Christianity had penetrated to the Far East by the 13th Century, it was not till the 1800s that Buddhism arrived in Western Europe. Things moved slowly till the mid-twentieth century when the Beat Movement,[300] and the counter-culture that arose from it all across the Western world in the 1950s, developed a deep interest in Eastern religions and spirituality, especially in the philosophy of Zen. At the end of the sixties, the Beatles made a much publicized, but rather unfortunate visit, to study TM with the Maharashi Mahesh Yogi.[301] It was only then that the interest in the Eastern Religions and their practices really took off in the West.

Hordes of young people from all over the Western world flocked to India along "the Hippie Trail." In a multitude of ways, they protested they were trying to escape what they saw as a thoroughly materialistic and hypocritical lifestyle. In India, they experienced transcendental meditation, ayurvedic medicine, yoga, experimentation with drugs, psychometry,[302] astral projection, psychic healing, spirit materializations, various other occult experiences, and what they described in general as a liberated style of life.

---

300 The Beat Generation was a literary movement started by a group of authors whose work explored and influenced American culture and politics, just after the Second World War. Most of their work was written and became well-known in the 1960s. Central themes in the works were rejection of materialistic values, embarking on a spiritual quest, non-conformity, experimentation with drugs, and sexual liberation. The movement is usually recognized as having originated at Colombia University in the mid-1940s.

301 January 1968.

302 The ability to discover information about a person or situation, by touching inanimate objects associated with them.

Apart from some slight acquaintance previously, this was the same time that I first encountered some serious accounts of the Eastern religions, especially Buddhism, Daoism and Hinduism. Many things struck me deeply in my reading, but perhaps nothing so much as the very obvious similarities there were between all the central teachings of Jesus and the central teachings of the Buddha.

I knew way back then that I must be missing some crucial part of the puzzle, but I had no idea what the solution to the puzzle might be. I felt however, that the most obvious explanation had to be, not that Jesus had plagiarized the Buddha, who had lived 500 years before him, but rather that the message of these two great beings must have somehow come from the same source. Needless to say, I also realized that the implications of that for the current form of the Western religious traditions would be almost incalculable.

The Elephant in the Room: Where Was Jesus between the Ages of 12 and 30, or Does It Matter?

We hear of Jesus in the Temple at the age of about twelve years, and hear nothing more about him till he is about age thirty. As noted in chapter five of this book, only two of the four Gospels tell us anything about the childhood of Jesus, but none of them tell us anything at all about those eighteen "missing years."

Nobody was teaching Buddhist and Hindu themes in Judea or Galilee at the time of Jesus, so there's been a lot of interest, and even more controversy, about where Jesus spent this long period before he began his public ministry. Naturally the most obvious explanation is that either Jesus went to India or Tibet himself, or the message came along one of the trade routes from the East, such as the Silk Road. Certain discoveries towards the end of the 19th Century gave credence to the belief that Jesus had travelled to India and Tibet, and several well-known works have dealt with the subject.[303]

I've noticed over the last couple of years especially, that certain, even well-established scholarly theologians have adopted a dismissive stance about the very suggestion that Jesus might have been in the East. In fact, I am not aware of any mainline scholarly theologian or Biblical expert these days who accepts the idea, even as a possibility. One subtle telltale sign that the 'experts' are getting uneasy is when a proposal is somehow regarded as beneath contempt and not worthy of consideration by any serious scholar, which is exactly what has happened here. However, this rejection without nuance, is certainly not something which the evidence would justify.

Some notable writers have put it dismissively in these terms: "He's alleged to have gone to Tibet to study with the Buddhists." Apart from the inconvenient fact that there were no Buddhists in Tibet until seven hundred years after the time of Jesus, no one has claimed that he went to study with the Buddhists anywhere. But it does appear he went there to study with an entirely different class of being.

The main source for this information comes from the account of a Russian War Correspondent, Nicolas Notovitch, who went to India in 1887. Near to the Tibetan border, at the city of Leh, he heard that a chronicle of the life of Jesus in India was preserved twenty-five miles away at the Monastery of Hemis. Notovitch visited this Monastery and managed to have the scrolls shown to him. He had the scrolls read to him, translated from the Tibetan[304] and when he returned to Europe in 1894 he had a French translation of the scrolls published. The book was quickly translated into English, German, Italian and Spanish. We will see more on this in the next section of this book, but it is a complex subject, and for a more full

[303] The movie, *The Lost Years of Jesus*, Shirley Maclaine's *Out on a Limb*, Janet Bock's *The Jesus Mystery*, Elizabeth Clare Prophet's *The Lost Years of Jesus* and Holger Kirsten's *Jesus Lived in India*. See also my two DVD set; "How Jesus Became a Christ." Sai Baba, Edgar Cayce and Bhagwan Shree Rajneesh have also claimed that Jesus went to India.

[304] The original scroll in the Pali language, was said to be held at the Library of Lhassa, capital of Tibet.

and detailed treatment than is feasible here, you are referred to my two-DVD set "How Jesus Became a Christ," published in 2006.

According to the account of Notovitch, and the testimony of Swami Abhedananda, who saw the scrolls in 1922, Jesus travelled from Jerusalem along the Silk Road to Damascus, Baghdad, Bactra (now Balkh in Afghanistan), went south from there to Kabul, and entered the Punjab. He crossed India from east to west, to Puri, and fleeing from his enemies went north to Kapalivastu, the birthplace of the Buddha Gautama. He studied for six years with the Brahmins at Puri, Rajagriha and Benares. He tried to teach the Vedas to the lower castes of people which was deeply resented by the Brahmins and Kshatriyas (high castes), since the Sudras (lower cast) were forbidden to read or even contemplate the Vedas. Jesus Issa denounced the Brahmins for this, and as a result a death plot was hatched against him. He escaped north, travelling west of Mount Everest, and on to Lhasa. Returning from India he followed the caravan route to Leh, and then on to Kabul. He followed the southern trade route through Persia where he survived an attempt to kill him by the Zoroastrian priests, who had tried to have him devoured by wild beasts.

Those who reject even the possibility that Jesus may have gone to India to study with the Masters, envisage him instead as spending those eighteen "missing years" years in Joseph's carpenter shop at Nazareth. If that were so, then, as I've already pointed out, apparently we should all have taken up carpentry years ago, since it is inferred by those who hold such views that it was in the workshop at Nazareth that he must have acquired all those wonderful insights and abilities that enabled him to heal the sick, walk on water and raise the dead, not to mention delivering the most splendid set of teachings on all major aspects of human destiny and purpose, that has ever appeared in human history.

Buddhism and Christianity: Striking Similarities, Bells, Rosaries, Holy Water, Images ... but above All, the Same Teachings

Almost a century and a half ago, T.W. Rhys Davids wrote that the earliest missionaries to Tibet observed similarities between Christianity and Buddhism that have been noticed since the first known contact:

> "Lamaism with its shaven priests, its bells and rosaries, its images and holy water, its popes and bishops, its abbots and monks of many grades, its processions and feast days, its confessional and purgatory, and its worship of the double Virgin, so strongly resembles Romanism that the first Catholic missionaries thought it must be an imitation by the devil of the religion of Christ."[305]

The recorded sayings of the three great Eastern Masters, Krishna, Lao Tsu,[306] and the Buddha, have many striking parallels with the themes that form the heart of the teachings of Jesus, but especially so in the case of the Buddha. The common theme in both Jesus and the Buddha is focused on compassion and love. The whole process in which we are involved here is described by them as some form of growth or evolution of what we are. To call that phenomenon "spiritual" would be both inadequate and misleading for both systems of teaching transcend religion. One thing is clear, however we may account for it: the teachings of these four great Masters must have come from the same source, however we may account for that, and however earth-shaking its implications might be for conventional Christianity.

It is thought-provoking and enlightening to look briefly at some of the more obvious parallels that exist between Jesus' teachings and those of the Buddha.

---

305 Rhys Davids, T. W: *Buddhist Birth Stories (Jataka Tales)*, 1878, Routledge, London.

306 Chinese mystic, 603-531 BC.

Jesus	**The Buddha**
1. Do unto others as you would wish done unto you.	
Do to others as you would have them do to you. Luke 6: 31.	Consider others as yourself Dhammapada 10:1.
2. Love Your Neighbor as Yourself.	
Love one another as I have loved you. John 13:34.	Let your thoughts of boundless love pervade the whole world. Sutta Nipata, 149-50.
My command is this: Love each other as I have loved you. John 15:12.	Consider others as yourself. Dhammapada 10:1.
Treat others the same way you want them to treat you. You shall love your neighbor as yourself. Luke 6: 31-33.	Hatred does not ever cease in this world by hating, but by love. Heartland Sangha.
3. Take Care of Others.	
He will reply, 'Truly I tell you, whatever you did not do for one of the least of these, you did not do for me.' Matthew. 25:45.	If you do not tend to one another, then who is there to tend you? Whoever would tend me, he should tend the sick. Vinaya, Mahavagga, 8.26.3.
4. Do Not Judge Others	
Why do you see the splinter in someone else's eye, but ignore the log in your own? Matthew. 7:3.	Pay attention to your own faults – those things you have done and those you have not. Overlook the faults of others. The Dhammapada, Section 4, 31-33.

5. Avoid Violence	
If anyone strikes you on the cheek, offer the other also. Luke 6:29.	If anyone should give you a blow with his hand, with a stick, or with a knife, you should abandon any desires and utter no evil words. Majjhima Nikaya, 21:6.
6. Turn the Other Cheek.	
If anyone strikes you on the cheek, offer the other also. Luke 6:29.	If anyone should give you a blow with his hand, with a stick, or with a knife, you should abandon any desires and utter no evil words. Majjhima Nikaya 21:6.
7. Disdain Possessions.	
Sending out his disciples, Jesus said, "Take no gold, nor silver, nor copper in your belts. No bag for your journey, nor two tunics nor sandals, nor a staff, for the laborer is worthy of his hire." Matthew 10:9, Mark. 6:8, Luke 9:3.	Like a bird which is content wherever it goes – its wings its only burden, the monks is content with one set of robes, and a bowl for his daily food. Wherever he goes, he takes only the bare necessities. The Kevaddha Sutra.
8. Need to Begin a New Existence.	
Unless one is born anew he will not be able to see the Kingdom of God. John 3:3	The cessation of the discriminating mind cannot take place until there is a 'turning-about' in the deepest seat of consciousness. Lankavatara Sutra.

9. Spread the Good News	
Go therefore and make disciples of all nations, baptizing them in the name of the Father and of the Son and of the Holy Spirit, teaching them to observe all that I have commanded you; and lo, I am with you always, to the close of the age. Matthew 28:19-20.	Teach the darma which is lovely at the beginning, lovely in the middle, lovely at the end. Explain with the spirit and the letter in the fashion of Brahma. In this way, you will be completely fulfilled and wholly pure. Maj. I, 179
10. By giving away we get.	
In everything I did, I showed you that by this kind of hard work we must help the weak, remembering the words the Lord Jesus himself said: 'It is more blessed to give than to receive.' Acts 20:35	"Hatred does not ever cease in this world by hating, but by love; this is an eternal truth. . . Overcome anger by love, overcome evil by good, overcome the miser by giving. Overcome the liar by truth." Heartland Sangha American Buddhism, "Parallel Sayings."

Acts 20:35:[307]

Burnett Hillman Streeter has suggested that the moral teaching of the Buddha has four major resemblances to the Sermon on the Mount.

As far as we know, Jesus left no written works. The Buddha himself wrote nothing either. He taught for over 45 years, modifying his presentations to suit the audience, so there are many repetitions in our present written records. Modern Buddhist scholarship seems to agree that the Buddha died

[307] The only words of Jesus that come from outside the Four Gospels.

somewhere within a 40-year time frame, centered on 480 BC.[308] His teachings were carefully memorized before they were put into written form, but that did not happen until more than four centuries after his death.

With regard to the New Testament, no autographs of any of its twenty-seven books have survived.

The teachings of Buddha were carefully memorized by faithful disciples who had heard them delivered. In fact, they regarded their accurate recitation of the teachings from memory, as a central spiritual discipline. By contrast not a word of the New Testament Gospels was penned by anyone who had known Jesus personally, and they were only committed to written form between forty to seventy years after his public ministry had ended. But as we saw in the "Jesus as Poet" section of this book, the same memorization processes as preserved the Buddha's message is likely to have occurred with the teachings of Jesus as well.

Despite all of the above, it is still possible to discern fairly clearly the fundamental principles of the teaching of Jesus before they were filtered through at least four decades of contemplation by the early Christian community, (especially in Jerusalem), and then written down. A major help in this exercise is to contemplate the extraordinary harmony between so many central themes in the message of Jesus and of Buddha. It is easy to see the comparison between them in the ten sets of equivalent statements or aphorisms that I laid out in table form a few pages back, but that is by no means the most important aspect of this theme. There is a far deeper harmony between the Buddha and Jesus than simply nearly identical wordings of the same message. There is also a whole background of understanding that is assumed by them both, and which we might never have realized if these aphorisms hadn't opened our minds up to the possibility of there being much more going on there than is apparent on the surface.

That harmony between these sayings gives us clues where to look further and deeper, and to search for the common presuppositions that underlie the entirety of both of their teachings.

---

[308] L. S *Cousins: "Journal of the Royal Asiatic Society,"* Series 3, 6.1, 1996: 57-63.

Unless we had been alerted by the similarity in the sayings of both Jesus and the Buddha, we would not have been alerted to the much deeper set of assumptions between them which has hardly ever been noted.

Close to the core of the fundamental teachings of Jesus was his emphasis on avoiding fear in all its forms. It is one of the most repeated instructions in the whole New Testament.[309] It is not difficult to detect twenty-five or thirty well known texts in which Jesus admonishes his followers in that way.

Planning Responsibly for the Future or Fearing the Future?

A little reflection will reveal why he had to emphasize this so strongly. We all have many concerns to deal with every day, not just personal concerns but concerns about the welfare of those we hold dear, and the fortunes of the various enterprises and causes, great and small, in which we are all involved. We are all prone to lapse into fear of the future: fear about finances, relationships, health, security, and a thousand other every-day items, and it was this that Jesus was targeting, for that kind of fear serves only negative purposes and preserves us in powerlessness and victimization.

There is a major difference between planning responsibly for the future and being afraid of the future. Fear is a powerful emotion, and what we fear we magnetize to us in the quantum field. We need to address and own our fears in a real sense, not just adopt some "whistling past the graveyard" attitude in their regard, else we will never escape from the state of powerlessness and lack.

It is worth noting that the God of whom Jesus spoke never inspired fear, but the contrary. It is obvious that Jesus in his teachings had in mind a vastly different entity than the traditional image of God in Western religion: "the judgmental Old Man with a beard in the clouds" concept, which I pilloried under the

309 See, for example, the list cited by Felix Just, S.J., "Have no fear! Do not be afraid!" http://catholic-resources.org/Bible/HaveNoFear.htm

"Hamburger Universe" image in one of my DVDs.[310]

Jesus said that the God of whom he spoke was within him, and within every one of us as well. So, it's obvious Jesus was referring to an entirely different kind of entity than the image the word "God" conjures up for the average individual today. It's been a long time since Ludwig Feuerbach expressed that great truth, to which I have referred a few times already: "God did not, as the Bible says, make man in His image; on the contrary man, as I have shown in *The Essence of Christianity*, made God in his image."[311]

This conventional image of God, which most Christian people tend to accept today, is not to be found in the teachings of Jesus.

The Buddha was accused of being an atheist because he rejected the conventional images of God held by the religions of his time. He correctly intuited that belief in God or gods evolved in human history, because it was a device that helped primitive humanity cope with the abundant threats and fears that menaced their everyday existence: threats to food supplies, natural disasters, and the forces of nature generally; threats from wild animals, accidents and disease. It was out of these situations that the primitive form of belief in gods or a God as a rescuer developed. It was this kind of fear-based God that Jesus came to expose for what it really was. Like the Buddha, Jesus could just as easily have been called an atheist by those who knew no better.

It is equally obvious that Jesus, like the Buddha, never taught the existence of some form of supernatural sphere, in which, for example, the miraculous might be considered to have its home. Jesus did extraordinary "miracles:" in the realm of nature, stilling a storm at sea; in the realm of health, healing all kinds of catastrophic diseases, and overturning all the accepted belief systems concerning human life and purpose, by raising people from the dead, including one who had been in the grave for several days in a warm climate.

But he inferred that these extraordinary phenomena came

---

310 Miceal Ledwith, The Great Questions in the Hamburger Universe. "Deep Deceptions", Vol. 1.

311 Ludwig Feuerbach, (28 July 1804 – 13 September 1872), *Lectures on the Essence of Religion.*

not from some realm called the 'miraculous,' but from a form of causation which he exercised in processes and dimensions of the "natural" world with which we were not yet familiar. It was to teach us how to understand such processes, and exercise such abilities, that he came. His purpose had nothing at all to do with being a "Suffering Savior." The human race certainly needed a Savior, as much then as now. But the Savior was needed to rescue us from our own crippling mindsets, not to protect us from the vengeance of a savage God.

The "miraculous" was never envisaged by Jesus as his exclusive preserve. Nor was his performance of the 'miraculous' done to engender reverence or awe. It was to demonstrate to us what he expected us to be able to learn to do ourselves. He admonished the witnesses of his 'works,' (as the Gospel of John called them instead of 'miracles'), that he expected them (and us) to do even greater things than he had done. In short, he wished to be imitated not to be venerated. "Truly, truly, I say to you, whoever believes in me will also do the works that I do; and greater works than these will he do, because I am going to the Father.[312]

It hardly needs pointing out that such phenomena are not characteristic of the communities that venerate his name today, so something serious has obviously gone wrong.

If the Buddha so wisely intuited that the type of God whom humans invented had its origin in the fears and insecurities plaguing the human condition, this then helps us to begin to notice that Jesus taught the same thing. The fact that the majority of believers might disagree with this analysis is really not of any great significance. The number of people who believe something is the case, is never a great indicator of whether that something is a fact or not. There was a time when it was believed that the world was flat, and despite that being accepted by 100% of the human population who were in a position to be aware, they were all wrong.

Unfortunately, many present-day belief systems, as a primary policy, veer towards emphasizing and inculcating those very

[312] John 14:12.

frightening images of God which Jesus had made it his business to discredit.

The contemplation of how closely the Buddha's sayings affirm the same message as those of Jesus, helps us to discern even deeper convergences between their foundational teachings. These convergences have not yet been pointed out in any significant way of which I am aware. Jesus' message about the origins of conventional belief in God was the same as the Buddha's: that belief in that type of God has its roots in human fear and powerlessness.

Addressing and breaking the grip of such fear and powerlessness is the first item on our agenda before we can attain anything of the magnificence in power that his message heralded for us.

A core principle of that position is that our insight into reality is, as yet, radically incomplete, almost as much now as it was then. When we attain the wisdom and abilities to interact with nature in harmony and power, then the purpose for which Jesus came, and for which we ourselves came, will at last be accomplished.

The Pot Is Stirred: a Russian Visits Kashmir

All this came to the forefront in the late 1880's to early 1890's, because a Russian aristocrat called Nicolas Notovitch claimed to have gone to India, Tibet, Kashmir and Katmandu. Near the Monastery of Hemis, which is near the city of Leh in Kashmir, he fell from his horse and broke a leg. He was taken in and nursed by the monks of the Monastery.

Apparently, he made a good impression, because the monks confided in him after a couple of weeks that they had very interesting documents in their possession in their library and that they were about 'his guru,' to wit, Jesus. These documents told an entirely different version of Jesus' life to what was accepted as fact in the West. They brought out the documents to him. As they were written in the ancient southern Indian language, Pali, the monks translated them, and Notovitch wrote down the entire contents of the scrolls. He came back to Europe, through Constantinople, and asked for guidance and advice there from a highly-placed ecclesiastic. That individual advised him not to have anything whatever to do with these documents, because they asserted all sorts of heretical things about Jesus. He was advised to go home and keep quiet about it all.

However, Notovitch was on his way to Paris, and when there asked the Pope's Nuncio (Ambassador) for advice about the Jesus Scrolls that he had seen at Hemis. The Nuncio was Archbishop (later Cardinal) Luigi Rotelli, who by coincidence had previously served in Constantinople before being assigned to Paris. Again, Notovitch was told by Archbishop Rotelli to go home and keep quiet. Fortunately Notovitch decided to ignore the advice and published the scrolls in 1893.

Over the last three or four years there have been all sorts of proclamations issued that Notovitch retracted his story, and that he had later confessed that he had made it all up. It was stated he was never in Leh or at the Monastery of Hemis. Many reputable scholars even today regard the Notovitch scrolls as fraudulent.

However, the guest book of the Monastery in the city of Leh has since come to light. This hand-written document registers that Notovitch was in Leh, and that he did break his leg, and was in the Monastery, and basically indicates that what he said in 1893 was true, despite whatever "retractions" he may have issued later, which if they were issued, were presumably under threat, or from a desire to be at last left alone.

Years after the publication of the scrolls, a distinguished Indian scholar who had spent a considerable time in the United States, heard of the Notovitch book and was intrigued by it.

His name was Swami Abhedananda.[313] He was a direct disciple of the renowned 19th Century mystic Ramakrishna Paramahansa. Swami Vivekananda sent Abhedananda to the West to head the Vedanta Society of New York in 1897. Fascinated by the account of Notovitch, Abhedananda was about to be reassigned to India in

---

313 Born in north Calcutta, 2 October 1866 and was named Kaliprasad Chandra.

1921. He diverted to Kashmir, and eventually undertook the very arduous journey from the plains of India to the snowy mountains, and eventually to the Monastery of Hemis itself.

A few high ranking officials of the British Raj had also gone to Hemis shortly after the publication of Novotich's book, including one James Archibald Douglas, who was the first Professor of English and History at the Government College in Agra, a distinguished scholar and high ranking official of the Raj. It's worth noting he had been tutor to the young Aleister (Edward) Crowley, the British occultist.

Douglas travelled from Agra to the Monastery of Hemis, to investigate Notovitch's claims. In typical colonial fashion we can imagine him banging on the door of the Monastery and demanding to see the scrolls that Notovitch had seen. Of course, the very wise porter at the door said: "There never was a visitor here called Notovitch and we don't have any scrolls."

It's well to keep in mind the precarious position that the Buddhist, Hindu, and Eastern religions generally, were in in British controlled India at that time. Anything that ran contrary to the traditional story of Jesus was going to be descended upon with a vengeance from on high, especially if it came from a non-Christian source. The various individuals who came over the following years, and demanded to see the scrolls at Hemis, were naturally told politely by the Monastery doorkeeper that there were no scrolls, nor had an individual called Notovitch ever been in their Monastery.

When Abhedananda, who was a Buddhist Monk, came to the Monastery of Hemis in 1922, he got a very different reception. He was welcomed and shown the Notovitch scrolls. The monks translated the scrolls for him, as they had also done for Notovitch, and Abhedananda transcribed the entire text. When he arrived home he consulted Notovitch's book and compared that text with the text he had copied down himself at Hemis. He found that the two texts were identical.

According to the scrolls shown to Abhedananda, Jesus went to India at 13, partially to escape his parents and keep them from forcing him to marry. He learned how to read and understand the

Vedas during his time in India. He later spent six years with the Buddhists, learned Pali and studied all the Buddhist scriptures. Now we can perhaps begin to understand better why there are so many parallels between the sayings of the Buddha and of Jesus, and why their foundational assumptions about God and human destiny are the same.

Abhednanda issued his version of the Issa or Notovitch scrolls, available today in the version "Swami Abhedananda's Journey into Kashmir and Tibet,"[314]

In 1927 the manuscript was published serially in *Visvavani,* a monthly publication of the Ramakrishna Vedanta Samiti, and subsequently published in a book form in Bengali. The fifth edition of Abhedananda's book in English was published in 1987, and it contains an English translation from the French of Notovich's *Life of Saint Issa.*

It's interesting that Abhedananda in his publication had omitted the trenchant criticisms of Buddhism and Hinduism that Jesus had expressed in the Notovitch version of the scrolls! He had published the good stuff, but he left out the criticisms! That omission by Abhedananda is in itself a strong indication of the authenticity of the scrolls. However, it is amazing how many reputable scholars in this field still continue to deny the reality of the Jesus scrolls from Hemis, presumably taking the alleged "confession" by Notovitch as the end of the matter.

A few years after Abhedananda had published his work, Nicolas Roerich, a renowned Russian painter and archeologist, who was at that time living in New York, became fascinated by the account of Notovitch and Abhedananda. Roerich was nominated for the Nobel Peace Prize three times. He has a museum dedicated to his artistic work in Manhattan.

Roerich went to Hemis in 1925, a couple of years after Abadananda had published his work. He had his wife and his son George with him when they visited the Monastery. George spoke fluent Tibetan, which was a distinct advantage, and Roerich reported that he had confirmed that Jesus had lived in India and Tibet and that that knowledge was everywhere in those

[314] Vedanta Press.

two countries. The native people, especially in India, were very reluctant to speak of that openly as it was calculated to offend the sensibilities of the powerful Christian Westerners who ruled their country and controlled most aspects of their lives.

In the Summer of 1939 Elizabeth Caspari went to Hemis with her husband Charles, and Mrs. Clarence Gasque, who was the head of the World Fellowship of Faith. Their party consisted of twenty-three people, and it required 112 ponies to carry their baggage up the trackless route to Hemis. No one in the party had ever heard of Nicolas Notovitch or the Jesus scrolls that he published. Apparently, like Notovitch, they made a very good impression on the monks of Hemis Monastery. Three or four days into their visit the Abbot said to them – it was on the eve of their departure: 'You know we have scrolls here that would be of great interest to you'. And they said 'Really'? He said 'Yes, they tell about <u>your</u> Jesus' ("your" was the word that they used). 'They tell of his time in India and Nepal and Tibet'. They brought out the manuscripts wrapped in silk. The Abbot said 'these scrolls tell that your Jesus was here.'

Madame Caspari took a picture of the monk displaying the scrolls, which has since become world famous. These were the scrolls that Notovitch had seen forty-five years before.

Daya Mata,[315] born Rachel Faye Wright, was President of the Self-Realization Fellowship (SRF) in Los Angeles, for fifty-five years. It was the organization that Paramahansa Yogananda founded to spread his teachings. In the early 1950s Daya Mata interviewed a visiting Buddhist dignitary named Krishna Tirta. To her astonishment he told her that Jesus had spent a considerable time in India and Tibet. He said that he himself, a high ranking official in the Buddhist and the Hindu traditions, had studied records in the ancient Temple of Puri, (just south of Calcutta), which confirmed these facts. He said not alone are those records kept in the Monastery of Puri, but similar records are to be found in many Monasteries all throughout northern India, Tibet and Nepal.

Why did the discovery of Nicolas Notovitch's arouse such controversy and opposition? Why were such efforts made to

[315] Sanskrit for "Compassionate Mother."

discredit the entire matter and bury it without trace? If I were a high official of the British Raj in India, and I went up banging on the door of the Hemis Monastery in the late 1890's, I would have been told: 'No, we never heard of Nicolas Notovitch, nor did we ever hear of his scrolls'. Why? Because our lives depended on it. Maybe the next day the Monastery would be disbanded. The situation in Hemis was very understandable when attempts were made to check the Notovitch saga.

But why is there still such a frenzy to disprove the claims of Notovitch? I think it's beyond doubt that he was at Hemis and saw and copied the scrolls. And did he retract his story about the scrolls later? I wouldn't be surprised at that for the same reason. Maybe he did say that he had made everything up, but I can find no proof anywhere that he ever did so. I'm sure if his retraction existed it would be trumpeted on high.

This would explain the major puzzle of the similarity between the teachings of the Buddha and Jesus. Did Jesus travel to India when he was a young man? As already noted, according to Notovitch the path he travelled was to go far north from Israel and then travel east, in terms of modern geography, through the South of Syria, through the middle of Iraq, right through the center of modern Persia, (Iran), and then they went into the north of Afghanistan. From Bactra they went South to Kabul, and then through the Khyber Pass to Taxila, the City of Stone, where Jesus' twin brother, Thomas, met King Gundaphores in the year 47 of our era. Apollonius of Tyana was also a guest of King Gundaphores at Taxila when Thomas was there.

Jesus and his brother were inspired to leave their native land by the tales of these people in India and Tibet and Kashmir who could do remarkable things. They could walk on water. They could produce matter out of thin air. Jesus and Thomas were fascinated by these stories. They wanted to learn how to control material things in this way, so they decided to leave, much to the chagrin of Mary, their unfortunate mother, and Joseph who was still alive, contrary to the rumors that he was 150 years old when they were married. Was it as reckless as it seems to go to India at age 12? Not quite, because their uncle, Joseph of Arimathea, was a trader who did a lot of business along the Silk Road. They went with one of those caravans, right down into the Punjab, the Land of the Five Rivers, and they spent some time there.

They were sorely disappointed in their expectation of hearing how all the gurus of India performed such wonderful phenomena. The gurus didn't teach anything. Thomas gave up after a year of being expected to wait on pompous gurus and went home. Jesus gave up too, but he went across the country in an easterly direction to an area south of Calcutta. He then went across to Puri. This is the site of the Monastery headed by Krishna Tirta, who had told Daya Mata in California in 1958, that Jesus had been in Puri on his way to Tibet, and that there were scrolls testifying to Jesus' travels in India as a young man, in many of the Indian Monasteries, not just at Hemis.

Jesus still didn't find anything at Puri either, except more pompous gurus. The scrolls tell us that Jesus learned to read and understand the Vedas, the sacred texts of the Hindus, which were written down between 500 and 1100 BC, especially the Upanishads and the Bhagavad-Gita. They are not for the casual reader, as you probably will gather quickly if you ever tried to read them. In the beginning, they were composed of a thousand hymns which served the priestly families. They contain the world's oldest music. Prose works followed to explain the ceremonies. Eventually, as so often happens, the Vedas became so complicated that they served no purpose. You can imagine the discouragement of Jesus, when everything he had journeyed all this distance to find, turned out to be nothing except pomposity.

To make matters worse in those days India was rigidly divided by the caste system. At the top level were the Brahmins or Priests. Below them were the Warriors. Below them again were the Merchants. And at the very bottom were the Shudras or the worker bees, who were destined to spend their lives in servitude to the upper classes.

When Jesus went north he eventually did reach real masters. The Brahmins taught him the theory of healing by prayer. As we understand prayer it's the best possible way <u>not</u> to get what you want. But the Brahmins had a different technique. You had to absolutely become what you wished to be. They taught him how to restore people's sanity by driving out possessing spirits. Are there such things as entities from frequency realms above this that cling onto us? There are, but we don't want to focus on them. We all have an unfortunate proclivity once "evil spirits" are mentioned, to think of nothing else for a very long time, and we know where that manifestation will take us.

Will we learn to heal the sick, walk on water and raise the dead while we have a fear and abhorrence for evil spirits?

Denunciation by Jesus of the High Castes of Buddhism, and Hinduism, as well as Zoroastrianism

According to Notovitch, Jesus was greatly loved by all who met him. He spent six years in the sacred cities of Juggernaut and Rajagriha, about 400 miles northwest of present day Calcutta, and at the sacred city of Benares, which is now called Varanasi.

The lowest class, the workers, weren't allowed to hear the Vedas or even to contemplate them. The merchants were only allowed to hear them on special feast days. But Jesus broke the rules. He taught the Vedas to everyone who turned up. You can tell how troublesome a child he was to his mother. He spoke out against the Brahmins and against the Warriors, for depriving the lower classes of their rights. "We are all equal", he said, "God the Father makes no difference between his children. All are equally dear to him."

He really set the cat among the pigeons when he started to deny the divine origin of the Vedas. And he also denied that Para-Brahma had incarnated in Vishnu, in Shiva and the other Indian gods.

The Hindus had filled their temples with abominations, he said, worshipping a collection of creatures, animals, stones and metals, while they were subduing the status of the human person that is greater than them all. He said it was an abomination to subjugate and humiliate people who worked by the sweat of their brows, in order to enable "an idler to sit at his sumptuous table".[316] The Warriors and the priests, he said, will become the workers and the workers will become dwellers with the Eternal. This is the law of reincarnation. Be careful what you are bringing down upon yourself. You can see that, even then, he knew how to make the choicest of enemies. As they say, people's worth can be gauged by the quality of their enemies.

Greatly encouraged by this, the lower classes, (who loved Jesus), the Merchants and the workers, asked Jesus how they should pray. He said, for God's sake get some sense. Stop talking to these carved images and statues because they can't hear you, they are deaf. Don't listen to the Vedas either because their truth is counterfeit. (Talk about magnetising trouble!). Don't humiliate your neighbor. Help the poor, support the weak, and don't covet. Don't do ill. And that was the same message of the Buddha that he brought back to Palestine a few years later.

Because of all this subversive teaching it comes as no surprise that the White Priests of Buddhism and the Warriors, conspired to kill him.

They made an attempt on his life in the city of Juggeraut – or they were planning it but he escaped. He travelled to Rajagriha, now Rajir, and eventually reached Kapilavastu, about 800 miles away. This is the city where the Buddha was born. This was where Jesus learned the ancient language of Pali, which had been the language of the Buddha Gautama. He applied himself to the study of the Sutras, the Path of Truth. These documents were supposed to be the faithful transmission of the teachings of the Buddha which, as mentioned earlier, were memorized while he was speaking, but only written down four centuries later. They were gathered in three woven baskets: the Vinaya Pitaka (rules and regulations for the monks), the Sutta Pitaka (mainly discources delivered by the Buddha himself), and the Abhidhamma Pitaka (the philosophy behind the Buddha's teaching).

From Kapilavastu, the Buddha's birth place, Jesus went north and he passed on the western side of Mount Everest, and

[316] Notovitch, Nicolas: The life of St. Issa: Best of the Sons of Men, V.

journeyed on into Nepal and Tibet. He stopped at the capital Lhasa, which of course is where the Dali Lama had his palace from late in the 17th century.

The Dali Lama and I were once speaking at the Conference for a Parliament of World Religions at Cape Town. The two of us were alone and chatting during a break. I said, 'I want to propose an heretical idea to you,' and he said 'I am the prophet of heresy'. 'I am glad to hear it' I said.

I said to him, 'Don't you think it was a good thing that you were kicked out of Lhasa and out of your palace, because in the intervening period you have travelled the whole world spreading your message, which otherwise would never had been heard by all those people?'

There was a very long, awkward silence. I thought he was going to ring the bell and have some of the heavies come and take care of me. Then he said, "You are right, you are right," and lapsed into thought.

Returning again to Jesus, he spent another six years with the Masters in those mountainous regions. There I'm sure he found a lot that was to his liking. In his twenty sixth year Jesus turned towards the West again and headed for home.

Everywhere he went history repeated itself. What did he do? He preached against idolatry. He sided with the oppressed and the poor. And the one thing that Jesus always did superbly was to upset every entrenched religious leader that there was, especially in Persia. So should it come to us as a surprise of any kind, that his message would upset every entrenched religious leader that exists today? That wouldn't be news, especially if you had your head buried in the metaphorical sand. Apart from not hearing anything when you have your head buried in the sand, it has also to be assessed as the supremely bad defensive posture.

In Iran, the priests of Zoroaster forbade the people to listen to him but of course Jesus wouldn't stop. The priests of Zoroaster[317] had Jesus arrested and they brought him before the Zoroastrian High Priest who interrogated him. Shades of what was to come.

[317] Ancient Persian Prophet. Also known as Zarathustra. Died somewhere between 1,000 and 500 BC.

The Zoroastrians didn't believe in capital punishment – directly. They liked someone else to do their dirty work for them. They cast him out into the wilderness one night near a lair of savage beasts, which they had done before with others, hoping he would be eaten by the beasts. But, of course, the beasts knew better than the priests of Zoroaster.

Earlier in this volume I noted the story of Polycarp. He knew John the disciple of Jesus. Apart from profound teachings, John had learned some things from Jesus, some things of practical usefulness. One of them was the control of reality to some degree, and for some reason or another Polycarp had specialized in the control of fire. There was once a famous incident in the city of Smyrna, near Ephesus, in the West of modern Turkey, half way down the west coast. There was a huge fire in the town. Polycarp was called and he extinguished the fire by command. That gets attention. And it wasn't the only thing he could do.

Later because of his heretical views, the people of the region decided to burn him at the stake about the year 155. They lit all of the faggots around him, the flames came up; they added more fuel to the flames, but Polycarp was untouched inside the flames. He wasn't even sweating apparently. The flames couldn't touch him because he could control fire. Fire is the most ethereal of all the physical elements. To control flames is one of the signs of the beginning of access to agape. Eventually somebody got a long spear and pushed it through the flames and killed him. Jesus couldn't just control fire, the most ethereal of the material elements. He could control a lot of other realities as well, including wild beasts, so he survived that adventure with the priesthood of Zoraster.

Jesus moved on. When he eventually got home, at the age of twenty-nine, he'd been gone for eighteen years, and they barely recognized him. The Jewish priests and elders at the beginning, according to the Notovitch Scrolls, were absolutely filled with admiration for what he was saying. Because he knew the urgency of the situation Jesus would not stop speaking, even in the direst of circumstances.

The Jewish priests asked him if it was it true that he had come to stir up trouble against the authorities?" Apparently, someone had complained to the Roman Governor, Pontius Pilate, about him. He replied: "I was painfully grieved when I saw how my brothers and sisters had forgotten the true God."

Who were the Jews worshipping? Jehovah of the Anunnaki. Jesus went on to say, "I tried to reorient them towards the real God. I tried to reestablish the Laws of Moses in people's hearts because they are in ignorance of what it really means. The laws have been subverted."

Notovitch's account squares with a lot of what we know from the New Testament about the life of Jesus in the Holy Land, but there are some major differences. All of the four Gospels of the New Testament blamed the Jews for the death of Jesus. Saint Luke, in particular, wanted to convey that Christianity was a pro-Roman movement, so he tried to portray Pontius Pilate in the best possible light: quietly ignoring the fact that it was Pontius Pilate who condemned Jesus to be mocked, scourged, and crowned with thorns, to be kicked around the place, abused by the soldiers and eventually given over to a horrible death. All of the four Gospels blame the Jews for that. But the Notovitch scrolls lay the blame where it really belongs, at the feet of Pontius Pilate.

There are some people who say Jehovah was the father of Jesus and Thomas but whether he was the physical father or not, he was certainly behind that incarnation. Why would Jehovah be interested in that? Because Jesus, given his previous incarnations, was the best person possible for Jehovah to bring into being, right at that period, since the people of Israel were waning in their loyalty to their pseudo-god. Jehovah needed an apostle to whip people back into loyalty to him, and he had chosen Jesus as the person to do this.

Jesus was interviewed on the Plane of Bliss about this and was asked, 'Do you really want to do this?' or 'Do you really know what you are letting yourself in for?' Jesus changed his mind. But if Jesus was incarnated at the bequest of Jehovah one of the candidates for being his physical father was either Tiberius, later Roman Emperor, who was a general in Palestine at that time, or one of his top people.

Attitude of Jesus towards Women

At a public lecture many years ago a speaker surprised me by saying that some of the most sexist organizations on this planet have been the world's great religions.

Indeed, many of them, he went on to say, claim to base such prejudiced attitudes on the inspired written word of God. It occurred to me then that the matter bore investigation.

Knowing how far apart the belief and practice of any organization can sometimes drift I wondered if this prejudice was a matter of fundamental doctrine for the great religions, or was it just how things happened to develop in practice for any number of the many reasons imaginable?

I began to look afresh at the principal writings that the great religions hold sacred, the Old and New Testaments, the Talmud, the Qur'an, and the sacred scriptures of the Buddhists and Hindus, to see how they estimated women. It was a discouraging investigation.

Some central streams of Buddhism believe that to be born a woman is due to bad karma. A woman ought to pray to be re-born as a man in a future existence.

The Qur'an regards a woman as 'half a man.' 'Forgetfulness overcomes a woman.' They are 'inherently weaker in rational judgment.' "The Prophet said, 'Isn't the witness of a woman equal to half of that of a man?' The women said, 'Yes.' He said, 'This is because of the deficiency of a woman's mind.'..."[318] Even the great western thinker Plato, quotes Socrates approvingly: "Do you know anything at all practiced by mankind in which the male is not far better than the female."[319] It's hardly surprising that Plato's pupil, Aristotle, the tutor of Alexander the Great, didn't even accept that women were legitimate human beings: they were "failed men"

---

[318] Sura 2:282.

[319] Republic, Book V, 455 c.

due to some mishap in the womb during the conception process.[320]

The most ancient source of all, the Hindu laws of Manu state: "In childhood a female remains subject to her father. In youth, a female is subject to her husband. When her lord is dead she shall be subject to her sons." 'A woman must never be independent.' Indeed, one of the major Hindu Sanskrit texts state that "It is the highest duty of the woman to burn herself after her husband's death."[321] It's been pointed out frequently that the number of women who died in this way have always been statistically small, but nevertheless, in an odd way, such a form of death and the individuals who endured it, are still revered in India today.[322]

There is no doubt that the influence of the Church has profoundly shaped our culture in the West, and that has brought many good things for which we should be profoundly grateful. But it does not take much research into either the sacred texts of the great religions, or the history of their practice down the centuries, to see that they have played a central role in fostering the disenfranchisement of women.

That did not stay within the Church's sphere, for its religious influence has come to be expressed in most bodies of fundamental secular legislation and practice around the world, not just in the West.

I came to see eventually that the facts of the matter were much more complicated even than this. This was not an influence that found an unwelcome reception in those over whom it was exercised. It seemed to me unmistakable that a pro-male and anti-female bias was buried deep within the human male psyche, independent of, and long prior to anything we would today regard as a religious influence. If this is the case then it should come as less of a surprise to find so much overt sexism in fundamental religious texts, given the traditions out of which those religions have themselves grown.

---

[320] "... is as it were a deformed male, " Περὶ ζῴων γενέσεως, On the *Generation of Animals*, 737a. 28.

[321] Brahma Purana 80.75.

[322] Leslie, Julia: "Suttee or Sati: Victim or Victor?" Reprinted from "Bulletin Center for the Study of World Religions," Harvard University, 1987-88. Motilal Banarsidass Publishers, Delhi.

A language's slang vocabulary can reveal a great deal of what prejudices lie deep at the heart of any culture, and Bishop Shelby Spong was one of the first to point out how so many popular words for sexual intercourse display enormous male hostility and contempt for the female

One of the greatest libraries that ever existed was established at Nineveh, beside Mosul in modern Iraq, by the last of the Assyrian kings, Assurbanipal (died about 627 BC). He was known as Asenappar in the Hebrew Bible and as Sardanapalus to the Romans. He was one of the few kings in antiquity who could read and write, and was the only literate monarch in fifteen centuries of Assyrian Kings. History regards him as forming the first deliberately collected library. Its significance for us here is that we can assume all ancient written works and records in cuneiform literature that existed in Mesopotamia, that most ancient cradle of civilization, were collected at Nineveh using all the resources of the mighty Assyrian Empire to do so.

Most reputable scholars today will admit that several of those documents are the precursors of seminal documents that later went to form the foundations of the Judeo-Christian tradition, in particular the Book of Genesis, which is central to understanding the estimate of the female in the Judeo-Christian tradition. Genesis is an immensely profound work despite having been turned on its head all too often by well-meaning preachers.

As pointed out earlier, Genesis wrestles with an age-old issue that must at some stage come to perplex every living person. If we persist in thinking of God and God's relation to the world, in the homely ways to which we have so long grown accustomed, then we are left with an insoluble problem, with which the opening chapters of Genesis wrestle.

The world as we know it is replete with more than its fair share of suffering, disease, old age, infirmity, natural disasters, frailty, disappointment, betrayal and ultimately death. That kind of world cannot have come from the hand of a good God who is also all-powerful, so either God did not create the world or something went wrong. Those indeed are the only two options we have in the mindset I have labeled "the Hamburger Universe."

That God did a good job originally but something went wrong was the explanation the authors of Genesis went for, but what is really notable is that the blame for what went wrong was laid fairly and squarely at the feet of Eve, the mother of the human race. So now from some of the earliest sources in the human record we have the female blamed for everything that's wrong with the world, (even though it should be noted that in the Nineveh documents a minor god is blamed as well). I had often noted in my Biblical studies years ago that whenever something went really wrong some woman was usually blamed.

This prejudice against women as the cause of all our woes has descended as an integral part of most of our cultures and history, and it's hardly surprising that eventually the distrust and avoidance of women became a central religious duty and indeed the very badge of holiness in the West.

But we have to ask if those ancient texts are the root of the anti-female bias in the male psyche, or did those texts themselves grow out of an already existing bias? If it's the former, then a major element in rectifying the situation would be to ask the religions to clean up their act as far as the female is concerned. If it's the latter, then we have a far deeper problem that originates way beyond the realms of rational thought and discourse, rooted in the shady realms of the unconscious, the subliminal and the taboo.

It probably also is connected to those aspects of the female that are related to the mysterious, their closeness to the facts of birth and the renewal of life, the unavoidable attraction they hold for men which undermines males perceived power, and those aspects of the female that have provoked cries of ritual uncleanness in every culture of which we have knowledge.

So even if the religions have historically been some of the most sexist organizations on Earth it seems they were more the agencies who exacerbated what was already there, rather than that they were the origins of it. In turn, that would mean that addressing the anti-female bias would have to be the first priority for any body of teaching that purported to be in the vanguard of spiritual evolution. It would also have to be the touchstone of its validity.

This raises some serious issues. Less than two decades after the Passion of Jesus, and some two decades before the appearance of the first Gospel of the New Testament, St. Paul started to put pen to paper. Over the next fifteen years more than half of the New Testament as we know it is attributed to him, and those writings preceded all the Gospels as I have already mentioned.

Rather curiously, Paul never mentions the quintessential Christian female, Mary, the Mother of Jesus, in his extensive writings. He states women will be saved only through motherhood (1 Tim. 2: 15); and that they ought to be subject to men. There is little doubt among scholars of the New Testament that Paul saw in the growing emancipation of women in the Roman world, a major strand in the breakdown of orderly society, and he believed that Christians should adhere to the traditional strict lines of family life. Peter says that women should be cherished because they are weaker, and the context implies he is not just thinking of physical weakness (1 Peter).

Things hardly improved when St. Jerome came on the scene and justified marriage only because it could produce more virgins. The highest praise Augustine could manage for women was to regard them as a "malum necessarium," 'a necessary evil.'

If we look back twenty or thirty years earlier than St. Paul's writings, we can see the cultural and religious background from which Jesus emerged. He had, of course, made enormous waves among the religious traditions of his day. It was a time when at every religious service the men prayed; "Blessed are you O Lord who has not made me a woman," or worse, "Blessed be God who has not created me a heathen, a slave or a woman."

It was a time when the women had to sit in separate sections of the Synagogues, and when they were not counted in the votes. It was unusual for them to be taught the Torah. Indeed, the writers of the Talmud added that it would be better to burn the words of Torah than entrust them to a woman. This very unpromising context is the background from which Jesus emerged, and there are strong hints that it might have been the general background which Paul and Peter wished to perpetuate.

If, as noted earlier, the emancipation of women has to be the touchstone for the validity of any leading edge spiritual movement for human liberation, then this raises disturbing questions because of these elements in the witness of Paul and Peter.

But before we ask those questions, we have to inquire if this version of things was in fact true to what Jesus taught and did, or not, or whether the structure erected on the foundation he had established had drifted from his message?

Indeed looking back over those previous twenty or thirty years we see a very different attitude in the teaching and practice of Jesus. The New Testament clearly acknowledges that women were among his earliest followers. Mary Magdalene, Joanna and Susanna accompanied Jesus during his ministry and supported him financially.

According to one account, an unnamed Gentile woman stated to Jesus without being contradicted, that the Ministry of God is not confined to particular groups or persons, but belongs to all who have faith. (Mark 7:24-30; Matthew 15:21-28)

Jesus ate with women as well as men, which would not have been customary, and spoke to them both in public and private. In the very early years of the church this trend continued and some of the earliest gathering places for the infant church were in the houses of such women.

Churches often grew up on those sites later, and have preserved their names in those locations even into our own times. Whatever may be said of the teaching of Jesus about women in the New Testament his conduct and practice would certainly have been branded as revolutionary.

However, the most poignant of all the teachings of Jesus on the dignity and nobility of women came to light just over one hundred years ago, from the famous scrolls discovered by Nicolas Notovitch at the monastery of Hemis. It is said that similar scrolls are to be found in many other monasteries scattered throughout India and Tibet.

Are we told nothing of those missing years by the New Testament because nothing of any account was happening. Or was something so significant happening that all mention of it had to be omitted, since it did not accord with the politically correct version of him which it had now been decided to preach?

Because of the tumult which his teachings provoked when he came back to Israel, he was constantly under scrutiny by the religious and secular authorities, and the spies of Pontius Pilate were constantly monitoring him. From the Notovitch Scrolls we learn that one day, an old woman who was listening to his teaching, was roughly pushed aside by one of those spies. He was rebuked by Jesus, and the statement of Jesus that followed must certainly rank as one of the most inspirational pronouncements on the dignity and nobility of woman that has ever emerged in human history. It merits quotation in full.

> "It is not good for a son to push away his mother, that he may occupy the place which belongs to her. Whoever does not respect his mother, the most sacred being after his God — is unworthy of the name of son.
>
> "Listen to what I say to you. Respect woman, for in her we see the mother of the universe, and all the truth of divine creation is to come through her.
>
> "She is the fount of everything good and beautiful, as she is also the germ of life and death. Upon her man depends in all his existence, for she is his moral and natural support in his labors.
>
> "In pain and suffering she brings you forth, in the sweat of her brow she watches over your growth, and until her death you cause her the greatest anxieties. Bless her and adore her, for she is your only friend and support on Earth.
>
> "Respect her, defend her. In doing so you will gain for yourself her love, you will find favor before God and for her sake many sins will be remitted to you.
>
> "Love your wives and respect them for they will be mothers tomorrow, and later the grandmothers of a whole nation.
>
> "Be submissive to the wife; her love enobles man, softens his hardened heart, tames the wild beast in him and changes it to a lamb.
>
> "Wives and mothers are the priceless treasures which

God has given to you. They are the most beautiful ornaments of the universe, and from them will be born all who will inhabit the Earth.

"Even as the Lord of Hosts separated the light from the darkness and the dry land from the waters, so does woman possess the divine gift of calling forth out of man's evil nature, all the good that is in him.

"Therefore I say unto you, after God, to woman must belong your best thoughts, for she is the divine temple where you will most easily obtain perfect happiness.

"Draw from this temple your moral force. There you will forget your sorrows and your failures, and recover the love necessary to aid your fellow men.

"Suffer her not to be humiliated, for by humiliating her you humiliate yourselves and lose the sentiment of love, without which nothing can exist here on Earth.

"Protect your wife, that she may protect you — you and your household. All that you do for your mothers, your wives, for a widow or for any woman in distress, you will do for your God."

The Link between Jesus and Mary Magdalene

But we do not have to go as far as ancient Nepal to gain this different view. A treasure trove of early Christian documents discovered in Egypt in the 19th. and 20th. centuries give us some amazingly fresh insights into Jesus' relation to women during his ministry. Several of these documents such as the *Pistis Sophia*, the *Sophia of Jesus Christ, the Dialogue of the Savior,* the *Gospel of Philip* and the *Gospel of Mary,* focus on one woman in particular, whom we already knew from the New Testament to be a prominent prophetic leader and visionary in at least one section of the early Christian movement, Mary Magdalene.

In the *Sophia of Jesus Christ* five women and twelve men are gathered to hear the Savior. Mary is entrusted with the most elevated teachings of Jesus and has a prominent role in handing on his message. In the *Pistis Sophia* she is also prominent among the disciples and asks more questions than all of the rest put together. Her high spiritual status is affirmed and she intercedes with the Savior as some of the disciples are despairing. In the *Gospel of Mary* the Magdalene is portrayed without doubt as a woman leader among the disciples.

She alone of all the disciples is not frightened and afraid. She is pre-eminently the one whom Jesus most esteems. *The Gospel of Philip* focuses on the special relationship between Jesus and her. In the *Dialogue of the Savior* Mary is named along with Jude Thomas and Matthew, as partaking in a prolonged dialogue with Jesus, and she questions Jesus on several matters as the representative of the group.

All of this evidence should settle the debate we often hear about whether she was an apostle or not.

The real question now is not whether she was one of the Apostles of Jesus but whether she was in fact, in the title often ascribed to her of late, the "Apostle of the Apostles."

Some churches still prohibit women from the ministry and the reason usually adduced is that the pattern of an all-male priesthood laid down by Jesus is not something that the Churches are at liberty to alter. Even when some churches do admit female ministers, to then admit them as bishops is seen as a further major barrier.

But what if the pattern of the priesthood established by Jesus was entirely different, and that the chief among the first such group was female? Certainly, if the primary duty of any true religion has to be to set about rectifying the inbuilt anti-female bias in the male psyche, no other initiative could ever hope to be as appropriate and successful as that.

And what of the personal side of things? As pointed out elsewhere in this volume, a succession of works such as "Holy Blood, Holy Grail," 'Bloodline of the Holy Grail,' "Rex Deus" and "The Da Vinci Code," have raised afresh the question of what kind of personal relationship there was between Magdelene and Jesus.

That inevitably leads to the further question of whether there exists any such thing as a Messianic Bloodline, and if there is, what does it entail? Is it simply a matter of historical physical descent from this preeminent pair, or would such descendants carry something in their physical or mental makeup that sets them apart?

We have to call Feuerbach to mind again: rather than God having created us in his own image, it is we who have created God in ours. In all the religions, what we are dealing with in the first place is human-style images of the Creator rather than with the real thing. As far as repression of the female goes those images of the Creator have to be recognized in the truest sense as nothing more than the Gods of Men.

Courting Rome: The Coloring of the Message to Suit the Taste of the Powers That Were

Pontius Pilate became the fifth Prefect of the Roman province of Judaea in AD 26, and served in that position for ten years under the Emperor Tiberius. Pilate was extremely insensitive to Jewish laws, customs and regulations, and on a number of occasions had almost driven the Jews to open revolt because of his crudeness. Philo of Alexandria,[323] the noted Hellenistic Jewish philosopher, was severely critical of his methods of administration. He states that Pilate was vindictive, had a furious temper and that he was naturally inflexible.[324] His administration, according to Philo, featured bribery, robberies, executions without trial, and wanton cruelty. It is not surprising that he feared complaints by the Jews to the Emperor.

His term as Prefect of Judea came to an abrupt end after a major atrocity recounted by Josephus. A large group of Samaritans had been persuaded to go to Mt. Gerazim to view newly discovered artifacts supposedly dating to the time of Moses. Before the group could reach the mountain, Pilate sent in a force of infantry and

[323] 25 BC – c. 50 AD.

[324] Philo, *On The Embassy of Gauis* Book XXXVIII 299–305.

cavalry, both heavily armed. Many of the Samaritan group were killed, the others were arrested, and most of the leaders were executed without trial. The Samaritans complained to Vitellus, the Roman Governor of Syria, who was Pilate's immediate superior in the region. Vitellus sent Pilate to Rome to explain his brutal suppression of the Samaritan uprising to Tiberius. Fortunately for Pilate he arrived in Rome shortly after the death of Tiberius on 16 March 37 AD.

As already mentioned the Notovitch or Issa scrolls credit the Jewish authorities with going out of their way to save Jesus.

A number of Jewish scholars have argued that the Gospels of the New Testament were in fact Gentile or Western documents, and were not Jewish documents in their origin and evolution at all. We also know, that with the possible exception of Mark's Gospel, all four Gospels were written after the fall of Jerusalem in the year 70 AD. At that point the Jewish nation was no longer a force to be reckoned with, so it's understandable the Gospels would have downplayed the significance of the Jewish authorities during the ministry of Jesus.

In ancient times you always needed to keep an eye on Rome. Most scholars believe that the Gospels were formulated with that end in view, and it's particularly obvious with Luke, as I emphasized earlier. In short, the big imperative was to spread the teachings of Jesus to the Greeks and the Romans in the western part of the Empire, and to do that successfully it was crucial that the Roman authorities would look on the early Christian communities with some favor.

It has been suggested, by some major scholars, that the whole purpose of this exercise was to win at least toleration for the early Christian movement, by taking the blame for what happened to Jesus off the Romans, where it rightfully belonged, and lay it on the Jews instead. In doing this they hoped not to upset the powers that were, or the new people to whom they were now preaching the message of Jesus.

In what did that eventually result? The unfortunate plague of anti-Semitism, which possessed Europe like a virulent disease for the next fifteen hundred years, and was in large degree due to

Christians blaming the Jews for the crucifixion of Jesus. That was the background that so many Christian movements down the centuries used to bolster up their campaigns against the Jews, Adolph Hitler being simply the most notable and recent tragic example.

This all came about because of where the blame was placed for the Passion of Jesus. How much suffering, how much injustice would we have been spared down the centuries if the blame for the death of Jesus had not been such a major factor in the evolution of the Western World.? How much distraction from agape or empowerment would we have been saved? If the teachings as contained in the Issa scrolls of the Hemis Monastery had held sway instead of the familiar Christian tradition, things would have been very different. Is that heresy? But be comforted, if Jesus were here today you'd be hearing exactly the same thing.

Chapter 21
A Final Perspective: The Temples of the Seven Seals in Egypt, Powerful Testament to the Real Mission of Jesus

We noted some intriguing suggestions about the years when Jesus was supposedly in India and Tibet. The other great gap in the life history of Jesus is his time in Egypt. Egypt in the days of Jesus was well past its glory. But it was still an extremely interesting place esoterically, mystically, spiritually. There's a great case to be made for saying that Egypt, together with Israel and some of the surrounding areas, were really all one country in effect, at that time. That means it wasn't that big a transition for the Holy Family to flee to Egypt during the infancy of Jesus to escape the paranoid attentions of Herod Antipas.[325]

Along the Nile in the days when Jesus and his father, mother and brother were refugees there, there was still a series of great

[325] Son of Herod the Great. Tetrarch of Galilee and Perea, 1 BC - 39 AD.

temples. Each temple was dedicated to the work of what you and I would refer to nowadays by using that much abused word "Chakras" or 'Seals'; age-old terms that come from the traditions of Hinduism, Jainism and Buddhism, and which were described from time immemorial in the Upanishads and later in the Vedas.

"Chakra" is a Sanskrit term which literally means a wheel or disc, and it is used to convey that there are seven main wheels of energy in the body, that are aligned along the length of the body from the base of the spine to the top of the head. The seven spinning wheels of energy are where consciousness and matter meet in the body. The energy is sometimes called "Prana," the Sanskrit word for the life force, the sum of all energy that permeates the entire universe, even inanimate objects, and which brought all reality into existence. It is the energy of the Creator. In the Jesus context, the equivalent term is 'Agape.' It is the flow of what God is.

Each of the seven spinning wheels of energy is associated with the complex nerve systems and major organs of the body. The condition of these centers affect all of our states, whether spiritual, emotional, or physical. Very often an ailment in one area of the body will call our attention to the fact that the spinning wheel of energy in that region of the body is out of whack and needs our attention. Thus, according to the Vedas, a physical ailment can help us detect a chakra or seal that is not operating freely, while a seal that is not operating properly will very possibly cause a physical ailment in that region of the body to which it relates.

The creation has descended from the Source by one singular method, the lowering of frequency. When we ponder this we realize how futile it is to picture God as some sort of human being enlarged.

It was on this paradigm of Agape that the whole of the teaching of Jesus was based, and all of our problems that stand in the way of attaining what Jesus taught, are in that condition because we have abused all these centers. Most of the negative religious concepts in the West further deepen that state of abuse. In fact, conventional religious beliefs can create chaos in the energy centers.

Obviously if this is the system that is operating in this universe we should want to get as unimpeded an access as possible to the source of that "prana," the life force or vital principle that pervades all things. To get this clearer conduit of power from where we really belong, Point Zero, we do not have to do anything heroic, in fact, surprisingly, it is even more important to do the negative rather than the positive. Why? Because the main intent of our journey consists in removing the blocks that exist between where we all came from, and still belong, and our material/spiritual incarnation on this plane. We have a lot of stuff to do negatively in taking out that garbage which blocks us from existing in the state of agape. When we truly exist in the state of agape the fullness of the power of the Creator starts to percolate down to us through the frequencies, because there is nothing to block it. That is what Jesus accomplished in a superlative degree. As already noted, that is how he did the so ineptly named "miracles," for they really were the application of the free flow of prana. That is what he taught us we also could and should do.

What would happen if I didn't take out the garbage from my house for a year? What would happen over two years, five years, ten years? How about a quarter million years? That's what we've done. We haven't taken out the garbage spiritually, from our beings, for a quarter million years. Is it any wonder things are in chaos?

Do we need to do acts of heroism to gain the power that attends the state of Agape? No, we just need to let stuff go. And to do that we have to basically address programs. How do we address programs? By attacking them? No, no. We have to transcend them. We have to rebuild and replace them with different materials. In other words, we have to sneak up on them and create new and better replacements. Then the old crippling programs will decay all by themselves. But meanwhile 95% of our lives are dictated by that quarter million years of garbage.

The ancient Egyptians regarded the Nile as the Kundalini force of the country, that represented the Kundalini in each living human being. There were seven temples along the Nile to mark the seven 'chakras' of Egypt. Spiritual garbage disposal was the business of those seven temples along the kundalini of the Nile.

If you were an initiate in those years you slowly progressed in a somewhat orderly fashion through these seven Temples, in each Temple addressing the issues that need to be 'owned' before access to our inner power can be realized. Long before the time of Jesus, if you were serious about your spiritual evolution, you enlisted in the first Temple, located at the bottom of the Nile at Aswan. What did you do there? Address the issues of the first seal, or chakra, that were keeping you dis-empowered. I can't go into detail about that as there may be pious souls reading this book in the future, so I leave it to your fertile imaginations!

What are the issues of the first three seals?

1. Procreation.
2. Pain and suffering, "Oh poor me," 'the world is not a fair place.'
3. Power.

We start at Aswan. It's about sexuality and its manifold uses and abuses.

When you had worked through all of those issues you had come into harmony with everything related to sexuality and procreation, but more than that, into harmony also with what those issues symbolized beyond that level.

Can we remember what the access to agape consists in? Harmony, the balancing the forces. The access to agape has levels, and the great access to power only comes when agape has been reconciled into harmony on at least four of those levels.

Achieving that balance and harmony in regard to the first seal was something the initiates worked on in the Temple at Aswan. How long did it take? It depended on how addicted you were to your limitations. Eventually, if you kept on, you would graduate.

Where would you go then? To the Temple dedicated to resolving the issues of the second seal. This is the most pitiful seal of all because all the victims are gathered there, piled high. "Oh, poor me, the world is not fair, if it weren't for 'a' and 'b' and 'c' what a wonderful person I would be." "How could they possibly do this to me?" These are the issues of the second seal — victimization, pain and powerlessness. Most unfortunately, this is what the sublime message of Jesus the Christ has been turned into in modern Christianity. It has been turned into a religion of the second seal based on a catastrophic Fall of Mankind at the very beginning, and reinforced with a massive misinterpretation of Jesus as a Suffering Redeemer. The constant focus is on making reparation in a spirit of guilt, powerlessness, victimization, worthlessness and fear.

It would be very difficult for believers that belong to any Western religion today, to get past the Temple of the Second Seal in Egypt at Kom Ombo, for there can be a great gratification and addiction in contemplating how we have been so victimized all our lives.

If I had graduated from the first temple at Aswan I was then brought up here to Kom Ombo, to work with the issues of the second seal, near the great "Un-Sympathy Temple." After whatever time it takes me to come to terms with those issues, and the priests in charge judge me to be ready, I am blindfolded and led to the massive façade of the Temple of the Second Seal for my test.

While the Temple itself is far older, the grand entry was constructed in the days of the Ptolemaic dynasty[326] and it still exists today. There are two grand openings in that facade. The door on the left-hand side was the entry to the Temple. The door on the right-hand side was the exit by which you went out if you had completed the initiation.

The Initiates who had been trained and tested in the issues of the second seal, probably for several years, were now judged to be ready for the great test.

You were led in through the great doorway on the left-hand side, and probably in times long gone, many of us did go in there, in other times, and in other bodies. This means you should be getting very uneasy reading about all this right now. All I will say for now is that more people went in the left-hand door than eventually came out the right-hand door at the end!

The initiates were led blindfolded into the heart of the Temple and then put standing, still blindfolded, on the edge of a pool, of

326 180-47 BC.

similar proportions to a large swimming pool.

This pool was in the temple of the God Sobek, Sobek being the ancient Egyptian word for crocodile. Standing on the edge of the pool the Initiates blindfolds are removed.

They were instructed to jump into the pool. But wait, as you might suspect in a Temple of Initiation, there's a catch. There are hungry Nile crocodiles in the pool – huge creatures. Specimens have been known to reach 20 feet in length and weigh 2,000 pounds.

If, despite your years of instruction you were still prone to think "Oh poor me, it's not fair," then this would be the moment when that deeply buried issue would come up. There is nothing, nothing, that can be compared to staring into the eyes of a Nile crocodile. It is guaranteed to bring up any residual feelings of the second seal that may have survived the intensive training up to this point.

In those days, you couldn't get into a fit of pique and go home and then come back two years later having re-assesed the situation. If you opted out of the test, then that was it for that lifetime. Consequently, most of the initiates, despite their misgivings, jumped into the pool. Some, or maybe even most of them, would wish they were anywhere else but there, which means they hadn't got the message of the previous few years instruction. So, once they jumped into the pool they started splashing around, trying to avoid the crocodiles snapping at them. It is not a career move to start splashing in a crocodile pool. Mercifully for the splashers, the whole experiment was over fairly quickly. Admittedly, there were some reddish stains in the water, but there were no files or records to keep, and there was no mopping up necessary. It was over.

But on the other hand, if your training at Aswan had taught you that you are the Lord God of your being, you know who it is who controls reality. And you were told that you can't control reality until you believe absolutely that that reality is so. Why? Because the Law of Cause and Effect works in reverse in the Quantum Field. So, if I'm a miserable sniveling creature, I am creating that same thing even though I am apparently begging to be released from it. The work of the Quantum Field is a reversal of the Law of Cause and Effect which is what Jesus always taught. So, if I want to be wonderful, prosperous, etc., I have to already live in that state of consciousness. If I want to be healed from cancer, in the example I gave earlier in this book, even racked with pain, I have to triumph over all of that, and in my mind I have to feel absolutely, and radiantly healthy. If so, I will become that state of health inevitably.

But if I am asking, "Oh somebody, whatever God is convenient, whether it's Jesus (who is usually the first casualty in such cases), or some other unfortunate deity, 'Oh Jesus, please, please help me to be healed from cancer.'" Whatever I am asking for, begging for, praying for, hoping for or beseeching for, that is what I will get. Not what I hoped for, but the state in which I actually expressed it is what will manifest in the Quantum Field. What does hoping, begging, praying etc., for something to manifest? It manifests the absence of what it is I believe I am trying to accomplish.

Those Initiates standing on the edge of the crocodile pool at Kom Ombo, probably had not ever had it formally stated to them that cause and effect in the Quantum Field work in reverse, which was also the heart of Jesus' teaching, but they still managed to put all of their doubts aside, focus, and jump whole-heartedly into the pool. Unlike perhaps some others who jumped in and said: 'Oh Jesus, help me to avoid these crocodiles'. (Before someone writes in to tell me this incident took place before the mission of Jesus, realize I'm using that hallowed phrase to make a point!).

The ones who had got the message during their training said 'Okay, I know the Lord God of my Being is in charge of my reality'. I know if I utterly believe I am safe, it will be so." They dove right into the crocodile pool wholeheartedly and headfirst. The pool was precisely designed so that if you did that you came down to the very bottom – it's only 14 feet deep – and you ended up at the entrance to a tunnel at the bottom of the pool.

The tunnel is dark, foreboding and claustaphobic (it still exists) but there is no better cure for claustrophobia then a couple of Nile crocodiles snapping at your heels. So, you swim for your life deep into the darkness of the tunnel. It is also fourteen feet long, wide enough for a slim initiate to pass through, but too narrow for a Nile crocodile.

At the end of that dark tunnel you emerge into the bottom of another pool, similar in every way to the one you left, except that there are no crocodiles.

What you had done showed you had grasped the teachings of the second seal. The crocodile pool at Kom Ombo is a heightened paradigm of everyday life. The lesson to be learned is that the most frightening or threatening reality can be changed if we are able to access that state that opens up our power to us. But as Jesus taught, once we start to hope, beg or pray for things to change, we only deepen the problem. That is the vocabulary of doom. What we have presented to the quantum field for manifestation is the absence of the reality for which we are hoping and praying, for we forgot: "Believe it is already yours." Instead all we will succeed in manifesting will be more hoping, begging and praying for what we want.

What did the initiation of the second seal symbolize? The transition from the sub-conscious programs that keep us all imperiled, that keep us marooned spiritually, and don't allow us to make progress. All of these seven temples were in different ways about the work of overcoming those things that keep us blocked and in particular becoming free from the sub-conscious limiting programs. That has always been the great journey.

Sometimes the path of spirituality has veered close to the path of the Great Work, and sometimes it has drifted far away from it, as it has in the main religions today. The essence of the ministry and teachings of Jesus was exactly aligned along the path of the Great Work for true spirituality and the Great Work are the same thing.

The Sixth Temple along the Nile is located in the so-called "King's Chamber," in the Great Pyramid of Giza. The inappropriately named "King's Chamber" was actually the Temple of the Goddess Nut, the Goddess of the Earth. In what did the Initiation of the Sixth Temple consist?

The Initiate now approaching the Temple of the Goddess Nut in the Great Pyramid, has progressed from the initiation of the second seal at Kom Ombo: and gone on to the Temple of the Third Seal at Karnak. Having graduated from there the Initiate would then have journeyed to the Temple of the Fourth Seal at Akenaton's new city, Amarna. After graduation there, the Initiate would then travel to the Step Pyramid at Saqqara, the Temple of the Fifth Seal. Then, at last at Giza, the initiate enters the Temple of the Goddess Nut, the Sixth Seal Temple, within the Great Pyramid.

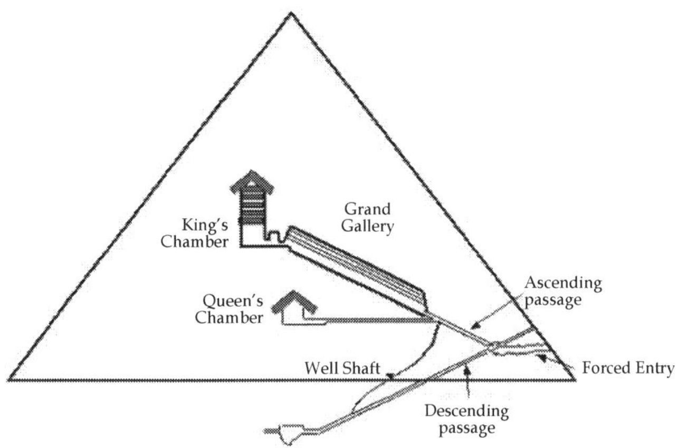

It's said that in its original design the Great Pyramid had no visible entrance. There was an entrance that responded to the mind. By the time you got there you should have been able to activate that entrance.

In 820 AD Caliph al Ma'mun, an Arab governor of Cairo, excavated a tunnel into the Great Pyramid, which suspiciously entered in to the Pyramid just where the ascending and descending passages meet. Some have suggested the original entryway to the Pyramid was known at that time and that the Caliph's men were actually digging out from inside in order to locate some other items of interest. If that were the case, then Al Mamum's tunnel emerged on the north face of the Pyramid and on the level of the 7th course of stone. The original entrance was placed ten courses of stone higher up, and 24 feet further east of the main axis than where Al Ma'mum's tunnel emerged.

The present entryway to the Great Pyramid is through Al Ma'mum's tunnel. It intersects a long, steeply sloping passage, closed to the public, into which the original entrance led. That descending passage is about 344 feet long and slopes down at an angle of approximately 26 degrees. It is almost four feet high and three and a half feet wide. That descending passageway ends up far below the pyramid, in a small chamber, carved by water over the aeons. That small chamber is directly under the apex of the pyramid almost as far beneath the floor of the desert as the peak of the pyramid is above. In the side of the chamber, opposite to where the descending passage enters the room, there is a little passageway, maybe two feet square — less than the size of the escape tunnel from the crocodile pit. For some reason, yet to be discovered, there is a null time frequency at work in that little passageway.

It's said that the Great Pyramid at Giza was built on this spot because of that small chamber. Originally, wooden pyramids were built there over that chamber, and eventually the present stone pyramid was erected in the 12th century BC. In November 2017 it was announced that a new chamber was detected in the Great Pyramid. It is approximately one hundred feet in length and lies above and parallels the Grand Gallery. It was found using a state-of-the-art scanning process called 'muography'.[327]

If you are extremely nice to the people showing you around in Egypt, they will allow you to go down that slope to the chamber, even though it is not open to the public. The sloping passageway is well over three hundred feet long and it's too low to stand up in. A ladder has been installed on the sloping floor of the tunnel, so you can, even with considerable loss of dignity, make the journey.

The Temple of the Goddess Nut[328] is exactly over this null time zone. And up above that you have the Queen's Chamber: so called. If you are on a regular tour of the Great Pyramid of Giza you will be ushered in through the hole that the Arab Sultan blew in the pyramid with dynamite six hundred years ago. You will go up a slope to the King's Chamber. As you go across from there to the chamber itself you may notice in the roof massive granite blocks suspended, for all the world like a set of portcullises in granite,

---

[327] Nature, Accelerated Article Preview Published online, 2 November 2017.

[328] Mother of Osiris, Seth, Isis, Nephthys and Horus. Her name means 'Sky'.

that are there in the ceiling waiting to fall down. I remember when I was going in there I said 'Let's hope there's not an earthquake while I'm in here, because if so I may be in here for eternity'.

When you enter the King's Chamber, to the right, and off-center is a sarcophagus, the famous great stone sarcophagus. If you are allowed to get into that sarcophagus, you will be lying down with your feet towards the nearest wall of the King's Chamber: your head will be extended out towards the middle of the room. In that position your head will be directly beneath the apex of the Great Pyramid, and in line with the null time zone beneath. The structure of the pyramid was designed to amplify the forces of that phenomenon.

If you and I were hypothetically back in the days of Jesus, and we were now promoted to being initiates of the sixth seal, what are the issues of the sixth seal with which we have to wrestle in this initiation? Let's not fool ourselves, we don't know. We knew what the issues of the first seal were. We knew what the issues of the second seal were. And we knew what the issues of the third seal were. Why? Because we are there.

With regard to the issues of the fourth seal, we have some vague dim half-remembered idea of what they might be. What do we realistically know of the issues of the fifth seal? Almost nothing.. The sixth seal? Not a clue. So all we can do is describe what went on in the Temple of the Sixth Seal in the King's Chamber of the Great Pyramid?

In times long gone initiates went in through the bottom of the pyramid blindfolded, and were brought up what we now call The Grand Gallery. You went across to the King's Chamber, entered it and turned sharp right. The priests led you to the side of the stone sarcophagus. You lay down on the floor and were then lifted up by eight priests, four on each side. They laid your body in the great sarcophagus. You were given the most strict instruction not to move, but nothing else.. They put the granite lid, (which was stolen later), on top of you. There were no further instructions.

The first hour goes by and the second hour goes by, and I have an itch somewhere and I can't scratch it and I'm uncomfortable. But above all else is the horrible thought, "How long am I going to be here?" An hour? It was already an hour. Seems like an eternity. Two hours, a day, two days? Maybe I'm supposed to leave my body here. Maybe I'm never going to be taken out, this is it.

Let's say that after two days, I begin to give in to my monkey mind. Instead of not moving my finger, I do. My right hand is lying on the base of this sarcophagus, and it's cold. And I move this index finger because it's at least under conscious control. I move my finger out two inches very cautiously, and I find a vertical obstruction of granite.

Then hoping the gods won't notice, I slide my hand vertically up the wall of granite, and of course at that stage the cause is already lost. I eventually find that there is a huge lid on my prison. Then, getting really alarmed, I pick up my second hand, and I find to my horror that there's this huge stone ceiling on my prison. It's too heavy and immobile for me to know if it is a lid. I try to lift it but it's far too heavy for a single person to lift it or even move. Colossal claustraphobia sets in. After that I speedily lose it altogether. I go into a complete panic. Most people died in that stage of the initiation.

But let's look on the positive side, supposing you didn't do that. How long were you actually supposed to be in the sarcophagus? Seventy-two hours. Why? Because apparently that is the amount of time required for the brain to allow the negative neuronets that create the crippling sub-conscious programs to die. So if I can maintain my presence of mind for seventy-two hours I will come out free of all of those limitations. Of course, I couldn't know that, because if I did know it, it wouldn't work. Why? Because I wouldn't be in agape: I'd be in an acute state of anxiety, waiting for the seventy-two hours to be up.

After the seventy-two hours the priests came back in, took the lid off, made sure my blinders were on properly, and led me out. I had graduated. But now the big difference was, I no longer had crippling programs.

After very careful instruction and preparation, being laid blind in the sarcophagus, with no idea of what was to come, it takes approximately three days and three nights for negative and dis-empowering sub-conscious programs to fade away.

In that perspective, our method of improving our knowledge about matters and allowing the crippling programs to be replaced by better ones, seems eminently more merciful!

Fear and Agape

We are told our DNA has 64 centers of which only a couple are activated. We have also been informed that the key to the activation of all 64 centers is to replace one of the great foundational emotions with the other. There are only two emotions fundamentally – fear and agape. If we can address fear, which is the root of all negative emotions, then we're free. The basic form of fear is the fear of death. Every other fear is rooted in that, according to Egyptian Wisdom. The initiation in Egypt I discussed was about addressing the fear of death. If we can remove that, all other fears will fall away and the greatest block to our spiritual empowerment will be gone.

It is customary to be treated much more gently these days than way back in those halcyon days in Egypt, when, literally we were thrown into the initiation head first. I am describing it in very basic terms as the removal of the fear of death. That was the purpose of the Temple of the Sixth Seal. Lying there for seventy-two hours and not knowing what, if anything, would happen, will surely bring up that fundamental fear.

What is the initiate desiring to attain? We don't know, because we are not able to understand or express it adequately. But we know what needs to be removed in order to understand what it is we are gaining. As mentioned above, we can understand the issues of the first and the second and the third seals, and the fourth to some degree. Beyond that we're still struggling.

The initiation of the sixth temple wasn't always done in the Great Pyramid. The same process was conducted in another center nearby. Jesus went through that initiation in the site near the Great Pyramid.

Many individuals going through that discipline lost their reason. Despite all the instructions, acute claustrophobia would set in, but once you moved your finger and started to feel the edges of the sarcophagus, in which you realized you now were, you were in deep trouble. Once you begin to try to lift the lid you're done for. Three days and three nights with the absolute minimum of sensory input is the required time for all the negative neuronets of the brain to lose their sustenance. Because they are not fed, they starve to death.

Where do we go next if we graduate from Giza? The Temple of the Seventh seal at the Temple of Heliopolis. Some traditions recount that Jesus was also there during the flight into Egypt away from the Tetrarch Herod Antipas, and also later when he was returning from the East to begin his public ministry in the Holy Land. The Temple of Heliopolis was about a real confrontation with what had been confronted symbolically at Giza.

We Are Already Immortal: What Are the Implications?

Graduating from the Temple of the Sixth Seal involved a symbolic confrontation with death in the sarcophagus. You didn't know if you would ever come out of it or even if you were supposed to come out of it. But if you could control your emotions sufficiently, then all the negative neuronets, all the programs, would be gone when the test was ended. That realization indicates the next step.

It's often said the biggest burden for a human being is the realization that we are mortal. But a little reflection will clarify that considerably, for we can see that in fact our really big issue is not the desire for immortality since at the level where it really counts, we are already immortals. We are all Gods. The heart and core of what I am will live forever. I cannot go out of existence, no matter how much I might want to in states of acute depression, nor how much I try. If I'm sufficiently neurotic, that could become my biggest nightmare — I can't die. I can't escape.

Some people commit suicide because they can't take life any longer. They think they're going to go into nothingness. By trying to end your life you have just made matters worse. Our biggest burden, or our biggest glory, depending on one's viewpoint, is that we are already immortal. It is impossible for us to cease to exist. Nothing can be done about that — it's already too late.

What then is our biggest challenge? Physical mortality. Normally we get to know each other, whether as partners, or even parents and children, or friends, only on the relatively superficial level of the personality. We often don't get to know each other in any deeper way than that. If that is the case, then, when someone dies physically, the person that we knew is gone, and gone for ever, for that personality ceased to exist along with the embodiment in the physical plane.

We have some very comforting beliefs about the loss of loved ones in death, in Christianity especially, but also in Islam. These beliefs teach us that even though the person has died, say my beloved mother, my beloved father, my beloved wife, my beloved husband or child, even though they are dead, they're still out there somewhere stacked up waiting for me to join them. Of course, they may well be, but if that's the case it's because they haven't gone on as they should. But at some stage they have to go on, and when they do, then that personality in which we knew them is gone, and it's gone permanently.

That's an horrific thought to people who never knew each other except on the level of the personality. In such a case, even if someone very close to them is reincarnated, and it is known of whom the individual is the reincarnation, there still isn't any strong bond or attraction between them any more, because the reincarnated loved one is no longer as we knew them. The bond or attraction vanished along with the personality of the physical body.

The great goal for us all, which is what Jesus came to address, was not to attain immortality of the person, but to attain immortality of the physical body. Is it possible? Yes. That is what this set of temples along the Nile was also designed to accomplish. So if I graduated from the Temple of the Goddess Nut in the King's Chamber, I'm now qualified to advance to the Temple of the Seventh Seal, at Heliopolis.

Persistence at Heliopolis

To day the ruins of the great Temple of Heliopolis, the Temple of the Seventh Seal, is not on the tourist route, to put it mildly. The area of Heliopolis is now in the north eastern suburbs of Cairo. In most versions of the Hebrew scriptures the city was called On. Heliopolis comes from the Greek, meaning "City of the Sun," and its Temple was the cult center for the Sun gods Ra and Atum.

The site of the Temple itself these days is marked by twenty-five acres of devastation covered with earth, about a mile west of the modern area named Heliopolis. An excavation was done in the 1960s which uncovered a stone doorway, a little larger than the average doorway, then a second doorway at right angles to the first. Straight ahead lies the ancient Holy of Holies of the Temple, a small room, and the remains of the walls are only about four to five feet high. This room was the center of the ancient Temple. In the excavation of the 1960's only the two gateways and the site of the Holy of Holies itself was excavated.

I was on a visit to Egypt in August 1996. The night before I departed for Egypt I got a short video which described the seven Temples along the Nile and the function. The video said that Heliopolis was the heart of the matter in Egypt, and that Jesus had been there. I had been given a gift of this trip to mark my retirement as President of our College in Ireland, and the gift included the services of a guide, a little minibus with a driver, and a third person, whose function I never quite figured out.

Over many protests, I managed to persuade my little party to take me to see the ruins of the Temple of Heliopolis. To say it wasn't on the tourist route was the understatement of all time. My guides did not know how to get there. Modern Heliopolis is one of the top grade residential areas of Cairo. But as you keep going towards the site of the ancient Temple, you enter some of the worst slums I've seen anywhere. There were no vehicles, just donkeys, camels and people. The guide was getting more and more nervous and said to me 'Look out there. We're the only vehicle within miles of here. Do you know what's going to happen to us; we're going to be attacked. They'll rob us, maybe kill us, and then burn the mini bus. What am I going to say to my boss?' Well I said 'Given what you've said, you won't have to say anything, because you'll be dead' That remark didn't improve matters.

We eventually arrived at an ancient obelisk in the heart of the slums, and they thought I'd be happy to see that, and that we could go home. But I insisted that I was looking for three doorways. There were several ancient doorways set into a concrete wall near the obelisk and the guide pointed those out to me in despair. and I said 'Not those, the doorways I am looking for you can walk through.' My relationship with my guides was now near irretrievable breakdown, but just at the right moment an old man wearing a dirty white robe and turban approached us and said he knew of another place. The driver unceremoniously bundled him into the front seat of the minibus. He said to the guides that he had never been in a motor vehicle before. We drove for a few minutes and came to a walled enclosure, which we discovered surrounded the ancient ruins of the Temple of Heliopolis.

Unfortunately, nobody is allowed to go in there. Three soldiers with automatic rifles were guarding the gateway. By now my guide was even more upset and uncomfortable. I asked him to speak for me to the chief military person at the gate as I didn't speak Arabic, and to tell him I would like to go inside to see the ruins. He went over to the person in charge and explained that I was a very distinguished person from Europe and I absolutely needed to go in there. The guard said: Sorry you can't go in here'. The guide came back and told me all this. I asked him to go back and tell the soldiers that I need to go in there and I'll be very grateful if they let me in'. He went back again and talked with the three guards and they all said "No."

Relations between European explorers and the Egyptian authorities in charge of the antiquities had not been good since the discoveries made by robots in shafts of the Great Pyramid under the guidance of the German Robotics engineer, Rudolph Gantenbrink three years before. He explored an 8" square shaft in the great Pyramid, that was 220 feet in length, that ended with a mysterious door with handles. No one could figure out what the handles were for in such an inaccessible space. The bottom line was that relations between Gantenbrink and the Egyptian authorities had deteriorated very badly, and the disagreements had left an antagonism against any Europeans trying to explore any of the Egyptians antiquities that were off the tourist track. Nothing could have been further off the tourist track than the ruins of the Temple of Heliopolis to which I was now trying to gain admittance.

The Egyptians are a very polite people and they don't easily tell you to get lost. The guide came back and told me there was no way the military were going to allow me to go in. I asked the guide, "Do any of them know some English?" I went over to the soldiers in the gateway and said 'I have come eight thousand miles to see this site and I absolutely need to get inside for a short while.'

I said I only needed five minutes, but they said 'I am so sorry, Sahib, so sorry'. I said 'You don't understand. I am not leaving here till I see these ruins.'"

The Egyptians, as I said, are a very polite and patient people. The soldiers brought out six chairs and placed them in the gateway, three chairs facing three. The three soldiers sat down on one side and the guide and I and the driver sat down on the other. They served tea. Then they sent a boy on a bicycle with a note to the Manager who lived about a mile away. He came on a bicycle within about fifteen minutes. I don't know what they said to him in the note: presumably, "We have this crank here who just won't go away." The Manager arrived just after we had finished our tea. The manager did speak English and I said to him 'You know this spot is the major archeological site in all of Egypt, this particular spot'. He laughed uproariously and said "You mean it's greater than Giza or Abu Simbel? Nobody comes here; there's nothing to see." I said 'Yes, this is the most significant site in Egypt, the last and greatest of the seven Temples along the Nile, representing the seven seals of the human body. I've come all of these thousands of miles to see this little area not even one hundred yards wide'.

The manger gave up the ghost and said: 'Okay, you can go in for five minutes; you will have a soldier on either side of you;

you can't bring your driver, and you can't bring the guide. You are to touch nothing, take no photos, and come back out pronto'. I said 'Deal'.

So, we went down the slope and through the first stone doorway, then the second stone doorway. The pathway then turned sharp left (a dimensional shift in sacred geometry) and led straight into the small enclosure of the Holy of Holies. The remains of the walls were only four or five feet high at most and the ruins of the room were no more than, at most, fifteen or twenty feet wide and long.

The previous night I had a dream that when Jesus accomplished what he was here to do he went back to his teachers at Heliopolis. They acknowledged what he had accomplished, and invited him to stand on a circular polished stone in the Holy of Holies, so that they could do him honor. That pedestal was reserved for the first person who would accomplish what the seven Temples of the Nile were constructed to facilitate: the overcoming of physical death.

I found out later that the substance of the incident is told in "The Aquarian Gospel of Jesus the Christ."

In my dream I had seen that circular polished stone, about three feet wide, on the left hand side of the room. I contemplated the sacredness of this spot for a moment, and then said to the two soldiers 'I need to go over here and dig with my hand in the dust'. They said 'You can't touch anything'. But I insisted on digging in the dust, so they called up to the Manager and he said to go ahead, but to hurry as I had only one minute left. I went over and dug down about three or four inches into the dry dust until I came to a polished stone. I dug out to the edge and along the edge: it was curved, I knew I had found the pedestal. So, I stood for a moment on the dust above the pedestal where long ago Jesus had stood to be acknowledged in the Holy of Holies of the Temple of the Seventh Seal.

The Manager called out that my five minutes were up, so we climbed back up the slope to the gateway. Honor was saved all round. I felt that by getting in at all I had somehow successfully undergone some of the initiations associated with the Temples of the Nile! The Manager, the soldiers, and the little boy messenger on the bicycle were happy to get a generous baksheesh; nobody was killed or robbed, the minibus wasn't burned, we all lived to tell the tale, and everyone went home happy.

Physical Immortality

What was the purpose of the Seventh Seal Temple at Heliopolis? In the King's Chamber at Giza you underwent a symbolic death in the sarcophagus. The experience cleaned out the crippling subconscious programs, albeit in a very merciless way. At Heliopolis you had to undergo a real physical death and raise your own body back to life, or raise someone else back to life. The first person to accomplish that would be invited to stand on the pedestal in the Holy of Holies while the achievement was honored. According to the Aquarian Gospel, Jesus was the first one to accomplish that goal.

Can we achieve physical immortality or is it even desirable? We can. What's the price? Giving up what by right we should already have lost anyway: my crippling limitations.

Why would I want to live on indefinitely when so many of those I love may have passed on before me? Why would I not wish to lay down the body to enjoy the much greater realms that exist in frequencies far above this material one? Have we forgotten that if we raise our consciousness as Jesus taught us, then we will access those same glorious realms without having to endure the body's physical decline, its eventual death and the loss of all its wisdom and memories? That is what true freedom and liberation consists in, and it is the ultimate possible experience of any incarnation.

Are some little bells beginning to ring now in our minds? Are we getting the hints of what Jesus was really about, and what he wanted us to be about? Remember he got this teaching in Egypt.

Other sources like the Aquarian Gospel say he was in Heliopolis a second time on his way back from India and Tibet. From there he went to meet John the Baptist at the Jordan when he was twenty-nine. I suppose Heliopolis was a sort of finishing school.

He went to Israel for his public ministry, which lasted only two years and nine months. The idea in the forefront of his mind was that the supreme test of human evolution and accomplishment was to have taken out so much garbage that the power of the spirit could come forth in all its power into your being on this plane. If so, the spirit could function without being impeded by the body, it could help the body and even raise the body back to life from catastrophic illness or even death. That was his agenda, it's his agenda for all of us. We are already immortal. What we need is immortality of the physical incarnation.

The destiny of Jesus was to live this out, and show that death was really a no thing. Death is the great primordial fear. The only thing that makes death a reality is grimly clinging to our own limitations.

The counterpart of fear is love or joy, which is the flow of what God is. As both the Book of Genesis and Saint Paul in the Epistle to the Romans said, death was never meant to be a natural thing.

That begins to give us another clue of what Jesus was really about. It really wasn't about him falling foul of the public authorities that brought him to his death. And somehow God raised him up because he didn't deserve to die. No. He came into the Holy Land with a very, very powerful agenda. He was on his way to an initiation of a most profound kind. It wasn't anything to do with being a Suffering Savior. It had everything to do with the transition process along the seven temples of the Nile. As Jesus said: "Whatever I can do, you too can do, and greater".

Fearing the Future or Planning for the Future?

Can we imagine the potentials for us if death and sickness, and all the fears and worries that are rooted ultimately in the fear of death were no longer of any significance? Do we yet realize the difference between responsibly planning for the future, and fearing the future?

What a change the realization of all this would bring to the world. We've more or less pushed things to the limit right now, so the achievement of imitating that example of Jesus seems perhaps more remote than ever.

What if we begin to get a suspicion, from contemplating those hidden years of Jesus, that there was much more going on in what he did, and what he said, and went through, than is conveyed by the sanitized, homogenized, pasteurized, versions of his teachings that we've been fed for so long. A lot more was going on than that. A lot of much more powerful stuff was being perpetrated. No wonder Mary his mother, that glorious, unfortunate, gifted being, was so puzzled. A lot more of unimaginable promise for you and me today was being accomplished.

The two great symbols from Jesus are Baptism and the Eucharist. Both precede Jesus by a very long time. Baptism symbolizes our return into the primordial substance from which everything was made, and emerging born into a new form.

The second great symbol, also from long, long, before Jesus, was the Eucharist, the sacred meal, which he enacted in his Last Supper with his disciples on the night before he was arrested.

This sacred meal goes back thousands of years to the great Mystery Schools of the high mountains of Kashmir, Tibet and India, and many other places. The elements in the enactment of the Eucharist symbolize the deepest realities about human nature, and its potentials for you and me. In those ancient schools the elements that made up the meal were extremely sacred. Bread, wine and water came directly from the Creator, Point Zero.

The bread, symbolized the physical incarnation. On this level, it represents the physical body we're looking at. On the level immediately above this, there is also a body, the infra red, and on the level above that, the light, there is a body, and in the level above that, the ultraviolet, there is a body and so on. To use a modern term, these bodies we all have are modems that interact with the specific frequency planes of our being, to which they belong.

The water, which is added to the wine in this symbolic meal, symbolized the soul, which keeps the memory of experiences from the sixth plane downwards. It is the recorder of the experiences and all the things we still need to own in order to be free.

Back to Quantum Physics. Whatever we accept, believe profoundly, truly, deeply, whatever we focus on, is going to manifest. Why? Because we ourselves are magnetizing it into our reality. The quantum field sees no difference between manifesting glorious things or misery; neither is there any difference in manifesting what we regard as small things or great things. One is not more difficult than the other in the quantum field, but we have mistakenly accepted that there is only so much we can hope to accomplish until we get really good at this. The quantum field does not recognize such a distinction. There is no difference in manifesting the small or the great. The difference exists only in our minds. The choice is entirely ours, but it takes a long time to truly realize that.

The Eucharist, the sacred meal of the bread, wine and water was the ultimately profound ceremony. It was designed specifically eons ago to unify the spirit, soul and the body, and to transmute it, as Jesus taught.

All of the seven sacraments were and still are profound rites of initiation if performed in the proper way. Are they normally performed nowadays in that way? Rarely.

I used to help out in a parish in this country during my Summer vacations. A Mass was scheduled at 6.00 am, we had another at 7.00, another at 8.30, another at 10.00, one at 12.00 and one at 1.00 pm. What was the focus of these re-enactments of the "Eucharist Meal" of the Last Supper of Jesus?

It is said when a Master breaks bread and hands it around to his disciples, he has the ability to convey his own DNA to the recipients through the bread. By eating that bread the disciples are elevating their own physicality in frequency. Jesus asked the participants of that Last Super to do this in commemoration of him. It is rightly assumed that the transformation of the bread through the power of Jesus still occurs in that ceremony.

Is this the normal focus in a busy parish on a Sunday morning, or is there too much emphasis on getting the parking lot empty before the next congregation comes in? How can you enact a sacred rite, a mystic initiation, in such a context?

What we do need to realize is that there is nothing ultimately wrong with Christianity. In fact, some of the most wonderful things done in human history have been done by Christian communities. Likewise, they have done some of the most horrendous things. But that doesn't say that their belief system is advantageous. It's not. So why are these rites not as powerful as they then were? Because we have to squash them into time frames and molds into which they don't fit.

The cross has become the symbol of Christianity for a very long time. Indeed it has become the very symbol of Jesus himself. But the cross is far more ancient than that. In ancient times it symbolized the harmony of the vertical and the horizontal. What's vertical? Coming down through the planes of frequency. What's the horizontal? What I experience, and own in living my life today.

But the symbol of the crucifix with the nailed body of Jesus is a different matter entirely. The crucifix is not the cross. It represents the execution by the Romans of criminals; it was most certainly not at the heart of what Jesus was about. We've come to venerate a symbol of an agonizing death, which I am sure would strike Jesus as very odd. Venerating the crucifix is the same thing as hanging an image of an electric chair or gallows around our necks.

It was only at the end of the seventh century, in the year 692 AD, that Emperor Justinian II said the crucifix should replace the bare cross, with no figure on it, which had been the symbol of Christianity up till then. That was an accurate representation of the ancient faith that came from Jesus, the bare cross, which was not a reminder of his passion, but of the reconciliation of the horizontal with the vertical: reconciliation of the descent and the experience. In that significance it's one of the most ancient of all symbols which you will find from the Near East, down into India, and South America, without having any reference to Jesus.

What did it symbolize in those ancient cultures? Certainly not an execution or a crucifixion, because there was no such thing in most of these cultures as crucifixion. It symbolized the harmony of the planes. It symbolized the transcendent and the immanent. The bare cross symbolized the unification of God-man, God-woman realized. It indicated a state of complete harmony had taken possession of all of the being of a living person, so that they became a Christ. The cross is the form or symbol of Spirit successfully incarnated into matter, to wit, Christhood. It was the key to how the universe worked.

Even mathematics later drew on this symbol: the cross became the symbol of increase, and when placed at an angle, it became the sign of multiplication, or progression in a forward movement.

In paganism and early Christianity the cross always symbolized life, never death. The first depiction of a being on a cross is of Orpheus from the third century before Christ. But sad to say, for a great part of the world's population the central religious symbol is a person impaled in agony on an instrument of torture. You might say, you know, this is an indication of how much Jesus was determined to die for us. But he didn't die for us in the sense of appeasing the anger of a very vengeful God.

In some warped way some religions say today that the crucifix is an image pleasing to God. On the other hand, an empty cross symbolizes the decent from spirit into flesh, and the seven bodies, and it celebrates the evolution of that life back into its return. What does the crucifix do by contrast? It idealizes suffering and death; an attitude which is fundamentally not of God. It would be hard to find a symbol that misrepresents Jesus so drastically as the crucifix does. It's a travesty that has now, unfortunately, become the central symbol of his mission.

In some archeological remains we find a serpent crucified on a bare cross. The cross has arms of equal length to symbolize harmony. It is common in illustrations in the hermetic and esoteric traditions.

What did the crucified serpent symbolize? As mentioned earlier, many ancient cultures regarded the serpent as having immortality. The serpent also symbolizes what we in the West would call the kundalini force, the life force that circulates through the human being. That force is impaled on a cross of equal arms. What does that symbolize? That we have brought the life force of immortality into harmony and expression in our lives. We haven't done it by repression, but by owning we've conquered ourselves.

Does the crucifixion of Jesus on the cross begin to take on a different impression? Much more than that he fell afoul of the wrong people? There was much more going on here than we think.

But there is even more when we ponder the times. In ancient times, puberty extended to the age of thirty-two. By that time, you had probably married and raised a family. Hopefully you had worked through a lot of your stuff. You were ready to move on to much more wonderful things. By the age of thirty-three you were really ready to take on the Great Work of human evolution, spiritually and materially.

The crucifixion of the kundalini force on the cross of resolution at the age of thirty-three, freed you for a new endeavor, so obviously the crucifixion and the time at which it occurred, has a much deeper symbolism, and we begin to see a different dimension to the passion; especially when we contemplate the time of year at which it occurred.

All the great festivals of the year are grouped around the time at which this happened in the life of Jesus. We have Passover in Judaism; Naw Ruz in the Persian culture. We have Maimuna in the Arab world. (We should not forget to note that the Persians are not Arabs). After the time of Jesus we have Easter.

Why are they all grouped around this time? What was the period that gives it significance?

The Spring Equinox used to be New Year's Day in saner times. Why do we have New Year's Day on the 31st of December now? Because January is named after the Roman God Janus, who had two heads, one looking one way, and one looking the opposite way. They felt that this was a good month to have us looking backwards at the past and onwards towards the future, and hence the year should change on that date. A much more logical time to have New Year's day would be the Spring Equinox, but it's too late to do anything about that now, so let's focus on more worthwhile objectives!

At the Spring Equinox and from there forward, the sun is waxing towards its full power, at least in the northern hemisphere. In ancient times it was reckoned to be an enormously propitious period in the year when the forces of nature were awakening and would favor any new enterprise. We would do well to remember that, especially if embarking on any creative new life. We all know gardeners are recommended to plant when the moon is waxing, not waning. How about when the entire year is waxing?

The ancients advised us to keep an eye on the sun in addition to the moon. The best time in the year to embark on a new endeavor, over and above gardening, is when the sun is waxing towards the Summer solstice, which is from the 25th of March into June. That's the time to start any new endeavor. I suppose you've noticed that Ramtha founded his school on Easter day.

The four great festivals of the ancient world, especially among the Druids, were interspersed between the solstice seasons and the equinoxes. For example, Samhain, the great new year feast of the Celts, was on November 1st, halfway between the Autumn Equinox and the Winter Solstice. The feast of Imbolc, on February 2nd, now Saint Brigid's Day, was the Spring festival, halfway between the Winter Solstice and the Spring Equinox. The feast of Bealtaine was halfway between the Spring Equinox and the Summer Solstice, while the feast of Lunasa was interspersed between the Summer Solstice and the Autumn Equinox. Christianity replaced all those festivals with a religious equivalent.

The most magnificent discourse of Jesus, in which he encapsulated all of his message, was what we now call the Sermon on the Mount. It was delivered during the time when he decided to commit himself to the experience of Passover that led to his arrest. But in the Sermon on the Mount, which was delivered on a grassy hillside on the Western side of the Lake, there is not a single idea that's not also found in the Jewish Mishmar, the Talmud.

Four great themes of the Buddha correspond to the central themes of the Sermon on the Mount.

Jesus' standing in the Old Testament tradition is recognized by all scholars. But what's not as widely accepted is how much Jesus stands in the dead center of other traditions as well, like the traditions of the Hermetic books of Egypt. The seventh book of Hermes was called The Secret Sermon on the Mount.

With fresh and informed eyes we can look back at so many things. Saint Francis of Assisi is credited with introducing the ox and the ass into the representation of the crib at Christmas. Would it surprise us to know that in ancient times in the Holy of Holies at the Temple of the Third Seal at Karnak, in Egypt, there is a depiction of a birth in a stable with angels singing, shepherds calling by, an ox and an ass? All of this took place exactly 1,700 years before the birth of Jesus.

All recognize that Jesus quotes Old Testament figures. Some scholars have recognized the allusions he makes. And at the bottom of every good translation of the New Testament today you may be happy enough to find references to them, maybe not. His audience would have recognized them without the footnotes.

The teachings of the Buddha Gautama and Jesus were both world-subverting. They taught a way of life that transformed themselves and everybody who followed them in that knowledge. It was about imitation of the path they had laid out. That way was far more important than knowledge, however important knowledge undoubtedly was. The similarity between Jesus and the Buddha lies mainly in the way. That was central to everything for both of them. The way would open up an entirely new way of being. What would it yield? The ultimate thing to be yielded would be physical immortality, but of course that is only the introduction to what is now made possible by this new dimension of existence.

There are of course also enormous differences between the teachings of Jesus and the Buddha. For instance, Jesus was an ardent campaigner for social change in a way the Buddha never was. He stood in the true tradition of the Prophets of Israel who campaigned to their great personal peril for social change. But the similarities are far more obvious.

Even if we had never heard of Nicolas Notovitch and the Issa Scrolls, you and I would be very dull people indeed, if we didn't suspect that Jesus had lived in Egypt, India and Tibet. The clues are all over the place. Does that mean that Jesus plagiarized the Buddha and the other great Masters that resonate to the same themes prior to his time? Obviously not. The truth is that each of them came from the same source that was prior to them all.

Buddhism arose as a heresy of Hinduism. The origins of Hinduism are lost in the mists of history. It is highly likely that its message originated in a famous instruction of 120 days, thirty-five centuries ago.

It was not the custom of Jesus to quote the Jewish prophets, and he never quoted the Buddha either. But some of the most famous elements of the teachings of Jesus are also found in the Buddha's writings, five hundred and fifty years previously.

Consider The Parable of the Sower. A sower went out to sow his seed and as he cast his seed some fell by the wayside and some were trodden down. The birds of the air devoured them. Some here and some fell there and some fell on fertile ground, yet yielded fruit a hundred fold.

The seed falls in very different soils.

What are the soils? They represent the level of tenacity with which I cling to my negativity as my identity, with which I cling to my sub-conscious programs.

The Buddha told that parable five hundred years before Jesus did. The Parable of the Treasure in the Field is also in the Buddha. So is the admonition that 'Though heaven and Earth pass away, my words will never pass away'. And the statement of Jesus about how easily we see the speck in our brother's eye, found in Luke 6:41-42, is also in the teachings of the Buddha. The faults of others are more easily seen than my own. Nevertheless, they offer a great clue to realizing that if I notice faults in other people it's very probable that I have those same faults, probably to a superlative degree, in myself. They are so deeply buried as a part of me that I can more readily see them mirrored to me in others. But that requires humility to acknowledge. The greater ability to see faults in others rather than in ourselves is taught in the Dhammapada of the Buddha[329], a collection of the Buddha's sayings in verse form; one of the most frequently read sections of the Buddhist scriptures.

The admonition of Jesus to 'do unto others as you would like them to do to you' is also in the teachings of the Buddha. Jesus said 'whoever looks at a woman with lust in our heart has already committed adultery with her' – in the quantum field, which is the only place where it really matters. The Buddha said 'Commit no adultery. The law is broken by even looking at the wife of another man with lust in your mind.'

Lord Krishna said in Hinduism 'I am the Alpha, I am the Beginning, I am the End, the Alpha and Omega', which Jesus

[329] Chapter 27.

said, of course, in the Book of Revelation.[330] And both Krishna and Jesus tell their disciples that he will dwell with them, and they with him forever.

Jesus said in the Gospel of Luke, Chapter 6, "If anyone strikes you on the cheek offer the other." Why? Because you're a patsy? No, because this is not the way to deal with it. There is another way. Buddha gives exactly the same advice and expands on it. Jesus said 'love your enemies, do good to those who hate you, bless those who curse you, pray for those that abuse you'. Why? Because if you don't you are just going to make matters worse. Rise to the state of agape and it will solve the problem, and also everything else that's trailing in its wake.

Buddha said 'Hatreds don't ever cease in this world by hating, but by love. Overcome anger by love, evil by good, the miser by generosity, the liar by truth'.

It is amazing how some Christians react to even attempting to show the close parallels between the teachings of the Buddha and the teachings of Jesus. It's almost as if they understand you to say that somehow Jesus was infringing the Buddha's copyright. The heart of the matter is that both were testifying to an ancient wisdom that preceded both of them by aeons.

---

[330] Revelation 22:13.

Chapter 22
Aligning Our Three Brains

As we have seen in this book, the greatest issue facing us when we try to make sense of human existence, is not about justifying the existence of an all-powerful and loving God faced with the tragically imperfect world we know. The greatest challenge facing us is to realize that what happens to me, and to humanity in general, is the result of a conspiracy of sorts between the deepest level of what we have accepted within us, and the quantum field.

Everything that exists in our frequency swims in a sea of energy emanating from its source, many levels above us. Everything has descended from that source. Our minds are constantly broadcasting to that sea of energy how we believe reality is or ought to be: in short, our accepted convictions are magnetizing their mirror images into my life. This magnetizing is occurring 24/7, not just in the all too rare moments when I manage to step apart from "the madding crowd."[331]

Enlightening us as to how best engage this reality was the heart of the message of Jesus. If we find this statement strange it is simply an indication of how far all of us have drifted from understanding, not just the core of his message, but the very framework within which it was elaborated.

If everything that happens to me is a result of this dance between the deepest levels of me and the energy of the quantum field, then obviously we should be alerted that we have a lot of housekeeping to do, and a lot of realities to which we need to awaken.

One of the most important of those is to realize what experts in the field started to understand not very long ago, that we just do not have a single brain in the cranium that is radiating these magnetizing thoughts to the quantum field. We apparently also

---

[331] Thomas Hardy, 1874, *Far from the Madding Crowd*, 1874. In 2007 it was nominated 10th on *The Guardian*'s list of the greatest love stories of all time.

have at least two other massive neural networks in our bodies, that equally deserve to be called "brains, but with very distinct roles." These two other centers exist in the heart area and the gut. This realization explains the unease we often sense between what we think and what we feel. These centers, particularly the heart brain, are also magnetizing reality to us out of the quantum field, just as really, and perhaps even more powerfully than the cranial brain.

On average, a cranial brain has nearly 80 billion neurons and is the seat of all our thinking, imaging, and verbal expression, which is probably why we have nearly always identified it as "the brain." We also know that the brain sends signal down to the heart to control its functioning, but were not aware until relatively recently that the heart sends far more signals up to the brain than the heart receives from the brain.

But if we ask someone to indicate where they feel emotion, they will not place their hand on their knee, or on top of their head, but above their heart. Deep down instinct tells us that this is the area where deep emotions are processed. The heart brain is the home of what we believe in, and of the things we value and treasure. It is the domain of feelings.

The electrical voltage of the heart brain is about 60 times greater than the electrical field of the cranial brain, and its magnetic field is approximately 5,000 times stronger than the magnetic field produced by the cranial brain.[332]

"This field can be measured several feet away from the body with sensitive magnetometers. These energetic emanations and interactions provide a plausible mechanism for how we can "feel" or sense another person's presence and even their emotional state, independent of body language and other signals."[333]

It should be obvious then that if the cranial brain and the heart brain are in conflict, what is profoundly accepted in the heart brain

[332] Energy cardiology: A dynamical energy systems approach for integrating conventional and alternative medicine. Advances, 12 (4), 4-24.

[333] McCraty, R. (2004). The Energetic Heart: Bioelectromagnetic Communication Within and Between People. In P. J. Rosch & M. S. Markov (Eds.), Bioelectromagnetic Medicine, (pp. 541-562). New York, NY: Marcel Dekker.

will very easily overcome what the cranial brain is radiating into the Quantum Field.

Or, to put it in another way, if I want to manifest something out of the quantum field it would seem to be imperative that I project it to the quantum field through the heart brain.

In short, from my conscious mind in the cranium, there is little point in loudly proclaiming that I am "radiantly happy," or 'fabulously wealthy,' if some other powerful centers within me may be radiating an opposite frequency into the quantum field. The plot thickens when we remember that the magnetic field of the heart brain is up to 5,000 times stronger than the cranial brain. I may shout out that I am "radiantly happy" from the conscious cranial brain, while suppressing how miserable I actually feel in my heart. But we must not forget that that energetic field of misery that I am, almost sub-consciously, radiating into the quantum field, is 5,000 times the strength of the cranial brain's proclamation of joy. No prizes for figuring what will manifest. In fact, the louder and more emphatically I shout out something positive and wonderful, the surer it is to be an indication of how doubtful I am about it ever manifesting.

Can we ponder from where those crippling programs and images of Jesus as the Suffering Savior are radiating their convictions to the quantum field? We can rest assured it is not solely from the cranial brain.

The third brain lies in the gut. The gut (or digestive system of the body) has approximately 500 million nerve cells and 100 million neurons, and it has been compared in terms of capability to the brain of a small animal, such as a cat or dog.

Here is where the line is drawn in the sand. The gut brain is where I know what is me, and what is definitely not me. It is the home of fear, self-preservation and security.

If, after two thousand years of indoctrination, I have come to accept that Jesus came here to suffer and die for my sins, to appease the vengeance of a vindictive God, and that the essence of Jesus is to be meek and mild, I now realize where those convictions, and the companion sub-conscious programs, have their home: in the brain of the heart, whose magnetic field is 5,000 times stronger than that of the cranial brain. Knowledge, research, learning of all kinds, is at home in the cranial brain. It is not enough. We have to engage the heart. But we cannot enlist the power of the heart on our side unless we can manage to embark on dissolving the crippling programs that over-ride all understanding and research.

There is another reason. If I can set up a situation in which I imagine myself speaking from the heart about some issue that confronts me, I will probably find that, speaking from the heart, I am speaking in the present, and that what I say feels authentic and real. Whereas, if I imagine myself speaking from my mind, (which has become our habit in the West, and is how we tend to assess objectivity), then I find I am speaking out of a sense of caution, fear, and do's and don'ts.

As mentioned a few pages back, our greatest challenge in making sense of human destiny and purpose, is not reconciling the kind of world we have with the existence of a benign and all-powerful God, which has been the central issue in almost all significant philosophical and religious movements. This is where we need the Copernican revolution referred to earlier; we don't just need more information and better perspectives, we need a paradigm shift.

The big challenge is to realize that what we have uncritically assumed is not what reality is about at all. It was this fact that Jesus came to teach us, and how to manifest reality ourselves, but of course it was distorted beyond recognition. The human race badly needed a savior when he came, every bit as much as we do now, not to save us from the vengeance of a savage God, but to rescue us from our own crippling programs and the conviction that other people, agencies and powers from outside me are what have decided, and continue to constitute, my reality. The heart of that process is the theme of this short chapter: enlisting on to our side the power of the heart and gut brains to create in the quantum field.

It was that which formed the heart of that embarrassing interlude on the lake shore at early morning, when Jesus basically asked Peter three times if he understood how crucial attaining the state of agape was to the successful manifestation of what he really wanted out of the quantum field. Peter's response was confined to 'figuring out,' to wondering what Jesus wanted, (cranial brain) with an overall profound sense of guilt for his three betrayals (gut brain).

The centrality of the heart brain was always prominent in the traditions of the East, but never really grasped to any degree in the West, except in the wisdom traditions. The realization of the three brains in the human body, with their very different functions, basically asserts three forms of intelligence in every human being. The wisdom traditions take for granted three forms of soul. In Christianity, we probably have a correspondence to that when we talk about 'body,' "soul" and 'spirit.'

Jesus placed an enormous emphasis on the paramount importance of forgiveness. It wasn't just to make us agreeable people, or to make sure we didn't go to Hell when we died. He emphasized it because the letting go of forgiveness is one of the great essentials for successful manifestation in the quantum field. Our sense of who we are resides in the gut brain, as mentioned already. In major matters needing forgiveness, it is our sense of who we are that has been assailed. So, it must be out of the gut brain that forgiveness comes.

Many people think that forgiveness for something serious is an affair of the heart, but it is not, for what has occurred that so sorely needs forgiveness is some form of trespass on our boundaries, something that has attacked my sense of security or identity. People who can't manage to forgive may come eventually to the realization that their hate or resentment is poisoning them, and that they can't move until it is released, and the release needs to come from the area of the gut brain.

In short it is not hard to see that forgiveness is really something we do for ourselves not for others, and it is equally clear that forgiveness is a characteristic of those who are strong. If someone has injured us we will almost certainly feel hurt and offended and almost inevitably bitter. That is what we feel, but somewhere deep down is probably an illusion that not forgiving will somehow teach the offender a lesson. Nothing could be further from the truth. The person who committed the injury may feel nothing, so, in effect,

I have become my own jailer by refusing to let the resentment and bitterness go. We are in effect serving a jail sentence for a crime somebody else committed. Recognition that the impact of the offense was felt most in the gut brain will help towards a resolution, because we begin to understand that no matter what particular shape it took, fundamentally as I perceived it, it was all about an attack on my self-worth whose home is in the gut brain.

Betrayal is something others do to us, but holding bitterness is something we do to ourselves, and bitterness and the holding of grudges are the ultimate agents that destroy Agape. Emmet Fox put it well back in the '30s: holding resentment is like drinking poison and waiting for another person to die. Or as the Buddha said: "Holding on to anger is like grasping a hot coal with the intent of throwing it at someone else; you are the one who gets burned."

That is a very high price to pay for some illusion of vengeance.

SUMMING UP

All the great Sages and Teachers of history have believed in an enormous power within the human person, into which we can tap to create reality. The most familiar method used to try to tap into this power is what became known as "the ascetic path:" renouncing the material world, and focusing our energies towards a God "up there." This is the framework within which the message of Jesus has normally been presented throughout most of Christian history, but in fact Jesus neither practised or taught the ascetic path, but rather something much more effective and powerful. His message has been radically dis-empowered down through Christian history by presenting it within this misleading framework.

Jesus taught that the enormous power to create reality existed within us all, not in some location "up there' towards which we must struggle by acts of repentance, mortification and renunciation of the material world, but within ourselves.

The age-old distortion of Jesus himself as a Suffering Savior, and categorizing his message as a path of asceticism, has warped what Jesus was and radically dis-empowered his teachings. It was almost inevitable that Jesus' message would have been so distorted since his Passion, the center of the Christian tradition's focus on Jesus, took place just before the Jewish Festival of Passover. The center of the Passover ceremonies culminated in the sacrifice of a lamb on the altar of the Temple. The lamb symbolized human sinners and the flowing of its blood down the stone altar of the Temple symbolized the washing away of our sins in the sight of God because of our repentance. The tradition of Jesus as a Suffering Savior who died to save us from the vengeance of an angry God has dominated the history of Christianity, which is tragic since the mission of Jesus had nothing to do with any such thing.

Jesus did indeed come to be our savior, not to deliver us from the punishment of an offended God, but to deliver us from something that has plagued the human race for all of its history:

the effects of our own crippling attitudes that constantly generatre dis-empowering and negative realities out of the quantum field.

Paradoxically, understanding Jesus to have been a Suffering Savior and his teachings as an ascetic path, in fact creates the very dis-empowerment from which Jesus came to deliver us. This tradition of understanding has set up a major set of sub-conscious blocks in us all which in effect makes it impossible for us to attain the power to create desirable realities which Jesus promised us.

Freeing ourselves from our sub-conscious programs is a delicate task, since apparently the first instinct of any sub-conscious program is to ensure its own survival. That means that any overt effort to get rid of our dis-empowering sub-conscious programs will only make matters worse.

The only successful way we know to alter or dis-empower the negative programs in our sub-conscious is to go back and examine the historical circumstances in which those negative programs were first formed. In our present case that involves going back to examine critically all of the historical sources and traditions that we have concerning Jesus, and make a concerted effort to see him as he really was, rather than how we have been told he is. This is essential if we want to remove a sub-conscious program. Every effort has been made in this book to provide that evidence in as simple and accessible a form as possible.

To do that, we looked at all the historical evidence relating to Jesus and his ministry, and also the myriad of evidence relating to the centuries of handing on a defective interpretation of what his teaching was about. In this way we begin to see a person who was as far as could be imagined from being a Savior from the consequences of our sins against God, a Suffering Savior, or a "Gentle Jesus, Meek and Mild."

The great British writer, Dorothy L. Sayers, put it classically and memorably:

"The people who hanged Christ, to do them justice, never accused him of being a bore. On the contrary; they thought him too dynamic to be safe. It has been left for later generations to muffle up that shattering personality and surround him with an atmosphere of tedium. We have very efficiently pared the claws of the Lion of

Judah, certified him `meek and mild', and recommended him as a fitting household pet for pale curates and pious old ladies. To those who knew him, however, he in no way suggested a milk and water person: they objected to him as a dangerous firebrand."[334]

But even as astute a commentator as Dorothy Sayers did not realize the true power and intent of the mission of Jesus.

Jesus taught that the divisions within us often cause us to create what we do NOT want out of the quantum field, when we believe we are doing precisely the opposite. He taught us in regard to creating reality, that when we pray for something, we should believe it is already ours. Instead of following his advice, we pray, we beg, ask, or beseech in prayer that God or Jesus will give us what we want. In short, instead of believing that what we pray for is already ours, we are proclaiming by asking *that we do not already possess it,* and that is what the quantum field will manifest: more of what it is we wish to be delivered from. In short, by this type of prayer we only make matters worse.

One of the most important elements in this process of recovering our power to manifest desirable reality out of the quantum field, is to make sure all levels of our conscious and sub-conscious mind are in harmony and completely aligned. Recent research has discovered two other major centers of neural activity within us, in addition to the cranial brain. We also have a 'brain' in the area of the heart and a third in the abdomen, with the heart brain emitting a field about 5,000 times stronger than the cranial brain.

Much of our awareness in the heart or abdominal brain is sub-conscious, and their state may be completely at odds with what we are aware of consciously in the cranial brain. In this lack of synchronization and harmony between these three brain centers, we see how this disharmony neutralizes and undermines our attempts to create the kind of reality we think we are creating consciously. If we only pay attention to what the cranial brain is broadcasting, the reality may well be that the other two centers are countermanding what we proclaim consciously, so that without realizing it we may be creating more of what it is we wish to be delivered from.

---

[334] Sayers, Dorothy L: Creed or Chaos, New York, Harcourt Brace. 1949.

It was on these issues that the teachings of Jesus centered: the need to clarify and expose the contradictions that we hold deep within us all without really being aware of them. We need to harmonize all these levels within us so that a clear and unified intent is sent out to the quantum field. This gives the true power of which Jesus spoke and it was what he primarily wished all human beings to have.

In this perspective, we can clearly see that 2,000 years ago Jesus did not come to save us from God's punishment for our sins but to rescue us from our own crippling programs. When this is accomplished then truly we will all begin to function as gods, as he so memorably taught. Jesus was often accused of blasphemy because he told human beings who they really were. Instead of aiming to start living like gods being a blasphemy, as so many have regarded it, it is instead a stark recognition of the state of how things are.

As we saw earlier, in its beginning stages, the human race was in contact with advanced humanoid beings whom they regarded as 'gods.' Despite their exalted status these advanced humanoids apparently had more than a fair share of very typical human failings, being prone to take offense, become angry or jealous, and to take vengeance. These very early experiences of our race unfortunately have percolated down through human history to still color the ways in which we think of God.

We accept "God" to be the source of everything, including, on the physical level, innumerable galaxies on an unimaginable scale, as well as being the source of a myriad of dimensions beyond the physical. If we contemplate in addition how we envisage God as perfect, lacking nothing, being all powerful, all-wise and all-goodness, it becomes extraordinarily difficult to conceive how God could either be pleased or take offense at something we humans may do. Essentially that amounts to envisaging God as some form of human being enlarged, and most assuredly however God may be imagined, God is not that. Instead of preoccupying ourselves with such matters we should instead be putting into practice what Jesus taught about changing the character of what it is we are creating from the quantum field every day. If we believe that some things we poor humans may do can anger such a God, and that we are destined to be punished or rewarded for what we do, then we have successfully made God in the image of those advanced humanoids our race knew long ago. In short, we have made God in our own image.

This in no way implies some form of moral free-for-all in which there are no standards, values or mores. If we perpetrate injustices or damage on others, the mechanics of the quantum field will adequately 'punish' us unless we address what we have done, just as the quantum field will "reward" in kind any wonderful things we do. The very same holds true if the individual we are short changing is myself. In short, there is no need to postulate that God has a function of rewarding or punishing human beings for their virtues or faults or failings.

Every aspect of the realities we experience every day, whether glorious or despicable, have been magnetized to us by what we accept deep down. All great achievements, whether negative or positive, have come from some great thought. All great thoughts come from great thinkers, and all great thinkers have evolved from realizing that what we profoundly accept deep down creates the reality we all experience every day. This is what is fundamental to an authentic life in this world, not just the struggle for peace, justice, truth and equality in so many forms, or to liberate the oppressed, but most basically of all, realizing that all reality is created by what we profoundly accept. How to take conscious control of this process was the kernel of the teachings of Jesus.

It is not hard to see that the system Jesus really taught, as opposed to what for so long we have been told he taught, is also the ultimate solution for all of the most intractable problems that we face in the world today, from hunger, injustice, want, disease, and discrimination, right down to personal unhappiness and lack. This would seem for all of us to be a much more worthwhile focus instead of expending so much effort on divisive issues such as various brand names for different ways of believing in what is often unfortunately an all-too-human version of God.

What better time to embark on this mission of rescuing ourselves by the methods Jesus taught, just as the 2,000th anniversary of the start of his mission is about to dawn. As pointed out at the beginning, the implications of implementing his teachings are enormous for every aspect of human existence, but also for the resolution of so many of the inheritances of a regrettable kind that we have inherited from our history.

INDEX

A

B

C

D

H

I

J

M

N

O

P

Q

R

S

T

U

V

W

Y

Z

SELECT BIBLIOGRAPHY OF WORKS RELATED TO THE THEME OF THIS BOOK

Abhedananda: Swami Abhedananda's Journey into Kashmir and Tibet, with "The Life of Jesus by Nicolas Notovitch," Vedanta Press, 2001 edition.

Alexander, Cecil Frances Humphreys, (1818-1895), Hymns for Little Children, 1848. Put to music by Henry Gauntlett (1805-1876) in 1849.

Alpert, Richard, Be Here Now, Published by the Lama Foundation, San Cristobal, New Mexico, 1971.

Baden, Joel; Moss, Candida: The Curious Case of Jesus's Wife, The Atlantic, December 2014.

Barnstone, Willis; Meyer, Marvin: The Gnostic Bible, edited by, revised and expanded edition, New Seeds Books, Boston. 2003.

Boulay, R.A: Flying Serpents & Dragons, the Story of Mankind's Reptilian Past, Google Books, 1990.

Bourgeault, Cynthia: The Wisdom Jesus, Shambhala Publications, 2008.

Bramley, William: The Gods of Eden, HarperCollins, 1989.

Bruno, Giordano: De Umbris Idearum ('The Shadow of Ideas'), 1582; Ars Reminiscendi ('The Art of Memory') 1583; De l'Infinito Universo et Mondi,1584, Giovanni Aquilecchia, Sansoni, Firenze, 1985; De Vinculis in Genere, 1588; De Magia, ('On Magic'), 1590; Opere Italiane, introduced by Nuccio Ordine, Torino, UTET, (2002) 2013: Twilit Grotto Esoteric Archives, HTML edition by Joseph H. Peterson, 1997.

Burney, C.F: The Poetry of Our Lord: An Examination of the Formal Elements of Hebrew Poetry in the Discourses of Jesus Christ, Wipf and Stock, 1924; The Aramaic Origin of the Fourth Gospel. Clarendon Press, 1922. Re-published 2004, by Wipf & Stock Publishers.

Carpenter, Edmund: (Editor), Upside Down: Arctic Realities, 2011.

Charles Burney: Chris M. Rands, Stephen Meader, Chris P. Ponting, Gerton Lunter. PLOS Genetics, July 24, 2014, http://dx.doi.org/10.1371/journal.pgen.1004525

Clark, Gerard, The Anunnaki of Nibiru: Mankind's Forgotten Creators, Enslavers, Saviors, and Hidden Architects of the New World Order, Google Books, 2013.

Clement, as testified by Eusebius, in Historia Ecclesiastica, 4.14.7.

Dalman, Gustaf: The Words of Jesus Considered in the Light of Post-Biblical Jewish Writings and the Aramaic language, T and T Clark, 1902, 1997.

Davids, Rhomas Rhys: Buddhist Birth Stories (Jataka Tales), 1878, Routledge, London.

de Leon, Luis: De los Nombres de Cristo,' 1574 - 1575; The Names of Christ, translation and introduction by Manuel Durán and William Kluback, Paulist Press, 1984; 'La Perfecta Casada,' 1583, translated and introduction by John A. Jones and Javier San José Lera, Lewiston, NY, 1999.

Dogmatic Constitution on Divine Revelation, promulgated by Pope Paul VI on November 18, 1965.

Edwards, Jonathan and Smolinski, Reiner, Editor, Sinners in the Hands of an Angry God, A Sermon Preached at Enfield, July 8th,1741. (1741). Electronic Texts in American Studies. Paper 54. http://digitalcommons.unl.edu/etas/54

Ehrman, Bart: Lost Christianities. New York: Oxford University Press, 2003.

Ehrman, Bart: Misquoting Jesus – The Story Behind Who Changed the Bible and Why. First paperback edition, Harper, San Francisco, 2007.

Eusebius, Historia Ecclesiastica. Eusebius; Deferrari, Roy Joseph: Eusebius Pamphili Ecclesiastical History, Washington, D.C.: The Catholic University of America Press, 1969.

Farris, Michael: From Tyndale to Madison, B & H Publishing Group, 2007.

Feuerbach, Ludwig: The Essence of Christianity, (Das Wesen des Christentums), 1841.

Frank Moore Cross, Canaanite Myth and Hebrew Epic, 1973.

Galton, Sir Francis: Statistical Inquiries into the Efficacy of Prayer, Fortnightly Review vol. 12, pp. 125-35, 1872.

Goleman, Daniel: Emotional Intelligence: Why it Can Matter More than IQ, Bantam Books, 1995.

Gossett, Thomas: Race: The History of an Idea in America, 1963; reprinted Oxford University Press, 1997.

Grant, Robert M: The Mystery of Marriage in the Gospel of Philip, Vigiliae Christianae 15.3 (September 1961:129–140).

Halloran, John A: Sumerian Lexicon: A Dictionary Guide to the Ancient Sumerian Language, The David Brown Book Company, 2006.

Hans Heinrich Schmid, The So-called Jahwist, 1976.

Herodotus: The Histories, Barnes and Noble, 2004.

Homer: The Odyssey, Barnes and Noble, 2003.

HUMAINE: Emotion, Annotation, and Representation Language, 2006. Shaver, P., Schwartz, J., Kirson, D., & O'Connor, C., 1987; Emotion Knowledge: Further Exploration of a Prototype Approach. Journal of Personality and Social Psychology, 52(6), 1061; Parrott, W. (2001), Emotions in Social Psychology, Psychology Press, Philadelphia; Plutchik, R. The Nature of Emotions, American Scientist, 2011.Robinson, D. L. (2009); Brain function, mental experiencer and personality, The Netherlands Journal of Psychology. pp. 152—167.

Hunger and World Poverty Sources: United Nations World Food Program (WFP), Oxfam, UNICEF.

International Theological Commission, The Hope of Salvation for Infants Who Die without Being Baptized, April 22, 2007.

Iraeneus: Adversus Haereses.

Jastrow, Jr., Morris: Aspects of Religious Belief and Practice in Babylonia and Assyria, G.P. Putnam's Sons, 1911.

John Van Seters, Abraham in History and Tradition, Yale University Press, 1975,

Johnson, Robert A: The Fisher King and the Handless Maiden: Understanding the Wounded Feeling Function in Masculine and Feminine Psychology. HarperCollins, 1993.

Josephus: The Works of Flavius Josephus, translated by William Whiston, William P. Nimm and Co., c. 1850.

Kelber, W.H: The Oral and Written Gospel, Indiana University Press, 1997; Jesus and Tradition: Words in Time, Words in Space," Semeia 65, 1995.

Knight, JZ: A State of Mind, Warner Books, 1987.

Kolosimo, Peter, Redfern Nick: "Giants and The Lost Lands of The Gods," Global Communications Conspiracy Journal, 2017.

Köstenberger, Andreas J, and Kruger, Michael J: The Heresy of Orthodoxy, Crossway Books, Wheaton Ill., 2010.

Lamot, Anne: Bird by Bird: Some Instructions on Writing and Life, Pantheon Books, 1994.

LaSor, William Sanford: Old Testament Survey: The Message, Form, and Background of the Old Testament, 1982.

LeDoux, Joseph E: Separating Findings from Conclusions, in "Psychology Today," August 10, 2015. Editors: James A. Sanders, Lee Martin McDonald

Ledwith, Míċeál: Maynooth at a Glance, Colomba Press, 1995; How Jesus Became a Christ, Edessa Code Publications, II, 2006; "The Great Questions in the Hamburger Universe, "Deep Deceptions," Vol. 1, Edessa Code Publications, 2005; How Jesus Became a Christ, Edessa Code Publications, 2, 2006; "Poisoned Prayer: Reversing the Law of Cause and Effect, 2007 (website articles series); The Orb Project, with Dr. Klaus Heinemann, Simon and Schuster/ Atria, Beyond Words, 2007; Clues to a More Exciting Universe, Edessa Code Publications, 2008.

Leslie, Julia: Suttee or Sati: Victim or Victor? Reprinted from "Bulletin Center for the Study of World Religions," Harvard University, 1987-88. Motilal Banarsidass Publishers, Delhi.

Leyton, Bentley: The Gnostic Scriptures, Bantam Doubleday Dell Publishing Group, New York,1987.

Lincoln, Henry: Holy Blood, Holy Grail. Jonathan Cape, 1982.

Lipton, Bruce: The Biology of Belief, Sounds True Publishing, Santa Rosa, California, 2005; The Wisdom of Your Cells — How Your Beliefs Control Your Biology, Audio Book, 2006; Spontaneous Evolution: Our Positive Future and a Way to Get There from Here (co-author Steve Bhaerman), 2009.

Marjanen, Antti: The Woman Jesus Loved: Mary Magdalene in the Nag Hammadi Library and Related Documents (Nag Hammadi and Manichaean Studies, 40), Brill, Philosophia Antiqua), 1996.

Martin, Laura: Eskimo Words for Snow, in "American Anthropologist," Vol. 88, no. 2, June 1986.

McCraty, R: The Energetic Heart: Bioelectromagnetic Communication Within and Between People. In P. J. Rosch & M. S. Markov (Eds.), Bioelectromagnetic Medicine, (pp. 541-562). Marcel Dekker, New York. 2004.

McDonald & Sanders, The Canon Debate, Baker Publishing Group, December 2001.

McDonald, Lee Martin and Sanders, James, editors, The Canon Debate, Hendrickson Publishers, Peabody, MA, 2001.

Meyer, Marvin (ed): The Ancient Mysteries: A Sourcebook, HarperCollins,1987; The Nag Hammadi Scriptures, HarperCollins, The International Edition, 2007; Meyer, Marvin, De Boer, Esther A: The Gospels of Mary: The Secret Tradition of Mary Magdalene, the Companion of Jesus, HarperCollins, 2004.

Meyers, Robin R: Saving Jesus from the Church, HarperOne, 2009.

Missick, Stephen: Christ's Words as Hebrew Poetry, 2011; Treasures of the Language of Jesus: the Aramaic Source of Christ's Teachings, Xlibris, 2000; The Words of Jesus in the Original Aramaic: Discovering the Semitic Roots of Christianity, Xulon Press, 2006; Mary of Magdala: Magdalene, the Forgotten Aramaic Prophetess of Christianity, Xlibris, 2006.

Nietzsche, Friedriche: Thus Spoke Zarathustra, Barnes and Noble, 2012.

Notovitch, Nicolas: The Unknown Life of Jesus Christ, translated by J. H. Connelly and L. Landsberg. The Project Gutenberg eBook, 2012.

Pagels, Elaine: The Gnostic Gospels, Vintage Books, New York, 1979.

Parks, Anton: The Secret of the Dark Stars, and Eden: The Truth About Our Origins, Pahana Books, published in English, 2013.

Philip, Gospel of: Nag Hammadi Library.

Phillips, J.B: Your God Is Too Small. A Guide for Believers and Skeptics Alike. Simon and Schuster, 1952.

Picknett, Lynn, and Prince, Clive: The Templar Revelation. Transworld Publishers, 1997.

Potkay, Adam. The Story of Joy: from the Bible to Late Romanticism, 2009.

Ramtha: I am Ramtha, Beyond Words, 1986; Last Waltz of the Tyrants, Beyond Words, 1989; Parallel Lifetimes, JZK Publishing, 2003, 2007; A Beginner's Guide to Creating Reality, third ed. JZK Publishing, 2004; Jesus the Christ: the Life of a Master, 2006; Love Yourself Into Life – The Magic Book, 2013 Jaime Leal Anaya (Editor), Pat Richker (Editor), The Brain – the Creator of Reality, Hun Nal Ye Publishing, 2014.

Ratzinger, Joseph: 'Dogmatic Constitution on Divine Revelation, Origin and Background' in: Herbert Vorgrimler (ed.), Commentary on the Documents of Vatican II, 5 volumes (New York: Herder and Herder, 1967-1969.

Rendtorff, Rolf: The Problem of the Process of Transmission in the Pentateuch, 1989.

Robert E. Van Voorst, Jesus outside the New Testament: an Introduction to the Ancient Evidence, Eerdmans, 2000.

Robert Temple, The Sirius Mystery, St. Martin's Press, 1976, and Destiny Books, Vermont, 1998. Author also of The Genius of China, The Crystal Sun, The Sphinx Mystery, and Egyptian Dawn.

Robinson, B A: Apologies by Pope John Paul II, (Galileo and Bruno), Ontario Consultants, March 2000.

Rose, Martin: Une Herméneutique de l'Ancien Testament, Comprendre, se Comprendre, Faire Comprendre, Labor et Fides, Geneva, 2003.

Sanders, E. P; Paul and Palestinian Judaism, 1977, and Just, Felix, S.J., Ph.D: The Deutero-Pauline Letters.

Sandlin, Destin: Website https://www.youtube.com/user/destinws2.

Sayers, Dorothy Lee: Creed Or Chaos?: and Other Essays in Popular Theology, Methuen, 1957.

Schmid, Hans: The So-Called Yahwist (1976) discussed in Antony F. Campbell and Mark A. O'Brien, Sources of the Pentateuch (1993), pp 2–11.

Scriven, Joseph M: "What a Friend We Have in Jesus," 1855.

Seife, Charles: "Vatican Regrets Burning Cosmologist," Science Now, March 1, 2000.

Sitchin, Zecharia: Genesis Revisited. Avon, 1990, The Wars of Gods and Men: Book III of the Earth Chronicles. 2007, Harper.

Soosalu, Grant, Oke, Marvin: mBraining, mBIT international Pty, Ltd., 2012.

Spiro. Rabbi Ken: A Crash Course in Jewish History: The Miracle and Meaning of Jewish History, from Abraham to Modern Israel. Targum Press in association with AISH.COM, Jerusalem, 2010.

Starbird, Margaret: The Woman with the Alabaster Jar, Bear and Company, 1993.

Tellinger, Michael; Slave Species of the Gods, 2005; African Temples of the Anunnaki, 201; The Secret History of the Anunnaki.

Thomas, Gospel of; "Hymn of the Pearl," in Acts of Thomas.

Tolkien, J.R.R: The Lord of the Rings, Allen and Unwin, 1954.

Truth, Gospel of, Nag Hammadi Library.

Ussher, James: Annales Veteris Testamenti, a prima mundi origine dedvcti: una cum rerum Asiaticarum et Aegyptiacarum chronico, a temporis historici principio usque ad Maccabaicorum initia productae. London, 1650. Modern English translation; "Annals of the World."

Von Daniken, Erich: Twilight of the Gods: The Mayan Calendar and the Return of the Extraterrestrials, New Page books, 2010; Remnants of the Gods: A Visual Tour of Alien Influence in Egypt, Spain, France, Turkey, and Italy, New Page Books, 2013.

Walter R. Mattfeld: The Garden of Eden Myth, Its Pre-Biblical Origins in Mesopotamian Myths. Nov 2010.

Wesley, Charles: "A Child's Prayer," First published in Hymns & Sacred Poems, 1742.

Williams, G. W: Highway Hypnosis. International Journal of Clinical and Experimental Hypnosis, (103): 143–151. 1963.

Yu Wu Song: The Wisdom of China: A Collection of Chinese Sayings, Collected and translated by Yu Wu Song.

Edessa Code, LLC
P.O. Box 1100
Tenino, WA 98589
USA
micealledwith.com

35878031R00333

Made in the USA
Middletown, DE
14 February 2019